ITALY

METHUEN'S COMPANIONS TO
MODERN STUDIES

SPAIN: A COMPANION TO SPANISH STUDIES. Edited by E. ALLISON
PEERS, M.A., Professor of Spanish in the University of Liverpool. With
3 Maps. Demy 8vo.   12s. 6d. net.

GERMANY: A COMPANION TO GERMAN STUDIES. Edited by J. BITHELL,
M.A., Reader in German in the University of London, Head of the
Department of German, Birkbeck College. With 2 Maps. Demy 8vo.
15s. net.

ITALY: A COMPANION TO ITALIAN STUDIES. Edited by EDMUND G.
GARDNER, M.A., Litt.D., F.B.A., Professor of Italian in the University
of London, University College. With a Map. Demy 8vo. 12s. 6d. net.

ITALY
A COMPANION TO ITALIAN STUDIES

EDITED BY

EDMUND G. GARDNER
LITT.D.

FELLOW OF THE BRITISH ACADEMY
PROFESSOR OF ITALIAN IN
THE UNIVERSITY OF LONDON

WITH A MAP

METHUEN & CO. LTD.
36 ESSEX STREET W.C.
London

First Published in 1934

PRINTED IN GREAT BRITAIN

TO

THE MEMORY OF

ANTONIO CHIARAMONTE BORDONARO

PREFACE

WHILE mainly intended for the increasing number of students of Italian, whether at home or in the Italian departments of English-speaking Universities, the writers of the following chapters have attempted at the same time to take into account the requirements of the general reader.

The political events of recent years have given a new and enhanced importance to Italian studies. What the great leader of contemporary Italy, Benito Mussolini, has finely and characteristically called " the accelerated rhythm of Italian life " is making Italian civilisation, and all that Italy represents, an increasingly predominant factor in the life and thought of the world to-day, and the traditional friendship and understanding between Great Britain and Italy has acquired a value and significance which could hardly have been anticipated in the past. We therefore dedicate this volume to the memory of the late Italian ambassador, Antonio Chiaramonte Bordonaro, who so ably promoted that friendship and understanding, and to whose sympathetic interest in the progress of Italian studies in this country all who were brought into personal contact with him will bear grateful witness.

EDMUND G. GARDNER

UNIVERSITY COLLEGE
UNIVERSITY OF LONDON
April, 1933

BIBLIOGRAPHICAL NOTE

Limits of space make it impossible to indicate more than a selection of books in the lists at the end of the chapters, to be supplemented by the ample bibliographies given in some of the works there mentioned ; as notably, in the case of literature, in V. Rossi's *Storia della letteratura italiana per uso dei licei* and the larger volumes of the *Storia letteraria d'Italia*, published by Vallardi of Milan, and, for history, in the *Cambridge Medieval* and *Modern History* and the volumes in the *Storia politica d'Italia scritta da una società di professori* (Vallardi). The reader is also referred to the articles in the *Enciclopedia Italiana* now in course of publication under the editorship of Giovanni Gentile (Rome : Istituto Treccani).

A list of some of the chief periodical publications useful to the student is here appended :—

Language and Philology : *Archivio glottologico italiano* (Turin) ; *Italia dialettale* (Pisa) ; *Studi glottologici italiani* (Turin) ; *Studi medievali* (Turin, of wider scope) ; *Studi romanzi* (Rome) ; *Studi di filologia italiana* (Florence, the *Bullettino della R. Accademia della Crusca*).

History of Literature : *Giornale storico della letteratura italiana* (Turin).

Political History : *Archivio storico italiano* (Florence) ; *Archivio della Società Romana di Storia Patria* (Rome) ; *Archivio storico lombardo* (Milan) ; *Archivio storico siciliano* (Palermo) ; *Archivio veneto, Nuovo archivio veneto, Archivio veneto-tridentino* (Venice) ; *Rivista storica italiana* (Turin) ; *Nuova rivista storica* (Milan) ; *Studi storici* (Pisa, Pavia) ; *Rassegna storica del Risorgimento* (Turin).

Cultural and General : *Nuova Antologia* (Rome) ; *La Critica* (Naples, ed. Croce) ; *Pan* (Milan) ; *Leonardo* (Florence) ; *Italia che scrive* (Rome) ; *Gerarchia* (Milan).

Art : *Bollettino d'Arte* (Rome) ; *Rivista d'Arte* (Florence) ; *L'Arte* (Turin).

Drama : *Scenario* (Rome).

Music : *Rivista musicale italiana* (Turin).

CONTENTS

ITALY

CHAPTER I

ITALY, THE ITALIAN PEOPLE, THE ITALIAN LANGUAGE

I

IN his letter on the advent of Henry of Luxemburg, one of
the landmarks in the development of the national idea in Italy,
Dante addresses the Italians as a single people : " incolae
Latiales."

Italy's peculiar shape suggests the image of a boot, just as
her larger islands suggested, even to very early geographers, a
triangle (Trinacria) and a footprint (Ichnusa—Sardinia). When
we consider the country in greater detail, we find hardly any
part of it that is not very definitely shaped, with characteristics
of its own that make it impossible to confuse it with any other.
Only the flatter regions of the Po valley, perhaps, and some
outlying districts of the South, can be said to be lacking in this
personality of landscape which has ever been the wonder of
visitors from every corner of the world. The labour of men
has added further distinctiveness to this natural variety, leaving
on the soil the stamp of different civilisations that range from the
prehistorical to the contemporary. The familiar image of the
boot (*lo stivale*) has led to a very common misrepresentation.
Geologically, as well as historically, Italy is not so much a peninsula
as a large crater or saucer, sloping down into the Mediterranean
from the heights of the Alps to the southern coasts of Sicily,
and partly submerged by the Tyrrhenian and the Adriatic seas.
On the eastern side the brim of the " saucer " is represented
by the definite line of the Velebic and Dinaric Alps, which encircle Dalmatia and extend as far south as the Mouths of Cattaro ;
to the west, by the mountainous ranges of Corsica and Sardinia.
From the points of view of geography, race, language and history
this huge crater may be considered as a unity, immensely varied
within itself, and yet stamped with certain deep general characters
that make this unity unmistakable.

Configuration and variety of external aspect, together with
certain unifying influences, find a counterpart in the temper
and mind of the people. Italy may be described as a country
where the *identical* is very rare, and the *indefinite* never exists.
Every minor valley of the Alps or the Apennines has its own
peculiar customs, its own exclusive and easily definable variety
of dialect, its own traditions and pride ; every small town in
the plains of the Po and the Arno, or along the sea-coasts,
has a history of deep and sometimes fierce rivalries with its
neighbouring centres, and peculiarities in mind, character and
activity which mark it out as if it were a small nation of its own.
The typical man of Pescia will speak of those of Prato almost as
an Englishman of the Scots ; and yet there are but a few miles
between the two townlets. In this " land of variety " it seems
difficult to detect the unitarian or unifying elements. Religion
and language naturally occur first to our minds (political unity,
as a whole, was only achieved in 1870). Yet many of the Italian
dialects are more distant from Latin or Tuscan than some that
are spoken outside the " crater " ; and Roman Catholicism,
almost universally accepted though less universally observed in
the peninsula, is by no means peculiar to it alone. Therefore
language and religion must be taken into account with reference
to historical and racial continuity during the last twenty centuries,
at least, of Italian history.

Italian thinkers themselves deplore the gratification of a
national bent towards rhetoric that makes modern Italians en-
large on their descent from Roman emperors and legionaries ;
but the opposite view, according to which there has been no
real continuity, either in race or civilisation, from the days of
Cæsar down to contemporary Italy, is nevertheless a total misrepresentation of facts. Whatever the pre-Roman population
of Italy may have been (certainly a Harlequin dress of Alpine
and Mediterranean types, Italics and Celts, Ligurians and
Illirians, Etruscans, Latins, Sabellians, Volsci, Calabri, Greeks,
and so many others), Rome undoubtedly brought to bear upon
them that unifying spirit that has left its indelible mark even
on much more distant and less deeply latinised peoples. Under
Augustus, for about forty years, the Roman citizenship was
extended to all the peninsula (or, more exactly, the " crater "),
and Virgil did not express a merely personal feeling when he
hailed Italy as his country. It is a commonplace, yet true,
that the Church of Rome inherited much that was inherent
and essential to Roman civilisation, and preserved it through
the mists of the Middle Ages ; and this, we would add, was one

of the deeper reasons why the Church played such a prominent part in medieval politics, and the people of Italy so often and so spontaneously identified its claims and interests with their own. The fact that the Church so often played Italian and non-Italian potentates one against the other, and even summoned foreign kings and emperors to restore its rights or maintain its claims against its own internal enemies, was the result of an *international* turn of mind that was shared by practically all Italians. Dante himself, in many respects the first prophet and founder of Italian unity, could only think of Italy as one nation within a universal empire, and saw nothing to deplore in the fact that a Germanic prince should be called to Rome as " King of the Romans " to be made " Holy Roman Emperor." Here and there, as notably in the latter part of the fourteenth century in a famous canzone of Fazio degli Uberti and an eclogue of Boccaccio, this is represented as a mere unfounded claim of a " barbarian," and there are traces of a national sentiment ; but we must come down as far as the early sixteenth century to find two enlightened and experienced politicians like Machiavelli and Guicciardini regarding the dominion of the priests as the chief cause of the misfortunes of Italy. The masses were even then, and to remain for a long time after, totally unconscious of the fact that all Europe was forming itself into large nations, and that Italy must follow their example or perish. There is no doubt that the variety of dialects, races and local conditions within the peninsula, its elongated and mountainous shape, and the fierce rivalries between its small states and cities, contributed very largely to that effect ; yet there is equally no doubt that the cosmopolitan spirit of Rome, continued in the Church and deeply absorbed by the people, was one of the causes of Italy's delay in forming herself into a unified nation.

The ethnical importance of incursions and invasions in the early Middle Ages has also been greatly exaggerated. The Ostrogoths, when they conquered the peninsula, were not numerous, and their rule was entirely wiped out within sixty years. The Langobards, who came and settled in Italy at the end of the sixth century, could not certainly total more than 200,000 souls, and the peninsula, although then at its lowest ebb in numbers of population, counted at least 7,000,000. Although these invaders held sway over large portions of the country for a little more than two centuries, none of their language survived there with the exception of a small number of words ; they gradually adopted the Catholic religion and what was left of Roman law. Only their barbaric spirit of lawless and turbulent individualism, and such crude ways of enforcing justice as the duel, private revenge, the *weregild* (money in payment of blood), were often imitated by Italians, and in some cases became so embedded in their habits that they appeared, in later centuries, as typical Italian customs, known outside Italy by their Italian names. But few will know or remember, for instance, that the *vendetta* first came into Italy as a lawful institution of Langobard law.

Traces of the Frankish, Norman, Angevin and Spanish dominations will be found here and there, especially among the nobility of Piedmont and the South. Sicily was for two centuries under Saracen rule, which brought some slight mixture of Asiatic blood into the veins of her people—and beautiful traces of Moresque as well as Byzantine influences in her architecture. The south-eastern parts of the peninsula, owing to vicinity and commerce, undoubtedly absorbed a certain amount of Levantine elements. Nevertheless, in the main, it may be safely concluded that the great bulk of the Italian population of to-day are the direct descendants of the inhabitants of the peninsula under the Roman Empire, and that, through the many and mighty events of intervening history, a continuous historical line may be traced from ancient Rome down to modern Italy.

II

Thus the people of Italy remain the purest representatives of the Latin race, and their language is the speech of imperial Rome grown to maturity.

Italian, with its various dialects, is an uninterrupted continuation and development of the Latin spoken by the inhabitants of the peninsula and its islands at the time of what, in loose phraseology, is called the fall of the Roman Empire. The other romance languages are similarly evolved, under various conditions, from " Vulgar Latin," which was practically the speech of the middle classes under the rule of Rome ; but Italian claims a certain pre-eminence in that, by virtue of its central type that has become the national and literary language, it has preserved more of the original character of Latin than any of its linguistic sisters. This, as Ascoli observes, is due to the fact that, whereas " Vulgar Latin " was adopted by the races that became subject to Rome, it originated in Italy where it was an ancient national fusion of the languages of the peoples conquered and absorbed by the Romans. The same cause made the development of Italian more tardy than that of the others. It is not until the early years of the tenth century that we find the Italian language (in a Latin poem on the coronation of the Emperor Berengarius in 915) recognised as something different from Latin, and sentences, intentionally in the vernacular and used as such for official purposes, first occur in a group of documents of the years 960 and 963 connected with the Abbey of Montecassino and referring to lawsuits about the possession of certain lands.

A certain number of words have entered the Italian language from non-Latin sources. The majority of these are Germanic. Some (as in other romance languages) come from words that had penetrated into Vulgar Latin from the contact between the Romans and the barbarian tribes in the latter days of the Empire : *guerra* (the dying out of *bellum* corresponding with the decay of the Roman military spirit when Germanic soldiers served in the legions and Germanic chiefs held high office in the armies), *biondo* (reflecting the admiration of the Roman ladies for the fair hair of Germanic women that led to the ousting of *flavus*), *borgo*. The substitution of *ricco* for *dives* suggests the spoliation of the Romans by the barbarian invaders. More Germanic words were introduced by the successive tides of conquest : Goth, Langobard and (in a minor degree) Frank. In general, words of Germanic origin refer to concrete objects : things connected with war (*elmo*), parts of the body and articles of utility (*guancia*, *schiena*, *guanto*), agriculture (*guidare*, from a Gothic verb meaning the yoking of horses or oxen) ; or, when referring to abstract ideas, with a suggestion of violence or abuse (*bramare*, *rubare*, *orgoglio*). Words beginning with *gu* and *sch* are almost always of Germanic origin. Among the borrowings from Greek (mostly through the medium of late Latin) is to be noted *zio* and *zia*, whereas a number of north Italian dialects preserve instead, for " aunt," the Latin *amita*, as in the Venetian *amia*. Arabic words entered Italian, partly through the Saracen conquest of Sicily, but more through commercial relations with the East (when they are frequently the same as in other western languages) : thus *cotone*, *ammiraglio*, *arsenale*, *dogana*, *fondaco*, *assassino*, *ricamo*, *baldacchino*, *liuto*. They are naturally more abundant in Sicilian, where geographical names (Alcantara, Marsala, Calatafimi) are frequently Arabic. With a very few exceptions, the Celtic element is confined to words that had already penetrated into classical Latin.

Apart from such " lexical contributions," Italian words are the continuation of Latin with various phonetic and morphological changes. But here we have to distinguish between so-called " popular " words, which proceed by spontaneous elaboration and oral tradition from spoken Latin, and so-called " literary "

words that have passed into the language from written or classical
Latin, and appear only slightly, or sometimes not at all, modified
by phonetic development.   Thus a Latin word may be represented
in two or more different forms, allotropes, one " popular," the
other "literary" or semi-literary.   More frequently the meaning
in the " popular " form has changed from that of classical Latin.
Thus, *iustitia* appears as *giustezza* (" exactness," " precision ")
and *giustizia ; vitium* gives both *vezzo* and *vizio ; causa* is continued by both *cosa* and *causa*, *occasio* by both *cagione* and
occasione.[1]   Further, the influence of French and Provençal upon
Italian, especially in the thirteenth century, has led to other
allotropes from the same Latin basis ; thus, *domina* is continued
by *donna* and (through the French) by *dama*, *gaudere* by *godere*
and *gioire*.   Similarly, the continuation of the Latin suffixes
-arius and *-aticum* by *-iere* (*o*) and *-aggio* respectively (*cavaliere*,
pensiero, *preghiera*, *viaggio*, *coraggio*) is due to their having passed
into Italian through the medium of French or Provençal, though
the suffix, once introduced, may have served for indigenous
formations.

In summarising the chief changes that Latin has undergone
in the passage to Italian, it should be kept in mind that phonetic
changes only in part affect " literary " words, and that even
" popular " words supply copious exceptions, through the influence of such factors as analogy, contamination, assimilation,
metathesis, and the like.

Tonic Vowels.—The place of the Latin accent is usually
maintained.   It has sometimes shifted through the classical *e*
or *i* in hiatus ceasing to be a vowel (*filíolus*, *figliuòlo*), or certain
parts of the verb, the first person plural of the imperfect
subjunctive and the third person plural of the strong perfect,
changing from paroxytone to proparoxytone in Vulgar Latin
(*cantassémus*, *cantássimo*, *fecérunt*, *fécero*).   The Latin tonic *a*,
long or short, is usually maintained unaltered.   The long tonic
e and short tonic *i* are alike continued as closed *e* (*vero*, *vede*).
" Literary " words often represent the Latin *ē* by an open vowel
(*crudèle*).   In hiatus and before certain consonant groups the
Latin *ĭ* is preserved : *via*, *famiglia*, *vigna*, *vince*, *lingua*.   In
southern Italian dialects, both *ē* and *ĭ* normally become *i*.   The
short tonic *e* normally develops as the diphthong *ie* in an open
syllable (*viène*), as open *e* in a closed syllable (*bèllo*, *vècchio*).

---

[1] In some instances, the "popular" and "literary" forms continue
different meanings of the Latin word : thus *exemplum* gives *scempio* and
esempio.

Long tonic *i* remains unchanged. Tonic long *o* and tonic short *u* are usually continued alike by a closed *o* (*pone, onda*). In the South both become *u*. In "literary" words, the Latin *ō* is often represented by an open *o* (*devòto*), and in some proparoxytones an open *o* may continue a Latin *ŭ* (*òmero, fòlaga*). The classical short tonic *o* normally develops as the diphthong *uo* in an open syllable (*uomo, muore*), though often reduced to a simple open *o*, which is the regular development in a closed syllable (*nòtte, òggi*). The long *u* remains unchanged. The diphthong *au* is normally continued as open *o* (*pòco, pòvero*), while *oe* and *ae* behave like a short tonic *e*.

Atonic Vowels.—In initial protonic syllables, *a* and *ī* are normally unchanged, *au* is reduced to *u* (*udire*).[1] *E* long or short, *ĭ*, *ae* and *oe*, show a general tendency to become *i* (*sicuro, nipote, cilestre, rispondere*). But *e* is often preserved, or *ĭ* becomes *e*, before an *r* followed by another consonant (*vertù* by the side of the literary *virtù*), or by analogy, especially in verbs where the first syllable is not a prefix (*vedere, venire*), and a following labial sometimes changes an *e* or *i* into *o* (*dovere, domani*). Protonic *o* and *u* are more frequently continued as *o* (*dolore, scodella*), but a *u* is frequent, especially when the Latin *u* was long (*uso*) or there is a tonic *i* in the following syllable (*uliva*). A median post-tonic vowel is often syncopated, thus giving rise to a new consonantal group (*occhio*); when preserved, it usually retains its Latin form, except that *u* becomes *o* (*popolo*), and certain following consonants produce sporadic changes. In the case of final atonic vowels, or vowels that have become final by fall of the Latin consonant, *a* normally remains except in the termination -*as*, where it becomes *i*;[2] *ī* remains; *ĕ, ae*, and *ĭ* normally become *e;* *ē* tends to become *i* (*oggi, vedi* imperative); *u* and *o* are continued as *o*.

Consonants.—Save in sporadic instances, where dissimilation or some other phenomenon has operated, the Latin consonant remains unchanged at the beginning of a word. The Latin *j*, whether classical or developed in Vulgar Latin from *de* or *di*, *ge* or *gi*, becomes palatal *g : giorno, giudice* (so with the Greek *z* in *geloso*). At the end of a word the consonant disappears, except in some monosyllables where there is usually epithesis

---

[1] In *godere, posare*, the open *o* instead of *u* is due to the influence of parts of the verb where the vowel is tonic : *gode, posa*.

[2] Thus the present indicative, second person singular, *ami* (*amas*). Somewhat similarly in monosyllables, the final *s* falls, with epithesis of *i* to the tonic vowel : *noi* (*nos*), *dai* (*das*), *sei* (*ĕs*), *sei* (*sĕx*). But a closed *e* absorbs the *i : tre* (*trēs*), *re* (*rēx*).

of a vowel : *sono* (*sum*), *miele, cuore*.[1] Medial consonants, or groups of consonants, are apt to show two or more developments, in some instances due to the position of the accent, in others to different local tendencies, in others to the period at which the word passed into the spoken language. Thus the Latin *j* (whether classical or developed in Vulgar Latin) gives both *ggi* and *i* (which generally fuses with a following tonic vowel) : *maggiore, oggi, raggio, aiutare, maestro ;* while, in a small group of words, a classical *dị* is continued as *zz* (dz) : *mezzo, rozzo*. This double development is noticeable in some of the consonant groups formed with " yod " (the Latin atonic *e* or *i* in hiatus). Thus, *sị* gives both *gi* and (through *sc*) *ci : Perugia, cagione, bacio, cacio ; tị* both *zz* (ts) and *gi : ragione, palazzo* and *palagio, prezzo* and *pregio, bellezza* (-*itia*), *cupidigia* (-*ities* with change of declension). With the group *rị*, the Tuscan tendency is for the *r* to fall : *muoio, febbraio, calzolaio ;* elsewhere, and particularly in the South, it is the *i* that falls : *moro*. The *i* frequently falls in literary words, as *impero*, while *danaro* is a fresh formation from the plural (-*arius* giving -*aio*, but -*arii* giving -*ari*). In the combinations *lị* and *nị* the result is the palatal *l* (*gli*) and the palatal *n* (*gn*) respectively : *figlio, voglio* (from *voleo* which replaced *volo*), *vigna, signore*.[2] A labial preceding the *i* is normally doubled : *vendemmia, rabbia, abbia ;* as also the palatal *c : faccia*. In these cases a *v* normally becomes *b* (*gabbia*), but a *vị* or *bị* is frequently continued as *ggi : soggetto, roggio* (*rubeus*), *pioggia* (*pluvia*), *aggio* (*habeo*), *deggio* (*debeo*). In some cases these are gallicisms, in others originally southern forms, or due to a Vulgar Latin change of *vị* or *bị* into *j*. In southern dialects *pị* is continued as *cci*, as in *saccio* (*sapio*) met in early Italian poetry : occasional instances, like *piccione*, have penetrated into standard Italian. Groups in which *l* follows *c* (or *t*), *p*, *b*, *f*, undergo important changes, the *l* changing to *ị :* *chiama, piano, fiore, biondo ;* when medial, whether from a classical group or, as more frequently, the result of syncope, the consonant is doubled : *doppio, occhio, vecchio*. But in some words, perhaps owing to French or Provençal influence, *cl* or *gl* gives *gli : veglio* and *maglia* as well as *vecchio* and *macchia, artiglio, coniglio*. The prefix *ex*, in " popular " words, becomes palatal *s* before vowels : *scempio* (*exemplum*), *scegliere* (*ex-*

---

[1] The *n* in final *nt* is similarly preserved in paroxytones : *cantano* (*cantant*).

[2] Forms like *doglio* (*doleo*), *vegno* (*venio*), have been replaced by *dolgo, vengo*, by analogy with presents like *colgo, piango*. The *ị* frequently falls in the first person to conform with other parts of the verb : *odo* (*audio*).

eligere) ; *x* gives both *ss* and palatal *s* : *visse, lasciare.* At the beginning of a word, *qu* loses the labial element before all vowels except *a* : *quale, che, chi, come, chiedere.* A secondary *qu* in Italian is developed from a Latin *cu* in hiatus, as in *piacque* (*placuit*), and in compounds of *eccum* before a tonic, but not before an atonic, vowel : *quella* (*eccum illa*), *coloro* (*eccum illorum*).

Nouns and Pronouns.—Prepositional constructions have replaced case distinctions by inflection. Many Italian nouns continue classical oblique cases, whether the accusative or one obtained by phonetic unification : *cagione, madre.* But not unfrequently the nominative is preserved in imparisyllabic nouns : *uomo, sarto,* the archaic *nievo* as well as *nipote,* the " popular " *orafo* by the side of the semi-literary *orefice.* So also the nominative-accusative in such former neuter nouns as *cuore, corpo, nome.* Although the neuter gender died out, neuter nouns becoming masculine, some neuter plurals have become feminine singulars (*spoglia, foglia, pecora, gioia* from *gaudia* through French or Provençal), while the Latin neuter plural of the second declension functions as a collective feminine plural to certain masculine nouns (*uova, mura, braccia, membra*), and the neuter plural of the third declension in the archaic feminine plurals in -*ora* (*le fuocora*) and still in certain southern dialects. Other traces of special Latin cases remain : the ablative singular in the typical romance adverb of quality, as *teneramente,* and the Latin genitive singular in the days of the week, as *lunedì* (*lunae dies*). Names of places frequently continue the Latin locative : *Firenze, Ascoli, Rimini.* In general, the Italian nouns represent the reduction of the five classical declensions to three in Vulgar Latin, the fourth and fifth being absorbed by the others, but there has been some further passage of words from one declension to another.

The definite article develops from *ille,* by weakening of its demonstrative meaning and reduction to a monosyllable.[1] *Ille,* and less frequently *ipse,* function as the personal pronoun of the third person, with changes due to Vulgar Latin : thus *egli,* through *elli,* from *illī, esso* from *ipsum.* Certain Latin adverbs have become atonic personal pronouns : *ci* (*ecce hic*), *vi* (*ibi*), *ne* (*inde*). *Is* and *hic* are preserved only in a few compounds, as also *iste.* A new demonstrative is formed by combinations with *ecce* and *eccum* : *ciò* (*ecce hoc*), *questo* (*eccum istum*), *quella* (*eccum illa*), *colui* (*eccum illui*). *Illorum,* become identical for both genders (*loro*), functions as subject and object, and also, retaining its genitive sense, as possessive pronoun.

[1] In Sardinian, the definite article continues *ipse* instead of *ille.*

Verbs.—The four Latin conjugations are continued by three, verbs in *-ére* and *-'ere* being treated as one conjugation. Some verbs from the Latin second and third have passed into the *a* and *i* conjugations (*tremare, abolire, fuggire*) ; the accent on the vowel in *e* verbs has sometimes shifted (*cadére, muòvere, rídere, sapére, rispóndere*). The passive has been replaced by a combination of the past participle with *essere* (or occasionally *venire, andare, fare*), and by an extended use of the reflexive construction (*si canta*) ; deponent verbs have become active. Italian preserves the present infinitive, the present participle (usually as an adjective), the past participle and the gerund ; the future participle only in a few literary words. In the indicative, it preserves the present (with the peculiarity that, from the thirteenth century onwards, the subjunctive functions in the first person plural, *avemo* being replaced by *abbiamo*), the imperfect, and the perfect ; in the subjunctive, the present is preserved, the pluperfect being continued to function as the imperfect but (with the exception of *essere, dare,* and *stare*) with the stem of the infinitive (*facessi,* not *fecissi*). In the imperative, the second person is continued from the Latin, except in *avere, essere, sapere* and *volere,* where forms from the subjunctive function. The lost tenses are supplied by combining the past participle with *avere* or *essere.* The Latin pluperfect indicative (apart from certain southern dialects) survives only in *fora* (*fueram*), a poetical conditional of *essere.* Similarly, the Latin future simple is preserved only in *fia* (*fiam*) which—together with forms from the present subjunctive—functions as a poetical future of *essere.* As in other romance languages, the Italian future is formed by the fusion of the infinitive of the verb with the present of *avere* (*cantare ho, canterò*). The conditional offers a notable peculiarity. Whereas the form exists (as in the majority of romance languages) showing the fusion of the infinitive with the imperfect of the auxiliary, this is originally a southern form that passed into poetry (*cantare avia, canteria*) ; the normal Italian form being that obtained by fusion with the perfect (*cantare ebbi, canterei*).

Several common verbs—*avere, fare, sapere*—have presents (*ho, fo, so*) due to analogy with *dare* and *stare.* In the indicative and subjunctive presents of many *i* verbs there has been an extension of the Latin suffix *-isco,* but with loss of its inceptive meaning. Weak perfects of *a* and *i* verbs continue the Latin, whereas those of *e* verbs are formed by analogy (*temei* replacing *timui*). The termination *-etti* (*credetti*) is due to the influence of *detti,* which developed as a perfect of *dare,* by the side of *diedi,* by analogy with *stetti.* *Dare* and *stare* are the only two

Italian verbs that continue Latin reduplicative perfects. The increase of strong perfects in *-ui* in Vulgar Latin is reflected in Italian : *conobbi, stetti, caddi, venni, viddi* by the side of *vidi ;* [1] as also the fresh formation of sigmatic perfects : *persi, uccisi, vinsi, lessi, mossi, apersi.* The weak past participle (*-áto, -úto, -íto*), besides continuing the Latin, has frequently replaced strong classical forms (*caduto, venuto, vivuto* and *vissuto*). The termination *-úto* has generally replaced *-ĭtus* (*avuto, piaciuto*), and in the South has taken the place of *-ītus,* whence forms like *vestuto* (as in Dante's description of Beatrice, " benignamente d'umiltà vestuta ") passed into early Italian poetry. In the main, the type of strong past participle in *-tus* has lost ground, and the type in *-sus* has gained, in the passage from Latin to Italian.

III

A literary language began to be formed in Italy during the thirteenth century, mainly in the sphere of lyrical poetry. The poets of the " scuola siciliana " wrote in what has been called a " siciliano illustre," which was not the vernacular of the people, but rehandled by men familiar with Latin who, in bringing their language closer to the Latin base, inevitably tended towards Tuscan, the Italian dialect that preserved the Latin linguistic tradition in its purest form. A certain southern colouring, both phonetic and morphological, remained, and penetrated into what became the traditional language of Italian poetry, together with elements derived from Provençal. This Tuscanism became accentuated after the fall of the House of Suabia, with the increased political and economic importance of Florence, and the fact that the Sicilian poets were succeeded by Tuscans, like Guittone of Arezzo and his school. The presence of Tuscan teachers and scholars at the university of Bologna, the political relations between that commune and Florence, was also a factor in this first partial unification of the language, in the circumscribed field of lyrical poetry, which was aided by the restricted sphere of subjects, the similarity of models, and the choice of words prescribed by the needs of the " poesia aulica." It is this that led Dante, in the *De Vulgari Eloquentia,* to his

[1] In such formations, the *u* falls and the previous consonant is doubled : *tenui, tenni ;* except when that consonant is a *c,* when the *u* remains : *placui, piacqui ;* or when it is an *s,* where the *u* already fell in Vulgar Latin : *posui, puòsi,* which became *pòsi* by analogy with the tonic vowel of the present.

conception of the " vulgare illustre," " the illustrious cardinal
courtly and curial vulgar tongue in Italy," which " belongs to
every Italian city and yet seems to belong to none, and by which
all the local dialects of the Italians are measured, weighed and
compared." He rejects Tuscan, as merely one among other
municipal dialects, in favour of this ideal literary Italian, an
abstraction free from local characteristics, which he seems to
find realised in the lyrical poetry of certain of his predecessors
and contemporaries—Sicilians, Apulians, Bolognese and Tuscans—
who, though natives of different regions of Italy, appeared to be
using a common " illustrious " vernacular in which the limited
linguistic knowledge of his times prevented him from recognising
the Tuscan basis. Nevertheless, in the *Divina Commedia*, Dante
represents the souls whom he meets on his spiritual pilgrimage
as recognising him as a Tuscan by his speech, and describes
himself as " parlando tosco." Thus the great masterpiece that
gave expression to the Italian genius is written in Tuscan by a
Florentine ; its syntax, phonetics and morphology (with sporadic
acceptance, usually for purposes of rhyme, of forms from other
Italian dialects, with Latinisms, and even occasional Gallicisms
and Provençalisms) are essentially Florentine, and the national
language " trovò la sua prima indistruttibile codificazione nel
genio immortale di Dante " (Guarnerio).

Simultaneously with the circulation of the *Commedia*, came
the other two members of the Tuscan triumvirate : Petrarch
and Boccaccio. The literary influence of these three before the
end of the fourteenth century established a Tuscan or Florentine
pre-eminence over other dialects throughout the greater part of
Italy. In the fifteenth century there was a certain check to
the development of Tuscan as the general literary language.
The influence of the classical revival led to the attempt to sub-
stitute Latin for the vernacular as the language of culture, and
the first struggle was to vindicate, against the humanists, the
rightful place of Italian as a literary language at all. Already
italiano and *toscano* were used as synonymous terms, and its
claims were maintained notably by Leon Battista Alberti and
Lorenzo de' Medici. When, in the latter part of the century,
the vernacular triumphed over Latin, there were (as Carducci
notes) three literary capitals : Florence, Ferrara and Naples.
In Florence pure Tuscan was naturally used and written, but
with no writer of such eminence as to impress himself upon the
whole peninsula as had done Dante, Petrarch and Boccaccio.
Nevertheless, the influence of these three was working elsewhere
in the other two literary centres. Here, too, was a feeling,

conscious or unconscious, that the language of these three was a thing to be desired. In both a type of vernacular for literary purposes arose that was not the spoken dialect, but a blending of what Dante would have regarded as an ideal courtly Italian with local forms and sounds. From this—through the study of the Tuscan triumvirate—emerged at Ferrara the *Orlando Innamorato* of Boiardo and at Naples the *Arcadia* of Sannazaro. Each, though in a different degree, represents the spontaneous development of the Tuscan tendency in non-Tuscan writers who are following in the footsteps of the great Florentines of the Trecento.

The " questione della lingua " took a more definite form in the sixteenth century, when Pietro Bembo arose as a kind of legislator for the literary language.   Himself a Venetian patrician and a Roman prelate, he nevertheless sought to fix the norm in the vernacular of Florence.   In his *Prose della volgar lingua* (published in 1525, but written earlier), he maintains that the language of Italy to be used in literary works is Florentine (with which he makes Tuscan identical), not the living language of the people, but as used by the great writers of the past, especially Petrarch and Boccaccio. His chief opponent was Giangiorgio Trissino, whose virtual rediscovery of the *De Vulgari Eloquentia* (which had been lost sight of since the fourteenth century) gave the authority of the greatest Italian name to his theory of the universal or " courtier " Italian language. Trissino—in his *Epistola* to Clement VII (1524) and in his dialogue, the *Castellano* (1529)—speaks of *lingua italiana* instead of *lingua toscana*, and distinguishes between *l'uso fiorentino* and *l'uso cortegiano*, frequently giving the preference to what he regards as Italian or " courtier," [1] arguing that, by removing the different pronunciations, modes of speech and words that characterise the various regions of Italy, there would remain " una istessa lingua italiana " which is what Dante and Petrarch wrote.   A similar view is put forward by Baldesar Castiglione in his *Cortegiano* (1528), where he pleads for a language that should include the nobler elements of the speech of the courts of the chief Italian cities, in which the use of words found in Boccaccio, but no longer current in Tuscany, and the rejection of all words that Tuscans do not use in the writer's own day, are alike to be regarded as pedantic affectations ; a language which, if not pure ancient Tuscan,

---

[1] For instance, in the conditional the forms derived from the perfect (as *sarei*) are Tuscan, those from the imperfect (as *seria* or *saria*) are Italian or " courtier " ; the pronunciation of *ogni* with a closed *o* is Florentine, with an open *o* " courtier."

would be "italiana, comune, copiosa, e varia." The theory
of the universal or courtier Italian is ably controverted by
Machiavelli, in his *Discorso* or *Dialogo*, an imaginary conversation between Dante and himself, in which he makes the poet
admit that there is no difference between the language of the
Commedia and Florentine, and declares that " there is no language
that can be called the common or curial language of Italy, because
all those that could be so called are based upon the Florentine
writers and the Florentine language." A somewhat different
position is represented by the Sienese, Claudio Tolomei, in his
dialogues, the *Polito* and the *Cesano*. His view in effect is that
the language of Italy should be called Tuscan, not Florentine
(which presents certain peculiarities to be rejected), and that the
actual standard should be, not the written works of the Tuscan
classics, but the usage of cultivated and lettered persons.

There was a certain unreality in the discussion, inasmuch
as the champions of the " common," " universal," " courtly "
Italian ignored the fact that this language, as employed by Dante,
Petrarch and Boccaccio, had its foundation in the Tuscan speech.
As Flamini observes, between Trissino demanding Italian citizenship for provincialisms and Tolomei seeking to impose the
actual usage of the cultured persons of a province upon the men
of letters of the whole peninsula, Bembo presented a mean that
would even conciliate the advocates of Latin. To make Italians
adopt in literary composition the language of Petrarch and
Boccaccio was quite a different thing from imposing upon them
the speech of a special province. True, it was Tuscan ; but
written for more than a century so as almost to be in the position
of a dead classical language and become common patrimony,
and likewise nearest to Latin. The triumph of Bembo is already
indicated by the greatest poet of the age, Ariosto, himself a
Ferrarese, submitting the definitive edition of the *Orlando Furioso*
(1532) to his judgment, and revising his diction so as to conform
with the written Tuscan tradition in accordance with the rules
laid down in the *Prose*.

The work of Bembo, in standardising and securing the recognition of Tuscan, or Florentine, as the literary language of
Italy, was continued by the members of the Florentine Academy,
which was founded in 1541. Its leading spirits were Benedetto
Varchi, Giambattista Gelli (the shoemaker), and Antonfrancesco
Grazzini (" Lasca "). Grazzini broke away from the Academy,
and founded the Brigata dei Crusconi which, under the auspices
of Lionardo Salviati, became the Accademia della Crusca, and
held its first regular assembly on 25th March, 1585. " Crusca "

means " bran," and the Academy took as its emblem the *frullone*, or sieve, with the motto " il più bel fiore ne coglie." Its labours crystallised into the famous *Vocabolario degli Accademici della Crusca*, of which the first edition was published in 1612. The *Vocabolario* was to establish the supremacy of the Tuscan vernacular, to be the barrier against corruption of the language, and to free it from accidental elements brought in by time. Its chief weakness was its exclusiveness ; it based the literary language primarily upon the great authors of the fourteenth century and certain of their successors, with only very slight attempts at conciliation with the actually spoken vernacular, thus tending to reduce its subject-matter to a condition not far removed from that of a classical dead language.

Subsequent editions of the *Vocabolario* somewhat enlarged its scope, but hardly modified its essentially eclectic character. Almost simultaneously with its first appearance, there was some Florentine reaction against the pedantry and exclusiveness of its compilers, and their neglect of the actually spoken tongue. This is represented particularly by Bernardo Davanzati (d. 1606), the author of the famous translation of Tacitus. Davanzati argued that to write, not in the living language, but in that " comune italiano " which is learned like a dead language in three Florentine authors, is " to cut the sinews of the language," whereby it remains poor and ineffective when compared with the actually spoken vernacular of Florence, and he defends the moderate use of popular Florentine idioms. With the seventeenth century begins the series of works not in " lingua," but in " dialetto," the attempts of non-Tuscan writers to raise a regional dialect to the dignity of a literary language, with Giambattista Basile in Neapolitan and Carlo Maria Maggi in Milanese.

The " questione della lingua " was revived at the end of the eighteenth century by Melchiorre Cesarotti, in his *Saggio sopra la lingua italiana*. Cesarotti attacked the *Vocabolario* for its limitations, whether regarded for the purpose of making the national language understood by foreigners or for that of serving for the use of writers. On the one hand, the traveller in regions of Italy other than Tuscany will meet words not registered in its pages, and, on the other, a man of science, in touch with the spirit of the age, will not find in it the words necessary to express his ideas. In particular, he criticised the excessive prominence given by the Crusca to writers of the Trecento and more modern writers in their manner. Against Cesarotti arose Antonio Cesari, with his *purismo*, maintaining that the Tuscan writers of the Trecento were still the insuperable models against the modern corruption of the Italian language. A new stage in the controversy was reached at the end of the Napoleonic period. In 1816 the Crusca, when about to prepare an enlarged and modernised edition of the *Vocabolario*, declined an offer of collaboration from the newly founded Istituto Nazionale of Milan. This brought Vincenzo Monti upon the scene, more or less on the lines of Cesarotti, but with a greater respect for the language of the past. Monti had an impassioned cult for the Italian language as the one remaining symbol of Italian nationality and unity. His *Proposta di alcune correzioni ed aggiunte al Vocabolario della Crusca*, published in instalments between 1817 and 1826, in collaboration with his son-in-law, Giulio Perticari, while admitting a certain pre-eminence of the Tuscan tradition, attempted to revive Dante's doctrine of "an Italian language different from all the dialects and common to all the cities of Italy." Monti, while denying that the national language was Florentine or that of any other region, admitted that Tuscan had a larger share than other regional vernaculars in the common and illustrious national language; but, as to the Tuscan of the Trecento, "live with the virtues of the ancients, but speak to me with the speech of the moderns." It is necessary to separate the living language from the dead, and *usage* is the absolute norm of speech.

This *uso* as norm leads us to Manzoni, though his main standpoint is in complete contradiction to that of Monti. Manzoni's great work was to free Italian prose from the academic character that it had borne since the days of Boccaccio. Like Ariosto with the final edition of his *Orlando*, Manzoni set himself to revise the language of his *Promessi Sposi*, "to wash his rags in the Arno"; but, in contrast with the method of the great Ferrarese, in accordance not with the written language but with the vernacular as spoken in Florence. His view was set forth later in the letter, *Sulla lingua italiana* (1845), and the report *Dell'unità della lingua e dei mezzi di diffonderla* (1868). He rejects the traditional phrase "lingua toscana" as not corresponding with the fact, and "lingua scritta" as implying a mere collection of words. His purpose is to have a language common to all Italy, to preserve the "carissimo nome di lingua italiana," and apply it to a real thing. "The Italian language is in Florence, like the Latin language was in Rome, like the French is in Paris." The literary language of Italy, what is vaguely called "lingua italiana," is not sufficient for all the needs of a modern society and nation, whereas the respective dialects of each city are richer. A single dialect must be extended to all the nation, and that must be the Florentine, not only because cultured Italians through-out the centuries have made it their own, but because " in it alone is found, united to what is common to all Italy, what is needed to give natural completion to the incomplete language of the nation." The norm and standard is therefore the *uso vivente* of Florence, the actual speech of contemporary cultured Florentines. Manzoni's excess was just the opposite of that of Bembo and the Crusca, inasmuch as he tended to neglect the effect and importance of literary tradition in the formation of a national language.

IV

In giving a summary account of regional differences in Italy we shall follow the track of spoken dialects, beginning from the centre where the popular language is nearer to literary Italian, and gradually passing thence to the North and South.

Tuscany will thus be our starting-point, although the per-petual " questione della lingua " may be taken to-day as settled, at least in the sense that it is generally agreed that there are bound to be differences between the spoken vernaculars of Tuscany and the officially recognised language. Where the boundary should be fixed remains, naturally, a matter of opinion. Nobody, perhaps, would now contend that the vernacular of the Florentines, full of marked aspirations of the guttural *c* and rich in local idioms, should be taken as a model of Italian, from the point of view either of construction or of pronunciation. Still less would the western Tuscan idioms, of Pisa and Leghorn, have a claim to be taken as models : there the guttural *c* very often disappears altogether. But in Lucca, and especially in some minor valleys of Garfagnana, in spite of a tendency to weaken guttural and labial consonants, and to use tones and cadences that remind one of the southern dialects, the local wealth in vocabulary and idioms is so marked as to attract the special attention of linguists, and a large vocabulary of Lucchese words has been compiled. Between Lucca and Florence stands Pistoia, where both pronunciation and vocabulary are very good and closer to the general standard of cultured Italians. Going southwards, we come to Arezzo and Siena, the latter being par-ticularly renowned for its clear pronunciation, and for having produced a literature of its own, different in style and character from that of any other part of Tuscany. Tuscan dialects in general give a fairly good clue to the temperament of the people : clear and realistic, slightly inclined to egotism and cynicism, extremely genial and inventive in finding forms of expression.

2

But nowhere as in Tuscany are local differences so marked : while the Pisans seem to have lost, with the sea, their old adventurous and warlike spirit, the Lucchese are very thrifty emigrants and successful merchants ; some minor centres in the Arno and Chiana valleys are industrialised ; Leghorn produces good sailors, and the peasants in most parts of Tuscany are very plucky and fairly well off.

Around Tuscany there is, as it were, a halo of minor dialects closely following the main characters of her speech.　Umbria, a high land of peasants, shepherds and mystics, and Corsica across the Tyrrhenian, have both developed semi-Tuscan dialects, with certain words, endings and phonetic characters already showing influences from the South.　Particularly in Corsican the *u* endings are very frequent.　Rome and Latium also dialectally stand half-way between Tuscan and Neapolitan, with a peculiar sweetness of their own ; the well-known proverb, " lingua toscana in bocca romana " (Tuscan tongue spoken by Roman), still holds good, in so far as a Roman will ever consent to speak a genuine " lingua toscana " ; which is not often the case.　The character of the real old Roman people is a puzzle to many travellers : it appears to be a mixture of nonchalance and passionality, of materialism and mysticism.　In fact the Romans enjoy a proverbial appetite, and they take life with a calm and sometimes joyous fatalism that is probably the result of their having seen too much of history where history was made.

Now, if we proceed eastwards and cross the passes of the Apennines, we experience a total change in the scenery and in the characters and languages of the inhabitants.　The air will be more crude and pungent, exposed as it is to the northeastern winds ; the landscape is less varied and picturesque, except for certain peculiar positions as that of the city of San Marino, a tiny independent republic.　We are in Romagna, historically a land of quarrelsome communes and of warlike and lawless noblemen.　Here, none of the calm, considerate, slightly selfish clearness of the Tuscans in speech and action ; the Romagnoli are passionate, enthusiastic and impulsive ; society means something positive and ever present to their minds ; they are born politicians, and they are likely to adopt extreme views and stand for revolution.　Yet there is kindliness in their hearts, loyalty, and the same elements of common sense and realism that are to be found more or less in all the peoples of the peninsula.　Their dialect is akin to that of the Emilians, though much more abrupt, with closer vowels and no slurring of the finals, and in certain respects is not so distinctly northern as the Emilian.   Yet Romagnoles and Emilians have their principal town in common, Bologna ; they can understand their reciprocal speeches ; and they are similar in their principal activity, which is agriculture brought to the technical perfection and intensity of a modern industry.   Emilia, reaching as far north in the Po valley as Parma and Guastalla, is one of the richest and most laborious regions of Italy.

In the North we find four main groups, both ethnical and linguistical.   Piedmont in the extreme north-west, a land of hard mountaineers and thrifty peasants, of feudal and monarchist traditions, has been for centuries the domain of the House of Savoy, and could thus become the cradle of Italian unity and independence during the Risorgimento.   It is a picturesque land, encircled by the highest ranges of the Alps and the Apennines, cut across by many clear and rapid streams and by the regal waters of the Po.   In recent times it has also achieved a great development in industry ; the motor-car industry in Turin, for instance, and the woollen manufactures of Biella, are of world renown.   The Piedmontese dialect, except for a few stems of Celtic or local, and certainly pre-Roman, origin, has formed itself largely under romance influence, and represents a linguistic link between France and Italy.   In fact, even the uncultured peasant of Piedmont can understand some French, and French was one of the spoken languages at the court of Turin until late in the nineteenth century.

Lombardy is the industrial and commercial heart of Italy, and Milan still holds her proud contention that she is the " moral capital " of the country.   From the low and once marshy and insanitary plains of the middle course of the Po, Lombardy rises, through the picturesque region of Brianza and the lakes, to the heights of the Lepontine Alps.   The Italian canton of Switzerland, Canton Ticino, reaches down from the watershed to Chiasso on Lake Lugano, not far from Milan : almost a symbol of Lombardy's historical and economical function as the main centre for the relations between Italy and Central Europe.   The people, racially a mixture of aborigines of the Alpine type, and of Celts, Latins and Langobards, are characterised by a great spirit of initiative in business, and a joviality and optimism of temper which are by no means universal in the peninsula.   Their dialect contains typically northern sounds, like the *ü* and *œ*, and is very abrupt, full of idioms and difficult to an untrained ear.

The Venetian districts are wider, more varied, and there-fore more difficult to be even summarily described.   The moun-tainous regions of Trento and Belluno reveal in their dialects the proximity of Ladin-speaking centres, like the valley of Ampezzo, whereas they seem to be almost immune from Germanic influences. In the region of Bolzano, German is commonly used both as a spoken and written language, and is taught in the schools. This is not the only example of a non-Italian linguistic " island " in the peninsula. In the valley of Aosta (the Roman *Augusta*), north of Turin, the spoken and officially recognised language is French ; and there are Slav-speaking centres near the north-eastern frontier, and Albanese and even Greek-speaking "islands" in the South and in Sicily. The dialect of Verona, Vicenza, Treviso, Padua, Venice, Trieste and Istria, with many local differences, could almost claim to be considered a language, in view of the remarkable amount of literature that has been written in it, and of its historical importance as the earliest and the principal western tongue known and spoken all along the coasts of the Levant. Its formation can be traced almost as far back as the origin of the " tosco-siciliano," or early Italian ; it derives from the meeting of romance and local Latin forms and sounds in the age following the Frankish conquest (eleventh century), when the tongue of the " Marca Trivigiana " began to be more widely known in Italy through the Carolingian and Arthurian tales and ballads of minstrels or " cantastorie." The growth of the Venetian Republic gave it, in time, more dignity, delicacy and refinement, and gradually combed it of many of its original solecisms. It is now, especially as spoken in Venice, a soft sounded and sweetly modulated dialect, rich in shades and subtleties, sometimes a little monotonous, but certainly quite suitable to the well-known conversational propensity of the Venetians. The glamour and elegance of Venetian life in the later centuries of the Republic seems to have survived in this tongue, so humorous and shaded and slightly melancholy, that lends itself well to poetry and song, and still inspires a considerable number of not unworthy vernacular poets.

The large and fertile plains north of Venice, Friuli (Latin, *Forum Iulii*), have a vernacular of their own, perhaps more direct in its Latin derivation, which keeps, quite peculiarly, the endings of the Latin datives *i* and *is* for the nominative case, and has the plural articles *los* and *las*. Along the Dalmatian coast, the island of Veglia had a dialect of her own, partly pre-Roman, now extinct and practically unrecorded ; but Venetian is known and spoken, though under the stress of political difficulties, as far down as Ragusa.

The Ligurians, on the north-western coasts of Italy, claim

that they have kept their race free even from Latin infiltrations, and that their racial characteristics have remained essentially unchanged since prehistoric times. Certainly, the physical conditions of their country are so peculiar that they alone might explain the persistence of the same habits and inclinations in the inhabitants. All along the coast, the Apennines slope down rather abruptly into the sea ; they are often barren and rocky, and they only yield a hard-won harvest of olives, some cereals and pine-nuts. The weather can be very stormy and very warm, according to the winds, and the large majority of the population are naturally merchants, sailors and fishermen. The Genoese are known to be hardened workers and business men, thrifty, unostentatious, conservative ; they travel the world, but they stick to their own habits and to their own dialect, which is a harsh and difficult one, more similar to the Lombard and the Emilian than to Piedmontese, but widely divergent from the neighbouring Tuscan.

To complete this rapid survey we must now go back to the eastern coast of Central Italy, where Romagna ends and the Marche present us with a dialect that is still fairly near the Tuscan model, but has much of the swing and softness of the southern group. The Marche are a region of low, green, fertile hills, inhabited by a population of quiet and conservative peasants. Moving west and southward we find the Abruzzi and Molise, which present us with the finest mountain sceneries of the Apennines.   It is here that the Apennines reach their highest summit in the Gran Sasso, the slopes of which are covered by dense secular forests inhabited by a varied fauna including the wolf and the brown bear. The people, mostly peasants and shepherds, keep their ancient picturesque traditions in dress and habits ; they have a repute for bravery, kindness and hospitality, and altogether live up to the old saying, "Abruzzo forte e gentile."   Abruzzo is fertile in men of letters, artists and politicians, and also produces dialectal writers able to show the adaptability to poetry of their very vocalic dialect, which is perhaps the most Tuscan-like of the southern group. Here we find that the Sicilian and Corsican ending in *u* is often substituted by *e*, although articles are *lu, la* and *nu, na ;* hard consonants are generally weakened as in Neapolitan, and not a few words show Greek or Levantine influence.

The southern ranges of the Apennines turn westwards from Abruzzo to form the high plateaux of Basilicata and Calabria. After the picturesque promontory of the Gargano, following the Adriatic coast, we find the low hills and barren plains of Apulia

(Tavoliere delle Puglie) surrounding a few ports, like Brindisi and Taranto, of great importance for Italian communications with the East. The principal city is Bari, with a modern and well-appointed university. Apart from seamen and fishermen, the majority of the population labour on the dry and often stony land. Their main produce is wheat, of which many parts of the Tavoliere are extremely fertile in good years ; but there are sometimes even three subsequent years of drought, drinkable water is everywhere scarce, and local conditions are sometimes insanitary. Peasants do not live in farmhouses scattered on the country, as is generally the case in Italy, but they group in small centres, and thence they depart every morning on a long, dreary journey, to reach the part of the land where they are appointed to work. Their language, akin in many ways to Calabrian and Sicilian, shows traces of Greek and other Levantine influences, and has also produced a certain amount of dialectal literature.

The tourist will generally find that the heel of the " boot " is less interesting than the southern Tyrrhenian coast. Here, after crossing the southern part of the Roman Agro and the Pontine marshes, he will find great beauty and variety in the green and rocky views of Campania. The Gulf of Naples and the remaining coast down to Calabria are so widely famous for their natural attractions that we need not attempt a description. The character of the inhabitants perhaps deserves a few words, if only to stultify the commonplace that represents Campania as the typical land of "dolce far niente." Naples had been for centuries the capital of a not well governed kingdom, and its rulers often found it expedient to have a loyal and quiet popu-lace in their capital, even by means of undeserved gratifications and bounties. The regular *lazzarone* was therefore, very often, an inferior type accustomed to rely on resources of a disputable character ; a distant cousin of the Spanish *pícaro*, and perhaps the result of similar circumstances, both natural and historical. But the *lazzarone* and the *camorrista* are very largely things of the past, much though this may displease a certain kind of romantic traveller ; yet the characteristics of Neapolitan life and manners are not so deeply changed, and probably will never be. As is so often the case in Italy, Campania is more pictur-esque than fertile ; the peasantry have a hard life, and they have to work more for their meagre food than those of most other lands. The townsmen of the middle and upper classes are generally in-telligent and cultured, hospitable and refined. Naples is an old centre of culture and lives up to its traditions ; it is also one of the most important commercial ports in the Mediterranean. The dialect was probably one of the earliest in its formation, and has a large and remarkable literature of its own ; together with Sicilian it is linked with the origins of Italian itself, and is very strictly grammatical. Its sound is soft and slightly dragging ; its idioms are quick and suggestive. Unlike many other peoples in the South, the Neapolitans are great talkers, and they possess a punctilious legal mind that has made them famous, though not always favourably, in every part of Italy.

Little can be said here of Basilicata and Calabria : two regions where many advantages of civilisation have long been wanting, and where nature seems to have spread with profusion its beauty and its curses. Much has been done, and is being done, by the Italian Government to improve sanitation, water supplies, elementary education and transports in those parts ; enormous dykes are being erected in the high Sila region to regulate the waters and produce electrical power. The inhabitants used to emigrate in large numbers, especially to America ; now they are beginning to feel that there is scope in staying at home. Their dialect presents two main varieties, being closer to the Neapolitan group in the inland and northern districts, whereas along the Ionic coast, down to the Straits of Messina, it still bears many obvious traces of the Greek influences, probably dating back to pre-Roman times.

From Lecce on the Adriatic coast of Apulia, and then following the Gulf of Otranto and the southern coast of Calabria as far as Reggio, and, across the straits, in many centres of the eastern part of Sicily, one finds the best archæological and linguistical survivals of Magna Græcia and of the Byzantine garrisons and ports of the Middle Ages. Sicily preserves otherwise, in architecture, in several place-names, and in a few tracts of its dialect, distinct reminders of its having been under Muslim domination for two centuries. The following Norman and Swabian period has left traces in buildings and in the names and physical types of ancient families ; but most of the nobility, and a good deal of the social habits and mentality of the people, are directly or indirectly of Spanish origin. The spirit of independence, and often unruliness, of the Spanish nobility that dominated Sicily for centuries reacted unfavourably on the jealous, thrifty, law-abiding character of a people that had known and absorbed something from all the greatest civilisations that ever flourished on the shores of the Mediterranean. The psychology of the ruled appeared to be dangerously incompatible with the habits and mentality of the rulers, and the results were serious and

far-reaching.   Changed conditions in the last seventy years have
done a great deal to direct along better channels the activities of
the island.   Sicilian is one of the most important dialects in Italy,
as, in the literary form which had developed among the men of
culture at the court of Frederick II, it is the linguistic basis of
the earliest phase of Italian lyrical poetry.   As thus adopted, it
was not so widely different from the dialects of Tuscany ; Latin
and Italian having been the cultured languages in the intervening centuries, Sicilian has developed its idiomatic and local
qualities, and is now a difficult dialect to understand, even for
southern Italians ; yet it prides itself on a literature of its own,
even contemporary.

Sardinia is to the traveller a source of continuous delight and
surprise ; a land of peasants and shepherds, very loyal and conservative, strenuous supporters of their king in war and peace,
faithful, hospitable, not over-imaginative and often lacking in
practical initiative.   Their race is a mixture of Latins, Cartha-
ginians and a more ancient stratum not clearly defined.   There
are small " islands " of Genoese immigrants, and in Alghero,
on the western coast, a Catalonian dialect is spoken.   Sardinian
can be described, very roughly, as a dialect standing between
Corsican and Sicilian, with many peculiarities of its own, pointing
to different influences.   It stands apart from the main Italian
linguistic system, and, more particularly in the dialect of the
central mountainous part (Logudorese), represents a more rudimentary type of romance vernacular.   To Dante it seemed
" imitating Latin like apes do men."

After all we have said, it would be perhaps contradictory to
attempt an explanation of what Italy " represents," or " stands
for," among the various nations of Europe.   One might elude
the question by suggesting that she stands for " variety."
Against such a conclusion an easy objection would be that, whenever the Italians had a chance to forge their, or other peoples',
destinies, they always brought a strong element of common
order, a unification to stamp itself on internal or external differences.   Unity was the very soul of the Roman Empire, as
it was and is of the Catholic Church ; and it was the Italian
Renaissance that gave a new meaning to the idea and the ideal
of unity of culture among the civilised nations of the world.

The contradiction is only apparent, and the puzzle is merely
a formal one.   Unity can only be an active principle wherever
there is a variety to be somewhat unified.   And the Italians
always found so much variety (of races, languages and cultures)
ready at hand within the borders of their own land, that they

were bound to develop a strong sense of unity and order whenever they had the energy and the occasion to play an important rôle in history. Even in our days, unity and order are two
essential principles to be kept in mind in studying the spirit
and growth of Fascism.

Another element that seems to be inherent to the Italian mind
is that of *form*. The word should not be taken in its common
everyday meaning ; it is here used more or less as in Scholastic
philosophy, to mean the principle that gives individuality to
particular things out of undifferentiated matter. The Italian
mind is not formal, but formative : as if it had absorbed into
itself the infinitely varied shapeliness of its country's sceneries
and the transparence of her sky. Italians have a great literature
of their own, a great tradition in music, and they have brought
a first-rate contribution to science and philosophy ; yet in one
field the output of their country can be said to have been unparalleled and almost prodigious, and it is that of the " arti
figurative " : architecture, sculpture, painting and all the minor
arts connected with these. It is here, perhaps, that the genius
of the race, since Etruscan and Roman days, showed itself un-
fettered and at its best. The Greek heritage could not be passed
on to more competent hands. But as it was so passed, before
and after the beginning of our modern era, it took on a different
value, a new meaning : the purely contemplative, sublimely
unpractical spirit of Greek art and philosophy was partly lost.
Italians are not altogether a contemplative or *lyrical* race. In
them and to them, *form* is an active principle ; a Madonna of
Raphael is not so much a thing *contemplated* as a thing *made ;*
as if man were taking from the hands of God his own free and
responsible share in the unending work of creation.

Italian art and Italian civilisation, whenever Italy could
follow and express her own instincts, alike bear the imprint
of this *forming* spirit : keen in the creation and definition, or
determination, of things ; keen in the achievement of unity and
order out of casual variety ; keen in the formulation of law out
of the shapeless and boundless multitude of human motives.
A *practical* inclination, perhaps, which has been discovered to
permeate even the most transcendental inspirations of Italian
poets ; an inclination which, in the periods of relaxation and
decadence, turns to empty and tiresome rhetoric, but in its days
of creative vigour is likely to produce, as it has produced more than
once, some of the most valuable, durable and universal institutions.

BIBLIOGRAPHY TO CHAPTER I

(i) C. Foligno, *Latin Thought during the Middle Ages.* Oxford, 1929.
P. Giacosa, *Stirpe italica.* Milan, 1918.
E. G. Parodi, *L'eredità romana e l'alba della nostra poesia*, in *Poesia e storia nella Divina Commedia.* Naples, 1921.
D. Randall-Maciver, *Italy before the Romans.* Oxford, 1928.
G. Volpe, *Momenti di storia italiana.* Florence, 1925.

(ii) G. Bertoni, *L'elemento germanico nella lingua italiana.* Genoa, 1914.
R. B. Bezzola, *Abbozzo di una storia dei gallicismi italiani nei primi secoli.* Zurich, 1924.
F. D'Ovidio and W. Meyer-Lübke, *Grammatica storica della lingua e dei dialetti italiani*, trad. Polcari. Milan, Manuali Hoepli.
P. G. Goidànich, *Grammatica italiana.* Bologna.
C. H. Grandgent, *An Introduction to Vulgar Latin.* Boston, 1907.
C. H. Grandgent, *From Latin to Italian.* Harvard University Press, 1927.
P. E. Guarnerio, *Fonologia romanza.* Milan, Manuali Hoepli.
D. Mauro Inguanes, *I placiti Cassinesi del secolo X con periodi in volgare.* Montecassino, 1930.
W. Meyer-Lübke, *Grammatica storica della lingua italiana e dei dialetti toscani*, ed. M. Bartoli. Turin, 1927.
P. Savi-Lopez, *Le origini neolatine.* Milan, Manuali Hoepli.
N. Zingarelli, *Vocabolario della lingua italiana.* Greco Milanese (new ed., 1931).

(iii) T. Casini, *Le forme metriche italiane.* Florence (2nd ed.), 1915.
F. D'Ovidio, *Versificazione italiana* (including essays on the *De Vulgari Eloquentia*, Milan, 1910). Republished in *Opere*, IX-X. Naples, 1932.
F. Foffano, *Prose linguistiche : la questione della lingua.* Florence, 1918.
P. E. Guarnerio, *Manuale di versificazione italiana.* Milan, 1913.
T. Labande Jeanroy, *La question de la langue en Italie.* Strasbourg, 1925.
C. Marconcini, *L'Accademia della Crusca dalle origini alla prima edizione del Vocabolario.* Pisa, 1910.
P. Rajna, *Le origini della lingua italiana*, in D'Ancona and Bacci, *Manuale* (see below).
C. Trabalza, *Storia della grammatica italiana.* Milan, 1908.
V. Vivaldi, *Storia delle controversie linguistiche in Italia.* Catanzaro, 1925.
F. D'Ovidio, *Le correzioni ai " Promessi sposi " e la questione della lingua.* In *Opere*, VIII. Naples, 1933.

(iv) C. Avolio, *Introduzione allo studio del dialetto siciliano.* Noto, 1882.
C. Battisti, *Testi dialettali italiani in trascrizione fonetica.* Halle, 1921.
C. Battisti, *Popoli e lingue nell'alto Adige.* Florence, 1931.
G. Bertoni, *Italia dialettale.* Milan, Manuali Hoepli.
G. A. Cesareo, *Le origini della poesia lirica e la poesia siciliana sotto gli Svevi.* 2nd ed. Palermo, 1924.
S. Debenedetti, *Testi antichi siciliani.* Turin, 1931.

CHAPTER II

MEDIEVAL ITALY TO THE DEATH OF HENRY VII

THERE is no clear line of demarcation between classical and medieval times, for the essential continuity between ancient Rome and modern Italy is the keynote of Italian civilisation. The so-called fall of the Roman Empire in 476—when the barbarian soldier Odovacar dethroned the last of the old Roman emperors in the West—is no longer accepted as marking an epoch. In 493 the great Ostrogoth, Theodoric, overthrew Odovacar and took Ravenna; henceforth for thirty years, with what may be called a mandate from the eastern emperor at Byzantium, he ruled as " King of the Goths and Romans in Italy." The Rome that welcomed Theodoric in 500, when he promised with God's help to keep inviolate all that the Roman princes in the past had ordained, was still—in spite of the ravages of Alaric's Visigoths and Gaiseric's Vandals—essentially the Rome of classical times. Theodoric died in 526. The prolonged horrors of the wars between the Goths and the Byzantines, the struggle between the successors of Theodoric, Totila and Teias, and the generals of Justinian, Belisarius and Narses, for the possession of Italy, from 535 to 553, when the last of the Gothic kings fell at Mons Lactarius, transformed the city into what became medieval Rome. We may conveniently take the sixth century as the beginning of medieval Italy. In 525 Boëthius—who may be regarded as the last man of classical times—had died in the dungeon of Theodoric, a martyr for the liberty of Rome if not for her religion. It is at least a striking coincidence that tradition has assigned to one same year, 529, the closing of the philosophical schools at Athens by the order of Justinian and the coming of St. Benedict from Subiaco to found Montecassino. The end of an epoch of classical thought would thus coincide with the opening of a new phase in medieval religious life. Between that date and the year of Benedict's death—according to tradition, 543, but perhaps as much as ten years later—the Benedictine rule was promulgated, which was to set the norm of medieval monasticism in the West. And with Gregory the Great, elected pope in 590, the medieval spirit becomes explicit and authoritative.

The end of the classical period had left Italy a political unity, though no longer the centre of the Roman Empire. This unity was preserved under Theodoric (whose kingdom included Sicily, Rezia, Istria, Provence and Dalmatia), and when the Byzantine conquest reunited it to the Eastern Empire. It was destroyed by the Langobard invasion that immediately followed, when, in the words of St. Gregory, " the barbarous and cruel nation of the Langobards, drawn as a sword out of a sheath, left their own country and invaded ours." It was in 568 that the Langobards under their king Alboin entered Italy, and the two centuries of Langobard domination witnessed the breaking up of that political unity which was destined not to be permanently restored until the Risorgimento. The Langobards— even under their greatest king Liutprand (712-744)—never succeeded in conquering the whole of Italy, although they penetrated down to the Ionian sea. Rome itself, a portion of eastern Italy centring in Ravenna, and continually diminishing parts of the South, remained still more or less subject to Byzantium, as also did Sicily, Sardinia and Corsica. While Langobard Italy had its capital at Pavia, Byzantine Italy had its at Ravenna, the seat of the Exarch until the city fell to the Langobard king Aistulf about 751. But neither the Langobard kingdom nor the Byzantine exarchate remained a single state. The Langobards failed to constitute their conquests into a real political unity. The kingdom was divided into duchies, and the most important of these—Friuli, Spoleto and Benevento—made themselves independent states. Similarly, portions of Byzantine Italy broke away from Ravenna. In the course of the eighth century Naples became a virtually independent duchy, and Rome " the republic of the Roman People " under the patronage of St. Peter represented by the pope, hardly yet a temporal sovereign. The Temporal Power was, in a sense, the creation of the Franks, to whom the popes appealed for aid against the increasing pressure of the Langobards. Pepin in 754 conquered the exarchate from the latter and bestowed it upon the pope ; his son Charlemagne, who took Pavia from the last Langobard king, Desiderius, in 774 and overthrew the Langobard kingdom, recognised the papal dominion over the duchy of Rome, the exarchate of Ravenna with the Pentapolis (Rimini, Pesaro, Fano, Sinigaglia and Ancona). The coronation of Charles as Holy Roman Emperor by Leo III on Christmas Day, 800, opened a new epoch for Italy as well as for the medieval world.

Already one of the chief glories of Italy had arisen. In the extreme eastern corner of the Peninsula, a race, by tradition descendants of refugees from Attila and the Huns (originally, perhaps, the Veneti were immigrants from Asia Minor, but romanised like the rest of the Italians), formed twelve communes on the banks and islands of the Adriatic lagoons, politically subject to Byzantium, and governed by tribunes elected by the people and confirmed by the emperor. In 697 these communities were confederated, and the first Doge—Paolo Lucio Anafesto of Heraclea—was elected. Henceforth, in spite of sanguinary feuds between the communities, Venice was a constituent state, with privileges and concessions from Byzantium which gradually amounted to independence. Though compelled to pay tribute to Liutprand by a treaty of 715, the Venetians formed no part of the Langobard kingdom, and in 729 they expelled the Langobards from a temporary occupation of Ravenna. When the Franks restored the western empire, the Venetians in 809 effected that concentration on the group of small islands called Rialto which marks the beginning of modern Venice, and answered the summons of the son of Charlemagne to acknowledge themselves his subjects with the words : " We will be the men of the Roman Emperor, not yours." This claim was recognised by Charlemagne, and Venice never became a part of the Holy Roman Empire.

Like the Langobard settlement, the Frankish conquest was only partial. Southern Italy remained intact, and from this point, as Villari observes, began to have a history different from that of the rest of the peninsula. There was still the Langobard duchy or principality of Benevento, from which Capua and Salerno broke off, while the rest of the South remained united to Byzantium, the maritime states of Naples, Amalfi and Gaeta preserving their independence. In the ninth century, between 828 and 878, the Saracens conquered Sicily, and on one occasion penetrated into Rome, only to be defeated by the fleets of Amalfi, Gaeta and Naples at Ostia in 849. The rest of northern Italy formed the " regnum italicum " of which the symbol was the " iron crown " of Milan, which was held by a member of Charlemagne's family until the extinction of the dynasty. Here, too, there was subdivision into duchies and counties under the feudal system ; and " marches " were constituted, such as the marquisate of Tuscany and the marquisate of Friuli. In the anarchy that followed the dissolution of the Carolingian Empire (the last of the dynasty of the great Charles died in 888), these potentates naturally tended to become independent sovereigns, even aiming at the crown of the Italian kingdom. In 915 the Marquess Berengarius of Friuli, after a struggle with Duke Guido of Spoleto,

was crowned emperor at Rome, and, towards the middle of the
century, there was a similar conflict between Hugh of Provence
and Berengarius of Ivrea. This anarchy, accompanied by unparalleled degradation of the papacy, was ended by the advent
of the Saxon king, Otto the Great, who was crowned emperor
at Rome in 962. Although Otto claimed southern Italy for his
Italian kingdom, neither he nor his successor could effect its
conquest. His direct line ended with Otto III, who died at Paterno
in 1002, dreaming of a new unity of civilisation under his sceptre,
but the " regnum italicum " remained henceforth associated by
a personal union to the " Holy Roman Empire " of the German
kings after Arduino of Ivrea (1003-15) had vainly struggled for
the crown of Italy against Otto's elected German successor,
Henry. Venice maintained her now purely nominal adherence
to the eastern empire, and had successfully resisted an attempt
of Otto II, in alliance with a faction in the republic itself, to bring
her into vassalage to the West. In the year 1000—a fitting
prelude to the fuller Italian life of the eleventh century—the
Doge, Pietro Orseolo II, led the fleet of the republic on the expedition against the Dalmatian pirates which was the beginning
of the Venetian hegemony of the Adriatic. Henceforth the Doge
bore the double title, " Duke of Venice and Dalmatia."

The eleventh century saw the rise of the city states, which
ultimately developed into the Italian communes in the North,
and the Norman conquest of southern Italy and Sicily.

There had been an increasing development of civic life in the
Italian cities from the last years of the Langobard domination.
To a large extent the descendants of the Langobards had fused
with the inhabitants of Latin stock, but the nobles were almost
entirely of Germanic race, whether Frank or Langobard or even
German followers of the Ottos. The feudal system introduced
by the Franks had declined, and, in accordance with the policy
of their successors, the power of the count or marquess in the
great cities had been replaced by that of the bishop. During
the eleventh century the trader and merchant, of purely Latin
descent, gradually came to the front ; the populations of the
towns increased, and the towns began to extend their juris-
diction over the neighbouring countryside, the " contado." The
German king Conrad, in 1037, found himself resisted by the people
of Milan under their Archbishop Ariberto (it is then that we
first hear of the *carroccio* or battle-car of the city), and this popular
consciousness was further stimulated by the reforming movement,
at first religious and social, in the latter part of the century, which
led to the war of investitures between Pope and Emperor in the

pontificate of Hildebrand as Gregory VII (1073-85). Between the end of the eleventh and the beginning of the twelfth century, we find communes evolving in the chief cities of north and central Italy, organisations based upon the general assembly of the citizens (*contio, arengum, parlamentum*), with consuls replacing the bishops as the representatives and elected governors of the city state. We have documentary evidence of consuls in Pisa about 1085, in Milan in 1087, and in Genoa in 1089 ; Pisa and Genoa were already strong enough to undertake enterprises against the Saracens in the western Mediterranean. Florence developed her commune after the death of the Countess Matilda in 1115 had led to the dissolution of the Marquisate of Tuscany.

A similar, somewhat earlier, development of municipal institutions in the cities of southern Italy was cut short by the Norman conquest. These Normans first appeared in the early years of the century as small bands of adventurers, each leader grasping territory for himself ; but they became united under the great Robert Guiscard de Hauteville, who, in 1059, was recognised by the pope as Duke of Apulia and a vassal of the Church. Bari, the Byzantine capital, fell in 1071 ; in 1072 Robert and his brother Roger took Palermo from the Saracens ; by 1080 all the South, except Naples, was in the hands of the Normans. Robert had been confirmed in his conquests as a vassal of the Church by the pope, and in 1084, when Gregory VII was besieged in Sant' Angelo by the Emperor Henry IV, he captured and sacked Rome, carrying off the liberated pontiff to Salerno. In the meantime his brother Roger completed the conquest of Sicily from the Saracens. There were thus two great Norman states : the dukedom of Apulia and the countship of Sicily. But, after Robert's death in 1085, his son and grandson were unable to hold their own against the Norman feudatories. In 1127 Roger's son, Count Roger II of Sicily, landed at Salerno ; within three years he united the entire Norman dominion, and in 1130 was crowned King of Sicily by the legate of the antipope Anacletus at Palermo. Naples, the last independent state in southern Italy, passed under his rule in 1137.

Thus, in contrast with communal Italy of the North, was established the monarchical Italy of the South, the title of the sovereign being " king of Sicily, the dukedom of Apulia and the principality of Capua." This " Kingdom of Sicily " has been called the first modern state. The Normans imposed upon their dominions the feudal system, but superimposed upon it an elaborate bureaucracy borrowed from Byzantium, with a theocratic conception of the king—in spite of the nominal suzerainty

of the pope—holding his crown immediately from God. Their
rule, especially in Sicily, was tolerant and eclectic, and their
capital Palermo became the most splendid and luxurious city
of the medieval world. Roger captured Tripoli in 1146, and extended the Norman power over the coast of northern Africa.
The power of the kingdom declined under his son and successor,
William I (1154-66), who had to struggle with a Byzantine
invasion and the revolt of the Norman feudatories ; but the long
and peaceful reign of the second William, William the Good
(1166-89), who led no armies in the field and lived secluded in
oriental luxury, gave what was afterwards looked back to as
a golden age to the southern kingdom.

In northern and central Italy, the main development of the
communes was in Lombardy (using the word to include Emilia
and what ultimately became the Venetian mainland) and Tuscany,
though there were states—like those of the Counts of Savoy,
the Marquesses of Monferrato, and the family of the Malaspina—
which stood apart from the communal system, as also did Venice.
Elsewhere, Perugia and Ancona were almost the only city states
that attained power and importance. From the outset, there
was inevitably mutual hostility among the communes. Each
was engaged in expanding its territory, annexing the contado,
suppressing smaller communities, subduing the feudal nobles of
the hills and countryside. This, and the geographical situation
by which one city controlled the trade outlets and checked the
commercial progress of another, led to what ultimately inspired
the stugggles between Guelfs and Ghibellines. Thus Milan
crushed Como and Lodi, and found rivals in Pavia and Cremona.
Verona found her expansion checked by Padua, Bologna hers
by Modena. Pisa was in constant rivalry with Genoa. A little
later, Florence found Siena blocking her way to Rome, and Pisa
barring the access of her commerce to the sea. The communes
did not aim at independence, but autonomy and local sovereignty.
With the exception of Venice and the kingdom of Sicily, all
Italy in theory acknowledged the suzerainty of the Holy Roman
Empire, and recognised the man chosen by the German electors
as the successor of Augustus and Trajan. But to Frederick
of Suabia, " Barbarossa," elected king by the Germans in 1152,
the claims of the communes seemed insolent usurpation of imperial prerogatives. When he came to Italy in 1154, to receive
the imperial crown and restore the power of the empire, he found
adherents not only in the feudal nobility, but in communes like
Lodi, Pavia and Cremona which dreaded and hated Milan.
Frederick crushed the incipient republican movement in Rome

associated with Arnold of Brescia, was crowned by the English Pope Adrian IV (1155), and compelled Milan to surrender on terms (1158). A second surrender in 1162 was followed by the partial destruction of the city ; but, in 1167, the famous meeting at Pontida resulted in the formation of the Lombard League, for the restoration of their fatherland to the Milanese and the recovery of communal privileges. The chief cities of northern Italy (except Pavia and Genoa) joined, and it was supported by Venice, Pope Alexander III, and King William II of Sicily. Milan rose again from its ashes, a new city Alessandria was built in honour of the pope and sustained a long siege. On 29th May, 1176, the decisive battle was fought at Legnano, in which the emperor and his Germans were completely defeated by the forces of the League. The Peace of Constance, in June, 1183, while recognising the suzerainty of the emperor, gave the communes complete autonomy and local sovereignty, within and without the city.

The Peace of Constance was followed by dramatic changes in Italy. William of Sicily, who was childless, in 1186 consented to the marriage of his aunt Constance, daughter of King Roger and heiress to the kingdom, with Henry, the son of Barbarossa. William died in 1189. Frederick was drowned in the third Crusade in 1190. Henry, crowned emperor as Henry VI in 1191, claimed the kingdom of Sicily, and, after a struggle with the Norman pretender Tancred, conquered the island with the aid of the Genoese fleet, and was crowned at Palermo on Christmas Day, 1194, the day before the birth of a son, Frederick, to him and Constance. Thus the House of Suabia succeeded the Normans in southern Italy. Henry died in 1197, leaving the child Frederick as King of Sicily under the guardianship of Pope Innocent III. His cruelty and bad faith had already produced a reaction in Italy. Genoa became anti-imperialist, and in 1197 at San Genesio the Tuscan cities (excepting Pisa and Pistoia) formed a *Societas Tusciae*, in which Florence began to play a part similar to that of Milan in opposing the imperial claims.

Simultaneously a change had come in the constitution of the Italian commune, corresponding with the growing advance of the burgher class in the city state, the consuls being replaced by a single magistrate, the podestà. The podestà was originally an official nominated by the emperor to exercise the imperial rights, but, after the peace of Constance, he became the elected chief magistrate and representative of the commune. To secure impartiality, he was normally a nobleman from some other Italian city, who brought with him his own household, and held office for six months or a year. To some extent it marks the beginning

of the process by which, especially in Tuscany, what became
known as the " popolani," the burgher class, were eliminating
the nobles from the direct government of the state.   The struggle
between Otto of Brunswick, of the Welf House, and young
Frederick of Sicily, the Weibling, for the imperial crown introduced the ominous names " Guelf " and " Ghibelline " into
Italian politics.   Taken vaguely to imply adherence to the cause
of Pope and Emperor respectively, their significance merely
covered the rivalries between commune and commune, between
factions and groups within the same city.   Thus in Florence
the murder of Buondelmonte in 1215, traditionally said to mark
the beginning of the Guelf and Ghibelline factions in the republic, was merely the coming to a head of a long-existing feud
between hostile associations of noble families.

In 1220 Frederick II was crowned emperor by Honorius III,
the pope who, three years later, confirmed Innocent's approval
of the Franciscan order.   He had promised to take the Cross
for the recovery of Jerusalem, and actually took the city in 1229,
but left the Holy Sepulchre in the hands of the Saracens.   The
union of the crown of Sicily with that of the " regnum italicum "
in the person of one man, himself by birth and genius an Italian,
threatened both the political independence of the papacy and
the whole existing constitution of Italy.   Thus when Frederick,
while splendidly continuing the Norman tradition in the southern
kingdom, attempted to renew the part of his grandfather and
father in the north of the peninsula, his reign became a prolonged struggle with the popes and the second Lombard League.
Though victorious over Milan and her allies at Cortenuova (1237),
and at sea with the Pisan fleet over the Genoese at Monte Cristo
(1241), the emperor—deposed by Pope Innocent IV in 1245—
was defeated at Parma (1248), and at Fossalta (1249), where his
son Enzo was taken prisoner by the Bolognese.

Florence had been compelled to accept Frederick's authority ;
but now—while he was on his deathbed in 1250—she established
her first democratic constitution, the *Primo Popolo*, in which
the " people " were organised into armed companies, under a new
magistrate, the Captain of the People.   Henceforth in Florence,
and somewhat less notably in other Italian republics, there was
a two-fold organisation of the state : the Commune with the
Podestà at its head, the People with the Captain (usually a
nobleman from some other city) who gradually assumed the chief
executive power, the podestà becoming little more than a chief
justice.   The *Primo Popolo* for ten years made Florence the predominant power in Tuscany, while Pisa and Siena adhered to

the Ghibelline cause ; in the North, Ezzelino da Romano, as imperial vicar, conquered Treviso, Padua, Verona and other cities until his defeat and death in 1259, and in the South Frederick's illegitimate son Manfred as King of Sicily carried on his father's policy. On 4th September, 1260, the Sienese, with the aid of Manfred's German mercenaries, the Florentine exiles, and other Ghibelline cities, annihilated the army of the *Primo Popolo* at the battle of Montaperti. The heroism of Farinata degli Uberti, the leader of the Ghibelline exiles, saved Florence from destruction ; but for six years the city lay under the domination of Manfred's vicar and the Ghibelline nobles, while the leading Guelf families went into exile.

The popes claimed to be suzerains of the kingdom of Sicily, and in 1265 Charles of Anjou, brother of St. Louis of France, came to Italy on the invitation of Clement IV as champion of the Church and the Guelfs. Crowned king by the pope, Charles—by his victory at Benevento (Feb. 1266), where Manfred fell—established an Angevin dynasty upon the Sicilian throne. The Ghibellines were expelled from Florence, the city received back the Guelf exiles and accepted Charles as overlord. The young Conradin, Frederick's grandson, attempted to win back the Sicilian kingdom, but was defeated by Charles at Tagliacozzo (1268) and beheaded at Naples. In the following year, the defeat of the Sienese by the French and Florentines at Colle di Val d'Elsa compelled Siena to abandon the Ghibelline cause and join Florence in the Guelf League under Charles's suzerainty. But the oppressive government of the king, who made Naples his capital and treated the island as a conquered province, led to the " Sicilian Vespers " (March, 1282), when the people of Palermo rose and massacred the French, and Sicily gave itself to the King of Aragon, Peter III. Henceforth the old Norman and Suabian kingdom of Sicily was divided, the Angevins reigning on the mainland as kings of Naples or Apulia (though still styling themselves kings of Sicily), an Aragonese dynasty in the island itself as kings of " Trinacria." Sicily was thus separated from the political and intellectual life of Italy, an intermittent war between Aragonese and Angevins further taxing the resources of the kingdom of Naples. Charles died in 1285, and was succeeded by his son, Charles II, then a prisoner in Spain,

From the beginning of the century, the trade organisations or guilds (" Arti ")—existing also in other cities, but nowhere attaining the same importance—had begun to play a predominant part in Florentine politics. They were the motive power in establishing the second democratic constitution of Florence in

1282, whereby—side by side with the two-fold organisation of Commune and People under podestà and captain with their respective councils—a new magistracy, that of the Priors of the Arts (later six in number, one from each *sesto* of the city, and holding office for two months), chosen from members of the guilds, formed the " Signoria." It is now that we meet one of the few striking figures in early Florentine politics : Giano della Bella, a wealthy Guelf noble who had become the leader of the people. Like Dante he ended his days in exile ; but, in 1293, he left his mark on the constitution by the Ordinances of Justice, by which members of noble houses, " grandi " or " magnati," were excluded from the priorate and chief councils of the state, and a new magistrate, the Gonfaloniere (Standard-bearer) of Justice, was added to the Signoria to enforce stringent regulations against such nobles as should commit violence against any of the people. Thus was completed the *Secondo Popolo*, by which the government was concentrated in the hands of citizens ascribed to the guilds, engaged in industry and commerce. This was secured by the organisation of the guilds, where there was a distinction between the *Arti maggiori* (mainly engaged in wholesale commerce, exportation and importation, and the mercantile relations of Florence with other Italian states and foreign countries), and the *Arti minori* (that carried on the retail traffic and internal trade of the city). There were seven of the *Arti maggiori* : *Calimala* (dressers of foreign cloth), *Lana* (wool), *Seta* (silk), *Cambio* (money-changing and banking), *Giudici e Notai* (judges and notaries), *Medici e Speziali* (physicians and apothecaries), *Vaiai e Pellicciai* (furriers).[1] The *Arti minori* were fourteen in number, and various industries, instead of having a guild of their own, were attached to one or other of the greater guilds. For a long time the minor guilds possessed a relatively small share in the state, and the mass of the *popolo minuto*, unskilled labour with no such right of association, was completely excluded. The nobles or magnates, whether the descendants of the old feudal nobility or families risen by wealth out of the " popolo grasso," could still sit in the Council of the Podestà and in the Council of the Commune, as well as in the offices and councils of the " Parte Guelfa " which represented a kind of conservative element in the republic.

[1] The painters constituted a section of the *Arte dei Medici e Speziali*. Dante matriculated in this guild, probably because of the close association of the liberal arts and philosophy with medicine. It corresponds, under a certain aspect, with the confederation of professional men and artists in the present Corporative Fascist State.

Siena—no longer, since the battle of Colle di Val d'Elsa, a territorial rival of Florence—from 1285 onwards had the government in the hands of the " Noveschi " : an oligarchy of " good merchants of the Guelf party," with a chief council or magistracy of the Nine, who held office for two months like the Florentine priors. To the complete exclusion of the lower orders as well as of the nobles, they were elected from the rich and enlightened burgher class, corresponding more or less to the " popolani grassi " of Florence. There was a similar organisation of Commune and People, but that of the latter was based, not upon the guilds, which (with the exception of the Arte di Mercanzia and Arte della Lana) were of little political importance, but upon the *societates armorum*, the armed militia of the wards into which the city was divided.

Apart from the loss of Sicily, the last years of the century witnessed a series of Guelf triumphs, such as the defeat of Pisa by Genoa at the naval battle of Meloria in 1284, and that of the Tuscan Ghibellines by the Florentines and their allies at Campaldino on 11th June, 1289. Boniface VIII, elected pope at the end of 1294, claimed to exercise imperial rights during the vacancy of the empire ; his intervention in Florentine affairs, where the Guelfs had split into two factions known as Bianchi and Neri, led to the coming of Charles of Valois to the city as papal " peace maker " on 1st November, 1301, and the revolution of which Dante was the victim. But the victorious party, though led by magnates, was unable to change the constitution of the republic or to abolish the Ordinances of Justice ; they could do little more than exile their opponents and place adherents of their own faction in power. In October, 1303, Pope Boniface succumbed, after the violence of the agents of Philip of France at Anagni. The attempts of his successor, Benedict XI, to procure the internal peace of Florence by the return of the exiles failed. In the first part of the fourteenth century, the unsettled condition of Florence was to some extent due to the fact that the " grandi " had not definitely abandoned their aspiration to dominate the state, while the lowest part of the popular element was still excluded from the government. In 1308, for the first time in Florentine history, we find a single man attacking the basis of the republican constitution, vaguely hankering after a tyranny in the fashion that was appearing in the Lombard cities. Corso Donati, who had led the faction that had expelled Dante and his associates, aspired to be the head of an aristocratic oligarchy supported by the populace, and looked for aid to the Ghibelline soldier, Uguccione della Faggiuola. But the

power of the commune was strong enough to crush his attempt
at the outset, as it was to prove able, a little later, to defend
the republic against the renewed imperial claims.

Bologna and Padua, both politically associated with Florence,
preserved their communal institutions and liberties. The republic of Genoa, under captains of the people, had crushed the
force of Pisa, and was beginning its long struggle with Venice
for supremacy in the near East. Elsewhere in Lombardy the
communes were passing under the control of single families,
beginning the period of the *signorie* or tyrannies. Ferrara at
an earlier date (1209 and permanently in 1240) had accepted
the rule of the Marquesses of Este, who added Modena and
Reggio to their dominions ; Verona fell into the hands of the
Della Scala ; the Visconti and the Della Torre struggled for
the lordship of Milan. Similarly with the smaller cities of
Romagna, the Marches, and Umbria, though Perugia remained
a free commune while nominally (like Bologna) acknowledging
papal suzerainty. Rome itself, abandoned by the popes for
Avignon after the election of Clement V in 1305, was at least
in theory a republic, ruled by aristocratic senators, usually two
in number, nominated by the absent pontiff. Almost every
Italian city was, like Florence, torn by faction, with combinations of exiled citizens awaiting any opportunity to return to
their homes by force of arms.

The two most powerful states in Italy were the Republic
of Venice and, though no longer comparable to the old undivided
Kingdom of Sicily, the Kingdom of Naples ; the former essentially aristocratic, the latter feudal.

In the earlier Middle Ages Venice had been a democratic
state with an elective sovereign ; the Doge (who all through
Venetian history held office for life) had been considerably more
than the mere titular head of the state, and, until the latter part
of the twelfth century, had been elected by the entire Venetian
community. But there had come into being a powerful class
of wealthy nobles—some possibly, as they claimed, descendants of
great Roman families who had taken refuge in the lagoons, others of
families who had acquired wealth during the centuries of commercial expansion—who curtailed the ducal authority by an increasingly stringent coronation oath, until, from the latter part of the
thirteenth century, the Doge was little more than a figurehead
in the republic, although a strong personality, like Pietro Gradenigo
(1289-1311), could at intervals impress himself upon its policy.
Simultaneously the people had been slowly thrust out of politics—
a striking contrast with what was happening contemporaneously

at Florence and (in a less degree) at Siena. The measure known as the *Serrata del Maggior Consiglio*, the " Closing of the Great Council," in 1297, stamped its oligarchical and aristocratic character upon the republic. The *Maggior Consiglio* was the parliament of Venice, in which the supreme authority of the state was vested ; its membership was now confined to members of noble families whose names were inscribed in the famous Golden Book, thus placing all political power in the hands of a single class. Henceforth the election of the Doge was confined to the Great Council, although—until the early years of the fifteenth century—there was still the formality of approval by the general assembly of the whole community. The discontent thus caused led to two conspiracies—those of Marin Bocconio in 1300 and Bajamonte Tiepolo in 1310—but they were instantly crushed. It was in consequence of the latter that the famous Council of Ten was instituted, though it was not made permanent until 1335. That this oligarchical constitution gave to Venice an internal peace and stability that no other Italian state enjoyed was due to the patriotism of the nobles, the impartial administration of the laws, the admission of ordinary Venetian citizens to various offices and posts of dignity, the general wellbeing of the people, and the encouragement of the trade guilds as long as their activities did not touch politics.

Until the fourteenth century the expansion of Venice had been exclusively to the East, where, after the first Crusade, she was the chief power in the Levant, though now challenged by Genoa, and she only slowly began to form part of the general Italian polity. It was as an external power, rather than as having a national interest in the matter, that she had supported the Lombard communes against Frederick Barbarossa. But her commerce and need of cornlands was driving her to acquire possessions on the mainland, and control of the rivers and roads to the Alps. A disputed succession in the House of Este in 1308 gave Venice the opportunity, urged upon her by Pietro Gradenigo, to embark upon what was practically her first war of aggression in Italy : an attempt to get possession of Ferrara. The resulting war with the pope of Avignon, Clement V, ended in 1311 to the disadvantage of the Venetians. Foiled at Ferrara, Venice turned to the policy of commercial expansion through Lombardy, which was to bring her into conflict with the newly established despots, and ultimately to make her mistress of the greater part of northeastern Italy.

While Venice stood outside the sphere of the Italian factions, the King of Naples was the natural and acknowledged head of the

Guelfs. He was also Count of Provence and lord of a portion
of Piedmont, but the resources of the kingdom were inadequate
for the great part that should have been his in Italian politics.
The prominent features of the " Regno," as the southern kingdom
was called, were the power and unreliability of the feudal nobles,
the privileges of the clergy, and the lack, even in Naples, of a
class of rich merchant burghers such as existed at Florence and
in other north Italian cities. The main commerce of the kingdom
was passing into the hands of foreigners, more particularly into
those of the great Florentine banking firms, which drew still
closer the bonds uniting the Guelf commune with the Angevin
monarchy, even as the papal suzerainty involved a certain submission to the policy of the pope. Charles II, a man far inferior
in ability to his father, died in 1309, and was succeeded by his
son Robert, one of the most striking and interesting figures of
the early fourteenth century, by no means devoid of high ideals,
but quite incapable of the great national rôle that he now seemed
called upon to fill.

    In October, 1310, the newly elected emperor, Henry of Luxem-
burg, crossed the Alps, his advent heralded by one of the most
splendid examples of political propaganda in history : Dante's
letter to the Princes and Peoples of Italy. He came with the
apostolic benediction and with the noblest intentions, hating
the very names of Guelf and Ghibelline, bent on peacefully
restoring the power of the Holy Roman Empire and maintaining
justice in the land. But he found material support in the
Ghibellines alone ; faced with the powerful opposition of a confederation of Guelf cities led by Florence in alliance with Robert
of Naples, he was reduced to employing the usual methods of
his German predecessors. As Henry VII he was crowned with
difficulty by the pope's legates in the Lateran on 29th June, 1312
(the forces of the Florentines and Robert held the rest of the
city), and unsuccessfully besieged Florence in the autumn. The
pope deserted his cause and fulminated excommunication, and
Henry died at Buonconvento on 24th August, 1313, on his way
south to attack the Neapolitan kingdom. His expedition had
merely intensified the factions that he came to quell. It did not
end the Guelf and Ghibelline contests, as he (and Dante with
him) had fondly hoped, but it was the last occasion in Italian
history when these names retained any trace of an ideal significance.

BIBLIOGRAPHY TO CHAPTER II

(a) GENERAL WORKS

Cambridge Medieval History, Vols. I-V, with very ample bibliographies.
In " Storia politica d'Italia scritta da una società di professori " (Milan) :
    G. Romano, *Le dominazioni barbariche in Italia*, 395-1024 (1909) ;
    F. Gianani, *I Comuni*, 1000-1300 (n.d.).
Italy Medieval and Modern, by E. M. Jamison, C. M. Ady, K. D. Vernon,
    and C. Sandford Terry. Oxford, 1917.
Janet P. Trevelyan, *A Short History of the Italian People*. 2nd ed. London,
    1926.

(b) A. M. Allen, *A History of Verona*. London, 1910.
B. Barbadoro, *Le finanze della repubblica fiorentina*. Florence, 1929.
Horatio Brown, *The Venetian Republic*. London, Temple Primers.
W. Butler, *The Lombard Communes*. London, 1906.
R. Caggese, *Firenze dalla decadenza di Roma al Risorgimento d'Italia*. Vols.
    I. and II. Florence, 1912-13.
R. Cessi, *Venezia ducale*, I-II. Padua, 1927-28.
P. Chalandon, *Histoire de la domination normande en Italie et en Sicile*.
    Paris, 1907.
J. Chapman, *Saint Benedict and the Sixth Century*. London, 1929.
R. Davidsohn, *Geschichte von Florenz*. Berlin, 1896-1927. There is an
    Italian translation of the earlier volumes.
R. L. Douglas, *A History of Siena*. London, 4th ed., 1915.
W. Hazlitt, *The Venetian Republic*. London, 1900.
W. Heywood, *History of Pisa*. Cambridge, 1921.
F. C. Hodgson, *The Early History of Venice* and *Venice in the Thirteenth and
    Fourteenth Centuries*. London, 1901 and 1910.
E. Kantorowicz, *Kaiser Friedrich der Zweite*. Berlin, 1927-31. (English
    translation by E. O. Lorimer, *Frederick the Second*. London, 1931.)
P. Molmenti, *La storia di Venezia nella vita privata dalle origini alla caduta
    della Repubblica*. Bergamo, 1905-08. English translation by Horatio
    F. Brown, *Venice : Its Individual Growth, etc.* Six volumes. London,
    1906-08.
N. Ottokar, *Il comune di Firenze alla fine del Dugento*. Florence, 1926.
M. A. Schipa, *Ducato di Napoli e Principato di Salerno*. Bari, 1923.
P. Villari, *Le invasioni barbariche in Italia* and *L'Italia da Carlo Magno alla
    morte di Arrigo VII*. Milan, 2nd ed., 1905, and 1910. Both translated
    into English.
P. Villari, *I primi due secoli della storia di Firenze*. New edition, Florence,
    1905. English translation from the first edition.
G. Volpe, *Medio evo italiano*. Florence, 1923.

CHAPTER III

ITALY FROM THE DEATH OF HENRY VII
TO THE INVASION OF CHARLES VIII

THE death of Henry VII (1313) and the settling of the
popes at Avignon (1305) may be taken as symbolical;
for thereafter these two great medieval powers ceased
for a long time to count as political forces in Italy, and the
Italian states only considered them when, and in so far as, they
were supported by armed forces. During the earlier Middle
Ages the popes as well as the emperors had claimed a universal
power, and the active supporters, as well as the theorists, of
these two political conceptions may be properly called by the
names of Guelfs and Ghibellines. But the rise of national states,
fully conscious of their national entity, such as the kingdom of
France, the gradual effacement of the empire, and the sub-
servience of the popes to France during their residence at Avignon,
contributed to render these parties names almost devoid of
meaning.

In Italy, moreover, it was not easy to reconcile the theory
of universal power with the actual independence and lively local
patriotism of the individual cities. We say cities advisedly, for
political life was in Italy centred in the cities. The feudal organisation had been wrecked by the at times merely passive,
but often active and always irreducible resistance of the citizen
population. At the beginning of the fourteenth century, practically every citizen community had developed trade and accumulated capital; capital looked for paying investments and trade
for expansion; and in some cities, such as Milan, Genoa, Venice
and Florence, so advanced a stage of economic development
was reached as to influence politics and call forth an interest
in intellectual and artistic pursuits. There was thus fostered
a keen love for the city that produced a tremendous awakening
of all human energies; the foundation of schools and universities,
the erection of magnificent churches and town halls. Strong
walls were built to protect the cities, castles and fortresses were
occupied which endangered the safety of the trade routes. Each

city desired peace, but each wished to prevail over its neighbours, to extend its political influence into the countryside
and over other cities ; so that peace was desired, but almost
every political development was conducive to conflict rather than
peace.

As was natural, the accelerated rhythm of activity caused
changes in the economic status of individuals, families and classes.
Landed gentry were impoverished by comparison with the rising
financial and commercial magnates ; house owners, on the contrary, could exact increased rents from their tenants, producers
of woollen cloth aimed at extending their custom in foreign
markets, while small tradesmen were only interested in the ex-
ploitation of internal markets, and all aimed at securing political
power so as to further their own political interests. These interests seldom coincided ; but there were points upon which
certain groups could usefully combine against others ; and the
groups and individuals themselves were occasionally interested
in more than one trade. Rich and noble families, moreover,
extended their protection to, and required the support of, less
powerful and fortunate cities, and in the keen struggle for pre-
eminence they relied on the strength of family ties. Powerful
families were perpetually at war over blood feuds and mixed
in the life of the cities with the object of crushing their rivals,
thus providing another cause, and by no means the least frequent,
of the constant troubles of the Italian cities.

Contemporary chronicles are ever enlarging upon the advantages of peace and stability ; and it was a longing for these that
had inspired the device of entrusting the executive power in
each city to the podestà. But this institution represented only
a transition. A yearly magistrate, whose choice was subject
to party and class considerations, could not produce stability
and peace. There were, moreover, of necessity too many people
who resented the political pre-eminence of their rivals, people
who were not strong enough to oust the dominant faction, but
sufficiently ambitious to consider their own inferiority an injus-
tice ; there were a large number of men excluded from citizenship
who could always be relied upon to take part in a riot, and
there were the inhabitants of the countryside and of the neighbouring villages and towns who felt aggrieved at being ruled by
a party in the dominant city. Thus by degrees, when the first
rush of political energy had partly exhausted itself in these
struggles, each city took a further step towards a more stable
government. There were in each city one or more families which
excelled owing to man-power and economic position, and they
occasionally happened to be represented by leaders endowed

with strong personalities. It needed but a little further progress
to entrust one such man with the executive power and to re-
elect him for a number of years. In Milan for a time the Torriani
had struggled against the Visconti; on the advent of Henry VII,
Matteo Visconti and his son Galeazzo succeeded in driving away
the Torriani as being disloyal to the emperor. From that moment
until 1447 the Visconti family ruled in Milan, at first as magistrates
(*Capitaneus Generalis*) elected by the citizen assembly and
strengthened by imperial support; when one of the Visconti
died, his successor went through the show of having himself
elected by the assembly; only later their position was legitimised
by the conferment of feudal titles. In Verona the Della Scala
secured for a time a similar position; and thus did the Gonzaga
in Mantua; the Carraresi at Padua; the Pepoli at Bologna.
In Ferrara the Este had long ago transformed their feudal position
into a " signoria "; at a later time, mercenary leaders secured
their election by force of arms; and, in Florence, the Albizzi
first, and later the Medici, ruled without any official title.

It appears from this that the rise of the despots, as they
have been called, answered a deep seated and generally felt
need. A powerful man, rich and enterprising, could be expected
to give a more continuous, and thus presumably more successful
direction to the state. His possible rivals were kept in check
or destroyed. All the rest of the citizens preferred to recognise
the pre-eminence of one man, than to bend before their political
foes; and there was a kind of bitter satisfaction in being no
better and no worse off than every other citizen. An even
greater advantage was to be found in an easier possibility for
expansion than the signoria permitted; for to be the subjects
of a " signore " was less galling for minor and neighbouring
cities than to be subjected to the citizens of the metropolis.
The main weakness in this system was that the link between the
different cities of the state was a purely personal one, and that
states could crumble as readily as they were built up, quite apart
from their complete dependence for success upon the personal
qualities of the ruler. It is obvious that Italians, by means
of the " signoria," tried to obviate the ill effects of a super-
abundance of energies, and tentatively obeyed the same centripetal
forces which were operating in other countries. First King John
of Bohemia, then Gian Galeazzo Visconti, and lastly King Ladislao
of Naples, appeared to be on the verge of forming a state so extended as to be almost national.

Another general feature that must be taken into account,
and explains many apparently inexplicable events, was the
universal employment of mercenary soldiers. It had often hap-

pened before that an emperor or another ally had lent a contingent
of troops to a particular state, or a particular party, this contingent to be fed, and sometimes paid, by the state or the party
that employed it.   The frequent wars fought by the cities which
were richer than they were populous, disturbed the citizens who
followed wealth-producing professions.   Moreover the art of war,
as well as other arts, was progressing, and soldiering had become
a specialised job requiring a training that few citizens could
afford ; so that individual mercenaries had often been enlisted
to supplement the citizen armies.   Despots had naturally no
liking for an armed population, and the " signore " was keen
on relieving the majority of his subjects from military duties
as irksome to the people as they were perilous to the despot
himself.   It happened at this juncture that considerable bodies
of troops were set free from the wars between England and
France, and, being unused to peace and unwilling to change their
manner of life, they passed into Italy and offered their services
to such states as were able to pay for them.   The first companies were loosely knit together and had no regular leader,
but soon they became strongly organised bodies, with a despot,
the commander, and a certain number of regular officials.   They
fought merely for gain, and, when no enlistment or " condotta "
was forthcoming, they plundered the country or held up minor
cities to ransom.   The White Company had in the end to be
paid off in order to free Italy from its unbearable exactions ;
the company of Sir John Hawkwood at one time seemed on the
verge of occupying Florence ; but by degrees these great bands
of foreign troops were eliminated and replaced by companies
led by Italians and mainly formed of Italians.   The " condottiere " enlisted and paid his men and hired out his own services
and those of his men.   Among the Italians, Alberico da Barbiano
became famous owing to his comparative fairness and the professional excellence to which he rose ; scientific warfare started
with him, and Muzio Attendolo Sforza as well as Braccio da
Montone learned their trade under his guidance.   Later Sforza
and Braccio became rival " condottieri " themselves and fought
constantly on opposite sides.   A well-organised company, with
soldiers loyal to their leader and to no one else in the world,
with no object but the acquisition of fame and wealth, with
secretaries who were almost diplomatists, and paymasters as
wily as ministers of finance, was a state without land, and many
a " condottiere " aspired at, and some even succeeded in, trans-
forming a roaming command into a " signoria."   And by the
side of them there were " signori " who, finding the revenue
of their states inadequate, eked out a living by accepting a

command of mercenary troops, as did some of the Gonzagas, Pandolfo Malatesta and others.

Keeping these general conditions before our mind, it will be less difficult to view the rapid flux of political events from the right angle. Henry VII had not one but two contending successors—Louis of Bavaria and Frederick of Austria; they paralysed one another for a time, and only later the Bavarian took some active interest in Italian affairs. No mention need be made of the events in the north-western provinces of Italy, for the states of the Counts of Savoy and the Marquesses of Saluzzo, owing to their geographical position astride of the Alps and the Apennines and their feudal organisation, were seldom involved in purely Italian affairs. By degrees the Counts of Savoy gained the upper hand, but their progress was slow owing to family dissensions, minorities and local struggles, particularly against Robert of Anjou, King of Naples, who had some possessions in Piedmont as well as in Provence.

The first years of the century were taken up by the difficult liquidation of the situation caused by the intervention of Henry VII. Matteo Visconti of Milan who controlled the whole of Lombardy, Cangrande della Scala who extended his rule from Verona through the whole of Venetia up to the Tagliamento, with the exclusion of Venice, Castruccio Castracani who had become despot of Lucca after Uguccione della Faggiuola's downfall in 1316, all claimed to act in the interests of the empire, while pursuing their own objects, and fighting their own foes. Against them were the forces of Robert of Naples, who hoped easily to secure a controlling power in Italy as the champion of the popes, with the help of such states as felt threatened by the ambition of the Visconti, the Scala and the Este who for a time took the imperial side. When Clement V died (1314), the cardinals had great difficulty in choosing his successor, and only in 1316, after much bargaining, they elected Jacques d'Euse of Cahors (John XXII), a man of ambition and energy. Robert freed Genoa from the troops of the Visconti (1318), and in 1320 there appeared in Italy as papal legate Bertrand du Poïet, a nephew of John XXII and a man of considerable ability, who started a crusade against all those who could be described as Ghibellines. He concentrated his efforts against the Visconti, particularly at the crisis created by the death of Matteo (1322), so that his son Galeazzo lost in 1323 almost the whole of his possessions; but, with the assistance of Louis of Bavaria, he rapidly regained them in 1324, when also Cangrande succeeded in repulsing the forces which had gathered against him. Meanwhile Castruccio defeated the Florentines (1325), and Robert of Naples was unable to

make any progress against Frederick of Sicily. Then, while
Bertrand du Poïet was holding Bologna for the pope (1327),
Louis of Bavaria decided to make an expedition into Italy.
Although excommunicated, he had found some spiritual support
among the Franciscan extremists who were denounced by the
pope as heretics, and he was accompanied by Marsilio of Padua,
who had dedicated to him his famous treatise *Defensor pacis*
(1324), which was mainly directed against ecclesiastical authority.
In the course of his ineffectual expedition, Louis, having become
suspicious of Galeazzo Visconti, held him a prisoner and deprived
him of his states, but pardoned him the following year and gave
his son Azzo the title of imperial vicar ; he occupied Pisa, recognised the Gonzaga as lords of Mantua, but succeeded in
little else save alienating the loyalty of his own supporters by
his ceaseless exactions. During the time spent by Louis in Italy,
several political leaders died : Galeazzo Visconti (1328), Castruccio
Castracani (1328), King Robert's son Charles of Calabria (1328),
and shortly later also Cangrande (1329), just when he had finally
succeeded in reducing the pertinacious resistance of Padua. An
epoch was ending. When Louis abandoned Pisa, some eight or
nine hundred of his troops refused to follow him, withdrew to
Ceruglio, seized Lucca, elected Marco Visconti as their leader,
and sold the city to a Genoese citizen. It was the first symptom
of a disease that was soon to become deadly.

That the old order was over was further shown by the meteoric
career of King John of Bohemia, the knightly and adventurous
son of Henry VII who died at Crecy (1346). While he was
at Trento, he was offered the lordship of Brescia by her citizens
who felt threatened by Mastino della Scala, Cangrande's successor.
He freed the town, recalled the exiles, and pacified the city (1330).
This success added glamour to his attractive personality, and a
number of Italian cities followed Brescia's example : Bergamo,
Como, Pavia, Cremona, Vercelli, Novara, Parma, Modena, Reggio,
Lucca ; Azzo Visconti requested himself the honour to hold
Milan as King John's representative. What was this ? King
John was so far from acting for Louis of Bavaria, as was feared
by some, that he sought an agreement with the papal legate,
Bertrand du Poïet. Their meeting caused the rulers of the
different cities to realise that there were dangers more real than
any imperial intervention ; so that old imperialists, like the
Scala, Visconti, Gonzaga and Este, hastened to join forces with
the upholders of the Guelf tradition, in order to extirpate this
new growth. King John's adventure was of no practical consequence, but it is extremely significant as showing the new
trend of events.

Politics in Italy, as no national monarchy had as yet been established, tended to crystallise in that curious and unstable situation that is now known as " balance of power." No single state was strong enough to absorb all others, for, as soon as one showed signs of becoming supreme, a general league was formed against it. Thus, when Mastino della Scala added Lucca to his possessions in the Po valley, the League of 1336 soon brought the Scalas to book (1339) ; they lost Padua to the Carrara (1337); Treviso to Venice (1338) ; Feltre and Belluno to the Dukes of Kärnten. Particularly notable in this league was the intervention of Venice. As Petrarch said, Venice constituted a world apart ; for centuries her interests had been purely sea-born and she had studiously avoided becoming enmeshed in Italian affairs. As we saw, Venice had occupied Ferrara during a disputed succession in the Este family in order to secure the means of navigation and to protect her trade on the Po ; and it was again a matter of trade that caused her intervention against the Scala, for so strong a neighbour on the immediate mainland was imperilling her free use of the water-ways, running into the Polesine of Rovigo ; and she agreed to the establishment of the Carrara at Padua in exchange for a treaty safeguarding her commercial interests. But she was now induced for the first time to hold Treviso on the mainland, so as to command the commercial roads from the Alps. Her main rival was, however, Genoa. The latter republic was rent by internal dissensions ; until 1339 her supreme magistrates were two and were called *Capitani ;* the popular revolution directed against the aristocracy caused the establishment of a Doge as in Venice, and the choice of the name is in itself significant of the rivalry with Venice. The first Doge was Simone Boccanegra, who was forced to resign in 1344 and was succeeded by Giovanni da Murta, under whose magistracy the privileges of the noblemen were further curtailed. It was at this time that commercial rivalry with Venice in the East developed into open warfare (1350). King Peter of Aragon helped the Venetians because of the Genoese aspiration to Sardinia, then in his possession ; on the other hand, King Louis of Hungary, who had tried in vain (1346) to deprive the Venetians of Zara in Dalmatia, favoured the Genoese. Despite Petrarch's eloquent letters, the war raged ; the Genoese, having been defeated on the coast of Sardinia (1353), gave themselves to the Archbishop Giovanni Visconti ; they conquered the Venetians on the coasts of Greece in 1354. The Venetians meanwhile had organised a general league against the Visconti whose fortune seemed to endanger the balance of power. But they had to face grave internal disturbances, for the new Doge, Marin

Falier, attempted to transform himself into a despot and was promptly beheaded (1354).

Florence was still keeping to her republican constitution, but there had been many indications that she could not hold out much longer. In 1325 she had summoned Charles, King Robert's son, as ruler for five years; and he sent Walter of Brienne as his lieutenant. Charles died in 1328, and in 1342 Florence, feeling sore at having lost Lucca to the Pisans, and ascribing this failure to the inadequacy of her officials, chose as her despot that same Walter of Brienne, the titular Duke of Athens; other Tuscan cities quickly followed her example; Walter tried to bolster up his position by favouring the noblemen and the people against the middle classes, which had hitherto held the state, but his tyrannical methods soon led to a rebellion by which he was dispossessed (1343); he died fighting at Poitiers (1356). Florence had lost most of her territory, and was faced by a serious financial crisis through the failure of the Bardi and Peruzzi banks, which had suffered great losses in England.

Naples and Rome were in no better position. King Robert was succeeded in 1343 by Giovanna I, his grand-daughter, but, lest dynastic questions should imperil her rule, the old king had arranged that she should marry Andrew of Hungary, who was also his grandson and a brother to King Louis of Hungary. His boorishness, Giovanna's waywardness and court intrigue brought about Andrew's assassination in 1345. This crime aroused great indignation and in no one more than in King Louis of Hungary who, in 1347, marched on Naples; the queen, who had meanwhile remarried, fled to Provence and was well received by the pope. Louis occupied her state, but on his departure, his troops could not hold out against the mercenary soldiers enlisted by the queen; who was thus left to misgovern, by the help of favourites, a country ravaged by the Black Death and by roaming mercenary troops.

Rome had lived through a strange adventure. During the absence of the popes, the cities of the papal dominions had fallen into the hands of local despots; brigands infested the Campagna; and Rome herself, with a shrinking population, saw her ancient monuments falling into utter ruin, while Colonna and Orsini fought within her streets. As there was no trade in Rome, and consequently no middle class, that element was lacking on which the life of the free cities depended. But the glories of ancient Rome had fired the imagination of a youth of humble descent: Nicola, the son of Lorenzo, Cola di Rienzo as he was called. His eloquence had endeared him to the Romans who

4

sent him to Avignon in 1343 as ambassador to the pope ; the
pope himself, no less than Petrarch, was struck with the young
man and gave him a public office. Cola unceasingly tried to
call back the memory of their former greatness to the Romans,
and he forecast the advent of a new period of glory. By a popular
revolution in 1347 he had himself elected to the office of Tribune ;
he checked the unruly noblemen, indited resonant letters to
announce his election, and planned to make of Rome the capital
of a confederation of Italian cities. Though he bewitched many
people as well as himself with his phantastic dreams, he was soon
compelled to take flight ; after living as a recluse for a couple
of years, he was arrested by Charles IV, the new emperor whom
Pope Clement VI had created in opposition to Louis of Bavaria
(1346), and was kept a prisoner by Clement himself. Clement's
successor, wishing to exploit Cola's popularity, gave him another
chance ; he was sent back to Rome, was created senator, lost all
sense of reality and was killed in a popular tumult (1352).

The second half of the fourteenth century saw two significant
events, the restoration of the temporal power of the popes by
Cardinal d'Albornoz, and the rise of the Visconti to almost
national importance. As if further to mark the end of the old
order, Charles IV, the pope's emperor as he was called, stayed
in Italy several months (1354-55), duly received the royal crown
at Milan and the imperial crown at Rome, extracted large sums
of money from several potentates, but failed to bring about any
results except showing that Italian states could now afford to
treat an emperor with scant ceremony.

Pope Innocent VI, having determined to restore papal authority in his Italian possessions, chose as his legate Cardinal Giles
d'Albornoz, a Spaniard who had fought against the Moors. By
the exercise of keen political sense and ruthless energy Albornoz
succeeded, by 1359, in crushing his most refractory opponents.
In the course of these operations he found time to work out a
set of regulations for the papal state (*Constitutiones Aegidianae*),
that is one of the first organic presentations of the political
theories developed by Renaissance Italy. In the end Albornoz
clashed with the Visconti ; Azzo had been succeeded by his
uncle Luchino (died 1349) and by the Archbishop Giovanni,
both able and enterprising rulers whose fortunes had prospered.
When Giovanni died (1354), his three nephews divided the estates
among themselves, and, as Matteo II soon ceased to live (1355),
only Bernabò and Galeazzo II need be considered. Neither of
them was a soldier, but they were both cunning and ruthless.
Since the days of Giovanni, Bologna had come into the hands
of the Visconti, though their hold upon her was never secure ;

in 1359 the occasion was offered to Albornoz to obtain the cession of Bologna from a disloyal governor, and war broke out. During the previous war the Visconti had lost Genoa and Asti, and had had considerable trouble with the insurgents of Pavia led by a fanatical monk of ultra-democratic tendencies, Fra Jacopo Bussolari, but on the whole they had successfully weathered the onslaught of a formidable league. They equally withstood the new attack, securing an ally in Amedeo VI of Savoy and wearing down the financial endurance of their enemies who were forced to disband their troops; for the Visconti fleeced their subjects, but paid their mercenaries well. Their wealth was such that they could form royal alliances; Galeazzo's son wedded Isabelle of France, and, in 1368, Violante was given in marriage to Lionel, Duke of Clarence. Thrice before 1374 were the Visconti assailed on all sides, and thrice did they succeed in making peace without serious losses, thus proving the solidity of their state; which very solidity, however, was ultimately the cause of the continued attacks. In 1378 Galeazzo II died, and was succeeded by Gian Galeazzo, who, living in fear of his uncle Bernabò, bided his time and affected to be entirely taken up with religious practices; but in 1385, by a trick, he imprisoned his uncle, and probably poisoned him. Thus began the rule of Gian Galeazzo, the greatest of the Visconti, the founder of the Cathedral of Milan and the Certosa of Pavia.

All these wars were fought by means of mercenary troops whose brigandage the country in general, and whose exactions the weaker states in particular, were forced to endure. And it was partly due to the consequent insecurity that Pope Urban V, who had returned to Rome in 1367 amid great rejoicing, was prevailed upon by his cardinals to go back to Avignon where he died in 1370, succeeded by another Frenchman, Gregory XI. Albornoz was dead, and the misrule of the papal legates led to a general rising of the cities of the papal states with the support of the Florentines (1375-78). Florence appointed a war council of eight members, the "Otto della Guerra," called the "Otto Santi" because of the intrepidity with which they defied ecclesiastical censures. An episode of the war was the brutal massacre at Cesena by the Breton mercenaries led by Cardinal Robert of Geneva. Gregory XI had finally returned to Rome (1377), against the will of the cardinals, of whom a large majority were French. His successor, Urban VI, an Italian, was elected amidst the clamours and threats of the Roman populace, which gave the French cardinals the pretext for declaring the election invalid and electing a rival pope, Robert of Geneva, who called himself Clement VII. There was thus (1378) originated a schism which was to last upwards of forty years, with one pope at Rome and another at Avignon. Beginning as a spiritual conflict, it soon degenerated into open hostilities in which national feeling played a part. Urban enlisted an Italian " compagnia " commanded by Alberigo da Barbiano ; its victory over the Bretons and Gascons of Clement at Marino (1379) was hailed by the Roman claimant as a national triumph, and he presented Barbiano with a banner inscribed with the significant motto, " Italia liberata dai barbari."

A notable movement took place at this time at Florence. The richer middle class, " popolani grassi," was in control of the government, and the lower middle classes were growing restive ; the latter were supported by Salvestro de' Medici, who obtained some concessions for them as a result of a popular disturbance. Then followed a general rising of the unskilled workers (the *Tumulto dei Ciompi*, 1378), led by the porters and wool carders subject to the " Arte della Lana," to demand the hitherto refused rights of political association. After a brief triumph, the insurgents were crushed by the defection of their leader, Michele di Lando, and the government ultimately passed back into the hands of the capitalists, the group headed by the Albizzi forming a kind of oligarchy.

The commercial competition between Venice and Genoa, and the growing power of the former, brought about another war, during which Venice was practically alone against her rival who had the support of the King of Hungary, the Duke of Austria, Francesco da Carrara and others. After serious reverses in which the city itself was threatened, Venice defeated the Genoese fleet at Chioggia (1380), and by the Peace of Turin (1381) obtained honourable terms, losing but few of her possessions.

In Naples the ageing Queen Giovanna was troubled by the succession between the Angevins of France and of Hungary ; she chose Louis of Anjou, a brother of the King of France, but the King of Hungary and Pope Urban supported the claims of her cousin, Carlo di Durazzo. Giovanna was defeated and murdered in prison by Carlo (1382), who was himself killed in Hungary where he was claiming the Hungarian throne, and was succeeded as King of Naples by his ten-year old son, Ladislao (1386).

In such general conditions, at the end of the century, the centre of political interest was to be sought in the North, where Gian Galeazzo Visconti was cunningly weaving his plots. Francesco da Carrara, flushed with recent success and unmindful of the unforgiving and watchful hatred of Venice, while pressing his advantage in Friuli, found himself confronted by a league of

Scala, Visconti and Venice ; Scala being weakened by a defeat, Visconti changed sides and, with the help of Carrara, swallowed up all the Scala dominions ; later, in agreement with Venice, he turned against Carrara and occupied Padua. Gian Galeazzo by characteristic means had thus become the master of the greater part of the Po valley (1387). It was at this time that the fateful marriage was concluded between Valentina Visconti, Gian Galeazzo's daughter, and Louis of Orleans, a brother of Charles VI of France. Gian Galeazzo then aimed at central Italy and at an outlet on the sea ; he lost again Padua to Carrara in 1392 who was allied to Florence, Venice and other states, but he kept to his plans and, refusing to side with either of the two popes, he meanwhile secured a diploma as Duke of Milan from Emperor Wenzel (1395).

The antagonism towards foreign troops had sentimental besides practical reasons ; and also the tendency towards larger political groupings must be considered a manifestation of a growing national feeling among Italians. Gian Galeazzo ruled over the whole of Lombardy, a large section of Piedmont and Venetia, considerable territories in Emilia and on the Apennines towards the Riviera. His lands completely encircled the Marquess of Mantua and threatened to encircle Carrara, so that these two princes fostered another coalition against him ; but the war caused no appreciable change (1398). Gian Galeazzo was in no hurry, for nowhere was there stability ; Venice was concerned with the progress of the Turks in the Balkans, Genoa was restive under French rule (1396-1409), Sardinia was just beginning to enjoy some sort of peace under the Aragonese domination, Corsica sulked against her Aragonese and Genoese masters, the royal Aragonese authority was not well established in Sicily, and only in 1399 the young king Ladislao was able to rid Naples of the French pretender ; Boniface IX was so pressed for money that he was forced to recognise the local despots of the cities in the papal states ; and the Romans only restively accepted the despotic rule of the pope (1398) ; many Tuscan cities were treating with Visconti ; and in Florence herself the middle class government was not stably organised. In the end Visconti, having purchased Pisa from her ruler (1399), advanced in Umbria, and Florence had recourse to the Emperor Robert of Bavaria who had been elected after the deposition of Wenzel. The imperial troops were defeated (1401) ; in 1402 Bologna, despite Florentine help, fell to Visconti, so that Florence appeared to be doomed, when Gian Galeazzo suddenly died before he had reached his fiftieth year (1402). His states which he had divided between his two sons, Giovanni Maria and Filippo Maria, seemed suddenly to melt. Pope Boniface IX recovered Bologna and Umbria, strengthening also his hold on Romagna, and Francesco da Carrara acquired several of the Visconti possessions in Venetia, so that the Regent Duchess easily secured the help of the Venetians, who promptly availed themselves of the opportunity and occupied the state of the Carrara family, whose surviving members were executed. Venice holding all the lands east of the Mincio river became a land power for the first time (1405-06). Pisa fell to Florence (1406) which was now the metropolis of the whole of Tuscany.

The new order was only stable in so far as Venetian and Florentine possessions were concerned, for the death of Pope Boniface IX brought about the election of Innocent VII, and, taking advantage of the uncertainty caused by the schism, King Ladislao interfered in the quarrel between pope and the Roman republicans and occupied Rome (1406), and a large portion of the papal state (1408). But by then the ecclesiastical situation had complicated the issue. The pressure brought to bear upon the two competitive popes had grown so strong that Gregory XII, the successor of Innocent, and Benedict XIII, the successor of Clement VII, agreed to meet at Savona (1407) ; when they failed to keep their promise, a number of the cardinals on both sides formed a council at Pisa where, having deposed both claimants, they proceeded to elect a third pope, Alexander V (1409). The different states recognised such of the three popes as seemed more likely to favour their interests ; as Ladislao supported Gregory XII, Alexander stirred up the old claimant to the Neapolitan succession, Louis of Anjou, who advanced on Rome with an army paid by Bologna, Florence and Siena, and led by Braccio da Montone and Sforza. The Romans were thus compelled to recognise Alexander V (1410), but at this moment Louis returned to Provence. Ladislao meanwhile, instead of seizing the opportunity offered to him, had been urging his claims to the Hungarian throne, and in 1411 he was faced by a new situation, for Alexander V died and the cardinals at Bologna elected John XXIII, who was recognised by the Emperor Sigismund and supported by Louis of Anjou. Despite this, Rome fell again to Ladislao (1413), but the emperor, who was also King of Hungary and thus an opponent of Ladislao, came to Italy that year with a view to arranging for another council. Sigismund was not allowed to enter Milan where, Giovanni Maria Visconti having been assassinated (1412), Filippo Maria had seized the power ; but he induced John XXIII to summon a council at Constance for 1st November, 1414. While the ambitious Ladislao was still pursuing his scheme, he, as a few years earlier, Gian Galeazzo, was struck down by an untimely death (August 1414).

The Council of Constance, which was attended by eighteen thousand clerics and a vast number of laymen, called upon all three popes to resign. John XXIII fled and was arrested (1415); Gregory XII abdicated, but the Spaniard Benedict XIII obstinately refused to yield. Finally Cardinal Colonna was raised to the tiara, and took the name of Martin V (1417). When the Council was dissolved in the spring of 1418, Pope Martin proceeded to Italy. In Piedmont he found that young Amedeo VIII of Savoy, who had been created a duke by Sigismund (1416), was well established in his position, the Marquess of Saluzzo being weak and that of Monferrato being friendly to Savoy. In Lombardy Filippo Maria had succeeded by luck, ability and treachery in building up his fortunes. He had married the wealthy widow of Facino Cane, his father's condottiere, though she was his senior by twenty-two years, and in 1418, a few days before the pope's arrival in Milan, having charged her with unfaithfulness, he had her executed. This domestic tragedy did not impair the magnificence of the reception given to the pope, who proceeded eastwards in order to pacify Malatesta, Gonzaga and Este with Visconti. Having avoided the rebellious Bologna, he found Florence (1419) at peace under the customary semi-oligarchical rule of the richer middle classes, now led by Gino Capponi and Niccolò da Uzzano. In Naples there reigned the wayward queen Giovanna II. Just as Filippo Maria relied on Carmagnola as his trusted condottiere, Giovanna relied on Sforza, who in 1417 fought for her against Braccio da Montone. Sforza's victory enabled Pope Martin to obtain the submission of Bologna and to enter Rome (1420).

Sforza and Braccio passed away almost at the same time (1424), just when two other important characters stepped on to the scene; the former's son Francesco and Alfonso of Aragon. The succession at Naples was difficult, for the queen had no direct issue; Louis of Anjou was again urging his claims with Sforza's support, and Giovanna turned for help to King Alfonso of Aragon, whose father Ferdinand had already ruled Sicily (since 1412), Sardinia and a great part of Corsica. Alfonso naturally accepted the Neapolitan succession and he soon forced Louis of Anjou to retire; but he was not satisfied with a semblance of power, and soon broke with the queen herself. In the North meanwhile Filippo Maria was pushing his opportunities; Genoa gave herself to him (1421); Carmagnola occupied the valley of the Ticino up to near the St. Gothard (1422), and shortly later gained a footing in Romagna; Florence felt her peril

particularly after the defeat of her army, and sought an alliance
with Venice.   The Venetians had occupied the whole of Friuli;
and, despite their increased power, were now urged by Francesco
Foscari, the new Doge, to add to their continental possessions,
thus abandoning their traditional policy.   Thus a league was made
between Venice, Florence, Este and Gonzaga against Milan
(1425), the army to be under the command of Carmagnola who
had fled from Milan in fear of his life.   The allies scored several
military successes, but in the end Visconti only lost Bergamo
and Brescia to Venice (1428).   Further intrigues of Filippo
Maria in Tuscany brought about a new alliance of Florence
with Venice and a new war against Milan, the war being mainly
conducted by the Venetians who, however, met with but scant
success, and, having apparently good reasons to suspect Carmagnola of intelligence with the enemy, sentenced him to death
(1432).   Peace was made in 1433, but the inconclusive results
of the war had caused dissatisfaction both in Venice and in
Florence ; and in the latter city the ruling faction endeavoured
to foist the responsibility on Cosimo de' Medici who had negotiated
the peace.   He was exiled, but, being the leading banker of the
day, he lived in Venice in a princely fashion, was soon recalled
and, from that day (October 1434), the Medici dynasty acquired
a decided pre-eminence in Florence.   Cosimo was merely the
richest citizen and had no official part in the government, but
he was considered the " signore " and nothing was done without
his wish.   Cosimo himself, Francesco Sforza and Alfonso of
Aragon controlled the complex events of the following years,
during which another schism divided the Roman Church.

When Queen Giovanna II died (1435), it was found that she
had chosen as her heir René, the brother of Louis of Anjou ;
he was supported by Genoa, through rivalry with Aragon, and
Genoa meant also the Duke of Milan.   In a sea battle Alfonso
was defeated and taken a prisoner ; the duke had him brought
to Milan and was fascinated by his charm and convinced by
his reasons.   It was perilous, Alfonso argued, for Visconti,
whose Lombard and Piedmontese possessions were in immediate
contact with France, that a French prince should also sit on the
throne of Naples.   Filippo Maria promptly changed sides, and a
long war ensued which ended with the victory of Alfonso
(1442), who made a triumphant progress into Naples in the
following year.

Pope Eugenius IV had good reason to fear Filippo Maria,
but he was prevented by his own difficulties from taking effective
measures against him.   Eugenius had summoned a council at
Basle ; the trend of the discussions, however, appeared to lead

to a curtailment of papal authority, so that the pope suspended the session of the council in December, 1431. This suspension was, however, bitterly resented by the Council of Basle, and there followed an open breach ; the most advanced ecclesiastics, who had alone remained at the council, summoned Eugenius before them, and refused to attend the council which the pope opened at Ferrara in 1437, where several representatives of the Greek Church came, including Bishop Bessarion and Gemistus Pleto. Finally the Council of Basle deposed Eugenius, and elected the old Duke Amedeo VIII of Savoy as Pope Felix V (1439). Eugenius was also confronted with political difficulties. At the instigation of the Duke of Milan, Sforza occupied several cities in the March of Ancona, and Piccinino fostered a revolution in Rome so that the pope had to take flight (1434) ; he relied mainly on the valour of Cardinal Vitelleschi, and on the frequent changes of allegiance of Sforza. Francesco Sforza looked upon himself as the successor of Filippo Maria who had no legitimate offspring, on the grounds of his being vaguely affianced to an illegitimate daughter of the duke. Characteristically, Sforza fought against Visconti without fearing to imperil his chances to become the duke's son-in-law ; in fact, it was through Sforza's mediation that a temporary peace was made in 1441, the treaty once again showing that a balance of power had been established which could not be altered while the greater states lived in fear of one another. Among these states it was necessary, however, also to reckon the principal " condottieri," in particular Sforza and Piccinino, for their military fame and the loyalty of their troops rendered them as powerful as if they had possessed real territorial bases. Sforza, who had finally married Bianca Maria Visconti, was in turn fighting for and against his father-in-law. In 1446 Sforza's fortunes were at a low ebb in central Italy ; but, the Duke of Milan having been defeated by the Venetians, and Sforza fearing lest the Venetians should definitely encroach upon the Visconti dominions, an agreement was made between father and son-in-law ; and Sforza sold to the new pope, Nicholas V, his possessions in central Italy and reached Lombardy just when Filippo Maria was dying (13th August, 1447). The Milanese set up a republican government, but the " Ambrosian Republic " could not cope with the difficulties of the situation ; many cities were lost to " condottieri," others to the Venetian army ; Sforza was chosen as commander, but it was soon apparent that his actions were intended to favour rather his own interests than those of his employers, and, while these hesitated, he seized the opportunity of a victory over the Venetians to turn front ; he allied himself with Venice against Milan, the Venetians recognising his claim to the Visconti succession in the hopes of having a large share of the spoils (1448). Encouraged by the support of Cosimo de' Medici, who desired to see in the North a state strong enough to keep the Venetians in check, Francesco Sforza hastened his operations, besieged and captured Milan (1450), and was hailed Duke of Milan.

Venice and Alfonso of Aragon, who still proposed to pursue the war against Milan, were induced to peace by the fall of Constantinople. The Venetians recognised Sforza as duke and retained the territory east of the Adda (1454). A year later the Duke of Milan, the republics of Venice and Florence, King Alfonso and Pope Nicholas V made an alliance guaranteeing each other's possessions for twenty-five years. A new stability was thus given to Italian life, from which the population reaped great material advantages, and artistic and literary development received a welcome assistance. The only regions of Italy excluded from these advantages were the Duchy of Savoy and the Marquisates of Saluzzo and Monferrato, where the still prevailing feudal institutions stunted economic development; their condition was rendered even less favourable by dynastic conflict and bad administration. In striking contrast, Francesco Sforza, a "condottiere" and the son of a "condottiere," proved himself to be a lover of peace and an administrator as able as he was enterprising; he died in 1466, and his son and successor, Galeazzo Maria, who had fought in the army of Louis XI, was only notable for his wanton cruelty and his moral profligacy.

Venice was enjoying this period of peace to the full, despite her anxiety at the Turkish advance. She had no longer any rivals in the eastern trade, and wealth poured into the city; it was spent lavishly on art, on amusement and on the development of her possessions. The arts and literary studies were honoured and enthusiastically favoured even in minor courts; such as those of Mantua and Ferrara, but the metropolis of the earlier Renaissance was Florence. Until his death (1464) Cosimo pursued a pacific policy and ever studiously refrained from any show of power, though he saw to it that his enemies received short shrift. Prosperity and peace produced an amazing output of artistic masterpieces. Pope Nicholas V, himself a scholar, was particularly notable as a protector of learned men; Manetti, Poggio, Valla, Decembrio, Filelfo were connected with the Roman curia and helped the pope to form a large collection of manuscripts which was to become the nucleus of the Vatican Library. His last years were saddened by the senseless conspiracy of Stefano Porcari and by the fall of Constantinople. The outbreak of wars in the South, following upon the death of Alfonso (1458), endangered the position of the new Pope Pius II (Enea Silvio Piccolomini). He strained every energy in order to organise a crusade, but was hampered by agitation in Rome and by wars particularly against the faithless, splendid and tragic Sigismondo Malatesta of Rimini (1463). Only a few thousand crusaders, lacking money, discipline and leaders, had assembled at Ancona, when Pius II died there (1464).

Alfonso was succeeded by his illegitimate son Ferdinando, who was engaged for several years in suppressing the opposition of the barons. The policy of the five major Italian states, with the possible exception of Venice, was now peaceful, for they feared losses more than they desired acquisitions. Venice, on the contrary, seemed to nurse the ambitious scheme of forming a national state. The deaths of Francesco Sforza and Cosimo occurring about the same time enhanced Venetian hopes, for the republic had some claim on Lombardy, and the Florentine exiles suggested that it would be easy to overthrow Piero de' Medici's rule. Venice was, however, prevented from continuing a profitable intrigue by a defensive alliance formed by Milan, Florence and Naples, and by the Turkish activities. In 1470 she lost some fortresses in the Balkans and in Greece; the acquisition of Cyprus was but small compensation, for, after sixteen years of continual warfare, in 1479 she was compelled to purchase peace from Mahomet II.

Meanwhile this fruitful period of peace was coming to an end. The profligacy and cruelty of Galeazzo Maria Sforza had stirred up a revolution in Genoa (1476), and provoked a few Milanese noblemen, aglow with a love of liberty learned in the classics, to murder him (1476). No revolutionary movement followed in Milan, thanks to the exertion of the Duchess Bona. She ruled for her son the Duke Gian Galeazzo who was eight years old, but she was opposed by her brothers-in-law, Ottaviano, Cardinal Ascanio, and Ludovico il Moro. Profiting by a Genoese rebellion, they succeeded in securing Aragonese and Florentine support, exiled the duchess, and installed Ludovico il Moro at the head of the government in the name of Gian Galeazzo.

Also in Florence the peace was disturbed; Piero de' Medici (d. 1469) was succeeded by Lorenzo and Giuliano; the old constitutional councils had lost power and were seldom summoned; but some members of the Pazzi family, with the cognisance of Ferdinand of Naples and Pope Sixtus IV, had recourse to a plot which failed because only Giuliano was murdered, Lorenzo escaping. The leaders of the plot, including Archbishop Salviati and Francesco de' Pazzi, were hung (1478), while the position of Lorenzo was consolidated by what had happened. The pope's passive participation in this affair was the result of his own insane partiality for his nephews, especially Girolamo Riario, whom he had made captain of the papal army, and Giuliano della Rovere whom he created a cardinal and who was later to play a great part in political events as Pope Julius II. It was partly due to this menacing state of things that in 1474 Venice, Florence and Milan formed a defensive alliance for twenty-five years, thus isolating the pope and Ferdinand of Aragon. But, when Lorenzo was attacked by the pope and the Aragonese, Venice was engaged in the east and Milan was paralysed by local troubles, so that he found himself dangerously isolated. He daringly went to Naples, charmed the king away from the papal alliance and made peace with him (1480). A general peace followed, in consequence of the general alarm caused in Italy by a Turkish fleet seizing Otranto, killing over 10,000 inhabitants, and carrying away many more thousands of them as slaves.

The peace was broken by the pope's irritation against the Aragonese of Naples and an attack upon Ferrara by the Venetians (1482), Sixtus first allying himself with Venice and then joining in a general league against the republic. The Venetians obtained a favourable peace, with increase of territory at the expense of the Duke of Ferrara in 1484. Sixtus died the same year ; his successor, Innocent VIII (Cibo), though a mild man, pursued the same policy, abandoning lofty claims to universal power and merely endeavouring to strengthen his hold on the papal state precisely as the other " signori " were doing. This tendency had a counterpart in the frequent murders of despots ; Galeazzo Maria Sforza, Giuliano de' Medici, Girolamo Riario and Galeotto Manfredi all met with violent deaths.

Meanwhile Innocent VIII and Lorenzo de' Medici maintained friendly relations ; Ludovico il Moro courted the Aragonese friendship and arranged the marriage of his nephew the duke with Isabella of Naples (1489), while he himself wedded the young Beatrice d'Este, a sister of the famous Isabella, Marchioness of Mantua. Lorenzo kept peace in Florence by strong means when necessary, but by preference trusted in his ability and in the fascination of the arts. He was the friend and protector of artists and poets—Botticelli, Poliziano, Marsilio Ficino, Luigi Pulci and young Michelangelo were among the many whom he could call his protégés. He died in 1492. His last years were disturbed by the violent sermons of Girolamo Savonarola, who bewailed the corruption of the age and forecast disasters untold.

Despite vast expenditure Florence was in a prosperous economic condition ; and prosperous were Venice, despite the strain of the eastern war, Genoa despite unceasing revolutionary trouble,

Milan, the states of the Este and even Naples, where the Aragonese administration was endeavouring to break down the economic structure of feudal days. Taxation was generally heavy ; and not all the people were enabled to participate in the heightened standard of living ; but the general prosperity, and refinement of life in the cities, were such as to strike foreigners with wonder and to surpass anything that could be seen in other countries. And the Italians were conscious of their superiority and naturally inclined to overrate it. War had become a mere nuisance for them ; it was fought by professional soldiers, and, though costly, its horrors only befell such people as happened to be in the way of the comparatively small armies ; professional war had, more-over, been hemmed in with rules such as might be dictated for duels. Most despots ranked diplomacy above valour ; Gian Galeazzo and Filippo Maria Visconti had shown a way that Ludovico il Moro, Cosimo and Lorenzo de' Medici successfully followed. Lorenzo's journey to Naples and his agreement with Ferdinand of Aragon could be taken as symbolical of this con-dition of things. The light of civilisation was so intense that men's eyes were blinded to the course of events outside Italy. Even the progress of the Turks, despite its impact upon Venetian and Italian trade, seemed a remote peril to which Italian di-plomatic ability would in the end find a remedy ; for Italian diplomacy had gained complete confidence in its own power, just as it had lost touch with morals and even with reality.

Lorenzo's death left his son Piero, a young and not very able man, in charge. The mild Innocent VIII was succeeded after a scandalous election by Rodrigo Borgia, Alexander VI, who pursued the same policy as his two immediate predecessors with even less scruples than they. Ludovico il Moro, ever anxious to enhance his power by tortuous schemes, had sought the support of an alliance with Venice and the pope ; but he did not trust his allies and, taking up an originally Venetian suggestion, he urged the young and heedless King of France, Charles VIII, to enter Italy in order to press his claim to the throne of Naples. And Charles welcomed this suggestion, concluded peace with England, Spain and the Emperor Maximilian, and made ready to start (1492). When the Italian leaders realised that Charles was really on the way, they felt some hesitation about the result of this unexpected complication ; Ludovico, fearing lest Louis of Orleans should dispossess him of Lombardy, and the pope feeling that his own possessions might be in danger. The pope was the only one, however, who showed his hand by an alliance with the Aragonese.

At this moment Ferdinand of Naples died and was succeeded

by Alfonso II (1494). Charles asked for a free pass for his armies and readily obtained it. Venice proclaimed her neutrality, Piero de' Medici sulked, but was unwilling to fight, only the pope replied with an open refusal, pointing out that Alfonso, pressed to extremity, was likely to seek the alliance of the Turks, particularly as the French king constantly proclaimed that he was only aiming at making Naples a jumping off board for an expedition against the Turks.

Charles reached Pavia (October 1494) where, after his visit, the Duke Gian Galeazzo suddenly died, probably poisoned by his uncle Ludovico, who succeeded him. Meanwhile the French army, well disciplined and ruthless in its methods, had scored some easy successes on the Riviera and in Romagna. Piero de' Medici, realising his own unpopularity in Florence, went to the French camp and offered a huge loan and a temporary cession of several fortresses to the king. This act caused great indignation in Florence, and Piero was driven away; the new republican government admitting Charles VIII into Florence, but securing far better terms than Piero had offered. The terrified pope allowed the king to pass through Rome; then, while Charles was entering Naples without resistance, Ludovico il Moro realised the danger of his own position and organised a league with Venice, the pope, Spain and the emperor against the invader (1495). The king and his advisers felt at once that he must return to France. He left a small army of occupation in Naples and marched back in the direction of the Alps, breaking through the encirclement of the army of the Italian League at Fornovo (6th July, 1495). Then Ludovico made peace, and the Aragonese (Ferdinand II) quickly reoccupied the Neapolitan kingdom.

The apparently fruitless expedition of Charles VIII had in reality destroyed the civilisation of the Renaissance. The unstable equilibrium, which had so long prevailed in Italy, was definitely ended. The classically inspired faith in their own superiority was shaken in the Italians. They were made unexpectedly to realise the untrustworthiness of mercenary troops, the inadequacy of subtle diplomacy against states which could rely on well organised forces. Above all, it had been shown to the foreign powers—France, Spain and emperor in particular—how easy an enterprise it was to invade the richest, finest and most advanced country in Europe, and how profitable it was to hold it to ransom. Another age had begun.

BIBLIOGRAPHY TO CHAPTER III

(a) General works. See works listed under (a) in Bibliography to Chapter II.

Also :—

P. Orsi, *Signorie e principati,* in " Storia politica d'Italia scritta da una società di professori." Milan, 1897.
Cambridge Medieval History, Vol. VI.
Cambridge Modern History, Vols. I-II.
L. Pastor, *History of the Popes from the Close of the Middle Ages.* English translation, London, 1891.

(b) See also works listed under (b) in Bibliography to Chapter II.

C. M. Ady, *Pius II.* London, 1913.
C. M. Ady, *History of Milan under the Sforza.* London, 1907.
Julia (Cartwright) Ady, *Beatrice d'Este* and *Isabella d'Este.* London, 1899 and 1903.
E. Armstrong, *Lorenzo de' Medici.* London, 1906.
R. Bacchelli, *La Congiura di don Giulio d'Este.* Milan, 1931.
R. Caggese, *Roberto d'Angiò e i suoi tempi.* Florence, 1922-32.
J. Dennistoun, *Memoirs of the Dukes of Urbino.* New ed. by E. Hutton. 3 vols. London, 1909.
N. Faraglia, *Storia della regina Giovanna d'Angiò.* Lanciano, 1904.
E. G. Gardner, *Dukes and Poets in Ferrara.* London, 1904.
M. F. Jerrold, *Italy in the Renaissance.* London, 1927.
A. Luzio, *Mantova e Urbino.* Turin, 1893.
A. Luzio, *Relazioni di Isabella d'Este Gonzaga con Ludovico e Beatrice Sforza.* Milan, 1890.
Yvonne Maguire, *Women of the Medici.* London, 1927.
F. Malaguzzi Valeri, *La Corte di Ludovico il Moro.* Milan, 1913-17.
D. Muir, *A History of Milan under the Visconti.* London, 1924.
R. Palmarocchi, *La politica italiana di Lorenzo de' Medici.* Florence, 1933.
P. D. Pasolini, *Caterina Sforza.* Rome, 1893.
Ester Pastorello, *Nuove ricerche sulla storia di Padova e dei principi da Carrara al tempo di Gian Galeazzo Visconti.* Padua, 1908.
G. B. Picotti, *La giovinezza di Leone X.* Milan, 1928.
E. Piva, *La guerra di Ferrara nel 1482.* Padua, 1893-94.
Laura M. Ragg, *Crises in Venetian History.* London, 1928.
N. Rodolico, *La democrazia fiorentina nel suo tramonto.* Bologna, 1904.
N. Rodolico, *Dal comune alla signoria* (Taddeo Pepoli). Bologna, 1898.
S. Romanin, *Storia documentata di Venezia.* Venice, 1853-61.
L. Soranzo, *Pio II e la politica italiana nella lotta contro i Malatesta.* Padua, 1911.
A. Solerti, *Ferrara e la Corte estense.* Città di Castello, 1900.
A. Sorbelli, *La Signoria di Giovanni Visconti a Bologna.* Bologna, 1911.
L. Tosti, *Storia del Concilio di Costanza.* Rome, 1887.
P. Villari, *Savonarola e i suoi tempi.* Florence, new ed., 1930.
C. Yriarte, *Autour des Borgias.* Paris, 1891 ; and *César Borgia.* Paris, 1889.

CHAPTER IV

EARLY ITALIAN LITERATURE

IT may be disputed whether Italy was retarded in developing her own voice in the vernacular by the pressure of the classical tradition and the consciousness of the Roman heritage, or by the practical character of the Italian genius that found its congenial expression in the many-sided life of the communes and in the revival of the study of Roman Law, or by the total conditions of Italian life producing a general ineptitude for literary production ; but the fact remains that we cannot speak of a " medieval " Italian literature as we can in the case of France or England, and that a " literature " in the vernacular, apart from a few poems or rhyming fragments, first appears in the early years of the thirteenth century : the *Duecento*.

Nevertheless something must first be said about medieval Latin works produced by Italians on Italian soil. It is with St. Gregory the Great, who professed to despise literary style, deeming it " most unworthy to restrain the words of the heavenly oracles under the rules of Donatus," that what had been classical Latin literature becomes unmistakably medieval ; particularly in his four books of *Dialogues* (593), " concerning the lives and miracles of the Italian fathers, and the eternity of souls." The one great man of letters in Italy during the eighth century is a Langobard who had acquired the Latin culture and the Latin veneration for the sacred name of Rome : Paulus Warnefridus. Some time after 783, in the peace of Montecassino, he wrote his *Historia Langobardorum*, the history of a conquered race destined to a larger life as part of the new Italian people, relating the legendary exploits of the Langobard kings with, as Ker said, " an unfailing sense of what is properly heroic." In the ninth and tenth centuries, Latin prose in Italy is mainly represented by ecclesiastical and monastic chronicles ; but Liutprand of Cremona, he too a Langobard by race, in his *Antapodosis* tells the story of his own times with vividness and biting humour. Some of the Latin poetry of the epoch reaches a higher level than the prose. Two lyrical gems are the *Carmen mutinense*, an exhortation to the soldiers keeping guard on the walls of Modena, which

anticipates the romance dawn-song, and the *O Roma nobilis* of a
Veronese poet, a salutation to the Eternal City guided by Peter
and Paul to a wider spiritual empire than had been hers of old.
An epic was attempted by an anonymous north Italian poet :
the *Gesta Berengarii imperatoris ;* four books of hexameters,
full of reminiscences of Virgil and Lucan, celebrating the exploits and coronation of the Marquess of Friuli who attained
the imperial crown in 915. The reforming movement of the
eleventh century is represented by one great writer : St. Peter
Damian (1007-72) ; a terrible rebuker of corruption and preacher
of asceticism, who, nevertheless, reveals a sense of humour in
his poem *De abbatum miseria*, depicting the daily troubles and
distractions of an abbot. His contemporary, St. Anselm of Aosta
(1033-1109), one of the founders of scholasticism, is associated
with Normandy and England rather than with Italy ; but his
last and best-known work, *Cur Deus Homo*, was composed among
the Alban hills while in exile from his see of Canterbury. There
was a great revival of monastic culture at the abbey of Montecassino, under the abbot Desiderius (1058-86), afterwards
Hildebrand's successor as Pope Victor III. Leo Marsicanus and
Petrus Diaconus compiled the *Chronicon Monasterii Casinensis*,
one of the most notable Italian histories of the Middle Ages.
Another of these monks, Albericus Casinensis, led the way in
the study of the *ars dictandi*, or *ars dictaminis*, the art of composition, which spread to the papal curia, and ultimately found
a fruitful field in the schools and in the public life of the communes.

Although Anselm and Peter Lombard (whose famous *Sententiae*
were produced at Paris about 1152) were Italians, the scholastic
movement centred in France rather than in Italy. The bent
of the Italian genius in the Middle Ages was practical rather
than speculative. What has been called " the first medical
renaissance " arose at Salerno, where, from the eleventh century,
there was a fully organised school of medicine, the first of its
kind in Europe. To have studied at Salerno was enough to make
the reputation of a practitioner in other lands. At the end of
this same century came the revival of the study of Roman Law
and Jurisprudence. This had never died out in Italy ; there
were famous schools of law at Pavia and Ravenna ; but these
were now eclipsed by that of Bologna, where the great Irnerius
taught from the last years of the century until about 1130, and
renovated the study of jurisprudence, delivering the word of
Justinian to the new life of the Italian commune. Simultaneously,
at Bologna, came the organisation of canon law, with the *Con-
cordantia* or *Decretum* of Gratianus about 1140. It was from this

revival of jurisprudence, and the throngs of students flocking
from all directions to hear Irnerius, that the first European
university came into being, and Bologna boasts the proud title
" alma mater studiorum." The year 1080 is traditionally accepted as that of the birth of the University of Bologna, and
we may regard it as definitely constituted by the middle of the
twelfth century.[1]

Already, in the first years of the eleventh century, the Deacon
Giovanni, chaplain to the Doge Pietro Orseolo II, had written
the *Chronicon Venetum*, in which " we are outside the life of the
cloister, and breathe the free and open air of the lagoons." At
the outset of the communal epoch the new Italian spirit is finely
exemplified in two Latin poems of 1087 and 1113 respectively,
celebrating victorious exploits of the Pisans against the Saracens
on the African coast and in the Balearic islands : the *Carmen
in victoria Pisanorum*, in rhyming rhythmical measure, and the
Liber Maiolichinus, in hexameters ; both associating the new
triumphs of Pisa with the glories of ancient Rome. The growing
self-consciousness of the young city state is seen in the municipal
chronicles. Genoa has a series of *Annales Januenses*, commissioned by the republic, the work of distinguished citizens and
men of action, beginning with Caffaro (d. 1166), running through
the twelfth and thirteenth centuries to Jacopo Doria in 1294. But
these Latin poems and chronicles of the Lombard cities unhappily
reflect the limitations of the national sentiment, which did not
prevent one commune from crushing another or invoking the
imperial aid to triumph over its neighbour. Thus, about 1127,
an anonymous poet of Como writes on the ineffectual struggle of
his native city against Milan, and, shortly before 1166, another of
Bergamo in more than 3000 hexameters relates, as an imperialist,
the Italian expedition of Frederick Barbarossa. In prose, chronicles of Lodi and Milan describe the struggle between the emperor
and the Lombard communes from opposite sides ; Ottone and
Acerbo Morena of Lodi being of the imperialist party, while the
anonymous Milanese, with burning patriotism, makes his work
centre round the destruction of Milan and its subsequent rebuild-
ing by the Lombard League.

A would-be epic in five books of hexameters comes from the
South at the beginning of the twelfth century : the *Gesta Roberti
Wiscardi* of Guglielmo Pugliese, celebrating the beginning of the

[1] The University of Padua was established by a migration of professors
and students from Bologna in 1222. Both these universities were ruled by
the students or scholars ; that of Naples, founded by Frederick II in 1224,
was controlled by the officers of state.

Norman conquest from the appearance of the first band of Norman adventurers on Monte Gargano to the death of Robert Guiscard. Under King Roger—at whose court Greek, Latin and Arabic were alike employed—the culture of the Sicilian kingdom was cosmopolitan, and for him Idrisi, an Arab from Spain, wrote in his own tongue the treatise on geography known as the " Book of Roger." In the reign of William I, Henry of Catania translated into Latin the *Phaedo* and *Meno* of Plato. But the most interesting literary productions of the South date from the end of the Norman domination. Ugo Falcando, in his *Liber de Regno Siciliae*, deals with the doings of the court in the reign of William I and the earlier years of William II, with a power of characterisation and a sense of Latin style that has gained him the inappropriate title of the " Tacitus of Sicily." His *Epistola de calamitate Siciliae* (1190) sets forth the view of the national party supporting Tancred, while that of the German imperialist side is represented by the poem in elegiacs of Pietro da Eboli, the *De rebus siculis* or *Liber ad honorem Augusti* (1195), celebrating Henry's triumph, hailing the birth of the child, grandson of Barbarossa and Roger, who shall be the glory of Italy. From the mountains of Calabria, at the end of the century, came the strange religious books of the abbot Joachim of Flora (d. 1202), a mystical reading of the story of the human race, which have exercised an extraordinary influence over religious thought through the idea of the coming third epoch of the Holy Ghost under the dispensation of the Everlasting Gospel.

Two writers must complete our survey : a poet and a rhetorician. Arrigo da Settimello, a priest in the Florentine contado, composed about 1193 the *Elegia de diversitate fortunae*, in elegiac verse, in which (like Boëthius) he laments his own misfortunes, disputes with Fortune, and is consoled by Philosophy, who instructs him on the corrupted state of the world and exhorts him to endurance. It has motives that anticipate Dante and Petrarch. Boncompagno da Signa, a Florentine who taught rhetoric at Bologna and other north Italian cities from the nineties of the century and died at Florence about 1240, was in his day the most renowned master of the " ars dictandi," every branch of which, from the composition of letters to the delivery of speeches, is covered by his various Latin professional handbooks. Among his other works are a history of the siege of Ancona (1201) and a treatise *De Amicitia* (1205). An amazingly piquant and vivid personality, Boncompagno has passages inspired by a keen sense of Italian nationality unsurpassed until we come to Dante.

Unquestionably there was popular poetry in the Italian

vernaculars long before anything that has come down to us ; the people in the fields and cities sang of love and other familiar topics, and the " giullare," or wandering minstrel, passed from place to place conveying the matter of romance. But the earliest extant Italian composition in verse is the much-discussed " cantilena " of a Tuscan giullare in praise of a bishop, " Salva lo vescovo senato," which some critics would place as early as the fifties of the twelfth century. To the nineties of the century belong the *Ritmo Cassinese*, an allegorical poem in which a spiritual man from the East instructs an unillumined western on the mystical way, and the so-called *Ritmo Bellunese*, four lines celebrating the taking of a castle by the people of Belluno, the earliest example of those pieces of popular vernacular verse on contemporary events of which others, later in date, are found inserted in chronicles of the thirteenth century. These pieces may represent the native poetry of Italy before elements came from beyond the Alps which the Italian genius assimilated to build up a new national literature. From France, first on the lips of the jongleurs, and then in poems and romances of the " lingua d'*oïl*," came the " matter of Rome," that naturally blended with the ever-living classical Latin tradition ; the " matter of France," the stories of the Carolingian cycle, that already had roots of its own in Italy ; the " matter of Britain," the Arthurian legends, that was more foreign to Italian soil. But more immediately fruitful was the influence of Provence. The troubadours, singers of the " lingua d'*oc*," began to frequent the cities and small courts of northern Italy. There is a " contrasto," shortly after 1190, in which Rambaut de Vaqueiras makes advances to a lady of Genoa in his own tongue and is repulsed by her in her native vernacular. Italian poets in northern Italy adopted the Provençal tongue. Pietro della Caravana or Cavarana, a Piedmontese or Veronese, in a Provençal serventese of 1195 exhorts the burghers of the Lombard cities to secure peace by opposing the emperor and his Germans with unity and firmness. He is the first of a school of " trovatori italiani," Italians writing Provençal verse, and greater poets of the kind appeared later—Sordello of Mantua, Bonifacio Calvo of Genoa, Bertolome Zorzi of Venice—who were still to use the " lingua d'*oc* " when the traditions of Provence had already passed into the new poetry of Italy. Simultaneously with the coming of the troubadours the Franciscan movement arose, and with it the *lauda*, the new sacred lyric of the people developing out of the sequence, the official Latin hymn of the Church. The earliest lauda preserved is the famous *Laudes creaturarum*, or *Canticum fratris Solis*, of St. Francis himself, composed about 1224, some two years before his death, in rhythmical prose with assonances and occasional rhymes, uniting all creatures from Brother Sun to Sister Death in a last song of love and praise.

Already, when St. Francis died, the new lyrical poetry of Italy had appeared in the South with its centre at the court of Frederick II. Following Dante, we speak of these poets, whether the individuals were natives of the island or of the Italian mainland, as forming the Sicilian school : " Because the royal throne was Sicily, it came to pass that whatever our predecessors produced in the vernacular is called Sicilian." Frederick's sphere of influence extended beyond the kingdom itself ; but the three chief poets of the school—Giacomo da Lentino (the " Notary "), Giacomino Pugliese and Rinaldo d'Aquino—were southerners. Frederick himself, his minister Pier della Vigna, and his son Enzo all wrote verse. This poetry imitates and develops that of the troubadours of Provence, but is more restricted in subject, as it treats almost exclusively of love with only very sparing allusions to contemporary events. It established a convention, a poetic phraseology, a repertory of images and similes, in dealing with the theme of the " service " of chivalrous love. These poets introduced the *canzone*, the stateliest form of Italian lyric, derived from the Provençal *chanson*, with the metrical modifications that the different genius of the Italian language demanded, and invented a new form, the sonnet, which is purely Italian in origin. The influence of French poetry, which perhaps preceded that of Provence, has been traced in the earliest lyrics of the school, including some of those of Giacomo da Lentino, whose production is the most copious and varied. At times, too, a more natural note is struck than that of the conventional chivalrous love, and from the outset there is an element that must needs be of native origin. These courtly singers had recourse to the (for us) lost poetry of the people to give fresh life to the matter that they derived from their Provençal models. Lyrical gems like Rinaldo d'Aquino's complaint of the woman whose lover has gone on the Crusade, or Odo delle Colonne's lamentation of the girl who has been betrayed and deserted for another, are manifestly elaborations of popular poetry rather than reflections from beyond the Alps. Noteworthy, in its mingling of courtly with popular phraseology, is the *contrasto* of Cielo d'Alcamo, shown by internal evidence to have been written between 1231 and 1250 : a dialogue, full of spirit and cynical humour, between the pertinacious lover and the lady

who ultimately yields to his suit.[1]   Although attempts have
been made to give an earlier date to certain poems, this first
phase of Italian lyrical poetry seems to run from about 1220.
The poets mentioned belong to the reign of Frederick, but a
small later group should rather be associated with that of Manfred.
Notable among these latter is Stefano Protonotaro of Messina,
by whom is a canzone in authentic Sicilian.   The last of these
Sicilians, Guido delle Colonne, highly praised by Dante and (for
his Latin prose version of the French romance of Troy) introduced by Chaucer into the *House of Fame*, was still living in
the eighties of the century ; his canzoni, notable alike for their
development of metrical form and a certain pregnant sententiousness, approximate in style to the poetry of the Tuscan successors
of the Sicilian school.

Simultaneously, though more slowly, Italian literary prose
developed ; not in the South, but at another centre of Italian
culture : the University of Bologna.   It began with the masters
of the *ars dictandi*, who, after setting models for elegant composition in Latin, turned to show how similar methods could
be applied to the vernacular.   The earliest example is found in
the *Gemma purpurea* of Guido Fava, or Faba, a younger rival
of Boncompagno at Bologna, written about 1230, in which he
gives a series of short formulæ for letters and compositions in
the vulgar tongue.   Somewhat questionably attributed to him
are the *Parlamenti et epistolae*, produced apparently at Siena
about 1242, an ampler collection in which the " parlamenti "
are Italian models for both speeches and letters, including an
admirable oration for a new podestà on taking office, and a flowery
communication from a student to his father asking for money
to enable him to complete the course for his degree.   A little later,
about 1250, Italian translations from French and Latin works
begin to appear ; one of the first is the *Liber Ystoriarum Roman-
orum* (or *Storie di Troia e di Roma*), translated from a Latin compilation of ancient history, and written in " romanesco," the local
dialect of Rome.

What may be regarded as a second phase of the Sicilian school
centres in Tuscany, while the South, under the yoke of the House
of Anjou, gradually becomes silent.   These poets are defined as
" rimatori siculo-toscani."   Chief among them, the acknowledged
master of this phase of Tuscan poetry, is Fra Guittone of Arezzo,
who died in 1294.   Obscure and rugged in style, abusing the
practice of " rime equivoche " which the Sicilians before him had

---

[1] A slightly later Tuscan counterpart, more " popular " in tone, is the
delightful *Gemma laziosa* of Ciacco dell'Anguillaia.

occasionally adopted from the Provençals, Guittone's poetry has the personal note lacking in that of his predecessors ; his lines have at times a pregnant sententiousness and efficacy rarely found in them, though the moralist and reformer too often suffocates the poet. To him and his followers is due the extension of the subject matter of the " poesia aulica " from love to ethical and political as well as religious themes, and Guittone's own great canzone on the overthrow of Florentine liberty at Montaperti (1260) initiates the series of canzoni on contemporary political events that is one of the glories of Italian lyrical poetry. Guittone is also the author of Italian letters, written in an artificial and mannered prose with Latinising constructions and showing the influence of the rhetorical models, but at times attaining genuine spontaneity and a certain austere simplicity. The poets of this group, besides giving popularity to the sonnet (which they employed *in tenzoni* on political themes), and developing the art of the canzone, introduced a new lyrical form, the ballata, composed not only for a musical setting, but also for the accompaniment of dancing. Notable among them are Bonagiunta Orbicciani of Lucca, an imitator of Giacomo da Lentino, introduced by Dante into the *Purgatorio* as the representative of the old school in poetry, and two Florentine rhymers, Monte Andrea and Chiaro Davanzati. The latter (if rightly identified) lived into the early years of the following century ; beginning under the influence of Guittone (his canzone on the submission of Florence to Charles of Anjou in 1267 is a worthy sequel to the Aretine's lament for Montaperti), some of Chiaro's later sonnets, clear-cut in style and beautiful in imagery, mark the transition to the " dolce stil nuovo." A place somewhat apart belongs to Rustico di Filippo (d. *circa* 1290), whose burlesque and realistic sonnets inaugurate a genre of composition that became characteristically Florentine.

While Guittone was at the height of his fame, the foundations were laid of a third phase of the " poesia aulica," which—echoing a line of Dante's—is called that of the " dolce stil nuovo." Its father was Guido Guinicelli of Bologna, who died in exile in 1276. Beginning as an ardent admirer of Guittone, Guinicelli developed a style of his own in certain exquisite sonnets that anticipate the *Vita Nuova*, and in his masterpiece, the canzone, *Al cor gentil ripara sempre amore*, in which a mystical interpretation is given to human love and a conception is set forth of the spiritual origin of true nobility that Dante was afterwards to make his own. He anticipates Dante, too, in his beautiful use of imagery, drawn mainly from phenomena of light and colour.

The "dolce stil nuovo" largely discarded the artificial word-play that Guittone (when beneath his better self) and his followers affected, and gave spiritual significance to what with the Sicilians had been poetic theory or convention. A new element drawn from scholastic philosophy becomes more prominent in Guido Cavalcanti, whom Dante was to call the first of his friends and who died in 1300. With Cavalcanti, the "dolce stil nuovo" becomes pre-eminently Florentine. In his famous canzone on the nature of love, *Donna me prega*, sentiment is smothered with metaphysics ; but elsewhere in his sonnets he elaborates Guinicelli's exaltation of womanhood, while discarding the religious and ethical aspect of the Bolognese poet's creed, and impressing his own strongly marked personality upon the whole. His ballate, for example, the *pastorella*, introducing a new genre from the French and Provençal, and the *Perch' io non spero*, composed during his last days in exile at Sarzana, are unrivalled in their kind. With Cavalcanti, Dante associates a younger poet, Lapo Gianni, as the best Florentine representative of the school.

This " poesia aulica " does not cover the whole field of early Italian poetry. In the Lombard cities, beginning in the thirties of the century with Uguccione da Lodi (who shows the influence of the Patarine heresy) and Gherardo Pateg or Patecchio, both Cremonese, there was considerable production of didactic and religious poetry, mainly in Alexandrine verse and in a language that is a literary elaboration of the local dialects. Notable among these are the poems on Hell and Heaven of the Franciscan friar, Giacomino da Verona (shortly after 1250), and the *contrasti* and *volgari* of the Milanese, Bonvesin de la Riva, who lived till 1313).[1] Brunetto Latini, the Florentine statesman and rhetorician, in exile in France after Montaperti, inaugurated the allegorical didactic poem with his *Tesoretto* (about 1262). The popular historical or political poem inspired by the factions of the day, in the form of the *serventese*, is preserved in a Romagnole piece in honour of Guido da Montefeltro (1273) and the Bolognese narration of the Geremei-Lambertazzi factions and the treachery of Tebaldello (1282) : themes that will recur in the *Divina Commedia*. In Umbria a great religious poet arose in Jacopone da Todi (d. 1306), the reputed author of the *Stabat Mater ;* his vernacular *laude*, with their intense personal note, are sometimes satirical, but more characteristic when they pass even beyond the Holy Poverty of St. Francis to a state of mystical annihilation in the ocean of divine love.

---

[1] Linguistically, we may associate with these Lombard poems the so-called *Lamento della sposa padovana* (1277), a Venetian poem, of which the " popular " origin has been disputed.

Italy in these years produced a supreme philosopher and theologian in St. Thomas Aquinas (d. 1274), whose monumental works—the commentaries upon Aristotle, the *Summa contra Gentiles*, and the *Summa Theologica*—are naturally in Latin, as are also those, more significant from the mystical standpoint, of his Franciscan contemporary, St. Bonaventura, who died in the same year. Latin still remained the usual medium of the chronicler, as with Rolandino of Padua (d. 1276), whose important chronicle of the March of Treviso shows the influence of the masters of the *ars dictandi*, and Salimbene of Parma (d. *circa* 1287), the wandering Franciscan, whose Latinity reflects the vernacular, in a unique medieval autobiography full of picturesque details and vivid characterisation. Italians also adopted French prose, the French speech being " more delightful and general than any other language "; thus Brunetto Latini, in the sixties, composed his vernacular encyclopedia, the *Trésor*, and, in the seventies, we have a chronicle of Venice by Martino da Canale, and two remarkable Arthurian compilations—the *Prophecies de Merlin* by an anonymous Venetian and the *Meliadus* of Rusticiano, or Rusti- chello, of Pisa. To Rusticiano is also due the original French text of the travels of Marco Polo—which he took down from the Venetian explorer's lips in prison at Genoa—known in its later Italian version as *Il Milione* from Marco's second name.

The majority of the prose works in Italian are derived, di- rectly or indirectly, from Latin or French texts which are some- times freely rehandled. Notable among them, in the last thirty years of the thirteenth century, are Brunetto Latini's *Rettorica*, a free translation of the *De Inventione* of Cicero ; the *Tristano Riccardiano*, a singularly interesting version of the story of Tristan and Iseult, apparently based upon a lost redaction of the French prose romance ; the *Libro della distruzione di Troia*, ultimately derived from the French poem of Benoît de Sainte-Maure ; the *Fatti di Cesare* and the *Conti di antichi cavalieri*, the first and perhaps the second from French compilations. A text of more original character and singular vivacity is the *Novellino*, or *Cento novelle antiche*, a collection of short stories drawn from the most varied sources, including the actual life of the thirteenth century. Scientific Italian prose has its rudimentary beginning in the *Libro della composizione del mondo* (1282) of a Franciscan, Fra Ristoro of Arezzo. A Florentine who must have been Dante's near neighbour, Bono Giamboni (d. *circa* 1292), besides translating various Latin works and the *Trésor* of Brunetto Latini, composed the *Introduzione alle virtù*, a kind of medieval pilgrim's progress, in a more developed style than attained by any previous writer in Italian prose. The historical compositions attributed to the Duecento are somewhat questionable. *Lu Rebellamentu de Sichilia* appears to be an authentic contemporary account of the Vespers of Palermo, though preserved in a relatively late linguistic form,[1] and a contemporary Sienese narrative of the battle of Montaperti has been recognised as the nucleus of a fifteenth-century *rifacimento*. The *Istoria fiorentina* of the Malispini—Ricordano and his nephew Giacotto—running from the tower of Babel to 1286, frequently regarded as a fabrication based on Giovanni Villani, is now held to be a fourteenth-century elaboration of a genuine work that was Villani's source. At the end of the century we have the anonymous *Cronica fiorentina*, at one time strangely attributed to Brunetto Latini. In both Malispini and the *Cronica* appears the well-known tradition of the origin of the factions in the city in the murder of Buondelmonte—of which there is no hint in the earlier Latin Florentine chronicle of Sanzanome.

It was in 1283 that the predestined national poet of Italy—Dante Alighieri, born at Florence in 1265—first appears as the writer of a sonnet in which he demands an interpretation of a dream from " all the faithful of love."

Thirty-one lyrics (canzoni, sonnets and a ballata) are woven together by a prose narrative with scholastic analyses of the several poems in the *Vita Nuova*, in which Dante tells the story of his love for Beatrice in her life and after her death (June, 1290), closing with an allusion to a " wonderful vision, wherein I saw things that made me purpose to say no more of this blessed one, until such time as I could discourse more worthily concerning her." The earlier lyrics show the influence, but slightly, of the poets of the " siculo-toscano " group, and more markedly that of Guido Cavalcanti, but this yields to that of Guido Guinicelli, and, with the " nuove rime " beginning with the canzone *Donne che avete intelletto d'amore*, Dante gives supreme and individual development to the Bolognese poet's idealisation of womanhood. Simultaneously there is a passage from love of the real woman to spiritual adoration of the image of virtue and beauty, of courtesy and humility, that the poet has created in his mind. Certain of the poems—the sonnets *Tanto gentile e tanto onesta pare* and *Vede perfettamente onne salute*, the canzone *Donna pietosa e di novella etate*—are among the most beautiful things in Italian poetry. The lyrics appear to have been composed between 1283

[1] With the doubtful exception of a fragment of the Gospel of St. Mark, no authentic texts of old Sicilian prose are earlier than the fourteenth century.

EARLY LITERATURE

and 1292, while the prose setting was probably written between 1292 and 1293. If Dante had a model before his eyes, it was that of the *razos* that accompanied the poems of the troubadours, and he seems also to have been influenced by the commentaries of Aquinas on Aristotle. As yet the influence of the Latin poets is slight, that of the new scholastic philosophy being much more obvious. Though some episodes are obviously symbolical, the *Vita Nuova* as a whole cannot be taken as an allegory, but rather as a mystical interpretation of the writer's early life and love in the light of the visionary experience with which it closes.

A number of Dante's other lyrics (known collectively as the *Rime* or *Canzoniere*) belong to the period of the *Vita Nuova*, written in honour of Beatrice or for one or other of the ladies who appear in the narrative, a few being more casual compositions for musical setting or in answer to other poets. Later than the *Vita Nuova* there is a small group of poems, among them the sublime *Amor che ne la mente mi ragiona*, which are allegorical, in praise of philosophy conceived as a spiritual mistress whose body is wisdom and whose soul is love. They were probably all written before 1300, as also were two didactic canzoni on nobility (*gentilezza*) and chivalry (*leggiadria*) which attempt to give lyrical form to transcripts from the Aristotelian *Ethics*. A remarkable group of canzoni, known as the " rime pietrose," including a masterpiece, *Io son venuto al punto de la rota*, seem inspired by a fruitless passion for a woman other than Beatrice ; they show the influence of the Provençal troubadour, Arnaut Daniel, from whom Dante introduced into Italian the new form of canzone that became known as the sestina. If these poems are rightly associated with another love canzone, *Amor, da che convien pur ch'io mi doglia*, they were written in the early years of Dante's exile. To this period probably belong an ethical canzone, *Doglia mi reca ne lo core ardire*, a denunciation of social corruption that anticipates the *Commedia*, and another lyrical masterpiece, *Tre donne intorno al cor mi son venute*, in which the Franciscan allegory of Lady Poverty and her companions mingles with imagery drawn from Isaiah in a hymn to justice which is also Dante's own apologia. This last canzone seems, perhaps about 1306, to have closed Dante's work in the pure lyric, though a few sonnets may belong to his later years.

With the poet's exile (1302), a wider horizon opened before his eyes ; no longer Florence, but all Italy, is the background of the *De Vulgari Eloquentia* (*circa* 1304) and the *Convivio* (1306-08). The former, in Latin prose but with vernacular quotations and illustrations, was left unfinished ; of the four projected books, only the first and a portion of the second were written. In the first book, starting from the origin of language, Dante seeks the " illustrious vernacular," the national language of Italy. For this purpose he examines all the Italian dialects, rejecting each in turn, including Tuscan, for what is practically an abstract literary language free from local characteristics. It has been said that Dante here makes the discovery that language is the symbol of nationality, and he already sees the Italians, though politically scattered, " united by the gracious light of reason." In the unfinished second book, Dante shows how this illustrious vulgar tongue should be employed in the noblest form of poetry : the canzone, " tragica coniugatio," a composition in the highest style, dealing with the exalted themes of arms, love and virtue. Taking his examples from the Provençal troubadours, from the best of his Italian predecessors and contemporaries, and from his own practice, Dante establishes principles for the structure of the canzone that are not only indispensable to the student of Italian poetic form, but of wider application in the sphere of æsthetics. The *Convivio* attempts, for practically the first time, to apply this illustrious Italian vernacular to prose, whereby " its virtue will be seen, how by it the most lofty and most novel conceptions are expressed almost as fittingly, sufficiently and gracefully as by Latin itself," when free from the incidental adornment of verse. In the form of a prose commentary upon fourteen of the poet's own canzoni, it was designed to make philosophy accessible to the unlearned by popularising the new Aristotelian science of Albertus Magnus and Thomas Aquinas. Only the introduction, mainly an impassioned defence of the Italian language and an apologia for the author's own life, and three other of the projected fifteen treatises were written, centring round the allegorical personification of Philosophy as a " donna gentile," of whom Dante became enamoured after the death of Beatrice. In the second and third treatises, the pyschological and mystical chapters, dealing with the nature of the soul and the significance of love, are particularly interesting. The fourth treatise is mainly ethical, discussing true nobility, moral virtue and human felicity, the goal of human life. And here the conception, that felicity (even here and now) is that for which man is born, which is the root of Dante's ideal imperialism, appears for the first time in his works : hence the necessity of the empire for establishing and maintaining peace, the divine election of the Romans to universal dominion, and the divine purpose in the history of Rome.

It is with this sense of Italian citizenship and this new Roman imperialism that Dante announces the advent of Henry of

Luxemburg in his letter to the Princes and Peoples of Italy (1310), a landmark in the development of the national idea, in which rulers and peoples are admonished as members of one body to accept the imperial deliverer from anarchy and oppression. The same spirit, though embittered by opposition, inspires his letter to the " most wicked Florentines " denouncing them for " shrinking from the yoke of liberty," and that to Henry himself, urging him to turn his forces against Florence (1311). The fullest and calmest exposition of Dante's imperialism is the Latin treatise entitled *Monarchia*, in three books. Its date is uncertain ; some scholars to-day hold that it was written in 1313, when Clement V had deserted Henry's cause and Robert of Naples was denying the whole imperial claim, while others assign it to 1318, when John XXII was carrying on a campaign against Louis of Bavaria, Henry's successor. In the first book Dante shows that the empire, or universal monarchy, is necessary for the well-being of the world, in order that the human race may attain the goal of civilisation—the actualising, or realisation, of the whole capacity of man's potential intellect—in peace and freedom. In his conception the empire is a permanent court of international justice, with means of enforcing its impartial decisions, the guiding power to represent law in a unity of civilisation within which nations and kingdoms and cities will develop along their own natural lines. The second book argues that history, supported by Christian faith, shows that the Roman People acquired this dignity of empire by the rightful judgment of God. In the third book it is shown that the emperor derives his authority, not from the successor of St. Peter, but immediately from God. The two cities—the earthly and the heavenly—of St. Augustine's *De Civitate Dei* become the two ends for which God has ordained man : blessedness of this life and blessedness of life eternal, to which the emperor and the pope, the one in accordance with the teachings of philosophy, the other in accordance with revelation, have to lead. The emperor is chosen by God alone, the electors being only the proclaimers of Divine Providence, but Cæsar must observe that reverence to Peter which is due from a first-born son to a father. To the later years of Dante's life belong the letter to the Italian cardinals, written shortly after the death of Clement V (20th April, 1314), urging them to bring back the Apostolic See to Rome, and the letter " to a Florentine friend," written probably in May, 1315, in which the poet, claiming to be " vir praedicans iustitiam," refuses to return to Florence under dishonouring conditions. Written at some date between 1318 and 1320 is the letter to Cangrande della Scala, containing

the dedication of the *Paradiso*, and what is practically a general
introduction to the *Commedia*, explaining its allegory and purpose,
insisting upon the power of the human intellect to transcend
the measure of humanity in mystical experience.   Probably
authentic, though unknown until the sixteenth century, is the
Quaestiv de aqua et terra, purporting to be a discussion on the
relative position of earth and water upon the surface of the globe
delivered by Dante at Verona in 1320.   Lastly we have two Latin
eclogues, composed at Ravenna in 1319 (or 1320) and 1321
respectively, prompted by an invitation from Giovanni del Virgilio
to write a Latin poem on a contemporary event and receive the
laurel crown at Bologna.   These delightful poems, revealing the
gentler side of Dante's character and throwing a pleasant light
upon his last years at Ravenna, may be said to have inaugurated
the pastoral poetry of the Renaissance.

The date of composition of the *Divina Commedia* is still a
disputed question.   Some have held that its germs are already
in the *Vita Nuova*, and that it is directly anticipated in the
" mirabile visione " and the promise to write of Beatrice " what
has never been said of any woman."   The vision of the other
world, upon which it is based, is represented as seen by Dante
in the spring of 1300, all that happened after the April of
that year being spoken of as future and by way of prophecy.
According to one theory, the *Inferno* and *Purgatorio* were composed before the death of Henry VII ; according to another,
the whole poem was both conceived and written between the
failure of the emperor's undertaking (1313) and the poet's own
death at Ravenna (14th Sept., 1321).   The recent discovery of
a reference to the *Inferno* by Francesco da Barberino, in his Latin
commentary to his *Documenti di Amore*, has been taken as proving
that the poem was known before 1313 ; but the date of the note
is uncertain, and we have no sure evidence as to the circulation
of the *Inferno* before 1317, whereas Dante's first eclogue proves
that, by 1319 or 1320, the *Inferno* and the *Purgatorio* had been
published, and the *Paradiso* was in preparation.   The internal
evidence is conflicting ; while portions at least of both *Inferno*
and *Purgatorio* seem considerably earlier, the close correspondence
between *Inf.* XIX and the letter to the Italian cardinals seems
to point to that canto having been written or revised in 1314.
The one indisputable fact is that the *Paradiso* is the work of
Dante's last years, and, if the late date of 1318 be accepted for
the *Monarchia*, we find the poet simultaneously building up the
earthly and depicting the heavenly city.

In the *Commedia*, the dual scheme of the *Monarchia* reappears, transferred from the sphere of Church and State to that of the individual soul : Virgil, representing human philosophy based on reason, leading Dante from the dark wood through Hell and Purgatory to blessedness of this life in the Earthly Paradise ; Beatrice, symbolising the divine science of theology in possession of revelation, guiding him through the nine moving spheres to the blessedness of eternal life in the true Paradise, the Empyrean. Based upon this vision of the world beyond the grave is an allegory of man, " as by free will, meriting and demeriting, he is subject to justice rewarding or punishing." Dante found a first sketch for the *Inferno* ready to his hand in the sixth book of the *Aeneid*, and filled this in with the current traditions of medieval eschatology, though, save, for occasional motives, he owed little to the medieval visions of the other world. His Hell, with its punishments, is essentially the eternal prolongation of the life of sin, chosen in time by abuse of free will. The *Purgatorio*, with its wonderful open-air setting and the voluntary nature of the purifying pains, is entirely his own creation, representing the soul's quest for purification of the spirit and moral liberty. The *Paradiso* transforms the current notions of astronomy into a mystical progress in love and knowledge that becomes an anticipation of the Beatific Vision, the transient experience of the perfect simultaneous and limitless life of Eternity.

The Latin poets, especially Virgil and Lucan, the Aristotelian philosophy, the mysticism of St. Augustine, the Victorines and St. Bernard, the scholasticism of Aquinas and Bonaventura, have all shared in the making of the poem ; but Dante's main source of inspiration is his own spiritual experience, his knowledge of the human heart, the contemplation of external nature, the observation of the life of his own times. His power of characterisation, more manifest in the great episodes of the *Inferno* than with the penitential spirits of the *Purgatorio* or the transfigured souls of the *Paradiso*, was a new thing in literature, and is naturally at its height when dealing with the men and women of the Middle Ages and his own contemporaries : Francesca da Rimini, Farinata, Pier della Vigna, Guido da Montefeltro ; though his Ulysses is also an unapproachable masterpiece. He seems to have invented little, but to have interpreted the facts and traditions as he had received them, revealing their real nature and moral significance. In the *Commedia*, Dante combines the fulfilment of the promise made to the memory of Beatrice at the end of the *Vita Nuova* with that of the charge he conceives laid upon him in the *Monarchia* of keeping vigil for the good of the world. The end of the poem is " to remove those living in this life from the state of misery, and to lead them to the state of felicity." Dante is the prophet of the Middle Ages, renewing for his own time the warnings and messianic aspirations of the Hebrew seers, but in the language and with the consummate art of the Latin poets.[1] The place of the *Divina Commedia* in literature is defined by Dante himself when, in Limbo, the great classical poets make him sixth in their band ; under Virgil's guidance, the modern vernacular poet has for the first time produced a work to equal the masterpieces of classical antiquity.

While Dante was thus creating the national literature of Italy, there was a large and varied production of minor poetry. Probably before 1300 we have a redaction in an Italian redolent of gallicisms of the *Roman de la Rose* in 232 sonnets, known as *Il Fiore*, ascribed to a " Ser Durante " whose name is simply that of the protagonist, and the *Intelligenza*, an allegorical poem in " nona rima," full of romantic colour, erroneously attributed to the Florentine chronicler, Dino Compagni. More or less contemporaneous with the *Commedia* are the dreary didactic poems, *I documenti di Amore* and *Del reggimento e costume di donna*, of Francesco da Barberino (d. 1348), and the *Acerba* of Cecco d'Ascoli, who was burned as a heretic in 1327. Lyrical poetry reaches a higher level. Cino de' Sigisbuldi of Pistoia, the friend and correspondent of Dante, who regarded him as the chief poet of love, was slightly younger than the Florentine, and died in 1337. The best of his love sonnets are only inferior to those of Dante among his contemporaries, and, unlike Dante, he employs the canzone for high political themes in two noble poems on the death of Henry of Luxemburg. Cecco Angiolieri of Siena (d. *circa* 1313) was called by Rossetti "the scamp of Dante's circle " ; his sonnets, in their grim and bitter humour, their crude realism and passionate railings against the world, reflect his life and reveal a power of no ordinary kind. Folgóre da San Gimignano (d. after 1316) painted vividly and minutely the blithe and delicate living of the young nobles of Siena in his *corona* of sonnets for the months of the year, and in four terrible sonnets denounces the cowardice of the Guelfs and hurls defiance at God for the victory of Uguccione della Faggiuola at Montecatini (1315). With these latter we may compare the beautiful and pathetic ballata, *Deh avrestù veduto messer Piero*, by an anonymous Guelf contemporary of the battle, which has something of the spirit of an old English ballad. Admirable, too, are the sonnets of the exiled Guelf, Pietro de' Faitinelli of Lucca (d. 1349). The jocose and familiar style of

[1] Its metre, the " terza rima," is a creation of Dante's own, adopted (but completely transformed in the process) from a form of serventese mainly used in popular poems of a satirical character or on contemporary events.

sonneteering is carried on by Pieraccio Tedaldi of Florence (d. *circa* 1350), the author of the first sonnet on the sonnet. Niccolò del Rosso of Treviso (d. after 1348), the compiler of an extensive manuscript collection of the lyrics of his contemporaries, in his political sonnets represents the Guelf dread of Cangrande and their futile hopes in Pope John and King Robert. The tradition of the " dolce stil nuovo " continues with two Florentines, Sennuccio del Bene (d. 1349) and Matteo Frescobaldi (d. 1348), of whom the former had been one of Dante's fellow exiles, and the latter was the son of the Dino Frescobaldi whom Boccaccio associates with the story of the recovery of the first seven cantos of the *Inferno*.

Prose developed considerably in the first half of the Trecento. Various " fiori " or anthologies appeared, such as the *Fiore di vertù*, on vices and virtues, by Tommaso de' Gozzadini of Bologna (d. after 1329), and the *Fiore d'Italia*, a kind of Roman history, with the story of Aeneas from Virgil, of the Carmelite, Guido da Pisa (d. after 1333), and the *Ammaestramenti degli antichi* of the Dominican, Bartolomeo da San Concordio (d. 1347). Two versions, representing different redactions, of the *Libro dei setti savi di Roma*, belong to the early years of the century. Florence led the way in vernacular history. Dino Compagni (d. 1325), who had played an honourable part in the political struggles that caused Dante's exile, wrote his *Cronica* of the factions of the city from shortly before 1300 to the coming of Henry of Luxemburg, inspired by an ardent love for his commune and a passionate sense of justice, in a vivid style that makes the small book a gem of historical literature. On a far larger scale, but with the same patriotic intention, Giovanni Villani composed his *Istorie fiorentine*, begun in 1300 and continued until his death in the pestilence of 1348 ; a work of unique value in depicting the life and development of the Florentine republic. It was continued by his brother, Matteo Villani (d. 1363), and completed by the latter's son Filippo. By an anonymous contemporary of the elder Villani is the *Istorie pistolesi*, a vivid account of the factions in Pistoia. The period is rich in ascetical and religious works, partly translations, partly original. Thus we have the sermons of Fra Giordano of Pisa (d. 1311), the *Vite dei santi padri* and other works of Fra Domenico Cavalca (d. 1342), and a complete version of the Bible, the *Bibbia volgare*, produced in the second half of the century. The *Fioretti di San Francesco* probably took its present shape shortly after 1350. Based in part upon an earlier Latin work (the *Actus beati Francisci et Sociorum eius*), and written from the standpoint of the party

6

of the strict observance, it completes the Francis of the *Commedia* in giving us the homely and legendary features in his personality that Dante omitted. From the Dominicans came the *Specchio di vera penitenza* (1354) by Fra Jacopo Passavanti of Santa Maria Novella, recasting in literary form the matter of his sermons to the people, with vivid " examples " intended to arouse the conscience of his hearers in the years of moral relaxation that followed the great pestilence. The *Libro*, or *Dialogo della Divina Provvidenza*, and the letters of Caterina Benincasa, St. Catherine of Siena (d. 1380), dictated by her to her secretaries and disciples, are still of profound significance to the student of religious experience, reflecting the personality of perhaps the only woman saint who has impressed popular imagination in something of the same way as St. Francis of Assisi.

Romance in prose is represented by the *Avventuroso Ciciliano* (after 1340), attributed to Bosone de' Raffaelli, describing the adventures of five Sicilian knights errant after the Vespers of Palermo, and, more notably, by the *Tavola Ritonda*. This remarkable work, as we now have it, seems to have taken shape between 1317 and the middle of the century. It is an attempt, anticipating the *Morte d'Arthur* of Malory, to fuse various branches of the Arthurian legend into a consistent whole, and contains much primitive matter freely rehandled by the author or compiler. There are also two fourteenth-century Italian romances of Merlin, of which one—the *Storia di Merlino* (1379)—is hardly less valuable to the student of Arthurianism. A body of romantic poems, in imitation of the *chansons de geste*, runs from the end of the thirteenth to the latter part of the fourteenth century, with its centre in the Veneto and the March of Treviso, in a hybrid Franco-Italian or in French by Italians. The most important of these are the *Entrée d'Espagne*, by an anonymous Paduan shortly before 1320, in which the adventures of Roland anticipate the fusion of the Carolingian story with the Arthurian tales of knights errant that will be characteristic of later Italian " poesia cavalleresca," and the *Attila*, about 1350, of Nicola da Casola, mingling romantic adventures of a hero of the House of Este with the invasion of Italy by Attila. In Italian, from the twenties of the century onwards, we meet the *cantari* in " ottava rima " : popular narrative poems, recited or sung to the people by the " cantastorie," who were the successors of the old giullari. The earliest preserved is the *Cantare di Fiorio e Biancofiore*, the French story retold in prose a few years later by Boccaccio in his *Filocolo*. These poems cover a wide and varied field, handling classical, romantic and religious themes, and even at times contemporary political events. The most attractive are those dealing with the Carolingian or Arthurian cycle, or representing the matter of the " Breton lays," or fantastic tales drawn from folk-lore. Thus the *Spagna*, on Charles' expedition and Roncesvalles ; the *Lancilotto*, the destruction of the Round Table ; *Pulzella Gaia*, the story of the love of Gawain for a daughter of Morgan le Fay ; *Carduino*, the Italian counterpart of the English *Sir Libeaus Desconus*. As a rule the *cantari* are anonymous, but we have several by the Florentine poet, Antonio Pucci (d. 1388) : notably *Madonna Lionessa*, with a variant of the pound of flesh motive that will appear in the *Merchant of Venice ;* [1] *Gismirante*, a medley of several fairy stories in an Arthurian setting ; the *Regina d'Oriente*, a harmony of fantastic romance and humour.

The two supreme figures of the middle of the century, Petrarch and Boccaccio, will be considered in connection with the Re-naissance. Among those who, by comparison, are minor poets, the first place belongs to Fazio degli Uberti, the great-grandson of Dante's Farinata, who was born in exile at Pisa and died at Verona about 1368. His *Dittamondo*, an unfinished poem in six books of terza rima, was intended " as an earthly parallel to Dante's Sacred Poem, doing for this world what he did for another " (Rossetti), as Fazio represents himself led by the geographer Solinus over the various lands ending with Jerusalem. Dreary as a whole, it has genuine poetical passages, as when the poet yearns to look upon Florence or describes the supposed sites of the Arthurian legend in true romantic colours. Several of his canzoni, on his loves and conditions of life, are admirable, and a famous political canzone (1355), in which Italy herself rebukes the baseness of Charles of Luxemburg, is a noble monu-ment of medieval Italian patriotism. The same spirit inspires the *Canzone di Roma*, attributed to Fazio but in reality by a Sienese, Bindo di Cione, which looks forward to a hereditary Italian monarchy. There was a considerable production of poetry at the courts of Lombardy, where, at Verona, Antonio da Tempo (1322) and Ghidino da Sommacompagna (1380) wrote treatises on the art of " ritmi volgari." The best of these northern poets was Francesco di Vannozzo, of Aretine origin but born at Padua, who became a courtier of the Visconti, was a friend and worshipper of Petrarch, and died about 1389. In a hybrid lan-guage in which Tuscan and Paduan are mingled, frequently rendered obscure by elaborate word-play, he composed *frottole* on public events, eulogies of his patrons, love sonnets occasionally of real beauty and originality (as one on the coming of the

---

[1] The same motive occurs in one of the stories of the *Pecorone* of Ser Giovanni Fiorentino (1378), an imitator of Boccaccio.

cuckoo), and a celebrated *cantilena* in eight tailed sonnets, in which the Italian cities offer homage to Gian Galeazzo Visconti as the national Messiah of Italy.　At Florence two remarkable poets—Antonio Pucci and Franco Sacchetti—combine what Carducci calls " poesia borghese," drawing inspiration from daily life, with patriotic exaltation of the commune.　The copious and varied verse of Antonio Pucci reflects almost every aspect of public and private life in Florence from the flood of 1333 to the acquisition of Arezzo in 1384, a monument of the vernacular of the people in the period when Petrarch and Boccaccio were establishing the norm of the literary language.　If Pucci is the poet of the piazza, his friend Sacchetti is the poet of the palace of the commune (he died about 1400).　He is at his best in lyrics written for music, or idealising Florentine country life, while his political canzoni give noble expression to the ideals and conflicts of the great Guelf republic in the latter part of the century.　Sacchetti is also the author of 300 prose *novelle*, of which only two-thirds have come down to us, dealing with the life of the middle and lower classes in Florence, full of the witty retorts and practical jokes in which the age delighted.　At the end of the century, between 1394 and 1402, a Dominican bishop, Federico Frezzi of Foligno, composed the *Quadriregio*, a somewhat pedestrian imitation of the *Divina Commedia*, in which Christian and mythological elements are mingled.　The friar's allegorical personifications are not without a certain imaginative power, and his meetings with the souls of his contemporaries in the other world are sometimes dramatic, but it would have needed a far greater poet to harmonise the eschatology of the Middle Ages with the spirit of the early Renaissance.

BIBLIOGRAPHY TO CHAPTER IV

Here, as in the following chapters on literature, we do not attempt to give full lists of modern editions of the principal authors.　In general, plain texts are provided in the series " Scrittori d'Italia " (Bari, Laterza), as well as in the cheaper collections such as " Scrittori nostri " (Lanciano, Carabba) and " Biblioteca classica economica " (Milan, Sonzogno).　Series with annotated texts : " Biblioteca scolastica di classici italiani "(Florence, Sansoni) ; " Classici annotati " (Milan, Vallardi) ; " Collezione di classici italiani con note " (Turin, Unione tipografica editrice, " Utet ").

(a) GENERAL WORKS

In the "Storia letteraria d'Italia " (Milan, Vallardi), with full bibliographies : F. Novati and A. Monteverdi, *Le Origini* (1926) ; G. Bertoni, *Il Duecento* (2nd ed., 1930) ; N. Zingarelli, *La vita, i tempi e le opere di Dante* (2nd ed., 2 vols., 1931) ; G. Volpi, *Il Trecento* (2nd ed., 1907).

G. Zonta, *Storia della letteratura italiana* (Turin, Vols. I-II, 1928-29 ; Vol. III, 1933.

On a smaller scale, with adequate bibliographies, V. Rossi, *Storia della letteratura italiana per uso dei Licei* (Milan, 3 vols., many issues).

A. D'Ancona and O. Bacci, *Manuale della letteratura italiana* (Florence, several issues), gives extracts as well as bibliographies.

With copious examples, T. Casini, *Letteratura italiana, storia ed esempi*, Vol. I. Milan, 1909-10.

La storia della letteratura italiana, of Francesco De Sanctis (Bari, 1913), English translation (Oxford, 1932), though out of date in some respects, is still invaluable for the insight it gives into the spirit of Italian literature.

(b) COLLECTIONS OF EARLY TEXTS

A. Schiaffini, *Testi fiorentini del dugento e dei primi del trecento*. Florence, 1926.

E. Monaci, *Crestomazia italiana dei primi secoli*. Città di Castello, 1913.

L. Piccioni, *Da Prudenzio a Dante*. Turin, several issues.

The first great early collection of Italian lyrics (compiled about 1300) is published diplomatically as *Il libro de varie romanze volgare, Cod. Vat. 3793*, ed. Satta and Egidi (Rome, 1902-08).

(c) We can only indicate a few works in the vast field of Dante literature, of which a copious bibliography will be found in Zingarelli's two volumes cited above. To keep abreast with the subject, the reader is referred to the periodical publications: *Studi danteschi diretti da* Michele Barbi (Florence) and *Giornale dantesco*, ed. L. Pietrobono (Florence).

Editions of complete works: *Le opere di Dante, testo critico della Società Dantesca Italiana* (Florence, 1921); *Le opere di Dante Alighieri*, ed. E. Moore and P. Toynbee (the "Oxford Dante," 4th ed., Oxford, 1924). A critical, but unannotated, edition of the *Commedia* alone, is edited by M. Casella (Bologna, 1923).

Annotated editions of the *Commedia : Divina Commedia con il commento Casini-Barbi* (Florence, several issues); with commentaries by F. Torraca (Milan, 1918, etc.), and C. Steiner (Turin, 1922); *La D. C. nella figurazione artistica e nel secolare commento*, ed. G. Biagi, G. L. Passerini, and E. Rostagno (Turin, 1921-31, the *Paradiso* not yet published).

Annotated editions of Minor Works: *Vita Nuova*, ed. M. Scherillo (Milan, Hoepli): *Canzoniere*, ed. G. Zonta (Milan, Vallardi); *Epistolae*, ed. P. Toynbee (Oxford, 1920).

P. Toynbee, *A Concise Dictionary of Proper Names and Notable Matters in the Works of Dante* (Oxford, 1914). The Concordances—E. A. Fay, of the *Divina Commedia* (Boston, 1888); E. S. Sheldon and A. C. White, of the Italian Works in prose and *Canzoniere* (Oxford, 1905); E. K. Rand and E. H. Wilkins, of the Latin Works (Oxford, 1912)—are still invaluable, although not based upon the *testo critico*.

For English readers, in the Temple Classics (London, Dent): the *Commedia* with text, translation and notes by H. Oelsner, T. Okey, and P. H. Wicksteed; *Vita Nuova*, with text, translation and notes by Okey and Wicksteed: *Convivio*, translation and commentary by Wicksteed; Latin Works, translation and commentaries by Ferrers-Howell and Wicksteed (Wicksteed's commentaries on the *Monarchia* and *Convivio* are notable). English introductions: C. Foligno, *Dante* (Benn's Sixpenny Library); E. G. Gardner, *Dante* (Dent, 1923). Good popular Italian introductions: U. Cosmo, *Vita di Dante* (Bari, 1930); M. Barbi, *Dante, vita, opere e fortuna* (Florence, 1933).

For special studies, see the bibliographies in Zingarelli's two volumes. An " edizione nazionale " of the works of Dante is in preparation, the first volume of which—the critical edition of the *Vita Nuova* by M. Barbi—has been published (Florence, 1932).

(d) In Order according to matter of Chapter

A. Gaspary, *History of Italian Literature to the Death of Dante*, trans. H. Oelsner. London, 1901.
E. Bonaiuti, *Gioacchino da Fiore, i tempi, la vita, il messaggio.* Rome, 1930.
F. Cuthbert, *Life of St. Francis of Assisi*, 2nd ed. London, 1921.
St. Francis of Assisi, Essays in Commemoration. University of London Press, 1926.
G. Bertoni, *I trovatori d'Italia.* Modena, 1915.
G. A. Cesareo, *Le origini della poesia lirica*, etc. (see Chap. I.).
E. F. Langley, *The Poetry of Giacomo da Lentino.* Harvard University Press, 1915.
Rime di Fra Guittone d'Arezzo, ed. F. Pellegrini. Bologna, 1901.
P. Ercole, *Guido Cavalcanti e le sue rime.* Leghorn, 1885.
F. Torraca, *Studi di storia letteraria* (includes essay on Fra Guittone). Florence, 1923.
V. Rossi, *Scritti di critica letteraria*, Vol. I. (with important essay on the " dolce stil nuovo "). Florence, 1930.
F. Massera, *Sonetti burleschi e realistici dei primi due secoli.* Bari, 1920.
E. Underhill, *Jacopone da Todi, a Spiritual Biography.* London, 1919.
E. Levi, *Poeti antichi lombardi* (Milan, 1921) and *Uguccione da Lodi* (Milan, n.d.).
E. I. May, *The " De Jerusalem Celesti " and the " De Babilonia Infernali " of Fra Giacomino da Verona.* Florence and Oxford, 1930.
Marco Polo, Il Milione, ed. L. F. Benedetto. Florence, 1928.
Il Novellino, ed. L. di Francia. Utet, 1930.
Les Prophecies de Merlin, ed. L. A. Paton. London and New York, 1926-27.
L'Entrée d'Espagne, ed. A. Thomas. Paris, 1913.
Il Tristano Riccardiano, ed. E. G. Parodi. Bologna, 1896.
La Tavola Ritonda, ed. F. L. Polidori. Bologna, 1864-65.
Fiore di Leggende, cantari leggendari, ed. E. Levi. Bari, 1914.
E. G. Gardner, *The Arthurian Legend in Italian Literature.* London, 1930.
I documenti di Amore di Francesco da Barberino, ed. F. Egidi. Rome, 1902-30.
Il Fiore e il Detto d'Amore, ed. E. G. Parodi. Florence, 1922.
L'Intelligenza, ed. V. Mistruzzi. Bologna, 1928.
Le Rime di Cino da Pistoia, ed. G. Zaccagnini. Geneva, 1925.
La Cronica di Dino Compagni, ed. G. Luzzato. Milan, 1906.
I Fioretti di san Francesco, ed. A. Della Torre (Turin, Paravia) ; ed. M. Casella (Florence, Sansoni).
R. Fawtier, *Sainte Catherine de Sienne.* Paris, 1921-30.
Rime di trecentisti minori, ed. G. Volpi. Florence, 1907.
Rime edite ed inedite di Fazio degli Uberti, ed. R. Renier. Florence, 1883.
Le Rime di Francesco di Vannozzo, ed. A. Medin. Bologna, 1928.
Il Quadriregio di Federico Frezzi, ed. E. Filippini. Bari, 1914.
Antonio Pucci, Le Noie, ed. K. McKenzie. Princeton University Press, 1931.
G. Gigli, *F. Sacchetti.* Messina, 1918.
L. di Francia, *F. Sacchetti novelliere.* Pisa, 1902.

CHAPTER V

THE LITERATURE OF THE RENAISSANCE

IN a certain sense Italians have always lived in a Renaissance
atmosphere, for even during the early Middle Ages the memory
of ancient Rome was not dimmed. During the thirteenth
century there were Latin writers such as Lovato and his friends,
and a little later the Milanese Giovanni da Cermenate, Mussato
of Padua, and Ferreto of Vicenza, who consciously tried to fashion
their style on that of the classics of Rome. And did not Dante
maintain that his " bello stile " was derived from Virgil ? These
were but signs of the coming revival, and the revival itself was
rendered conscious of its object and scope by Francesco Petrarca
(1304-74). He was born at Arezzo as the son of a Florentine
exile, was educated in Provence, read law for two years at the
University of Bologna, and then lived for some time at Avignon
as the protégé of the Colonna family. But he felt an exile
and had the exile's passionate longing for his home and traditions.
As he regretted the beauty of landscape when it struck him elsewhere than in Italy, so was he unable to see any perfection but
in the works of the Latins. He reacted against the corruption
of the papal court, as he reacted against the philosophical theories
of the thirteenth century. Petrarch, introspective by nature,
could not rest content with the philosophy of Aristotle as interpreted by Aquinas ; his favourite authors, St. Augustine and
Cicero, extolled Platonic philosophy, and Petrarch set his faith
in this doctrine though he could but indirectly become acquainted
with it. Solitary meditation, communion with nature, friendship
with a few exemplary men, familiarity with the works in which
great men of the past had revealed their message, were to be
the means by which men could improve themselves and heal the
ills of the age ; but the works of ancient writers were written
in Latin and Greek ; it behoved him, therefore, to study these
languages (though he never had the opportunity of making himself
master of Greek), and to express his own thoughts in a style not
unworthy of the classical age. In so doing he was revealing to
himself and to his contemporaries that the lucid Latin style of

87

the Middle Ages could not pass muster if judged by ancient
standards ; literary imitation of old models thus became the necessary means to the achievement of the moral and political reform
he had in view ; and he considered it his duty to divulge the
works in which he had recorded his own experiences in as classical
a language as it was possible for him to compose. His works
took the form of long letters on every conceivable subject which
he revised and collected into orderly series ; of introspective con-
fessions (*Secretum*), the praise of solitary life (*De vita solitaria*),
eclogues and other Latin poems. His masterpiece was to be
an epic poem, *Africa*, and, though this poem was left unfinished
and was never published during his lifetime, it gained for him
the coveted prize of the poetical laurels in Rome (1341). In
order to discover the secret of ancient craftsmanship, it was
necessary to know all the classical works that were still traceable,
and to read them in the best and oldest manuscripts. Petrarch
felt that disinterested admiration for beautiful books that is
peculiar to the born book-lover, but this passion was kindled
in him by his love for scholarship, no less than his scholarship
found its ultimate justification in his aim at a moral reform.
Thus he spared no labour and no expense, though he was never
richly provided with worldly means, in order to discover forgotten
works of the classical age and to become possessed of the best
manuscripts available. But Petrarch had another side. He was
human and susceptible to the charm of beauty in nature and
man ; and his heart was principally fascinated by Laura, who
was certainly a married lady of Avignon, but whose real name
can only be conjectured. He was overcome with her charms
when he first set eyes on her in a church at the age of twenty-
two ; he loved and sang her praises as long as she lived (she
died of the Black Death in 1348), and after that until the last
days of his own life. These poems he wrote in Italian, and
he considered them with a certain amount of complacency as
trifles (*nugellae vulgares*) ; for his fame, he held, depended upon
his classical scholarship ; despite this, he never ceased to polish
his Italian lyrics, to dispose them into an orderly sequence,
dividing the poems written during Laura's lifetime from those
that were inspired by her memory, intermingling with them some
occasional and political verses, and closing the volume with a
moving hymn to the Virgin Mary. He cherished his love, but
he also regretted this bondage, for no man is free and dare aspire
to heavenly beatitude who is trammelled by human love and
by desire of fame. And he persuaded himself, after Laura's
death, that she had striven by her unapproachable coldness to

dissemble her love and avoid sin, so as to render possible their reunion in heaven. But even then his mood was constantly changing, and these contrasting sentiments found expression in verses so hauntingly melodious as to become the heartbreaking model for all the poets in the future. But if his imitators may at times have loved as ardently as he did, they could not recapture, and indeed mostly failed to discover, the mainspring of his inspiration.

When, in his later years, he attempted to describe Laura in glory in a series of *Trionfi*, his learning rather stunted his inspiration. His friends admired no doubt his Italian lyrics, but, taking the cue from him, they mainly discussed scholarly or philosophical subjects in their letters ; and few among them realised that scholarship was for Petrarch a means to an end, not an end in itself. They gradually lost sight of his ultimate object, and became fully enraptured by the contemplation and admiration of the ancients ; they became pure scholars and, having acquired a familiarity with the classics and a mastery of style incomparably greater and more polished than his, they were emboldened to affect a certain superior commiseration for his efforts ; and the thoroughness of their learning concealed from their contemporaries that the movement, which Petrarch had initiated, was thus turned from its course, and that the Renaissance was, to a certain extent, deprived of its most promising elements.

Among his friends was Giovanni " Boccaccio," the son of Boccaccio di Chellino and of an unknown Frenchwoman (1313-75). His father, a fairly prosperous merchant, could neither get him to pursue his trade or to study canonical law ; while he was in Naples the young man became a favourite with the ladies in the easy-going Angevin court, and he lost his heart to one of these ladies, Maria d'Aquino, an illegitimate daughter of King Robert, who was called Fiammetta by Boccaccio ; thereafter he divided his attention between literature and love. In order to please Fiammetta, he turned an old French love story into a wearisome Italian novel (*Filocolo*) ; to bewail a separation from her, he composed in " ottava rima " a romantic poem (*Filostrato*) ; and to try to win back her fickle favours he wrote, again in " ottava rima," which thus became the accepted metre of narrative poetry, a heroic poem (*Teseide* or *Amazonio*) ; and later he harped back on his love in a psychological novel (*Fiammetta*). Under the spell of the Tuscan landscape and of classical mythology, he wrote a charming pastoral poem (*Ninfale fiesolano*), but he failed to attain the same measure of success in a pastoral novel interspersed with eclogues in "terza rima" (*Ameto*). In this work there are passages which are evidently based on Dante as model; Boccaccio's whole-hearted admiration, however, did not enable him successfully to imitate the *Commedia*, and the poem in "terza rima" in which Fiammetta is exalted as the means to reach heavenly beatitude (*Amorosa visione*) lacks vigour and consistency. Also the *Decameron*, written between 1348 and 1353, probably contains many stories with which Boccaccio had entertained the ladies of the Neapolitan court; but it is the work of his maturity and shows him at his best as a story-teller to whom nothing came amiss; tragic adventures, romantic tales, good jests and coarse anecdotes. He portrays the society of his days with its vices and its dreams of earthly rather than heavenly happiness. With the exception of a gross satire against women (*Corbaccio*), the *Decameron* closes the period of Boccaccio's creative activity. In 1350 he had met Petrarch, and the rest of his life was spent by him in paying a modest tribute to Dante, writing his life in Italian and publicly commenting the *Inferno*, and in pursuing the scholarly ideals which were championed by Petrarch; by compiling a laborious mythological encyclopedia (*De genealogia deorum gentilium*) and writing Latin lives of illustrious men and women of the past.

Scholarship so dominated the successive generations as to stunt the development of creative literature. To write in Italian was considered beneath their dignity by these devotees of the classical ages; the glamour of which was daily enhanced by the discoveries of old manuscripts and ancient statues and medals. Once again Italy, they felt, was taking the lead. Rome had ruled the universe; later popes and emperors (the successors of the bishops and of the emperors of Rome) had contended for universal pre-eminence; now the humanists, as they are called, were establishing a new culture, based on classical ideas, and expounded in the language of Rome. Petrarch realised that the Middle Ages lacked a sense of perspective, and dealt with classical works as if they were medieval, with classical heroes as if they were paladins of Charlemagne's court; he had endeavoured to visualise the classical ages with a closer adherence to historical truth; he had discovered some speeches of Cicero and his letters *ad Atticum*. Soon the humanists, beginning with Salutati, made rapid strides towards accurate scholarship. Coluccio Salutati (1331-1406) was a profuse correspondent and a skilful editor of classical texts. Poggio Bracciolini (1380-1459) discovered complete texts of Quintilian and Lucretius, poems of Silius Italicus and Statius, besides nine of Cicero's speeches.

The rhetorical works of Cicero were discovered at Lodi ; the comedies of Plautus were found in Germany. But even more important were the diligent comparison of different texts and the discussion of variants for, by these means, the humanists acquired a detailed information about ancient history and mastered the secret of Latin style. Some among them trusted in the nicety of individual taste, and judged by impression ; others were more methodical and comparative in their studies. The earlier humanists favoured impressionism, but against them the Roman Lorenzo Valla (1405-57) and later Angelo Poliziano (Ambrogini) (1454-94) brought scientific scholarship to such a standard as to conquer all opposition. From the outset these scholars had felt the need to acquire Greek as well as Latin ; Manuel Crisolora was summoned from Constantinople to teach in Florence ; later Greek ecclesiastics came to Italy to the Council of Ferrara, and Greeks who fled before the conquering Turks spread the knowledge of their language and literature in Italy. Petrarch had instinctively realised the greatness of Plato, now Gemistus Pleto (1355-1450) expounded platonic philosophy, and Marsilio Ficino (1433-99), on the advice of Cosimo de' Medici, worked out its Christian interpretation, thus giving origin to Italian neo-platonism, a doctrine which was accepted by Giovanni Pico della Mirandola (1463-94), and has left its mark on the works of Lorenzo de' Medici, Michelangelo and, to a certain extent, on the whole of the literary and artistic group of Lorenzo's court.

The position of these scholars was curious. Petrarch had not hesitated to claim for himself the right, and to shoulder the duty, of giving advice to ruling princes ; his followers, holding themselves to be the true exponents of the classical spirit, considered no reward adequate to their merits. They could interpret the ancients, write eloquent speeches and distribute glory to their contemporaries. Hector, they said, was indebted to Homer for his fame ; and thus, being poor and ambitious, they became often importunate ; but the signori, who well understood the spirit of the age, took pride in having famous humanists in their service. Many of them became as mercenary and as quarrelsome as the " condottieri," hurling vulgar invectives against one another on the slightest provocation ; not even Poggio, Leonardo Bruni (1370-1444) and Lorenzo Valla proving above such an unseemly practice. But their activities were many-sided and their contribution to the Renaissance of great value. Becoming entirely steeped in classicism, they imitated Latin and Greek erotic poems, and affected stoical, aristotelian and epicurian tendencies, thus impairing their Christian zeal ; and

Valla dared to disprove the historical truth of the Donation of
Constantine to Pope Sylvester ; they wrote eloquent and occasionally penetrating histories, as did Bruni and Biondo Flavio
(1388-1463) ; they became the interpreters of the politics of their
age, as Pontano (1426-1503) ; they fully reformed the system
of education by founding model schools such as the " casa zoiosa "
of Vittorino da Feltre (1378-1445), and by becoming, as did
Guarino Veronese (1374-1460), the teachers of typical Renaissance
princes such as Leonello and Borso d'Este.   And it is significant
that Pope Nicholas V (1447-55) drew inspiration for his actions
from humanistic ideals, and that a professed humanist (Enea
Silvio Piccolomini) ascended the throne of St. Peter under the
name of Pius II (1458-64).   By that time the popes had become
aware that the claim to universal power had no longer any chance
of being accepted owing to the secession of the reformers, and
they shifted their ground, supporting humanistic ideals and thus
championing a new universality, which was also Latin and was
based on Latin traditions.

This was the deep-seated cause of the opposition of zealous
Catholics towards vernacular literature and of their partiality
for Latin and scholarship.   There were many, however, who kept
loyal to the traditions of the fourteenth century ; belated imitators of Dante, as Matteo Palmieri (1406-75) in his neoplatonic
poem, *La città di vita*, and Giovanni Gherardi (d. *c.* 1445) da Prato ;
spiritless imitators of Petrarch, as Giusto de' Conti (d. 1449) and
Buonaccorso da Montemagno (d. 1429), later the more artificial
Antonio Tebaldeo (1463-1537) and Serafino Aquilano (1466-1500).
And there were poets who continued more popular themes ; authors
of *novelle* in verse, of legendary *cantari*, burlesque poets as
Burchiello (1404-49) and Antonio Cammelli, " il Pistoia " (1440-
1502), and the large group of dramatists who composed *Sacre
rappresentazioni* to be acted by religious guilds, some of them
spontaneous and simple as Feo Belcari (1410-84) and some aping
popular simplicity like the Magnifico Lorenzo (1449-92). The lack
of original exponents soon brought this dramatic form into decay,
particularly after Poliziano's innovation ; he had cast a heathen
and pastoral story in the form of a sacred drama (*Orfeo*) and thus
started the fashion of pastoral drama which was very accept-
able to courtly circles in Italy and later also in England, but only
occasionally produced works of real merit ; the court poets also
transformed the popular *canzonetta* and madrigal (well represented
in the works of Leonardo Giustinian, 1388-1446) into a refined
form of lyrical poetry (Lorenzo de' Medici, Poliziano, etc.) which
had also its less gifted practitioners.

With the exception of some imitators of Petrarch, as the Spaniard Benedetto Gareth, "Cariteo" (1450-1514), at Naples, vernacular poets did not allow Latin to influence their style ; but prose writers, to whom Boccaccio had shown the way, were wont to force Latin syntax and vocabulary on their works ; and few were able to keep this fashion within reasonable bounds, as did Belcari, Palmieri and, to a certain extent, Vespasiano da Bisticci (1421-98) in his important *Vite di uomini illustri*. And this tendency was particularly noticeable among non-Tuscan writers who wished to write in literary Italian, for, lacking familiarity with the spoken language of Florence, they could only base their vocabulary and syntax on literary examples. Thus, if Masuccio Guardati of Salerno still retained a certain directness in his *Novellino*, and Sannazaro of Naples in his famous *Arcadia* (1481-1504) achieved some laborious polish, there were many who debased Italian to a kind of literary jargon, as the Trevisan Francesco Colonna who wrote the *Hypnerotomachia Poliphili*.

There was greater ease and directness in the Latin poems of Pontano or in Poggio's *Facetiae* than in most works written in Italian. Even men of surpassing and many-sided genius, as Leon Battista Alberti (*c.* 1404-72), who upheld with Lorenzo de' Medici the claims of Italian against Latin, and who could write in a simple style when he wished (*Della famiglia*), are mostly laboured and involved.

An exception must be made for the poems of chivalry. Since the thirteenth century, at least, songs on the knights of Charlemagne and, less frequently, on the knights of King Arthur, had been recited in public squares and in castle halls, at first in French and later in Italian dialects. Some of the paladins had become such firm favourites with the people as to be " naturalised " ; thus Roland, or rather Orlando, was reputed to have been born in Italy, and Rinaldo was considered Italian ; in the new clime their features were altered ; the tales in which their deeds were recounted were elaborated and modified, abridged or expanded according to the taste of the audiences and the lapses of the memory of the songsters. Only the immense popularity of these tales could justify Andrea da Barberino (b. 1370) in writing his long compilation in prose, *I reali di Francia*, in which several French poems are so successfully strung together as to form a story that has been a popular favourite to this day. For some reason the characters as well as the events acquired a characteristic uniformity in these tales : Charlemagne would be old, his knights rebellious and divided into two factions ; some loyal knights would be wrongly accused, travel to far-off lands, accomplishing wondrous feats and return to France, mostly with some converted and love-sick princess in their train, just in time to save the king from the precarious position in which an enormous hoard of heathen assailants had placed him.

This popular form of poetry was not welcome in literary circles. Poliziano in 1475 endeavoured to ennoble it in his *Stanze per la giostra*, which is a pastoral poem rather than a poem of chivalry ; but the credit for raising the *cantari* to a higher level belongs to another of Lorenzo's friends, Luigi Pulci, a man, witty, gifted and endowed with an easy turn of verse (1432-84). He stumbled upon success while merely aiming at the entertainment of the Medici circle. He just dovetailed into one another two unrelated stories, and refashioned them in his own way ; but the inimitable flow of his lines, the skilful drawing of characters, the rapid development of the episodes which are told with rollicking fun, bare-faced exaggerations and sly thrusts at the less decorous qualities of the heroes, everything contributed to his success. There is scarcely any connexion with chivalry, and particular attention is paid to the giant Morgante and the treacherous " little giant " Margutte, the embodiment of grotesque evil. Pulci was at pains to show that he was a sceptical Florentine of the Renaissance and no candid believer in these fables still so generally admired.

Count Matteo Maria Boiardo (1441-94) would have resented such an attempt if he had known of it, for this proud nobleman was fond of the beautiful stories of the past. He could not wholly believe in them, but he almost regretted his own inability. When harassed by the wearisome duties which were thrust upon him by the princes of Este, and sore at heart owing to personal disappointments and distressing political events, he took refuge in this dream-world of his own fashioning—not in a pastoral land peopled by cultured shepherds, but in the world of chivalry in which he felt at home among noble knights and beautiful if fickle ladies. He cherished them as dream people, and would chide them and smile at them occasionally because he was aware that the dream was his own dream. Taking the cue from some simple *cantari* where a confusion between the Arthurian and the Carlovingian cycles had occurred, he intentionally mixed up the heroes of the two separate stocks, turning the dour paladins of Charlemagne into love-lorn adventurers ; and this transformation engendered a paternal feeling on his side towards his characters. He was a well-read gentleman, but not a full-fledged scholar. So that if he italianised Herodotus and Xenophon to win the favour of his prince, he did his work with the help of a Latin translation ; and he had, perhaps, less Latin than his elegies would lead us to suppose. He had been thwarted in love and, for the lady who had preferred a more powerful suitor, he composed sonnets and canzoni of rare merit. His language lacked purity and his style originality, but his love was real and his anguish profound, so that his lines, despite an occasional lack of polish, rank among the best love lyrics of the fifteenth century. His lady jilted him ; later his aunt, it would appear, was cognisant of an attempt on his life ; need we be surprised if his opinion of women is low and his judgment of them bitter ? The story of the *Orlando innamorato* is too complex to be told in detail. Orlando, the stern hero of the French chanson, goes with Ranaldo to the East in pursuit of Angelica ; they love her and hate her in turn as the result of drinking from a bewitched spring, and meet with extraordinary adventures. And, entwined with this central story, there are hundreds of episodes in which there appear damsels and knights, giants, monsters, magicians ; there are wonderful descriptions of wonderful places and there are amusing tales. The poet was partial to the trick of breaking off an episode at the most interesting moment in order to take up another thread, which was also interrupted before it was all spun out. The heroes keep to their traditional characters, but they are drawn by a cultured courtier of the Italian Renaissance who smiled at their simplicity, just as he disbelieved in some of their greatest feats ; and his smile, which is not ironical or completely detached, but affectionate and almost sympathetic, has none of the ribald coarseness of Pulci's. The *Orlando innamorato* was begun in 1482 and written at intervals until the descent of Charles VIII ; the sight of foreign troops caused Boiardo to pause, and probably the worry connected with their misbehaviour hastened his death (1494). His poem attracted at once great attention ; it was imitated by Francesco Cieco of Ferrara (*Mambriano*) ; it was rewritten by Francesco Berni (1497-1535) in polished Tuscan and in a different vein, and it inspired Ariosto to write his masterpiece.

Ludovico Ariosto (1474-1533), having shown early promise as a student, was compelled by family needs to follow his father and become a protégé of the Este princes, first of Cardinal Ippolito and later of his brother Duke Alfonso I of Ferrara ; while undertaking such official duties as were entrusted to him, he also took part in some theatrical performances. As a poet, he soon forsook Latin for Italian, and, owing to the no mean view which he took of his literary gifts, he was ever a restive if an able official, holding that his genius entitled him to a privileged position.

After some lyrical and dramatic experiments, he planned to complete and recast Boiardo's story into a perfect poem, trusting to the inspired craftsmanship of his versification, his polished mastery of the Italian language, and his close if dissembled adherence to the principles of classical epics. The haphazard composition of Boiardo's poem became an ordered complexity by means of the skilful entwining of numerous threads into a perfectly harmonious pattern ; the heroes lost some of their original charm, but gained much in composure and refinement. The *Orlando Furioso*—incomparably the greatest poem of the Italian Renaissance—is not the reconstruction of an ideal world, but the beautiful medium by means of which Ariosto expressed his feeling and ideals : his sensuousness, his love for the classics, his loyalty to his masters, the sorrow he felt at the course of political events, his literary preferences. And he was never tired of polishing and perfecting his creation, from its first edition in 1516, to the second in 1521 and the third in 1532 upon the revision of which he was still engaged when he died.

By that time, however, Italy was in the thralls of foreign invasion ; the age of the scholars was over ; the printing press (since its first appearance at Subiaco in 1469) had become well established and Italian was asserting itself against Latin. Latin was, of course, still carefully studied and excellently written ; Cicero and Virgil were the accepted models ; the hurt pride of Italians found solace in claiming the privilege of the Roman tradition. Foreign soldiers could conquer in the battlefield, but no " barbarian " could vie with Italians for the possession of the genuine heritage of Rome. This claim to the citizenship of an ideal Rome was so well recognised that Erasmus was prompted to retaliate by battling against Ciceronianism, and the Belgian Longueil craved the honorary citizenship of Rome with so ardent an enthusiasm as to commit suicide when that honour was denied to him. Classicism rallied to the Roman Church and was protected by the popes just when the voices of the reformers were becoming louder. The scholars, who in a previous age had appeared to regret the charm of the heathen myths, wrote Christian poems in Latin (Sannazaro's *De partu Virginis*, Battista Mantovano's *Parthenicae*, Vida's *Christias*), and Latin poems on scientific subjects. But the day of Latin was over ; there were grammarians who worked as carefully on Italian as their predecessors had worked on Latin, and a celebrated scholar, the Venetian nobleman and Roman prelate, Pietro Bembo (1470-1547), solemnly championed the formation of a classical language in Italian on the basis of the works of Petrarch and Boccaccio. By supposing a literary foundation of the Italian language, he made it possible for non-Tuscan Italians, as he was himself, to stand up to the Tuscans in linguistic discussions and to challenge their reputed superiority. And this champion of the language of Petrarch and Boccaccio, who were Tuscans, hailing from Venice was welcomed, particularly as he acted upon his principles and employed Italian with so consummate an art as to be greeted a master by the Tuscans themselves. His theories did not triumph without a struggle, however, for native Tuscans as Machiavelli (1469-1527) argued that literary style must be based on the spoken language of Tuscany and not on ancient models ; and Castiglione (1478-1529), among other provincial writers, refused to forego his right to employ words and form of his native dialect when he considered them authorised by courtly usage ; just as Dante had maintained in the *De Vulgari Eloquentia*. So keen were men of letters upon securing a measure of uniformity, that G. G. Trissino (1478-1550) of Vicenza felt impelled to come to the assistance of non-Tuscans by writing a grammar, and he went so far in his printed works as to adopt different types for open and closed vowels, for voiceless and voiced sibilants. This discussion on language is of interest as showing the triumph of Italian over Latin, and the clear consciousness the Italians possessed of their linguistic unity precisely at a time when foreign domination accentuated the rift between the different provinces. And it is significant in this respect that Machiavelli, a political thinker, considered this discussion so important as to intervene in it himself.

Machiavelli's later achievements indicate that this poorly provided son of a family of some standing had been carefully taught ; Greek he had not, and perhaps his Latin was not up to the standard of the age, but he must have shown some early signs of literary proficiency if he secured the protection of so polished a scholar as Marcello Adriani, who was chancellor of the republic when Machiavelli, during the rule of Piero Soderini, was elected to a minor post in the chancery. He had lived through, and kept scornfully aloof from, the Savonarola experiment, and, as soon as he was given employment, he threw himself whole-heartedly into his task ; although, what is particularly notable in so restless an age, he never seems to have entertained any personal ambition. He rightly considered himself the intellectual equal of the best, but he showed no wish to be more than a successful and influential official ; and it is possible that, with certain exceptions, he would not have written his principal works but for his dismissal from office. His early works are in point of fact official

7

letters and reports which he wrote while he was entrusted with diplomatic missions (*Del modo di trattare i popoli di Valdichiana ; Descrizione del modo tenuto dal Duca Valentino ; Rapporto delle cose della Magna ; Ritratti delle cose dell' Alemagna ; Ritratti delle cose di Francia*).   As an official, however, he knew his worth, formed definite opinions and tried to win over his government to them.   And he met with a considerable measure of success, for his ability was appreciated by Soderini and even more by Soderini's brother, the influential Bishop of Arezzo.   He soon became convinced that the main cause of Italy's weakness was to be found in the exclusive employment of mercenary troops ; no state could thrive that had no adequate and reliable forces at its disposal, and no forces were reliable except national levies. His first *Decennale*, the history of 1494-1504 in " terza rima," he wrote in 1504 mainly with a view of bringing home to his fellow-citizens the weakness of the state ; and he exerted all his energy in persuading Soderini to organise a conscript army. Only a limited experiment was agreed upon, and then this chancery official became fired with military enthusiasm ; he saw himself transformed into an army man, and took upon himself the difficult and thankless task of organising the levies from the countryside ; he also wrote an important report on the subject. He gloried in a small success of this improvised force, and did not lose faith in it even when it was ingloriously routed at Prato on the Medici's return.   This return (1512) spelt the end of Machiavelli's active life, and he was forced to reside in the country at S. Casciano.   There was a touch of vulgarity in his character which was brought into relief by straitened circumstances, so that this man, who was a loving husband and a good father, made rather a show of his coarseness and his unseemly behaviour.   But it was during his enforced leisure that, partly as an outlet for his intellectual activity and partly in the hope of convincing the Medici of his merit, and thus of regaining his position, he undertook his greater works.

Unusually observant and penetrating, Machiavelli was in the habit of looking deep beneath the surface of events ; he detected their causes ; in fact, he was so enamoured with his discoveries that he occasionally so arranged the exposition of historical facts as to emphasise unduly the lesson which they appeared to him to contain.   He was an observant, but so passionate, a witness as to be unintentionally misleading.   A close student of the realistic policy of ancient Rome, he constantly paralleled current events with the data of Roman history, particularly as they were told by the pessimistic Tacitus ; and he was divided between his theoretical tendency to democracy and his practical realisation of the necessity of despotism. So that he could illustrate Livy in his *Discorsi sopra la prima deca di Tito Livio* in the light of contemporary events, and draw a picture of the possibilities of despotism in *Il Principe* practically at the same time (1513). What mattered in his opinion was the close study of reality and the choice of the means suited to the attainment of the object in view ; a choice that he called *virtù*. He was so convinced of the necessity of successful action, that he could extol Cesare Borgia as a model in his *Principe*, though he had made slighting remarks about Borgia's conduct in his letters from Rome at the time of Borgia's downfall. It gave him a coarse satisfaction to parade the low opinion of mankind he had learned from experience to form. For the sake of driving home the lesson he wanted to teach, he did not mind shocking his readers, for it was consistent with his outlook that the least scrupulous among his readers, and the readiest to act upon his less guarded advice, would be the first to affect horror at his " immorality." His ideal was Italy's independence, and independence must follow upon military victory ; in the political conditions of the age only a prince could bring about such a result, and no man could become a prince who was not prepared to act in conformity with the needs and the practice of the age. What he had to say he said in a forcible language, which, despite some affectation of indifference to literary tradition and slight irregularities, is a miracle of lucid and eloquent presentation. Characteristically he also composed a treatise on military art (*Discorsi dell' arte della guerra*, 1516), so that a minor government official was at one and the same time the first exponent of political science, and the initiator of the modern conception of strategy. He also wrote two comedies, of which the *Mandragola*, a merciless satire of middle class and ecclesiastical corruption, stands out as the finest play of the Italian Renaissance. Though he prided himself upon close attention to facts, and indifference to literary adornment, in neither case would it be wise to take him at his own valuation ; for, if he had little liking for empty phrases, he was so well aware of the literary merit of his work as to feel hurt when Ariosto overlooked his name in a list of contemporary writers ; and he was so keen upon the discovery of the causes by which political events are brought about, that he was not above envisaging facts with certain preconceived ideas, as is visible in his historical works (*Vita di Castruccio Castracani* and *Istorie fiorentine*). By nature and training he was led to stress the vices rather than the virtues of his contemporaries and to formulate certain bitter dicta, by

which he has stood condemned in the eyes of many who chose
to consider him, quite unjustly, as the embodiment of evil. About
his patriotism there cannot be two opinions : he was the first
man of the sixteenth century openly to advocate Italy's unification
and liberation.

No other political writer was as significant in his days ; not
Donato Giannotti, a well-meaning constitutional theorist of
Florence ; and not even Francesco Guicciardini (1483-1540), despite
his almost uncanny realism. Guicciardini was as ambitious as he
was devoted to Florence, in whose service he was often employed ;
with his keen practical sense, he ably served the Medici family
in Florence and in Rome, incurring on their behalf the hostility
of his fellow-citizens during their rebellion against the Medici
rule. But, whether in office or out of office, he never ceased from
writing ; and his works are historically more trustworthy than
Machiavelli's, for, being free from political preconceptions, he saw
things as they were and set them down in a lucid if at times
complex style. Perhaps the first was the most valuable of his
works (*Istoria fiorentina*, 1378-1509), but his *Discorsi politici* and
the dialogue *Del reggimento di Firenze* are almost as illuminating
as his cynical *Ricordi politici e civili*, or his interesting criticism
of Machiavelli (*Considerazioni sui Discorsi del Machiavelli*). His
famous *Storia d'Italia* (1492-1534) is notable for its comprehen-
siveness, its veracity, and the elaborate style which he fashioned
on Livy's and which was well suited to the meditative bent of his
mind. Next to these two Florentine giants comes the Venetian,
Paolo Paruta (1540-98), a devoted patriotic historian in his
Guerra di Cipro and *Storia veneziana* (1513-51), and a notable
political thinker (*Della perfezione della vita politica ; Discorsi
politici*). In these works he endeavoured to reconcile political
theory with Christian ethics as the spirit of the Counter-Reformation required. But the best exponent of the political doctrine
of the age was the Piedmontese priest, Giovanni Botero (1533-
1617), a profuse writer who had much experience of practical
politics ; in his *Ragion di Stato*, Machiavelli's views are openly
antagonised and often tacitly imitated, if this be done with the
then necessary precaution of subjecting politics to the control
of religion. Around these, the outstanding historians and political
writers, there were numbers of notable craftsmen ; the Florentines
excelling as writers of a prose comparatively free from the tyranny
of Latin, as Jacopo Nardi (1476-1563) (*Istorie della Città di Firenze*, 1375-1494), the outspoken Benedetto Varchi (1503-65) who
was also a poet, playwright and essayist, the eloquent P. F.
Giambullari (1499-1555) who attempted to write in Italian a

Storia d'Europa, the elegant and concise B. Davanzati (1529-1606) who translated Tacitus. In other parts of Italy there excelled P. Bembo who translated his own *Historia veneta* (1487-1513) ; Angelo di Costanzo (d. 1591) and Camillo Porzio (d. 1580), in Naples, the Latinist Paolo Giovio (1483-1552) in Milan. Mention should also be made of the interesting works of travellers and ecclesiastics about foreign countries and of the diarist Marin Sanudo who, collecting all the documents which came to his notice in the Venetian chancery, put together a work (*Diari*, 1496-1533), that is an incomparable source for the history of this period.

In other departments of literature the burden of classical tradition, as revived by the Renaissance scholars, appeared distinctly to thwart the literary development and to stunt inspiration. This was particularly noticeable in drama. There had been written mystery plays during the Middle Ages, and also Latin plays which did not slavishly conform to classical standards. At the courts the love of display had favoured the fashion of pageants which sometimes attained artistic refinement ; but, since drama was to find its home in the courts, a particular character was impressed upon it. After Poliziano's example, pastoral drama, essentially artificial and remote from contemporary reality, began to enjoy a great vogue ; it was later to achieve perfection with Tasso (*Aminta*), but meanwhile, in the course of about a hundred years, there were written many dramas on pastoral subjects. The pastoral fiction was based on classical examples. Dante had himself reintroduced Latin bucolic poetry to Italy ; Petrarch and Boccaccio had followed in his steps, and as this form became well established among writers of Latin, it was natural that pastoral works should also be written in the vernacular. Boccaccio's *Ameto* provided an excellent model ; and, at the end of the fifteenth century, Sannazaro composed in Italian his *Arcadia* that was to call forth a lasting echo in European literature. With him the pastoral fiction definitely became an outlet for feelings and dreams that could not find an adequate expression in direct language ; there vaguely came into existence a land of refuge, a kind of fictitious Golden Age, in the description of which poets gave expression to their dreams and found escape from the increasingly distressing realities of Italian political life. The *Arcadia* was too learned and too complex a work to be closely imitated, but it marked the success of pastoral literature and fostered the fashion of pastoral drama.

Drama, however, was by no means restricted to shepherds and nymphs. The study of Plautus and Terence was bound,

in an age so steeped in classicism, to encourage the production
of their plays : at first they were acted in Latin; soon, later,
in incredibly bad Italian translations, particularly at the court
of Ferrara. And it was but a small, if a decisive step, to pass
from these translations to the staging of original plays written
in Italian. " Original " is scarcely a suitable adjective, for though
five among the earliest of these plays were written by Ariosto
himself, they were so closely imitated from their classical models
as to allow little room for the portrayal of actual life. There are
signs in Ariosto's plays of a possible departure from his models ;
and there are characters and scenes inspired by contemporary
life ; but classicism and imitation prevailed. Almost alone,
Machiavelli dared to write a play (*Mandragola*) on a true or life-
like incident giving full scope to his acid realism. Other playwrights, however, fell too readily into the habit of dramatising
short stories, and thus failed to exploit the possibilities of drama.
Real life and dramatic technique were sacrificed ; for drama
remained a department of literature and was not the work
of specialised craftsmen. Some of the best comedies were due
to " novellieri " as Lasca (1503-84), philosophers as Giordano
Bruno (1548-1600), and pamphleteers as Pietro Aretino (1492-
1556). Many of these plays have good points, but only one,
the *Mandragola*, comes near to perfection, and almost all, the
best as well as the worst, are frankly immoral in subject and
execution. From this angle the *Calandria* by Cardinal Dovizi is
no better than Ariosto's *Lena* or Aretino's *Marescalco ;* the immorality of the subjects depending as much on the environment
as upon the desire of keeping within the classical tradition.

It would be impossible even to mention here the names
of the principal playwrights, for they are legion ; the output
was stupendous in quantity and strangely uniform in technique
and subject matter ; and though many of these plays were
repeatedly printed in Italy and occasionally imitated by foreign
playwrights, the general standard was fair without ever attaining
high artistic merit. Most of these plays were meant to be read
rather than performed ; for the theatres were few, and the mass
of the people preferred another form of drama. There had been
professional entertainers throughout the Middle Ages, and during
the Renaissance there were produced some farcical plays in different places ; at Cava, near Naples, at Asti in Piedmont, and
in Venetia, where they took the form of uncouth dialogues between
country yokels. All were dialectal. At Siena there was formed
a guild of amateur actors, " I Rozzi," who proved very successful
and occasionally performed outside their city. In Padua there

appeared a professional actor-playwright, Angelo Beolco, called Ruzzante (1502-42), of outstanding merit. He acted plays of his own fashion or written by the Venetian Andrea Calmo (1510-71), and it was in these plays that a variety of dialects was first introduced. The gentleman spoke Venetian and the lawyer Bolognese ; the servant (Harlequin) spoke Bergamasque. Gradually these characters who wore masks became fixed, and the actors specialised in impersonating particular masks. They found it convenient to improvise the dialogue from a written *scenario*, for they were thus free to introduce topical jests and acrobatics, and to suit the jests to the audiences before which they happened to be performing. This professional and impromptu comedy was called " Commedia dell' arte " and met with great favour not only with popular, but also with educated audiences ; and professional companies of " Comici dell' arte " were soon touring in Italy, in France, England and Germany. The value of their plays is difficult to estimate from the bare *scenarios* we possess in considerable numbers ; it is clear, however, that success depended mainly on the histrionic proficiency of these actors, and also that these plays lacked originality, being mostly framed upon classical and later upon Spanish models. During the course of the sixteenth century the " Commedia dell' arte " rivalled and often overshadowed the learned comedy and the pastoral drama, and perhaps contributed to stunt the development of tragedy.

Seneca's tragedies had alone come down to the Renaissance from the Middle Ages ; they were acted in Latin and in translations at Rome and Ferrara on the threshold of the sixteenth century ; but meanwhile the progress of classical studies had brought to light some Greek tragedies, and in 1515 Gian Giorgio Trissino, who unfortunately fancied himself as a poet, constructed a tragedy painstakingly imitated from the Greek models : *Sofonisba*. He strictly observed the unities and used the " endecasillabo sciolto " as his principal metre. His work lacked fire, inspiration and dramatic power, but it was the first of its kind and became the standard to which Trissino himself and the later poets (Rucellai, Alamanni and others) endeavoured to conform, with no greater measure of success ; until another scholar G. B. Giraldi Cintio (1504-73), aiming at more dramatic power, returned to the Senecan model. His tragedies, which occasionally violated the unities, attained some forcefulness by means of the gory representation of terrible misdeeds. A year after Giraldi's *Orbecche* (1541) was produced, yet another scholar, Sperone Speroni (1500-88), even less endowed with poetical gifts than Giraldi, published his *Canace*, a play horrible in its imaginary violence, faulty in composition and quite undeserving of the unending discussions to which it gave occasion. It was left to Aretino to compose a more successful tragedy (*Orazia*, 1546), in which, as was his wont, he seemed perversely to aim at breaking all the rules his competitors set themselves to observe. He was thus as much influenced by classical theories as his competitors, but he possessed originality enough to produce a remarkable drama.

Aristotle's *Poetics* had, by the middle of the century, acquired a tyrannical hold on the Italian Renaissance. Tragedies were composed by scholars who had no other aim in view but to conform to Aristotle's theories. The deadening effect of foreign domination, the restrictions imposed by the Counter-Reformation and the close adherence to Aristotelian principles are sufficient to explain the lack of success of tragedies and of regular epics. Such success as the authors of the later Renaissance achieved is found in those literary forms that were necessarily less affected by these restrictions : in comedy, satire in which Italians gave outlet to their discontent, and in lyrical poetry.

Lyrical poetry during the Quattrocento was dominated by Petrarch and his imitators, whose works soon showed signs of decadence. These poets wrote on a cliché ; they caught the most obvious and most external features of their models to adorn their own superficial and artificial sentiments. The result was graceful enough on occasion and sufficiently melodious, as in the poems of Antonio Tebaldeo of Ferrara (1463-1537), but it was an insult to the memory of Petrarch. In an age in which the principle of authority prevailed, even lyrical poetry was bound to be regulated. Its reformer was Bembo ; he maintained that Petrarch alone was the master to imitate, and that the weaker productions of his followers must entirely be discarded. As it was a frequent practice to write Latin by constructing sentences which were mosaics of deftly connected quotations, it followed almost inevitably that Petrarch's lyrics should also become a quarry of apt quotations to be welded together in clever combinations. The flaccid facility of earlier Petrarchists was replaced by the fastidious sternness of scholarly poets whose form was perfect and whose heart was cold. Bembo's dictatorship was so generally accepted and so uncompromising, that a rebel, the Venetian Antonio Brocardo, was hounded to death. Thus rigidly Bembism ruled. The smoothness of formal perfection was so readily achieved as to give a sense of repletion, but, within the enormous mass of the " rime " composed in this age, there must be singled out some truly excellent lyrics. They were not written by Bembo himself or Annibale Caro (1507-66), who never seemed to be moved out of their composure ; not by Berardino Rota (1509-75), Angelo di Costanzo (1507-91), or Bernardo Accolti, the former of whom is noticeable for his laboured metaphors and conceits ; but by Bernardo Tasso (1493-1569), who feelingly bewailed the death of his wife, by Galeazzo di Tarsia (d. 1553), and above all, perhaps, by the impassioned Luigi Tansillo (1510-68). The lyrical fashion affected the whole of society ; ladies could not resist it : Veronica Gambara (1485-1550) showed some ability, and Vittoria Colonna (1492-1547) was inspired by a refined and feminine idealism. Also courtesans seem to have considered poetry a necessary adjunct to their charms ; Tullia d'Aragona probably relied on professional help for the production of her unimportant poems, but Gasparina Stampa (d. 1554), whatever her position may have been, was moved by strong feeling and bequeathed to posterity some of the most moving love poems of the Cinquecento. Among all these polished practitioners it seems strange to mention the brooding and solitary Michelangelo (1475-1564) ; his poems are inspired by feelings so strong and deep that their expression is often rugged, if it is always original ; he corresponded in verse with Vittoria Colonna, and was inspired by his devout friendship with her, his religious feeling and his patriotic sorrow.

Political events cast a deep gloom upon men's spirits ; for obvious reasons of expediency it was not often expressed, but is reflected in a certain despondency traceable in many works. These sentiments are found, too, in popular songs mainly inspired by the wars against the Turks, in the laments of exiles such as Galeazzo di Tarsia and Luigi Alamanni (1495-1556), and in the sonnets of F. M. Molza (d. 1544) and Giovanni Guidiccioni (d. 1541) on the sack of Rome and the condition of Italy. Despite this, political poetry was but a rivulet as compared to the streams of verses on other subjects.

Following upon the classical example also didactic poetry was elegantly cultivated by Bernardo Rucellai (*Le api*), Alamanni (*La coltivazione*), Tansillo (*Il podere, La balia*), Erasmo da Valvasone (*La caccia*), and Bernardino Baldi (*La nautica*, 1590) ; the first and the last of these reaching real excellence. Virgil was their master, precisely as Juvenal and Horace were chosen as models by satirical writers, stern as Antonio Vinciguerra (d. 1502), facile or humorous. Ariosto gave a profoundly human representation of his own character and outlook in his satires. The native zest of Italians could not be fully repressed by political and ecclesiastical domination ; extraordinary witty and bitter political skits

(*Pasquinate*) were published anonymously, and Pietro Aretino (1492-1556) exploited this form as a means to blackmail his powerful and wealthy patrons. His venomous pen was so dreaded that he could pride himself upon being the " scourge of princes," and he used his lash so effectively as to make a handsome income. But his was a quite exceptional case, for this unscrupulous wretch was endowed with remarkable literary gifts. On the contrary, the learned Francesco Berni (1497-1535), by mixing satire with burlesque and using a language that was considered excessively free even in his day, succeeded in creating a well-defined sub-species of satire, " rime bernesche "; which have no high aim, their object being only to entertain or insult, seldom to satirise ; it was probably for these reasons that he found many imitators, among whom A. F. Grazzini (Lasca) was the most successful. Another aspect of satirical poetry is seen in the *Baldus* of " Merlino Cocaio " (Teofilo Folengo, d. 1544), a parody of the romantic epic in a language, " lingua macheronica," which is itself a parody of classical Latin.

Equally free in tone were the *novelle*. Italians have often excelled in this form which was brought to perfection by Boccaccio. During the fourteenth century Franco Sacchetti, though influenced by Boccaccio, was less ambitious than he in his themes and less elaborate in their development ; Ser Giovanni Fiorentino in his *Pecorone* was drab ; Giovanni Sercambi, coarse and ungrammatical, was only interesting because of the many popular traditions which he collected. During the fifteenth century Boccaccio's influence was clearly traceable in the works of Giovanni da Prato, Jacopo Caviceo and particularly in the collection of Masuccio Salernitano (1476). The latter did not lack a certain vivacity and a moralising purpose, though he did not refrain from excessive realism ; Gentile Sermini was frankly lewd, just as in the next century was Fortini ; isolated *novelle* were written by Machiavelli, Luigi da Porto (*Giulietta e Romeo*), amusing accounts of often cruel jests were composed by Lasca (*Cene*), fantastic stories occur in the *Piacevoli notti* of Straparola, and heavy, tragic and intentionally moral tales in Cinzio Giraldi's (1504-73) *Ecatommiti ;* Agnolo Firenzuola (1493-1543), if lacking originality, must be credited with the refinement of Tuscan diction ; and Matteo Bandello (1485-1561), a voluminous and artless writer, deserves mention on account of the great variety of the themes which he treated and the interesting dedicatory letters which provide a precious source of information about social life during the Cinquecento.

It was a strange and complex life, harassed by a succession of political disasters, and yet greedy for enjoyment and extraordinarily sensitive to the appeal of the arts. The refinement to which the art of living had been brought by the Renaissance can nowhere be better appreciated than in the many treatises dealing with education and social manners. Just as the Paduan Alvise Corner wrote a famous booklet on simple life (*La vita sobria*), Baldesar Castiglione (1478-1529), a nobleman and a courtier, summed up the ideal which the best among Italians set themselves to attain (*Il cortegiano*) ; this ideal is Stoic rather than Christian, cultured and refined rather than deeply human ; great emphasis is laid on manners, but the importance of more solid qualities is never lost sight of. The immediate success with which this book met was significant, and certainly helps us to understand the deeper tendencies of the age. The *Cortegiano* was by no means an isolated work ; good manners formed the subject of the *Galateo* of Giovanni della Casa (1503-56), just as love, and particularly Platonic love, which was the subject of one of the dialogues of the *Cortegiano*, was dealt with in almost countless treatises in Latin as well as in Italian, such as the *Asolani* of Bembo, Speroni's *Dialoghi* and many other works. The literary output of the sixteenth century was as stupendous as its wealth of artistic production. There were so many writers of merit, if often hide-bound by classicism, and they dealt with so wide a variety of subjects, that no summary can do justice to this age.

A few examples must suffice. We have mentioned treatises on love and manners, but also more technical subjects were discussed. There had no sooner appeared a translation of Aristotle's *Poetics* than there followed a long series of acute interpretations which exercised a great influence upon literary criticism in Italy, in France and in England, as well as in Germany and Spain. The names of Castelvetro and Scaligero, who were by no means the most penetrating writers on this subject, became familiar in England. We have already mentioned the long polemic on the Italian language, but it must be remembered that language gave occasion to interesting works even apart from that discussion, such as Varchi's *Ercolano* and Salviati's *Avvertimenti della lingua sopra il Decameron*. On the subject of language Caro and Castelvetro had a violent quarrel. Others wrote on Dante ; Trissino discussed spelling ; there were grammarians and there were historians of art. The excellent *Vite* of Giorgio Vasari (1511-74), though sometimes lacking in insight and occasionally prejudiced, will ever remain an invaluable source for the history of Italian art ; and the autobiography of Benvenuto Cellini (1500-71) stands alone as a mixture of vain glory and impudence, but also as a highly significant portraiture of his environment.

In a way it is a piece of special pleading, no less than the *Apologia* of Lorenzino de' Medici (1514-48), who, having killed his cousin Alessandro, the tyrannical ruler of Florence, set about in an eloquent speech to explain the lofty reasons which, according to him, had driven him to commit so vile a murder. Eloquent speeches were not uncommon during this period, and also in the many collections of letters which are preserved there are excellent examples of oratorical power, notably in Tasso's.

Torquato Tasso (1544-95) well sums up in himself the literary development of the later Renaissance ; with the exception of satire, comedy and *novelle*, he touched upon most other forms of literature and left his mark upon each. He was born while the Council was assembled at Trent, and grew to precocious manhood while the Counter-Reformation was getting Italy into its grip, with the assistance of Spain in political life and of the interpreters of Aristotle's *Poetics* in the sphere of literature. While a student at Padua, in 1561-62, Tasso came under the influence of the dreary Speroni. The charm of Ariosto's *Orlando* was strong upon the young man, but, if Ariosto had put classical order in the matter of chivalry, he had not conformed to the type of epic that Aristotle described. Gian Giorgio Trissino, in his clumsy way, had illustrated Aristotelian principles by a poem (*L'Italia liberata dai Goti*) that is only a poem in name, and Luigi Alamanni had attempted a regular epic with his *Avarchide ;* but Tasso was too well endowed with native genius to be unaware of the worthlessness of the former. He attempted in his eighteenth year to cast the story of Rinaldo, a Carlovingian paladin, into an Aristotelian mould, an attempt which could not be successful. While still a student at Padua he was elected to a local academy, took part in its debates on poetry, and began his almost unceasing production of lyrical poems strongly influenced by Petrarch and Bembo. He was in the service of Cardinal Luigi d'Este from 1565 to 1571 and, after 1572, in that of Duke Alfonso II, and it was in 1573 that he created the masterpiece of pastoral drama with his *Aminta*. But even then his mind was not creating in joy, and was not free from the deadening influences of theoretical prejudice. The dramatic structure and the versification of the *Aminta* are based on Speroni's *Canace ;* the young poet had already become deeply involved in philosophical and æsthetical discussions, and, in his characteristic chorus on the Golden Age, one does not only listen to the man who longs for an age less harassed by religious and political restrictions, but also the poet who dreams of the world in which poetry might be the direct expression of feeling, free from rules and critical trammels. He was writing about the nature of love and, above all, he was meditating and discussing the possibilities of creating a Christian epic not bereft of the adventurous charm with which the poems of chivalry were endowed. Having been strongly impressed by the menacing advance of the Turks, he chose a subject connected with the Crusades, and by 1575 he had completed the poem which we know under the title of *Gerusalemme liberata ;* but he was ever tormented by doubts as to its religious orthodoxy and its conformity to Aristotelian principles, and he submitted his poem to some learned pedants for their consideration. They took their task so seriously as to criticise the structure, the episodes and the sentiments of the work. He wrote long letters in its defence, but he was not sure of himself, and the strain told upon his highly sensitive system ; his mind became deranged ; he reasoned most lucidly in his treatises and his letters, but often acted insanely ; he fled from the court repeatedly, wandered throughout Italy begging his way, turned up at court again, until the Duke had him shut up in the monastery of St. Anna. There is no truth in the legend of his love for Leonora d'Este, and no truth in the story of his persecution ; he was treated no better, and certainly no worse, than lunatics were in his days, but his was an intermittent affection of the mind, and there were days and months during which he felt sane, and suffered intensely owing to the restrictions which were of necessity imposed upon him. The pirating of his poem further distressed him. It was published under the titles of *Goffredo* and *Gerusalemme liberata*, neither of which was of his choosing. In his age, in Italy, a man of Tasso's character could not but fail to recapture the power of primitive epic ; and there were in his poem idyllic sentimentality and sensuousness ; but the violent criticism which was at once levelled against his work was absurdly excessive. When he was freed from his prison, he wrote two tragedies of no great value (*Torrismondo* and *Galealto*) in which he attempted to give expression to modern sentiments in classical form ; he revised his poem and republished it under the title of *Gerusalemme conquistata*, but the revision satisfied the requirements of the Inquisition to the detriment of poetical perfection. He also wrote many moving lyrics on religious subjects and a wearisome epic on the Creation (*Il mondo creato*, 1594). With him closed the last period of the Renaissance ; he had transformed the epic, often indulged in conceits, created pastoral drama, a form of poetic production that was to originate the opera, and he had instilled a tender musicality in all his verses such as only Petrarch and Leopardi could equal. Pastoral dreams, critical restrictions, a tendency to conceit and an over indulgence in the pure music of verse were his legacies to the age to come.

BIBLIOGRAPHY TO CHAPTER V

GENERAL WORKS

In the "Storia letteraria d'Italia" (Milan, Vallardi): F. Flamini, *Il Cinquecento* (1902), belongs to the first issue of the series. In the new issue have appeared V. Rossi, *Il Quattrocento* (2nd ed., 1933), and G. Toffanin, *Il Cinquecento* (1929). See also the general works listed under Chapter IV.

FRANCESCO PETRARCA.
  Canzoniere or *Rime*, ed. Carducci and Ferrari (Florence, Sansoni), ed. Scherillo (Milan, Hoepli), ed. N. Zingarelli (Florence, 1925); *Trionfi*, ed. C. Calcaterra (Turin, 1923); *Epistolae de rebus familiaribus et variae*, ed. Fracassetti (Florence, 1859); *Petrarchae Epistolae selectae*, ed. A. F. Johnson (Oxford, 1923); *Poemata minora*, ed. D. Rossetti (Milan, 1829-34); *Epistolae sine nomine*, ed. P. Piur (Halle, 1925); *De sua ipsius et multorum ignorantia*, ed. L. M. Capelli (Paris, 1906). In the "Edizione Nazionale" have already appeared the *Africa*, ed. N. Festa (Florence, 1926), and *Le Familiari* (*Epistolae de rebus familiaribus*), ed. V. Rossi, Vol. I (Florence, 1933). Among works on Petrarch may be mentioned :—
G. A. Cesareo, *Francesco Petrarca, la Vita.* Palermo, 1922.
A. Foresti, *Aneddoti della vita di Francesco Petrarca.* Brescia, 1926.
H. C. Holloway-Calthorp, *Life and Times of Petrarch.* London, 1907.
Maud F. Jerrold, *Francesco Petrarca, Poet and Humanist.* London, 1909.
P. Mazzei, *La vita e le opere di Francesco Petrarca.* Leghorn, 1927.
P. de Nolhac, *Pétrarque et l'humanisme*, 2nd ed. Paris, 1907.
BOCCACCIO.
  Editions of Works. *Opere Latine Minori*, ed. A. F. Massera (Bari, 1928); *Decameron*, ed. Massera (Bari, 1927); *Rime e la Caccia di Diana*, ed. Massera (Turin, 1914); *Filocolo*, ed. E. de Ferri (Turin, 1920); *Filostrato, Fiammetta, Corbaccio*, in *Bibliotheca Romanica* (Strasbourg); *Ninfale fiesolano*, ed. Massera (Turin, 1927); *Il Comento alla Divina Commedia e gli altri scritti intorno a Dante*, ed. D. Guerri (Bari, 1918).
  Life, etc.: E. Hutton, *Giovanni Boccaccio* (London, 1909); H. Hauvette, *Boccace, étude biographique et littéraire* (with a good select bibliography. Paris, 1914). For Boccaccio and his imitators, L. di Francia, *La Novellistica*, in "Storia dei generi letterari" (Milan, Vallardi).

HUMANISM AND CLASSICAL STUDIES

J. Burckhardt, *The Renaissance in Italy*, English trans. London, 1930.
F. Novati, *La Giovinezza di Coluccio Salutati* (Turin, 1888); *Epistolario di Coluccio Salutati* (Rome, 1892-1911).
R. Sabbadini, *Il metodo degli umanisti* (Florence, 1922); *Storia del Ciceronianismo* (Turin, 1886); *Vita di Guarino Veronese* (Genoa, 1891);

La Scuola e gli studi di Guarino Veronese (Catania, 1896) ; *Epistolario di Guarino Veronese* (Venice, 1915-19) ; *Le scoperte dei codici latini e greci* (Florence, 1905-14).
G. Zippel, *Niccolò Niccoli.* Florence, 1890.
E. Walser, *Poggius florentinus.* Leipzig, 1914.
G. Mancini, *Vita di Lorenzo Valla* (Florence, 1891) ; *Vita di Leon Battista Alberti* (2nd ed. Florence, 1911).
V. Zabughin, *Giulio Pomponio Leto* (Rome, 1909-12) ; *Vergilio nel Rinascimento italiano* (Bologna, 1921-25).
W. H. Woodward, *Vittorino da Feltre and other Humanist Educators.* Cambridge, 1905.
G. Gentile, *Studi sul Rinascimento.* Florence, 1923.
G. Saitta, *Filosofia italiana e umanesimo.* Venice, 1928.
G. Toffanin, *Che cosa fu l'umanesimo* (Florence, 1929) ; *La fine dell'umanesimo* (Turin, 1919).

THE QUATTROCENTO

Vite di uomini illustri del secolo XV scritte da Vespasiano da Bisticci, ed. L. Frati. Bologna, 1892-93.
F. Flamini, *La lirica toscana del Rinascimento anteriore ai tempi del Magnifico.* Pisa, 1891.
A. D'Ancona, *La poesia popolare italiana.* Leghorn, 1906.
Lorenzo de' Medici, *Opere*, ed. A. Simioni. Bari, 1913-14.
E. Rho, *Lorenzo il Magnifico* (Bari, 1926) ; *La lirica di A. Poliziano* (Turin, 1923).
A. Momigliano, *Poliziano.* Turin, 1921.
G. Vaccarella, *Saggio sulla Rinascenza e la poesia di A. Poliziano.* Palermo, 1921.
Luigi Pulci, *Morgante Maggiore*, ed. G. Volpi. Florence, 1900-04.
F. Foffano, *il Morgante di L. Pulci.* Turin, 1891.
Matteo Maria Boiardo, *Le poesie volgari e latine*, ed. A. Solerti (Bologna, 1894) ; *Orlando innamorato*, ed. F. Foffano (Turin, 1927) ; *Rime*, ed. G. Reichembach (Turin, 1929) ; G. Reichembach, *Matteo Maria Boiardo* (Bologna, 1929).
Jacopo Sannazaro, *The Piscatory Eclogues*, ed. W. P. Mustard (Baltimore, 1914) ; *Arcadia*, ed. Scherillo (Turin, 1888) ; ed. Carrara (Turin, 1927).
A. Sainati, *La lirica latina del Rinascimento.* Pisa, 1919.

THE CINQUECENTO

MACHIAVELLI.
    Tutte le opere storiche e letterarie, ed. G. Mazzoni and M. Casella (Florence, 1929) ; *Il Principe*, ed. G. Lisio (Florence, 1901) ; *Le istorie fiorentine*, ed. P. Carli (Florence, 1927) ; *Lettere*, ed. G. Lesca (Florence, 1929) ; O. Tommasini, *La vita e gli scritti di Niccolò Machiavelli* (Rome, 1883-1911) ; P. Villari, *Niccolò Machiavelli e i suoi tempi* (new ed., Milan, 1927) ; F. Ercole, *La politica di Machiavelli* (Rome, 1926) ; *Le opere maggiori*, ed. P. Carli, with commentary (3rd ed., Florence, 1932).
GUICCIARDINI.
    Istoria d'Italia, ed. A. Gherardi (Florence, 1919) ; ed. C. Panigarda (Bari, 1929) ; *Storie fiorentine*, ed. R. Palmarocchi (Bari, 1931) ; A. Rossi, *Francesco Guicciardini e il governo fiorentino* (Bologna,

1896-99) ; E. Benoist, *Guichardin historien et homme d'état* (Paris, 1892).

G. Lisio, *La storiografia*, in " Storia dei generi letterari " (Milan, Vallardi).

ARIOSTO.

Orlando furioso, ed. F. Ermini (Rome, 1909-13) ; ed. S. Debenedetti (Bari, 1929) ; *Le satire*, ed. C. Berardi (Campobasso, 1918) ; *Le commedie*, ed. M. Catalano (Bologna, 1933) ; Pio Rajna, *Le fonti dell' Orlando furioso* (2nd ed., Florence, 1900) ; G. Bertoni, *L'Orlando furioso e la Rinascenza a Ferrara* (Modena, 1919) ; H. Hauvette, *L'Arioste et la poésie chevaleresque à Ferrare* (Paris, 1927) ; M. Catalano, *Vita di Ludovico Ariosto ricostituita su nuovi documenti* (Geneva, 1930-31) ; A. Momigliano, *Saggio sull' Orlando furioso* (Bari, 1929).

Il Cortegiano del conte Baldesar Castiglione, ed. V. Cian (3rd ed., Florence, 1929) ; Hoby's translation, ed. W. Raleigh (London, 1900) ; Julia Ady, *Baldasarre Castiglione* (London, 1908).

F. Rizzi, *L'anima del Cinquecento e la lirica volgare*. Milan, 1928.

M. F. Jerrold, *Vittoria Colonna*. London, 1906.

Pietro Aretino, *Lettere*, ed. F. Nicolini (Bari, 1913) ; E. Hutton, *Pietro Aretino, The Scourge of Princes* (London, 1922).

Matteo Bandello, *Novelle*, ed. S. Brognoligo. Bari, 1910-12.

Novelle del Cinquecento, ed. G. Fatini. Turin, 1929.

Trattati d'amore del Cinquecento, ed. G. Zonta (Bari, 1912) ; *Trattati del Cinquecento sulla donna*, ed. G. Zonta (Bari, 1913) ; T. F. Crane, *Italian Social Customs of the Sixteenth Century* (Yale, 1920).

TORQUATO TASSO.

Gerusalemme liberata, ed. S. Ferrari (Florence, 1890) ; ed. L. Bonfigli (Bari, 1930) ; *Opere minori in versi*, ed. A. Solerti (Bologna, 1891-95) ; *Rime*, ed. Solerti (Bologna, 1898-1902) ; *Prose diverse*, ed. C. Guasti (Florence, 1875) ; *I discorsi dell' arte poetica*, etc., ed. Solerti (Turin, 1895) ; A. Solerti, *Vita di T. Tasso* (Turin, 1895) ; V. Vivaldi, *La Gerusalemme liberata studiata nelle sue fonti* (Trani, 1901-07).

THE DRAMA (also for subsequent periods).

A. Mortier, *Ruzzante* (Paris, 1925) ; Winifred Smith, *The Commedia dell'Arte* (New York, 1912) ; C. Miclachewski, *La Commedia dell'Arte ou Le théâtre des comédiens italiens des XVI, XVII et XVIII siècles* (Paris, 1927) ; M. Apollonio, *Storia della Commedia dell'Arte* (Rome, 1930). In " Storia dei generi letterari " : E. Bertana, *La Tragedia* (Milan, 1906) ; E. Sanesi, *La Commedia* (Milan, 1911).

CHAPTER VI

ITALY FROM THE RENAISSANCE TO THE UNIFICATION

(a) From the Invasion of Charles VIII to the French Revolution

AFTER the descent of Charles VIII, events followed one another with so breathless a rapidity that the Italians were scarcely able to realise the full import of what was taking place. In Florence Piero de' Medici's faintheartedness in dealing with the French king caused the establishment of a new republican government; its dominating spirit being a pious and fanatical friar, Savonarola, who was moved to a frenzy of indignation by what he considered the immorality of the age. The government was organised on the model of the Venetian constitution; and Savonarola, who had often vaguely forecast disasters or victories, was hailed as a prophet when Leghorn was freed from the siege of the Venetian and imperial forces, thanks partly to storms. But, contrary to the agreement, the French retained Pisa; the pope, who had incurred great losses, endeavoured to strengthen his position by announcing his determination to reform the Church (1497); he could no longer countenance the attitude of Savonarola; for the friar, after bringing the zeal of his adherents to fever-heat and causing them to make a solemn bonfire of pictures, jewels, masks and playing cards as a token of reform, attacked the morality of the papal court with so outspoken a violence, that Alexander VI forbade him to preach, and later threatened to excommunicate Florence. The very excess of Savonarola's zeal laying him open to ridicule, caused him to lose favour with the people, and, the supporters of the Medici helping towards this end, he was prosecuted, tortured and ultimately done to death (23rd May, 1498). The fall of this strangely untimely reformer did not bring about the return of the Medici, despite the efforts of their supporters. On the contrary, the weakness of the government and the ineffectual attempts at reconquering Pisa caused the establishment of a kind of dictatorship (*Gonfaloniere a vita*) in the person of the good-natured Piero

Soderini (1502), in whose chancery Machiavelli took service; Soderini was, however, unable to restore the fortunes of the republic.

While Savonarola was undergoing his trial, there died at Amboise Charles VIII; he was succeeded by his able cousin Louis of Orleans, as Louis XII, who assumed the titles of Duke of Milan and King of Naples, thus proclaiming his decision of urging his hereditary claims. And he found some support in Italy, for the Venetians were so disgusted by the tortuous policy of Ludovico il Moro that they felt disposed to overlook the danger that the French domination in Lombardy must imply. Also Alexander VI, who schemed to build up a state for the Borgias, promised his assistance in return for a dukedom to be conferred on his son Cesare Borgia, who thus became Duke of Valentinois (Duca Valentino), and military help in his endeavours. Florence was neutral. There followed French victories in Lombardy, the flight of Ludovico il Moro (1499), and a solemn entry of Louis XII into Milan, where he was welcomed by the representatives of all Italian powers except Naples. The Milanese, however, rebelled in 1500, and Sforza returned only to be defeated at Novara, where his Swiss troops withdrew to Bellinzona and Locarno, occupying the territory which became the Canton Ticino of the Swiss Confederation. Sforza died as a prisoner in France in 1510. Meanwhile Cesare Borgia was pursuing the conquest of Romagna, but the situation was further complicated by the events in the South. Ferdinand the Catholic, King of Spain, had some pretension on Naples as being an Aragonese possession; the Kings of France and Spain agreed therefore to a partition of southern Italy, and a French army under D'Aubigny and a Spanish one under Consalvo of Cordoba quickly brought about the downfall of the Aragonese and the surrender of Frederick of Aragon to Louis XII. Frederick was made Duke of Anjou and with him went the poet Sannazaro (1501). Cesare Borgia had been compelled to participate in this war; he soon returned to his task in central Italy, where, after crushing a rebellion of his troops, he only refrained from attacking Florence owing to the French veto. The heavy costs of this campaign were defrayed by Alexander VI, the richest cardinals having developed the habit of dying most opportunely to replenish the papal exchequer. Diplomacy and politics were seldom so openly divorced from good faith. Just as the " condottieri " had long been accustomed to change their allegiance irrespective of their engagements, now kings and popes broke without compunction their most solemn promises. The crimes of the Borgias are proverbial;

King Ferdinand of Spain agreed with Louis XII to the partition
of Naples, while still pretending to consider Frederick of Aragon
his ally ; Consalvo of Cordoba took a solemn oath to allow Prince
Ferdinand of Aragon to go free, and kept him a prisoner ; it
is not surprising therefore that the two allies, France and Spain,
should have turned against one another. Hostilities began in
1502, and it was during this war that a celebrated *Disfida* took
place at Barletta between Italian and French champions (1503).

In the end the French were routed on the river Garigliano,
where Piero de' Medici was drowned, and by the beginning of
1504 Consalvo was at work at organising the administration of
the kingdom. A few months earlier (August, 1503) Alexander VI
had died, and Cesare Borgia, who was ill at the time, had lost
his state, and when, after the short papacy of Pius III, Cardinal
della Rovere became Julius II, Borgia fled to Consalvo, who sent
him as prisoner to Spain. He died there fighting in 1507.

Julius II was sixty years old, but possessed youthful energy
and strength. It was his ambition to build up a strong state
for the Church, availing himself of the dissensions between Spain
and France. The Venetians, though constantly at war with the
Turks, having occupied some cities of Romagna and Apulia,
called upon themselves the ready wrath of the pope. He quickly
recovered the Romagna up to Bologna (1506), and when Venice,
through friendship to France, refused to allow the Emperor
Maximilian to proceed with his army to Rome where he meant
to receive the imperial crown (1508), the way was prepared for
a general league against Venice. It was signed at Cambrai in
December, 1508, and contained detailed articles concerning the
partition of the Venetian territories. Besides the emperor, the
Kings of France and Spain, the pope and minor Italian powers,
also the King of Hungary was invited to collaborate in the suppression of the only power that was acting as a bulwark against
Turkish invasions. Venice was defeated at Agnadello (1509),
and each of the allies hastened to occupy his part of the loot,
but the population, as distinct from the aristocracy, regretted
the change ; and the lack of co-ordination in the operations of the
allies, and their jealousy of one another, allowed sufficient scope
to Venetian diplomacy for manœuvre. Padua was suddenly
seized and successfully defended against the emperor (1509), the
pope was induced to peace (1510) ; the King of Spain following
his example ; only Alfonso d'Este resisted the pope's orders and
continued operations ; the pope lost Bologna to the French
(1511), and, being threatened with the convocation of a council
at Pisa, he retaliated by organising a holy league with Venice

and Spain against France (October 1511), the papal war-cry
" fuori i barbari " arousing a significant enthusiasm among the
Italians.

Thanks to the valour and ability of Gaston de Foix, the operations culminating in the battle of Ravenna (1512) were favourable
to the French, but later Swiss troops helped to drive them from
most of their possessions except a few fortresses, and a congress
of Mantua placed Maximilian Sforza, son of Ludovico il Moro
on the ducal throne of Milan, and sent an army to Florence in
order to re-establish the Medici rule.   Prato was brutally sacked
by the allies, and Cardinal Giovanni de' Medici with his brother
Giuliano returned to Florence.   Cardinal Giovanni, who controlled
the government, was raised to the tiara in 1513 on the death of
Julius II, as Leo X ; he was less energetic and more peace-loving
than his predecessor, but he was no less keen on protecting the
arts.   He was faced, however, with another general confederation,
because the Venetians, distrusting Sforza, combined with the
French against the emperor, but the French were defeated at
Novara, 1513, and the Venetians had to bear the brunt of the
war in Friuli.   The succession of the brilliant Francis I to
Louis XII gave a new impetus to the war ; Francis won a great
battle at Marignano (1515), received the surrender of Maximilian
Sforza, and made peace with the pope as well as with the new
King of Spain, Charles I.

A new era had set in.   Leo X was pope, the Venetians, severely
hit by the rapid decay of their trade brought about by the discovery of the South African route and by Portuguese enterprise,
withdrew from the fray ; the stage was held by Francis I and
Charles I, who became emperor as Charles V on the death of his
grandfather Maximilian (1519).   He was king of the Low Countries,
of Spain, of the lands across the sea, and of the Romans ; and
Francis I, as well as the pope, realised that a clash with him was
inevitable.   In 1520 Charles sailed to Dover to meet Henry VIII
and Cardinal Wolsey previous to the meeting at Calais where
the English king was to get into touch with Francis I.   The
two rivals were courting external support ; the pope meanwhile
threw in his chances with the emperor in order to secure his help
against Luther.   The victories of the imperial troops in Lombardy
were not interrupted by the death of the pope (1521), who was
succeeded by a pious and unworldly Dutchman, Adrian VI
(1522), after whose brief pontificate Cardinal Giulio de' Medici
was elected pope as Clement VII (1523) and ruled in Florence by
the intermediary of Cardinal Passerini.   The war between Francis
and Charles went on, the famous knight, Bayard, dying on the

Sesia in 1524; at Pavia, in 1525, Francis himself was defeated and taken a prisoner.

The imperial triumph made the Italian pause. Owing to the number and the ruthlessness of the foreign armies, the populations had never suffered so intensely; the rulers felt powerless even though they took pride in the empty title of allies of the emperor. The old balance of power was unsettled, and diplomacy was at work to seek for another equilibrium. On the liberation of Francis I after the peace of Madrid in 1526, another holy league was formed between the pope, Francis, the Venetians and Florence, with the object of driving the imperial troops out of Italy. The league was in so far popular as the Spaniards had proved themselves to be the most avaricious of masters; but the allies showed little enterprise. In 1526 there died the most famous Italian leader of the age, Giovanni dalle Bande Nere (the son of a Medici and of Caterina Sforza), and imperial troops, ill-paid and riotous, reached Rome and sacked the eternal city in 1527; many among the soldiers were Lutherans, but the Lutherans were scarcely more cruel than the Spanish troops and Italian adventurers. Clement VII, who had not foreseen his danger, was further hit by the revolution in Florence against the Medicean rule. The republican government was re-established, while French and imperial troops with alternating fortunes continued hostilities. During the period of French prevalence the Genoese admiral, Andrea Doria, passed from the French to the imperial service, and succeeded in freeing Genoa from the French domination. The war was lagging, Clement VII, rather than lose his Florence, made peace with the emperor (1529) who, a little later, also came to an understanding with Francis I. Florence was left isolated; the republic anxiously made defensive preparations, but she stood no chance against the forces which faced her. There was held at Bologna a general assembly of princes where Charles met Clement VII. Francesco Sforza was made Duke of Milan; the Venetians surrendered some harbours in the Adriatic, the knights of Rhodes were given Malta, up till then a Sicilian dependency; Charles V was portrayed by Titian and crowned by Clement VII (1530). The emperor had undertaken to crush the republican government in Florence on behalf of the pope. Despite the valour of her leaders, notably Ferrucci, and the efforts of Michelangelo as a military engineer, Florence was forced into submission by the disloyalty of her commander Malatesta Baglioni, by famine and disease, and Alessandro de' Medici became the ruler of Florence.

Of Italy's prosperity there was little left. The rich Lombard

plains were deserted ; the sea trade was starved by the discovery
of new routes ; excepting Venice and Savoy, the various states
were all more or less dependent on Charles V, and all were directly or indirectly sucked dry by his governors and agents.
Hereafter Italian history is little more than the account of some
petty quarrels between members of one family who are all ground
down by general conditions and whose life-long agony is too
uniform to call for a detailed description.

In order to raise the fortunes of his family, Clement VII
arranged a marriage of his niece Caterina de' Medici with Henry,
a son of King Francis ; this wedding (1533) was, however, the
last success of his policy, for he died a year later. He was succeeded by Paul III (Farnese), a " nepotist," but a man of keen
political sense. It was at his behest that Charles V defeated
the corsair Barbarossa, who laid waste the coast of southern
Italy (1535), a much-needed enterprise, which was followed,
however, by a new war with France for the possession of Milan
when Francesco Sforza died. Charles was ready for concessions ;
but the murder of Alessandro de' Medici by his cousin Lorenzino
(1537), the plots of the Florentine exiles against the new ruler
Cosimo (the son of Giovanni dalle Bande Nere), and the onslaught
of the Turks against Venice offered Francis I new opportunities
for intrigue (1537). The pope arranged for a truce in order to
organise the war against the Turks ; instead the most Christian
King of France became an ally of the Turks, and Venice and the
Italian coast towns suffered in consequence. Italy was scarcely
affected by the peace of Crespy (1544), which was concluded as a
necessary premise to the convocation of the fateful Council of
Trent. It was intended to reconcile the Protestants and to reform
the Church, but its labours were further complicated by the conflicting interests of pope and emperor, both of whom were anxious
to increase their prestige ; by the death of Francis I (1547) and
by conspiracies in Lucca, Genoa and Piacenza, by an insurrection
in Naples (1547) which occasioned a crushing defeat of the imperial
navy by the Turks ; in all of which events Spanish and French
agents had part.

Siena which had rebelled against the Spanish occupation was
spared reprisals, thanks to a Turkish attack on Naples. It was
during these hostilities that a Turkish fleet, allied to France,
laid bare Elba and helped the Corsican insurgents to drive away
the Genoese forces and to hand over the island to France (1554).
Cosimo de' Medici, a peace-loving and able ruler who was making
successful endeavours to restore Florentine prosperity, was drawn
into the war and occupied Siena (1557). The election of Pope

Paul IV (1555) brought to the throne a member of the Carafa house, who, owing to his family's traditional hostility towards Spain, induced Henry II to restart the fray. But the luck of war was unfavourable to the pope, and the Duke of Alva was threatening Rome when the army of Philip II (who had succeeded on the abdication of Charles V in 1556), under the leadership of Emanuele Filiberto of Savoy, completely routed the French at St. Quentin. The peace of Cateau-Cambrésis (1559) brought at last some stability ; France renounced her claims in Tuscany, in Corsica and in Piedmont, where she retained, however, some fortresses, including Turin. Thus Emanuele Filiberto, who had succeeded his father, Carlo III, as Duke of Savoy when his state was entirely at the mercy of foreign troops, took the first step towards the reconstitution of his hereditary domains.

What was the condition of Italy at this time ?

Spain possessed the duchy of Milan and the whole of Lombardy, the kingdom of Naples and Sicily, Sardinia and some coastal fortresses on the Tyrrenean sea (Stato dei Presidî). Emanuele Filiberto had Savoy and Piedmont, less Turin, Chieri, Pinerolo, held by France, Vercelli and Asti held by Spain. The Venetian possessions extended west as far as the Adda river and comprised Istria, Dalmatia, Cyprus and Candia. Genoa had a few coastal towns and Corsica. The Duke Gonzaga ruled over Monferrato and Mantua. Ottavio Farnese had Parma and Piacenza ; Alfonso II d'Este had Modena and Ferrara ; Cosimo de' Medici (Grand Duke of Tuscany from 1569) ruled Tuscany except the republican Lucca ; Francesco Maria della Rovere ruled Urbino, and Pope Pius IV ruled the states of the Church, but all were more or less dependent on Spain. The Spanish administration varied in form, not in substance ; there were local magistrates and councils, but, on the whole, the country was considered a source of revenue, and was gradually becoming impoverished owing to excessive taxation and general mismanagement. Of the other states the only ones that showed some progressive tendencies were Tuscany and Savoy. In Tuscany Cosimo did not reduce taxation, but endeavoured to achieve a more equitable distribution of its incidence, and in Savoy Emanuele Filiberto with a firm hand organised agriculture and justice, built up an army, and encouraged education. Ferrara was annexed to the states of the Church in 1598, the House of Este retaining Modena and Reggio ; Urbino similarly passed to the popes in 1624.

Everywhere the decrees of the Council of Trent (closed in 1562) were taking effect. Protestant tendencies, which had

sporadically flared up in different parts, were to be suppressed by
the Inquisition ; the liberty of education and of the printing press
was stunted by the Inquisition and by the Index of forbidden
books ; several new orders of religious, particularly the reformed
Franciscans and the Jesuits, became the agents of the Counter-
Reformation. There was a vast improvement in the moral
standard of the higher ranks of the Church and an ardent zeal
for reform ; but this zeal was rather enforced from above than
springing from a sincere re-awakening of religious feeling. Where
the Spanish rule prevailed a great impetus was given to punctilio
and prerogatives, to form rather than substance. The Spanish
magistrates considered their period of office a legitimate opportunity to acquire wealth ; when they were not avaricious, they
were incapable, and often were both. Poverty caused agriculture
and industry to decay ; destitution and political unruliness
produced banditry. When the populace had a chance and was
particularly pressed, it rose. Riots and insurrections occurred
everywhere at different periods in the Spanish domains ; the
philosopher Campanella himself led a conspiracy in Calabria
in 1599.

The papal states were particularly fertile in brigands. Thus
while the states of the Duke of Savoy were rapidly progressing,
and while Tuscany was once again coming to the fore, there was
stagnation in the Venetian territory, disorder in the papal states,
scant progress in Parma and Piacenza, and everywhere else decadence and misery. Plague and other diseases made frequent
ravages. The only wars that Emanuele Filiberto fought after
he returned to Savoy were against his non-Catholic subjects in
the district of Pinerolo, and he was driven to this persecution
unwillingly by the pressure of ecclesiastical authorities. He
died in 1580.

In Venice stagnation was followed by decadence. The Turks
never relieved their pressure ; the noblemen had ceased to go
sea-faring and lived on their accumulated wealth ; Venice became
a pleasure city famous for its pomp, its merry life and its gambling ;
the subjects on the mainland enjoyed the benefit of a fair administration of justice, but were ground down by heavy and ill
distributed taxation; the population was decreasing. So that
when the Turks threatened Cyprus and Candia, Venice sought
the assistance of allies ; a league was formed, but its help was
scanty and grudgingly given, and there was no unity of command ;
despite this the grand fleet of the allies scored a great victory
at Lepanto (7th October, 1571), which did not crush the Ottoman
power but dispelled the legend of its invincibility on the sea,

though the allies were prevented by petty jealousies from pressing their advantage. Venice made peace in 1573 and for some years was free from Turkish attacks.

When Carlo Emanuele I of Savoy succeeded his father (1580), he soon became the most important figure in Italian politics. The Spanish governor of Lombardy had tried in vain to prevent the organisation of an army in Savoy, and now Carlo Emanuele, finding himself wedged in between French and Spanish possessions, craftily decided to exploit so perilous a position, offering his help to whichever of the two powers gave him better terms, and consistently aiming at his own advantage ; he went so far as to aspire to the leadership of all the Italian powers, joined in a league against the foreigners, and showed some vague national consciousness. But if he kept his own interests in view, he was the means of stirring up national aspirations among the intellectuals of his age. He was as restless as he was crafty, and as crafty as he was daring; so that his schemes and his actions form an almost inextricable sequence. On the ground that Geneva had become the centre of Protestantism, he intrigued and fought with a view to occupying this city ; he failed in 1589 in an open attack, and he failed in a *coup de main* in 1602 ; in the meantime, taking advantage of the troubled condition of France, he seized Saluzzo (1587) ; in 1591 his attempt at invading the south of France brought him into a parlous position, for Spain did not come to his assistance ; and it was only in 1601 that, after many vicissitudes of war and many diplomatic discussions, France renounced Saluzzo and allowed a corridor connecting Savoy to Burgundy, then a possession of Spain. Carlo Emanuele had thus initiated the new policy of the House of Savoy, which aimed at excluding France from Italian territory, and transferring the centre of the Savoy states to the south and east of the Alps. So active a participation in warfare entailed, of course, heavy taxation and much hardship for his subjects ; but the duke was not unmindful of the need of a good administration, and he endeavoured to curtail ecclesiastical privileges in his state, thus coming into conflict with the papacy.

Pius V, the pope of Lepanto, was succeeded by Gregory XIII whose chief claim to remembrance was the reform of the calendar. He was followed by that remarkable Pope Sixtus V, a man of tireless energy, who rid the Roman state of the scourge of brigands, accumulated great wealth, ably organised the administration of the Church, and had a shrewd dislike for international leagues. He aimed at preserving peace in Italy and at fighting the Turks and the Protestants ; for this reason he supported Philip II against England, and countenanced the attacks on Geneva on the part of Carlo Emanuele. He died in 1590. Clement VIII (Aldobrandini), elected in 1592, was a high-minded pontiff, anxious to increase the glory of the Church in spiritual and temporal matters ; it was he who absolved Henry IV of France, who finally condemned the philosopher Giordano Bruno (1600), and first came into conflict with Carlo Emanuele owing to his ecclesiastical reforms. Neither Clement nor his successor ever gave way, but the Duke of Savoy was as persistent as they were, and his edicts were not repealed. A similar conflict occurred between the Church and Venice, for Paul V (Borghese), as zealous an upholder of Church prerogatives as Clement VIII, resented the insistence of Venice to subject two criminal priests to the civil courts and pronounced an interdict upon the republic. This quarrel gave occasion to the publication of a number of pamphlets, and brought into prominence the learned monk Paolo Sarpi who championed, at his peril, the rights of the civil power (1606). Carlo Emanuele, resenting the disdainful protectorate of Philip II of Spain, came to an agreement with Henry IV which might have produced great changes in Italy ; but the assassination of the French king (1610) left the Duke of Savoy at the mercy of the Spaniards. He had to forego the hope of occupying Monferrato, and, as neither England nor Venice or France was willing or able to help him, he was compelled to face alone the greatest power of the age. He ultimately acquired more renown by his heroic exploits than he lost power by his defeat.

At this time the control of Spain over her Italian provinces grew less stringent. Charles V had been emperor as well as King of Spain ; on his abdication the Hapsburg possessions were divided between his Austrian and his Spanish heirs ; when Philip II of Spain died, his successor Philip III was unable to exercise an adequate control of his governors in Italy ; they pursued independent policies of their own, sometimes even rebelling against their king. With the cognisance of the Spanish ambassador in Venice and the unofficial intervention of other great powers, an attempt was made to crush the Venetian republic (1618), and Carlo Emanuele hoped that at last the republic would dare openly to stand up against treacherous Spain ; his hopes were not realised, because the Venetian government avoided an open breach and was satisfied with the removal of the Spanish ambassador, Bedmar, and the execution of other conspirators.

Cosimo's successor, Francesco de' Medici, had always lived under the ægis of Spain. When his brother Ferdinando I (1587-1609) succeeded him as grand duke, he vainly tried to follow an independent policy; he succeeded, however, in improving the condition of his subjects, profiting by the growing trade of the port of Leghorn that his brother Francesco had widened. Both Ferdinando I and Cosimo II were constantly forced to assist Spain with money, and Cosimo, weak and effete, became the chief prop of the Spanish domination in Italy; when he died in 1621 an inept regency was established, during which the last vestiges of Tuscan prosperity were swept away.

The Italian states were not directly concerned in the events of the Thirty Years War, but the Hapsburg hold on Italy was so strong, and the pretensions of France were so insistent, that the whole of Italy was shaken by that long conflict. The pope was interested in it in so far as the pretext of the war was religious; Carlo Emanuele concerned himself in it with the hope of extending his domains towards Lombardy. By then the fortunes of the empire were rising, thanks to the energetic guidance of Ferdinand II. At first the ferocious rebellion of the catholic Valtellina against the protestant Grisons, brought about a conflict in which the pope, Venice, Carlo Emanuele, France and Spain took part (1620-21). Later, when Richelieu had seized the government of France, Carlo Emanuele joined forces with France and Venice, though in so doing he had to renounce his set policy to keep the French out of Italy; he fought valiantly, but the peace of Monzone was settled without regard to his or to the Venetians' claims. Disaster came when, in 1627, Vincenzo Gonzaga of Monferrato and Mantua died without leaving male issue, and France supported Carlo Gonzaga of Nevers. The control of this state was desired for military reasons by all parties; despite the valour of the Duke of Savoy, Richelieu was too much for him, and the French secured the Alpine passes and gained a stronghold in Piedmont; Mantua resisted the imperial troops for several months, but was finally captured and subjected to one of the most barbarous sacks that are known to Italian history (1630). The plague described in the *Promessi Sposi* was a consequence of this war. A few days later Carlo Emanuele died, when his fortunes were at their lowest ebb. He had struggled for fifty years and shown outstanding military and diplomatic gifts, he had aspired to the thrones of Spain, of the empire, of the East, and had found time to protect men of letters and to exploit them as propagandists; he had also composed poems himself. Tassoni was in his pay, Marino stated his case. His son, Vittorio Amedeo I, was as wax in the hands of Richelieu; by the Treaty of Cherasco, the duke ceded Pinerolo and was forced into an unprofitable alliance with France. When the duke died (1637) and the regency was assumed by the duchess, a devoted sister of Louis XIII, the situation was worsened, the new duke, Carlo Emanuele II, being only four years old ; a long civil war gave further occasion to France and to Spain to occupy Piedmontese fortresses ; and the conditions did not improve when the civil war ended, for the duchess still retained a great influence ; the soldiers lacked discipline, money was wasted on luxuries ; justice was venal, and the population no less harrassed by the administration in peace than by the armies in war.

The growing influence of France was as noticeable in other parts of Italy. It had been the policy of Richelieu to weaken the Hapsburgs by harrassing their Italian possessions ; the same policy was pursued after his death by Mazarin, who took advantage of every occasion to interfere. In order to support the candidature of a prince of the House of Savoy to the Neapolitan throne, in 1646, a fleet commanded by Tommaso of Savoy appeared before Naples ; lacking money for the defence, the Spanish viceroy increased taxation, and the populace rose (1647) under the leadership of Masaniello, the rebellion lasting long after his death ; though Naples was finally occupied on 5th April, 1648, further riots occurred in 1649 and had to be ferociously repressed. Similar events took place in Palermo. The later revolution of Messina (1675-76) was due to other causes, but France was more deeply implicated in it, for Louis XIV sent a fleet to support it and its ultimate withdrawal was the occasion of a merciless repression.

Even at Rome events were in some way determined by France. The popes had in general sided with Spain ; Clement VIII favoured France instead ; and Urban VIII, fearing the Hapsburg supremacy, also sided with France, but, when he attacked the Farnesi of Parma and Piacenza in order to deprive them of Castro (1642), Richelieu successfully supported the Farnesi. Urban, who had prosecuted Galileo, was forced by French pressure to condemn Jansenius. Pope Alexander VII (Chigi, 1655) was involved in a quarrel with Louis XIV and was forced to accept humiliating conditions (1662). Whenever the papal throne became vacant, the cardinals were constrained to deal with the French, and occasionally the Hapsburg emissaries ; despite the entreaties of Pope Innocent XI, Louis went so far as to order the Italian states to abstain from supporting the emperor against the Turks besieging Vienna (1683).

This siege of Vienna was an episode in the Turkish drive to the West that had begun some years previously. A quarrel had been picked with Venice in 1645 ; Candia was attacked ; despite several naval successes and heroic efforts, the Venetians were unable to cope with the inexhaustible military resources of the Turks. After a siege lasting seventeen years, Candia fell in 1669. A last effort was made by Venice when her fleet occupied the coast of Greece, besieged Athens (1685-87), and gained a great victory in 1697 which contributed to the Turkish rout sanctioned by the peace of Carlowitz (1699). Venice, however, had long ceased to have any importance in Italian politics ; the whole peninsula had fallen into foreign subjection ; and it was only towards the end of the century that the state of Savoy resumed its advance.

Carlo Emanuele II had come out of minority in 1648, but his mother still controlled the policy of the state. The peace of Westphalia had brought little relief ; French and Spanish armies were continuously overrunning the country ; even Turin was for fifteen years in French hands ; at the peace of the Pyrenees Carlo Emanuele could not get a reasonable hearing (1659) ; religious fanaticism involved him in a bitter repression of his Vaudois subjects (1664). The duke did much, however, towards improving the administration, controlling the violence of the aristocracy, evenly distributing taxation, organising the army, and giving some attention to the arts. His death in 1675 was deeply regretted by his subjects who had to go through another period of regency and of subserviency to France. At last his son, the young duke, Vittorio Amedeo II, seized the power and began a long struggle against French pre-eminence. He still yielded to Louis XIV by persecuting the Vaudois (1686), but he secretly joined the league of Austria, Poland, Russia and Venice against the Turks who were allied with the French king. Louis XIV became aware in 1690 of the Piedmontese secession, and war broke out. Despite perilous vicissitudes and defeats, the assistance of his cousin, Prince Eugene of Savoy, who was in the imperial service, the loyalty of the population, his own valour and able diplomacy extricated the duke from his difficulties so as to allow him to make peace at favourable terms and obtain the withdrawal of the French from Italian territory (1697).

The struggle for the Spanish succession involved Italy in another war. The Hapsburgs of Austria protested against the choice of Philip V, a grandson of Louis XIV ; Venice, Genoa and Parma remained neutral ; Gonzaga supported Louis XIV ; Vittorio Amedeo joined forces with him, but, owing to personal slights, he turned in 1701 to the other side ; after many vicissitudes Turin was besieged (1706) and liberated by the timely arrival of the imperial army of Eugene. Finally at Utrecht, where the candidature of Vittorio Amedeo II to the throne of Spain was also considered, Vittorio Amedeo received Sicily, thanks mainly to England, and the title of king ; he retained some cities in Lombardy and was no longer overruled by his French neighbours. The Hapsburgs of Austria were loath to give up the pretensions to the Spanish succession and were compensated at Rastadt with the Spanish dominions in Italy—Naples, Sardinia, Mantua, a large section of Lombardy and the fortresses of the Presidî (1714). Vittorio Amedeo was reluctantly forced to give up his claim to Milan ; but he obtained royal rank and seemed to have achieved an outstanding position. Peace did not last long, thanks to the activities of Alberoni, the minister of the new queen of Philip V of Spain, Elizabeth Farnese of Parma, whence also Alberoni hailed. It became Elizabeth's wish to carve out states for her children in Italy, since Philip's son by his first queen would succeed to the Spanish throne. Parma and Tuscany seemed fair game, for the Duke of Parma, who had no male issue, was heir-presumptive to Gian Gastone, the last and effete scion of the Medici. Alberoni, who was more daring in his schemes than scrupulous in the choice of his means, sent a fleet to attack Sardinia by surprise and to occupy Sicily. This action irritated the great powers, who enforced Alberoni's dismissal and induced Vittorio Amedeo to accept Sardinia in exchange for Sicily, which was handed over to Austria (1720). But Elizabeth of Spain clung to her plans, and by long negotiations succeeded in wrenching the assent of the emperor : her son, Charles, should succeed in Parma and in Tuscany in return for the Spanish recognition of the pragmatic sanction. Charles took possession of Parma and was accepted as heir of the Medici (1732). Austria, despite her fairly efficient administrative system, was unpopular in the South and disliked in the North of Italy, so that, as soon as the emperor fell out with France over the succession in Poland, the war spread to Italy. Vittorio Amedeo had trouble with the administration of Sardinia, but he showed there, as well as in his dealings with the Church and in his local reforms, extra-ordinary ability, nursing finance and fostering education so that the country recovered during the last years of his rule. A year after his abdication in favour of his son (1730), he tried to seize the power again, but he was arrested and died as a prisoner in 1732 ; a strange and ill-fitting end for one of the most brilliant princes of the House of Savoy.

The succession to the throne of Poland plunged the principal Italian states into war again, and caused Carlo Emanuele III of Savoy and his advisers much uncertainty. He was not anxious to have the Austrians as neighbours, and sided therefore with

France and Spain ; Lombardy was occupied by his troops and by a French contingent, and Charles, the son of the King of Spain, entered Naples, almost without opposition. When peace was signed, however, the interests of Carlo Emanuele and the wishes of Elizabeth Farnese were scarcely considered. The duke was given some cities on the right of the Ticino ; Charles became King of Naples, surrendering Tuscany to a Hapsburg who was Duke of Lorraine. These pacts, which had been previously agreed, were ratified by the third Treaty of Vienna in 1735.

Charles set about at once to remedy some of the ills of the previous misgovernment of Naples ; he endeavoured to curtail feudal and ecclesiastical privileges, to reduce taxation and to spread education ; he chose as his minister a Tuscan professor, Tanucci, a man of great administrative ability. But new complications were at hand. When the emperor died (1740), despite the trouble he had taken in getting the legitimacy of his daughter's succession acknowledged by the powers, the Austrian succession brought about a general war. Maria Theresa was attacked by Prussia ; the Bourbons of France and Spain also threatened her possessions ; and they summoned the Duke of Savoy to assist them, while England pressed him instead to join forces with Maria Theresa. He held his hand for a time, dreading the Bourbons and being aware that the Spanish queen looked upon him and his states with jealous and greedy eyes ; for she was now aiming at providing a state for her second son Philip. When he finally waged war against the Bourbons, he soon found himself in great difficulties. The Austrians were defeated by Charles of Naples ; the French and Spaniards occupied Lombardy and overran most of the Sardinian states ; later, the fortunes of war favoured his own and the Austrian forces, so that, when Philip V of Spain died, and the French and Spaniards withdrew, Genoa was occupied by the Austrians. At last the treaty of Aix-la-Chapelle (1748) brought a respite ; Carlo Emanuele acquired a further slice of Lombardy ; Philip was given Parma and Piacenza, Carlo Emanuele being later appeased by a pecuniary compensation (1763) ; Charles retained Naples and Sicily, which, when he succeeded to the throne of Spain as Charles III in 1759, he passed on to his son Ferdinando ; Austria controlled Milan and strengthened her hold on other states by marriages, for daughters of Maria Theresa were married to the son of Philip and to Ferdinando of Naples ; Leopold of Hapsburg-Lorraine finally succeeded to Tuscany when the last of the Medici died. Only small territorial changes were caused by later events. The most notable was the sale of Corsica to France in 1768. Both Sardinia and Corsica were not fortunate with their rulers. The Dukes of Savoy were too much occupied in war, and in the administration of their continental possessions, to command the necessary leisure and resources to improve the very backward condition of Sardinia. Corsica was even less fortunate, for the republic of Genoa, split by political factions, only cared for the collection of the revenue. The administration was corrupt and the proud islanders hated the Genoese ; they often rebelled. Once a German adventurer became their king ; later Pasquale Paoli so harrassed the Genoese that they first asked for French military assistance and later sold the island to France. As for Sardinia, under the rule of Vittorio Amedeo III, who succeeded Carlo Emanuele III, her conditions did not improve, for the king, upright but narrow-minded and mainly concerned with Spanish ceremonial and with the care of the army, did not fully realise his obligation towards his island subjects.

The popes were confronted with serious difficulties. Their administration was bad, even though the scandal of nepotism had ceased ; and during the eighteenth century on one side Jansenism and, on the other, disbelief contributed to rendering ecclesiastical privileges intolerable. The kings of Sardinia, as the dukes of Savoy were now called, had a long struggle with the Church on this point, and they were ably assisted by the minister D'Ormea. Also Charles of Naples tried to curtail privileges. When the Bourbons of France and Spain demanded the suppression of the Jesuits, who were charged with pecuniary greed and political interference, Naples and Parma followed suit ; Clement XIV dissolved the Order (1773), but the Italian states demanded and exacted more ; Venice, Naples, Tuscany, abolished immemorial rights and suppressed convents ; their relations with Rome had become strained when the French revolution broke out and caused all these conflicts to become obsolete. By that time the conditions of the kingdom of Sardinia were less prosperous, through the inefficiency of the king and his ministers ; in Lombardy the scheme of reform which the emperor, Joseph II, spurred on by the liberals, had brought in, even though too rigidly conceived, was sufficient to stir the natural resources of that province to an economic revival. Leopold of Tuscany, though suspicious, was well intentioned and sufficiently keen to bring in some very welcome reforms ; in Naples instead, Ferdinando, who was dominated by his queen, quarrelled with his father, dismissed the able Tanucci, and totally trusted a narrow-minded Irishman, Acton. In Parma Maria Amalia, more frivolous and capricious but as wilful as her sister, the Queen of

Naples, caused the dismissal of Du Tillot, an able minister, and plunged the little state into the thralls of reaction.

(b) FROM THE FRENCH REVOLUTION TO 1870

The treaty of Aix-la-Chapelle settled the condition of Italy for a considerable time. It was a period of intense intellectual activity during which new philosophical ideas, by no means all imported from foreign countries, and the example of foreign rulers contributed to arouse a new interest in internal affairs. Unfortunately, the men who would have been able to take advantage of this period of peace were removed from positions of trust, or not allowed to reach them. King Vittorio Amedeo III was too proud and too narrow-minded to choose ministers of the calibre of D'Ormea and Bogino ; Joseph II succeeded in suppressing all local initiative in Lombardy ; in Parma Du Tillot had been removed, as Tanucci in Naples, to make place for the influence of the wayward daughter of Maria Theresa ; the Grand Duke of Tuscany crabbed his reforming efforts by suspicion of his subjects ; Venice had lost the old spirit of initiative, and was content to vegetate as a pleasure city surrounded by a territory in economic decay ; of the islands, Corsica was lost, Sardinia was the Cinderella of the state of Savoy, and only Sicily enjoyed for a time the privilege of being ruled by a clever viceroy ; the popes were far too concerned with resisting the flow of liberal vindications in foreign lands and with the Jesuit trouble to be in a position even to consider the necessary reforms of their states.

Seldom, however, had Italians more actively participated in the intellectual life of Europe. Travellers, geographers, mathematicians, musicians, painters, architects, essayists, poets went to and often found a home in foreign countries ; most of them, however, returned to Italy, and their activities provided a suitable background for the liberal reforms which were advocated or carried out, and for that onslaught on privileges and on traditional ideas that was characteristic of the age. Much more than an echo of French ideas, there was in Italy a parallel movement ; if it did not effect a political revolution, it was mainly because the necessary conditions were lacking, above all because the country was still divided into some dozen states besides a number of minor centres which claimed feudal exemptions ; though the concept of national unity was the implicit, and often explicit, premise of much that was written and done. Thus, when the revolution started in France, it was looked upon with sympathy by many Italians of liberal ideas often belonging to the privileged

9

classes, and with horror only by the upholders of ecclesiastical privileges, of traditional religion, of aristocratic pre-eminence and by the ignorant masses. Even in Venice, the movement towards a democratic reform made itself felt. The governments were necessarily hostile, in Turin because of the restricted outlook of the king, in Rome for obvious reasons, and elsewhere because of the predominant influence of Austria. Austria was the most uncompromising opponent of revolutionary ideas, and it was the Austrian dominance in Italy, and the Austrian occupation in Lombardy, that occasioned the French expedition in Italy and thus the triumph of the revolution in the peninsula. During the long peace the Italian states had economised on the armies, or, as Vittorio Amedeo, had only paid attention to uniforms and parades. Vittorio Amedeo refused the offer of Milan in 1792, allied himself with Austria, and came into conflict with the French, who aimed at crippling Austria on the Po as well as on the Rhine. The French advance was easy, if not very deep, until the command was entrusted to the young Bonaparte (1796). In a few days he opened himself the way into the Po valley, secured it by a treaty with Vittorio Amedeo, drove the Austrians out of Lombardy, and besieged the great fortress of Mantua. Each of three relieving armies was destroyed at Castiglione, Arcole and Rivoli, and by April, 1797, having crossed the Alps into Austria, Bonaparte signed the treaty of Leoben by which Venice lost her mainland territory to the emperor though she had preserved a cowering neutrality. The French were greeted with enthusiasm, and soon cordially hated because of their intolerable exactions and violent repressions. The realisation, however, that French " fraternité " meant the tyranny of bayonets, did not prevent the spreading of revolutionary ideas ; Bologna and Ferrara rose against the pope, Reggio and Modena against the Duke of Modena ; the pope was granted a truce, but he proclaimed his antagonism to France, and the French army enforced the treaty by which the pope was humiliated, lost Romagna and Avignon, surrendered a hundred works of art and paid an enormous indemnity (1797). Against Venice Bonaparte was even more ruthless ; he had marched through her territory and handed it over to Austria ; though there was a party in Venice which was ready to move with the times, he was never more curt than when dealing with the old republic. In a very short time every single state of Italy collapsed. Milan received a constitution on the French model, and was fused with Emilia and Romagna to form the Cisalpine republic. Genoa remained independent as the Ligurian republic until 1805 when she was incorporated into the French empire.

Rome was transformed into the Roman republic (1798), the pope being exiled to Tuscany and later to France, where he died; Naples having ventured to attack the army of occupation in Rome was subjugated, and, the court having fled to Sicily on Nelson's ships, was turned into the Parthenopean republic; King Vittorio Emanuele was forced to take refuge in Sardinia (1799), after having handed over his mainland territories to the French. The Grand Duke of Tuscany was asked to withdraw. The absence, however, of Bonaparte, and the victories of the Austro-Russians under General Suvarow in 1799 drove the French out of Italy except Genoa which was defended by Massena; Naples was reconquered by Cardinal Ruffo, and Nelson consented to the abrogation of the capitulation and to the murdering of the liberals who had merely been sentenced to exile, among them patriotic women, Admiral Caracciolo and the philosopher Pagano.

This bloody interlude was concluded by the return of Bonaparte, his election as First Consul, and his victory at Marengo (1800); and then began in Italy the real domination of Napoleon. Venice and the land west of the Adige were still retained by Austria until 1806; the Duke of Modena was driven away; Tuscany became the kingdom of Etruria under the Bourbons of Parma. French troops occupied Apulia; the Cisalpine, restored as the Italian, republic elected Bonaparte as president. On Napoleon's accession to the empire, a kingdom of Italy was formed and entrusted to Eugene Beauharnais, his stepson; the republic of Lucca was given to Napoleon's sister, Eliza Bacciocchi; the kingdom of Etruria was annexed to France (1808) and then transformed into a grand duchy and given to Eliza Bacciocchi; Joseph Bonaparte was created King of Naples (1806), and two years later handed over a much reformed state to his successor Joachim Murat; and Murat was enabled to carry on the good work which was nowhere more necessary, thanks to the charm that his personality exercised upon the Neapolitans.

Two facts need to be noted during the Napoleonic era; the conflict with the pope and the rise of national feeling. The pope in Rome steadily refused to take sides in the war; he protested against the Napoleonic code and proclaimed his feudal rights upon Naples; by instalments the emperor deprived him of his possessions; even Rome was occupied (1808), but Pius VII, shut up in the Quirinal palace, kept up his resistance. When the emperor decreed the end of the temporal power (1809), Pius excommunicated him and was arrested and taken to Savona, but he did not yield to force as he did not yield to the offers of compromise, and he only returned to Rome in May, 1814, when the star of Napoleon was setting.

The disappearance of the ancient states showed of a sudden that these obstacles to the dream of all patriots from Petrarch to Alfieri were not unsurmountable ; the kingdom of Italy which was created by Napoleon, comprising the whole of North Italy, except Piedmont and some duchies given to his marshals in Venetia, had a constitution and an army ; its independence was illusory, but it gave scope to an Italian administration, and it was large enough to create a certain pride in its existence and bitter regret for its incompleteness ; the regiments of Italians fought valiantly in the continental war and suffered grievous losses in Russia. Italians could talk once again of their national army, and the limited realisation of their aspirations rendered their desire for further satisfaction at once keener and more poignant. Beauharnais was loyal to Napoleon, but Murat hesitated in his allegiance during the years 1813-15 ; after Dresden he negotiated with Austria, and he deserted after Leipzig (1813). When the return of all legitimate princes to their states was decided (1814), the fate of Murat was still in the balance, until he blundered by supporting Napoleon during the hundred days ; later he summoned the Italian patriots to his flag by the proclamation of Rimini (30th March, 1815) ; but he was defeated, compelled to take flight, and shot when he attempted to land at Pizzo in Calabria. The echo of his actions among Italians showed that national aspirations were no longer considered mere dreams. National feeling had always existed among Italians, but, by showing the possibility of their immediate realisation, the Napoleonic era brought Italian hopes within the scope of practical politics, as an object for which it was worth fighting and preparing. But the Italians had not really reached political maturity, and when Napoleon disappeared from the stage, Italians, exhausted by war and irritated by the despotic rule of the French, either favoured the return of the ancient rulers or allowed their supporters to take the lead. They lacked a centre and a flag ; the Milanese reactionaries engineered an unseemly riot during which a minister was lynched (20th April, 1814) ; and the other cities welcomed or sulkily accepted the return of the old princelings. Austria, holding Lombardy and Venetia, and thus all the gates of the central and eastern Alps, controlled Italy by force of arms and by political influence. Francesco IV of Modena, Ferdinando III of Tuscany, Napoleon's empress, Marie Louise of Parma and Piacenza, belonged to the Hapsburg family ; the Bourbon of Parma, who had become

Duke of Lucca, looked to Austria for the reversion of his old state
at the death of Marie Louise ; Pius VII held his states under the
protection of the Austrians, and Ferdinando IV of Naples looked
to Austria for guidance and protection. Only Vittorio Emanuele
I of Sardinia claimed a semblance of independence ; but he was
impervious to modern ideas as he was blind to the signs of the
times ; his first decree after his return was characteristic ; it
simply abolished all laws and statutes that had been brought
in by the French, as if it were possible to cancel twenty years of
history by a stroke of the pen. The inhabitants of the Lombardo-
Veneto, who had been flattered by the hope of retaining some
autonomy, were quickly undeceived ; Austria called this province
a kingdom and this was the limit of her concession. Its administration was efficient if harsh, and its economic condition materially
improved, despite the large sums which were made over to the
central exchequer ; the population increased. Tuscany was
barely prosperous ; the papal territories on the Adriatic were
economically active and politically restive ; the central Italian
states were too small to exercise any influence.

The kingdom of Sardinia was considered a sentry against
France and thoroughly reactionary, but it counted some 4,000,000
of hard-working inhabitants ; it possessed Genoa, an added source
of prosperity, and it soon felt the call of liberal ideas. Larger
and more populous was the kingdom of the two Sicilies, but
Ferdinando IV had no army and no will except Austria's. The
ideas of freedom and equality had taken too stong a hold to be
easily suppressed ; as their expression was forbidden in the open,
it was natural that they should be discussed and advocated in
secret. During the French Revolution freemasonry, which had
already been imported into Italy at an earlier period from England,
was fostered by government circles ; it possessed secret rites and
formulas, and served as a model to other societies, and in the first
place to the Carboneria. After 1815 the number of its adherents
increased and its motto became " Union, Liberty and Freedom " ;
it was split into a number of conflicting varieties with different
political tendencies, mostly anti-clerical ; so that there were also
brought into existence other secret societies having catholic
sympathies. These conditions were not peculiar to Italy, and
the international connexions of the secret societies ensured a
certain co-ordination of revolutionary movements in different
countries. On the example of Spain, a military revolt occurred
in Naples (1820) resulting in the acceptance by the king of the
Spanish constitution of 1812. Sicily followed suit with a separatist
rebellion. The king was summoned to Laybach by Austria,

and though he had taken his sacred oath to the constitution, he asked for Austrian assistance, and an Austrian contingent easily defeated the Neapolitan troops ; then the treacherous king repealed the constitution and began the persecution of all liberals (1821).

A tragic drama was staged in Piedmont, where the Carbonari had their principal upholders among the aristocracy and were befriended by Carlo Alberto, the heir to the throne. The army openly asked for a constitution ; Vittorio Emanuele I, faint-heartedly abdicated in favour of his brother, Carlo Felice, who was absent, and Carlo Alberto, as regent, with the reservation of the king's approval, yielded to the liberal demands. His action was disallowed by the king who returned with the support of Austrian troops, and Carlo Alberto was compelled to submit. In Milan trouble was brewing among the intellectuals, who advocated reforms in a thinly veiled language on the pages of a literary paper, *Il Conciliatore*, of romanticist tendencies. Timely arrests forestalled every outbreak ; Silvio Pellico, Confalonieri and their friends were the principal victims ; they suffered for many years in Austrian dungeons, while exiles from Lombardy, Naples and Piedmont made Europe acquainted with the conditions ruling in Italy.

During the following years political persecution was in full swing. The ranks of the Carbonari were depleted by executions, imprisonment and exiles. They regained hope when, in July, 1830, Louis Philippe was carried to the French throne by a revolutionary movement and stood forth as the champion of liberal principles. He announced that he would prevent foreign intervention in internal agitations, and this declaration instilled hope into the liberals. The treacherous Francesco IV of Modena flirted with them, and then betrayed them, seeking Austrian help (1831) ; in Bologna, Ferrara and many other cities of the papal states there were risings against papal tyranny in which all classes of citizens had part. Louis Philippe, however, was browbeaten by Austria, and let it be known that the principle of non-intervention had been adopted by France, but was not going to be upheld by France in other countries ; and in less than two months Austrian soldiers re-established the old order and began the usual persecutions. The Carbonari sect had shown its lack of organisation ; a young Genoese, Giuseppe Mazzini (1805-72), who had been arrested as a Carbonaro in 1830 and sent into exile in 1831, realised the inadequacy of the Carboneria. He was sensitive and idealistic and yet possessed of an energy that could not be daunted ; the association which he founded in 1832 at Marseilles was the direct expression of his own character. A devotee of religious and democratic ideas, he chose as a motto "Dio e popolo"; Italy must be freed as a united republic, "Unità e repubblica," and this end must be attained by thoughtful action, "Pensiero ed azione." Many of his followers were arrested in Piedmont in 1833; and he made an ill-fated expedition in Savoy in 1834 in order to come to their rescue. There never was a more resilient character than Mazzini's; failure inspired him to new efforts; it was his creed that a handful of energetic conspirators could cause a whole city to rise, and that, whenever the remotest chance of success was offered, an attempt must be made to seize it. The upshot was that, after 1834, the outbreaks in the different Italian states in which Mazzini's society, the "Giovine Italia," was concerned, were too many to be enumerated here. The Giovine Italia had its martyrs. Two young officers of the Austrian navy, the brothers Bandiera, Venetian by birth and the sons of an Austrian admiral, sacrificed themselves for the sake of Mazzinian ideals when a revolt in Calabria seemed to need, and promised to reward, assistance. Their end caused much commotion, and increased the following of another section of the liberals.

Among the intellectuals in the North some trusted in progressive reform and in the gradual wearing down of political barriers, rather than in open insurrection. Confalonieri and Pellico, who suffered in the dungeons of Spielberg, Capponi in Tuscany, Balbo and Massimo d'Azeglio in Piedmont shared similar views. They were less rigidly organised, and in fact D'Azeglio, for one, spurned secret societies, but they found an eloquent mouthpiece in Vincenzo Gioberti, once a court chaplain in Turin, and afterwards an exile in Paris and in Brussels. As the result of long meditation he brought out in 1843 a book, *Del primato morale e civile degli Italiani*, that claimed Italian pre-eminence in all branches of human activities, and advocated reforms and the constitution of an Italian confederation under the presidency of the pope, military defence being entrusted to the Piedmontese army. This scheme had the advantage that it contained nothing of an openly seditious character, so that it called forth discussion and made many recruits among men to whom sedition and secret societies were repellent. On economic grounds alone, now when peace and ordinary administration had brought about a considerable revival, the petty regulations of the police and the hindrance constituted by the barrier of protective tariffs had become unbearable; and most governments felt that reforms were overdue. Such a feeling had been strengthened and spread by the frequent congresses of scientists in which political matters were almost openly discussed. Gioberti's work was followed by others in which slightly different views were upheld, and this movement gained strength when Massimo d'Azeglio was instructed by Carlo Alberto, king since 1831, to tell his friends that he shared their views and would take their lead as soon as the moment came. Carlo Alberto was unpopular among many liberals, because his behaviour in 1821 had been grievously misconstrued ; but since he had become a king he had laboured unceasingly at improving the condition of his state, had used moderation in repressing Mazzinian movements, and had occasionally revealed his loathing for Austria. Liberal hopes were kindled when Cardinal Mastai-Ferretti became pope as Pius IX (1846), for he was known for his religious zeal and his political moderation. He seemed to be the pope whom Gioberti advocated, and the enthusiasm with which his election was received was a sign of his individual popularity, and of the hold that Giobertian ideas had on the people. Popular enthusiasm forced the pope's hand and, despite the warnings of Austria, he conceded certain of the constitutional reforms for which the liberals were clamouring—a partly elective council and a civil militia. This papal action encouraged the liberals in other states to ask for similar concessions. The Piedmontese and the Tuscans obtained the freedom of the press and a civil militia ; Austria and Naples did not yield ; when the pope seemed threatened by Austria, Carlo Alberto from Turin and from Nice Garibaldi, who had won some fame through his daring exploits in South America, offered their help ; Mazzini from London wrote his encouragement (1847).

In the Austrian provinces riots were frequent and repressions were violent ; a strike of smokers had recently provoked a good deal of bloodshed in Milan, Pavia, Padua and Venice, where some of the leaders were arrested. The spark came whence least it was to be expected ; the Sicilians rebelled against the Bourbons, fighting heroically they drove the royal forces from the island ; then also Naples demanded a constitutional charter and suddenly King Ferdinando gave way (29th January, 1848). There was no stopping now ; the Grand Duke Leopoldo II (17th February), Carlo Alberto (5th March), and even Pius IX (14th March), whose position was naturally more difficult, were compelled to follow this same course. Meanwhile Paris had revolted against Louis Philippe, riots had occurred in German towns, Vienna had rebelled. It was time for the Italians under Austrian domination to fight ; Venice expelled the Austrians and constituted herself into a republic under the presidency of Daniele

Manin (18th March). On the same day, independently, there started the Milanese revolution, and in five days an army of 13,000 men was driven out of the metropolis of Lombardy. Insurrections took place in other cities, and the Austrian army only retained the four co-ordinated fortresses of Verona, Peschiera, Mantua and Legnago. The flag of the revolution was white, red and green ; Carlo Alberto, moving at the head of his army against Austria, flew the same flag with the cross of Savoy in its centre. The Grand Duke of Tuscany, the pope and the King of Naples could not resist popular enthusiasm, and were forced to send contingents to the Po valley. It was a holy war, but there was no agreement between the allies. In Milan the republicans rapidly gained the upper hand over the moderates ; the people voted the annexation to Piedmont as other cities had done, but Carlo Alberto agreed to put off any political settlement until the end of the war ; and the republicans, no less than the sovereigns of other states, fearing lest his success were to add to his popularity, stinted their support. The inhabitants of the countryside were openly opposed to war ; the pope had soon realised that the army of the Church could not take part in a war against a catholic country ; his troops were recalled, and, only in opposition to his orders, some of them remained in the field. There followed quick changes in Rome, and the flight of the pope to Gaeta. In Naples reactionary riots gave the opportunity to the king to recall his troops and to repeal the constitution ; there were riots also in Tuscany. Meanwhile the Piedmontese army attacked the Austrian fortresses, and, after some initial successes, was pushed back by the reinforced enemy (Custoza, 25th July), beaten again near Milan where factious disorders were rife, so that the king, with a heavy heart, signed an armistice (9th August). Defeat caused political agitation in Piedmont itself. The Austrians quickly reinstated the old sovereigns in their capitals, and only Rome, Venice and Tuscany remained free. In Tuscany the grand duke had fled to Gaeta, and the government was in the hands of the extremists led by Guerrazzi : in Rome a republican government was established of which Mazzini was the controlling personality ; the defence was entrusted to a small army of volunteers under Garibaldi ; Venice revoked her annexation to Piedmont, and constituted herself into a republic under the dictatorship of Manin. Gioberti was minister in Piedmont, but he was rapidly losing popularity. The natural anxiety to assist Venice, Tuscany and Rome precipitated a new war, though the Piedmontese army was not ready. At Novara the Sardinians were routed (23rd Ma

and Carlo Alberto abdicated hoping that his son, Vittorio Emanuele
II, might obtain better terms from the Austrians. Brescia, which
had risen again, was barbarously treated by General Haynau.
After a long siege the heroic defenders of Venice, decimated by
the ravages of war, famine and disease, were forced to capit-
ulate (22nd August). The Austrians had already reinstated
the old sovereigns in central Italy, and Rome had capitulated
after a magnificent defence on 2nd July to a French army sent
by Louis Napoleon who had replaced Louis Philippe. The revolution in Sicily had been crushed by the Bourbons in May.

Reaction was apparently triumphant, but the rift between
the reactionary governments and the people had become irre-
mediable. Of all the sovereigns only the King of Sardinia
had been loyal to liberal principles. Vittorio Emanuele had
accepted the harsh conditions imposed by Austria, but steadily
refused to repeal the constitution. The peace was grudgingly
ratified by the Sardinian Parliament after a dramatic debate.
The prime minister was then D'Azeglio, Gioberti having resigned,
and in 1850 there entered the cabinet a young cadet of a noble
family, Camillo Benso di Cavour, who had left the army because
of his liberal principles some years previously. Level-headed,
tireless and endowed with a keen sense of reality, he was fated
to become the guiding force of the Risorgimento. He soon replaced D'Azeglio as prime minister (1852), despite some hesitation
on the part of Vittorio Emanuele, and he controlled parliament
in so masterful a way that in a very short time he was able to
introduce far-reaching reforms in all departments of the state
with a view to consolidating its economic structure, improving
the resources of the people, reorganising the army so as to render
the kingdom of Sardinia capable to fulfil its mission in Italy.

The failure in 1848-49 had struck a serious blow to the Giovine
Italia, but Mazzinian outbreaks were sporadically occurring and
causing victims ; there had been a revolt in Genoa (1849) ; in
1852 the Austrian police discovered some Mazzinian agents in
Lombardy, and a few saintly patriots died on the scaffold at
Mantua (1852) ; there were riots in Milan (1853) and a daring
expedition in Cadore (1855) ; the Dukes of Parma and Modena
and the King of Naples subjected the liberals to merciless persecution. It was then that Gladstone was inspired to write
his famous indictment of the Neapolitan Bourbons. In Tuscany
the rule, if milder, was in no way more liberal. Turin swarmed
with political refugees, and Cavour risked an open breach with
Austria in order to champion their cause. He dared more in
1854 when he proposed and arranged an alliance with England

CHAPTER VII

ITALIAN LITERATURE FROM THE END OF THE RENAISSANCE TO 1870

(a) THE LITERATURE OF THE SEICENTO

THE period that runs from the latter part of the sixteenth to the end of the seventeenth century—broadly speaking from the death of Tasso to the foundation of the Arcadia—has been traditionally represented as one of decadence and corruption in the history of Italian thought, art and letters, and the word " barocco " or " secentismo," applied to the productions of the age, has become synonymous with bad taste, insincerity and pretentiousness. This has been attributed to the exhaustion of the creative energy of the Italians by the Renaissance, to the Spanish domination that the events of the preceding century had imposed upon Italy, to the influence of the Counter-Reformation guided by the Jesuits. But, although art and letters inevitably reflect what Croce calls the " ritmo lento e fiacco " of the Italian national and social life of the time, and prose and verse alike are correspondingly infested with inflation and artificiality, this general condemnation is only in part justified. It was an age of preparation and of seeking for novelty, of keen interest in political theory and history, of tentative progress in the study of æsthetics, of reaction against outworn conventions (with germs of the future romantic movement), and of great advance in the field of natural science.

Already the Calabrian, Bernardino Telesio (d. 1588), in his *De rerum natura iuxta propria principia*, had combated the authority of Aristotle, insisting that the investigator of natural phenomena should question nature herself rather than follow her commentators. This revolt from accepted authority is personified in another southerner, Giordano Bruno of Nola, with his ideal of philosophical liberty, who perished at the stake in Rome in 1600. And now we meet one of the most heroic figures in history. Galileo Galilei (1564-1642), born at Pisa of an old Florentine family, not only opened new fields of scientific triumphs

but popularised his results in vernacular works in dialogue form,
the *Dialogo de' massimi sistemi* (1630) and the *Dialoghi delle
nuove scienze* (1638), that are written in a simple and robust
Italian prose, absolutely free from the turgid and artificial style
of the age. News of his epoch-making discoveries—as first
announced in a small Latin treatise, the *Sidereus nuncius* (1610)—
penetrated into a Neapolitan dungeon, to a Dominican friar
who wrote to urge him not to restrict himself to physical science,
but to reveal a universal philosophy that should be known as
Italian. This was Tommaso Campanella (1568-1639), a follower
of Telesio and like him a Calabrian, who for a quarter of a century
was imprisoned by the Spanish government at Naples for a wild
conspiracy to establish a theocratic republic, the " City of the
Sun," with laws based upon nature, among his native mountains.
This fantastic utopia, a state based upon communism and what
we should now call eugenics, is idealised in Campanella's Italian
dialogue, the *Città del Sole* (1602), or, as he called it in the later
Latin version, *Idea reipublicae philosophicae*. Campanella looked
to the renovation of the world by basing every sphere of human
thought and activity upon natural principles, turning from " the
books and dead temples of men " to " the original book of Nature."
This philosophy, in elaborate Latin prose works, he attempted
to harmonise with the orthodox Catholic faith. But Campanella
is above all a poet : the one great poet of the Seicento. His
Poesie filosofiche, almost all composed in prison and hardly known
until the present day, give lyrical utterance to his metaphysical
creed of God and nature, his messianic and utopian dreams for
the renovation of mankind (with himself as destined liberator),
his hatred of oppression, hypocrisy and corruption, his own
sufferings and spiritual experience. The " Salmodia metafisi-
cale," the " Canzone del pentimento," " Della possanza del-
l'uomo," and certain sonnets, are among the masterpieces of
Italian lyrical poetry.

In general, poetry is the side of literature that most reflects
the superficiality and perverted taste of the Seicento. Already
the tendency to elaborate conceits, to sentimental sensuality,
and to a somewhat empty musicality, is found in the *Pastor
fido* (1590) of Giambattista Guarini, like Tasso a courtier of
Ferrara (though the work, showing the changed political temper
of the time, is dedicated to the Duke of Savoy), which, while
mingling comedy with tragedy, attempts to surpass the *Aminta*
by developing the pastoral play along the lines of classical drama.
The typical poet of the early part of the period is the Neapolitan,
Giambattista Marino (1569-1625), who expressed his artistic creed

in the line " è del poeta il fin la meraviglia." In his pastorals
and other lyrics, and particularly in his huge classical epic of
frigid sensuality, the *Adone* (1623), he set himself to dazzle the
reader by prodigality and excess, by lavish abuse of imagery,
and startlingly incongruous metaphors and antithesis, though
he can at times in his sonnets strike a simpler note. Even his
opponents, like Tommaso Stigliani (1573-1651), are affected by
the same spirit. To some extent, " Marinismo " was a reaction
against the conventional Petrarchism of the latter part of the
sixteenth century (as represented, for instance, by Giovanni
Della Casa), but had a basis in Petrarchism, materialising its
conceits to the point of absurdity. The " Marinisti," mostly
southerners by birth or adoption, carried on their master's cult
of " ingegnosità " and " sensualismo," with selection of far-
fetched, incongruous, and sometimes perverted subjects—though
occasional sonnets or other lyrics, notably those of Girolamo
Fontanella (d. 1644), have a genuine charm. Simultaneously
in northern Italy, poets were treading a more austere lyrical
path, though with hardly higher artistic results. Gabriello
Chiabrera (1552-1638) was attempting novelty in form and expression by following the Greek poets, seeking, like Christopher
Columbus, " trovar nuovo mondo o affogare," with *canzoni
eroiche* in imitation of Pindar to celebrate the triumphs of the
Counter-Reformation, and *anacreontiche*, lighter lyrics that owe
more to Ronsard and the French poets of the Pleiade than to
his professed Greek model. The earlier poems of Fulvio Testi
(1593-1646), a famous ode and the *Pianto d'Italia*, give worthy
expression to the brief period of national hope in Carlo Emanuele
of Savoy as Italy's champion against the might of Spain ; his
later moralising canzoni, more or less on Horatian lines, are
somewhat dreary. Another northerner, Ciro di Pers (d. 1662,
but his poetry is mostly early), though at times lapsing into the
conceits of the Marinisti, strikes a nobler note in free canzoni on
the conditions of Italy and in a singularly beautiful sonnet on the
old theme of Platonic love.

The invention of " una nuova sorte di poesia " was claimed
by Alessandro Tassoni (1565-1635)—notable also for his eloquent
expression of the anti-Spanish feeling of Italians in his prose *Filip-
piche contro gli Spagnuoli* (1615) and for his critical attack upon
the fame of Petrarch—with his *Secchia rapita* (1622), the mock
epic, " poema eroicocomico," on the carrying off of a bucket from
Bologna by the Modenese in one of the petty wars of the thirteenth century, in which the reader is bidden see " Elena tras-
formarsi in una secchia." A finer poetical spirit, though with

less satiric fertility, Carlo Dottori imitated Tassoni with the *Asino* (1652), likewise in ten cantos, in which the subject of contention is a banner with a painted ass, " dentro un'insegna un asinel dipinto," taken from the Vicentines by the Paduans ; a comic poem with serious romantic episodes, among which that of the death of Desmanina, the repudiated wife of Ezzelino, at her husband's hands has true beauty and pathos. A third poem of the same genre, the *Malmantile racquistato* of the painter, Lorenzo Lippi (1606-65), was mainly composed for the purpose of illustrating the wealth of the Florentine vernacular—which likewise gives what permanent value they possess to the comedies in prose and verse, the *Fiera* and the *Tancia*, of Michelangelo's nephew, the younger Michelangelo Buonarroti (1568-1646). Satirical poetry is well represented in the North by the *Sermoni* of Chiabrera, who takes Horace as his model, and in the South by the *Satire* of the Neapolitan painter, Salvator Rosa (1615-73), as vigorous with the pen as with the brush, the Juvenal of the seventeenth century, particularly effective in the pieces dealing with music, poetry and painting. A large number of serious epic poems were composed on heroical religious or crusading themes in imitation of the *Gerusalemme liberata*, such as the *Croce racquistata* of Francesco Bracciolini (1611), who also wrote the burlesque *Scherno degli Dei*, the *Conquisto di Granata* of Girolamo Graziani (1650), and the *Boemondo* of G. L. Sempronio (1651) ; with the possible exception of that of Graziani, these works have no great poetic merit and are dreary reading, though saved by Virgil and Tasso from the more flagrant barocchism of the age.

While the comedy of the century is worthless, the tragic drama is noble and elevated in tone, and frequently of a high quality. The *Adamo* (1613) of Giambattista Andreini, the son of an actor, may well have influenced Milton. Federigo della Valle composed three tragedies—*La Reina di Scotia*, *Judith* and *Esther* (1628)—free from all traces of barocchism and with true lyrical beauty. These dramas on religious themes (the death of Mary, Queen of Scots, is treated as that of a Catholic martyr) follow the classical model, as also do other tragedies, notable among which are the *Aristodemo* (1657) of Carlo Dottori and the *Cleopatra* of Giovanni Delfino (1617-99). In the latter work Cleopatra is a noble figure, though hardly suggesting Shakespeare's " Serpent of old Nile," while the magnanimity of the love-sick Augustus anticipates the Roman heroes of Metastasio. Other tragedies anticipate the romantic drama in their revolt from the fetters of the unities of time and place. Conspicuous among

these, and announced as " una tragedia di nuova moda," is the
Cromuele of Girolamo Graziani (1671), with a singularly powerful
and impressive presentation, however impossible historically, of
the great Protector of the English Commonwealth, whose utter-
ances are full of maxims of statecraft, the " ragion di stato "
that the proscribed Machiavelli had elevated to the rank of
a science, and Paruta and Botero, in their different ways,
had attempted to harmonise with the principles of religion and
morality.

These questions of " ragion di stato " play no small part in
the most vital and attractive prose work of the seventeenth
century, the *Ragguagli di Parnaso* (1612-13) of Traiano Boccalini
(1556-1613), a native of the papal states who had found refuge
in the friendly shelter of Venice. In the shape of reports or
news-letters from Parnassus, an imaginary realm under the king-
ship of Apollo, in which personages from all the centuries jostle
pleasantly together and which has diplomatic relations with the
actual states of the world, it is at once satire and literary criticism,
inspired by keen insight, a noble sense of Italian nationality,
and a humour that at times seems curiously modern. Paruta
is Apollo's professor of political science at the university, but
the work of Botero is refused admission into the Delphic library.
Among the most admirable of the *Ragguagli* is the one satirising
the Counter-Reformation dread of Machiavelli, and another,
defending Tasso from the pedantry of his critics, which is in effect
a plea for poetic liberty that contains the romantic creed in germ.
Boccalini's *Pietra del paragone* (published posthumously in 1615)
is in form a continuation of the *Ragguagli*, but more political
in matter, its main purpose being an attack upon the Spanish
predominance in Europe and a denunciation of Spain's treatment
of her Italian possessions, the author—like Fulvio Testi and
others—looking for the liberation of Italy to the valour of Carlo
Emanuele of Savoy.

Among the targets for Boccalini's wit is the excessive production of histories. A vast number of works appeared, especially
in the earlier part of the century, dealing with the history of
European countries other than Italy, such as those of the civil
wars in France by Enrico Caterino Davila (1575-1634), who follows
the historiographical tradition of the Cinquecento, and the struggle
of the Netherlands against Spain by Guido Bentivoglio (1579-
1644), whose style is more the artificial one of the Seicento. A
place apart belongs to the Servite friar, Paolo Sarpi (1552-1623),
the official theologian of the Venetian Republic in its struggle
with Paul V. One of the most virile spirits of the age, his *Storia*

del Concilio di Trento (1619)—in opposition to the Counter-Reformation which he regards as a fresh corruption rather than a regeneration of the Church—is written in a prose as free from barocchism as is that of Galileo. In answer we have the more artificial in style, but (allowing for the different point of view) equally candid history of the Council as regarded by the Roman Curia, of the Jesuit cardinal, Sforza Pallavicino (1607-67). Another Jesuit, Daniello Bartoli (1608-85), was characterised by De Sanctis as the " Marino della prosa " for his *Storia della Compagnia di Gesù*, written in a rhetorical and diffuse style that is the counterpart of the barocco churches of his Order. Yet another Jesuit, Paolo Segneri (1624-94), a famous preacher and skilled director of souls, composed ascetical treatises and series of sermons, such as the *Manna dell'anima* and the *Quaresimale*, that have not entirely lost appeal and efficacy. Noticeable among the writers on political science are the Bolognese, Virgilio Malvezzi (1595-1654), praised to the skies in his own time for his *Romulo* and *Tarquinio superbo*, and Lodovico Zuccolo of Faenza (d. 1630), whose reputation has been revived of late years. Zuccolo's dialogue, the *Repubblica d'Evandria*, under the form of a Utopia, links up with Machiavelli's ideal of Italian unity. The same writer, in his *Discorso delle ragioni del numero del verso italiano*, and Sforza Pallavicino, in his *Del Bene*, show themselves pioneers in æsthetic theory, in claiming that the judgment of a work of art pertains to a special faculty, and insisting on the domination of intuition and imagination.

The prose romances that abounded in the Seicento, some on the lines of the outworn romances of chivalry, others satirising contemporary matters under the guise of fiction, are among the most worthless products of the age ; the most popular in their day were the *Dianea* of Gianfrancesco Loredano (1627) and the longer *Calloandro fedele* (1640) of Giovanni Ambrogio Marini. A would-be Boccaccio of the century is Giovanni Sagredo, whose *Arcadia in Brenta* (1667) depicts a company of Venetians, three cavaliers and three ladies, spending eight days in disport in a houseboat on the Brenta, entertaining themselves with quips and conundrums, short stories and singing. In spite of the barocco style of the introduction, the book brings us into touch with the actual social life of the period. A far more significant work—ranking, though on a different and lower plane, with the *Ragguagli* of Boccalini as one of the few prose works of the century that still have real vitality—is the *Pentamerone*, or *Cunto de li Cunti*, of Giambattista Basile (d. 1632). Written in the Neapolitan dialect, which Basile thus elevated to the rank of a literary

language, it is mainly a collection of fairy stories including such
old and valued friends as Puss-in-Boots (though without those
pedal adornments), Cinderella and Rapunzel.[1]

Meanwhile scientific academies had come into being : the
Accademia dei Lincei at Rome in 1603, the Accademia del Cimento
—with its Dantesque motto, " provando e riprovando "—at
Florence in 1657. The new scientific spirit, inaugurated by
Galileo, was continuing its triumphant course, with men like
Marcello Malpighi (1628-94) and Lorenzo Magalotti (1637-1712).
It was reflected in Italian literature—notably in Magalotti's *Saggi
di naturali esperienze*—and, as Croce observes, contributed to the
literary reaction that put an end to barocchism also in prose.

While Marinismo was finding its last expression in the sheer
"ingegnosità" of the Neapolitan Jesuit, Giacomo Lubrano, and the
Sicilian swashbuckler, Giuseppe Artale, a reaction in poetic ideals
was tending to a return to the models of the past and to a more
refined taste, though hardly, save in isolated cases, producing
poetry worthy of the name. But it is significant that the pioneer
in this reform should have been an eminent Tuscan scientist,
the physician Francesco Redi (1626-98). A student of the classics
and early Italians, Redi represents something of the old Tuscan
spirit alike in burlesque and in love poetry, where he echoes the
dolce stil nuovo and Petrarch. His masterpiece, the " ditirambo,"
Bacco in Toscana, published in 1685 after more than ten years
labour, a poem in various metres in praise of Tuscan wine, has
at least lyrical movement and an amazing buoyancy that should
quicken the pulses of the most rigid prohibitionist. In Lombardy,
Francesco di Lemene (1634-1704) is still largely a victim of
the " ingegnosità " of the century ; but Carlo Maria Maggi
(1630-99), besides comedies and lyrics in his native vernacular
(in which he shows himself the founder of Milanese dialectal
literature), composed a series of noteworthy sonnets on the state
of Italy in 1690, slumbering in " la moderna viltà " while the
thunderbolts of war were looming beyond the Alps. With these,
but on a higher level, may be placed the magnificent sonnet of
the Jesuit, Giambattista Pastorini, on the bombardment of Genoa
by the French in 1684. Vincenzo da Filicaia (1642-1707), a
Florentine senator, and Alessandro Guidi (1650-1712), a native
of Pavia settled at Rome, close the epoch with what De Sanctis
characterises as " eroismo rettorico." Filicaia, though no longer
regarded as rising above mediocrity, is the better poet of the

[1] " Puss-in-Boots " had already appeared in Italian in the *Piacevoli
notti* of Straparola (1550-53).

two. His lyrics are all devoted to worthy themes, and his religious sonnets express the faith that ruled his life ; but his six canzoni on the relief of Vienna by Sobieski and the Poles, his once famous sonnets on Italy, have more artifice and rhetoric than spontaneous inspiration. The same excess of emphasis and rhetoric, the constant straining after sonorousness, is still more marked in Alessandro Guidi, particularly in his once admired canzone *La Fortuna*—" quella grandiosa ode " which even Alfieri read " with unspeakable transport "—and his pompous canzoni celebrating the foundation of the Arcadia. Redi and Filicaia were associated with Guidi in the foundation of this famous academy in 1690 at Rome—thus closing a century from that of the Crusca in Florence—which marks the final defeat of secentismo in poetry and the beginning of a new period in Italian literature.

(b) From the Beginning of the Eighteenth Century to 1870

During the seventeenth century the French openly rebelled against the literary pre-eminence that Italy had maintained so long, and during the later period so undeservingly. This rebellion, which was led by the Abbé Bouhours and Madame Dacier, was deeply resented and caused a critical revaluation in which many scholars took part : Maffei, Muratori, Gravina, Calepio, Martelli, Conti among others. They naturally reasoned with a prejudiced mind and from classical premises ; despite this, their work was productive of many fruitful suggestions which seem to have affected the earlier theorists of German romanticism. The eighteenth century has been called the century of Arcadia from the name of the academy founded in Rome in 1690 under the auspices of Queen Christina of Sweden, of which Gravina was one of the founders, Crescimbeni the leading spirit, and practically every man of note a member. This academy had puerile formalities and a ludicrous ritual, but its justification and merits must not be overlooked. In the endeavour to discard all the excesses of the Seicento, it aimed at classical simplicity and mostly attained only thinness. But its labours were not all wasted. In its assemblies there were read numbers of vapid poems and orations on unimportant subjects, precisely as it often happens in our days at the meeting of literary societies and at public lectures ; but it ought not to be overlooked that the Arcadia stimulated the rise of other learned societies and indirectly promoted very valuable investigations ; above all, that men like Gravina

(1664-1718), the founder of the history of law, Maffei, a most gifted innovator of archæological studies and the real founder of modern paleography, Muratori (1672-1750), the tireless researcher of medieval history, and Tiraboschi (1731-94), the first historian of Italian literature, were all ascribed to this society and prided themselves on being members of it.

Among their colleagues were historians of merit, great mathematicians, astronomers, geographers, explorers, essayists and philosophers. For if, in considering this period, one looks beyond the boundaries of pure literature, one cannot but be amazed that decadence should be imputed to an age in which Italian architects adorned the capitals of Europe, from St. Petersburg to Lisbon, with magnificent buildings, Italian travellers and geographers turned up in the remotest parts of the world, painters, such as Tiepolo and Guardi, were summoned to foreign countries, musicians expressed the tragedy of the nation in works of lasting appeal, and Vico (1668-1744), the lonely giant, built up one of the great philosophical systems of mankind. In creative literature there was no doubt a crisis ; the country was exhausted by continuous wars and by Spanish misgovernment ; and, while sorrow found expression in music, sensuous sentimentality appeared to provide an escape, and inspired poetry and painting. Madrigals and canzonette are minor forms of literature, but Zappi (1667-1719), Rolli (1687-1765), Manfredi (1674-1739), and Metastasio (1698-1782), brought them to perfection, and Frugoni (1692-1768), lazy and lacking ambition, showed truly amazing possibilities and achieved a considerable measure of success in metrical reform. These men did not possess the moral energy to rise above the fatuity of contemporary society with its wigs, its frills, its lace, its powder and its gorgeous buttons and buckels ; and often they composed verses in Berni's style on most frivolous subjects, as did Fagiuoli (1660-1742). More seriously-minded satirists were prone, as Menzini (1646-1704) and Sergardi (1660-1726), to mix up personal spite with moral indignation ; but their works showed symptoms of dissatisfaction with the prevailing condition, and even Forteguerri's (1674-1735) mock heroic poem *Ricciardetto* has traits well worthy of attention.

The first half of the century was the age of the theatre ; Italians, as if dreading to express themselves fully, wore masks on every occasion, and found relief in music the meaning of which cannot be clearly deciphered. The mummeries of fashion transformed the whole life of society into a huge show, even the practice of having officious friends in attendance on married women (*cicisbei*) was the result of the general make-believe.

And thus the theatre was naturally the rage ; the opera above all, in the performance of which, further to complicate the fiction, specially trained and treated males sang the feminine parts. The opera, or "melodrama" as it is properly called, had risen to great heights with the early masters of the sixteenth century and had degenerated during the seventeenth owing to its excessively facile melodies and frivolous subjects. A learned critic, Apostolo Zeno (1668-1750) of Venice, attempted a reform by choosing better subjects for his libretti, but he lacked the dramatic power and the poetic graces to bring this reform to perfection ; such a success was to be the privilege of Pietro Trapassi, the son of a Roman cook. Gravina discovered his parts, trained him and altered his name to that of Metastasio. He was made to work at philosophy and law, but, when his teacher died in 1718, he was soon drawn into his natural field of activity, and by 1724 he had composed one of his masterpieces (*Didone abbandonata*). It was his aim to compose libretti having a literary and dramatic value apart from their musical setting, and, as he possessed an uncanny gift of producing melodious lines, he rose at once to great fame ; he was later called to Vienna as imperial poet in succession to Zeno, and there poured out a long series of *melodrammi*. His was on the whole a lucky life, for Gravina, the singer Bulgarelli, and Countess Althann generously assisted him, but he was too ready to relieve his feelings in tears or in verse when sorrow afflicted him ; and he was inclined to see Roman dignity and Greek pathos under the aspect of eighteenth-century ceremoniousness and sentimentality. Such deficiencies as well as the melodiousness of his verse, which could not be imitated, caused his example to exercise less influence than would be expected, and soon the prevalence of the musical element in opera became overwhelming and the importance of the drama itself proportionately indifferent.

Another branch of dramatic literature requires no less attention. Through its long vogue the "Commedia dell' arte" had exhausted its possibilities and had become barren and stale. Some playwrights tried to keep up interest by a rapid succession of unexpected events, and in Tuscany G. B. Fagiuoli (1660-1742), G. Gigli and Jacopo Nelli (1670-1767) were already groping after character drama ; Gigli's *Don Pilone* (1711) was in fact an adaptation of the *Tartuffe*. But the honour of consciously bringing about a dramatic reform belongs to Goldoni (1707-93), for, compared to his life-long and single-minded devotion to his ideals, the attempts of Tuscan and Lombard playwrights pale into insignificance. Carlo Goldoni was born to his profession ;

he sketched a play when he was eight years old ; he acted in one when he was a student at Perugia and, though he became a lawyer, he kept up his interests in acting and, after many vicissitudes, threw in his lot with a famous company of actors for whom he wrote at first scenarios, mock-heroic plays, musical comedies and interludes, until four years later (1738) he persuaded his actors to perform a character play of which he wrote the scenario and the part of the hero. Success encouraged him to pursue on these lines until, in 1743, he produced a fully written character play (*La donna di garbo*). His most fruitful period, 1748-62, was spent in Venice ; later he went to Paris, having been driven from Venice by the irritating imitations of the Abbate Chiari (1711-85) and by the satire of Carlo Gozzi (1720-1806), who disapproved of the innovation of Goldoni, of his antagonism to improvisation, and his preference for middle-class heroes. Of Goldoni's 250 plays a large proportion met with success, being simple and life-like and well attuned to his kindly, honest and optimistic nature. G. G. de Rossi (1754-1827) and G. Giraud (1776-1834) were the most notable among his followers.

Just as Goldoni wished to reform dramatic art, other Italians worked for the reform of historical and critical studies, of philosophy, tragedy, journalism and satire. It was the period during which the encyclopædists were paving the way to the French Revolution, and they had their often independent counterparts in Italy. It would be impossible to exaggerate the influence upon literature of these political and philosophical tendencies, and it would be equally impossible to summarise their manifold manifestations. History and historical documentation were restlessly cultivated by Muratori, the number and importance of whose works is amazing : collection of documents, twenty-eight folio volumes of medieval chronicles (*Rerum Italicarum scriptores*), *Antichità estensi*, *Annali d'Italia* up to 1749. The Veronese S. Maffei (1675-1755) extended his activities beyond the Middle Ages and to creative literature ; but his greatest achievements were his *Verona illustrata* and some of his paleographical essays. With them must be mentioned G. Tiraboschi, whose history of Italian literature is still valuable despite lack of critical insight. Solitary and misunderstood, G. B. Vico absorbed Latin scholarship, refuted the philosophy of Descartes, and built up a theory of history (*Principî di una scienza nuova*), partly based on linguistic and literary considerations, that was to have a sweeping influence at the end of the eighteenth century and again at the end of the nineteenth. In the days of triumphing "Reason and Reasonableness," this gloomy book of Vico's, difficult to read owing to its tortured conciseness, and difficult to understand, was an untimely apparition. It rises up as a mountain enshrouded in mist which is rent by sudden flashes.

In Naples, where economics, legal and philosophical studies were actively pursued by A. Genovesi, F. Galiani, G. Filangeri and M. Pagano, another lawyer, Pietro Giannone, in his *Storia del Regno di Napoli*, so openly attacked ecclesiastical privilege as to draw upon himself the attention of the Inquisition, in whose hands he landed some thirteen years later (1736), thanks to the offices of a minister of Sardinia. In other parts of Italy there existed a similar activity, particularly in Milan where a few young noblemen attempted to spread the ideas of the French encyclopædists by issuing a periodical (*Il Caffè*, 1764-66) as the mouthpiece of their *Accademia dei pugni*. Among them were the economist and historian, Pietro Verri (1729-97), who later took a great part in the reform of the financial administration of Lombardy, his brother Alessandro, a gifted man of letters and an admirer of the English poetry of the tombs, Cesare Beccaria (1738-94), the penetrating author of *Dei delitti e delle pene* (1764), in which capital punishment, torture and prison administration were effectively attacked.

These young men assailed tradition in all its forms, and advocated novelty of any kind ; modern literatures were to be studied instead of the classics, and the Italian language was to be rendered more pliable by the wholesale introduction of Gallic forms and words. Thus the *Caffè* provided an interesting contrast with the many literary periodicals of the age which all had a strictly traditional character ; and it can be only paralleled by the purely literary periodical edited by Baretti, *La Frusta letteraria* (1763-64). Apart from the great treatises of Muratori and Gravina, criticism had been brought to the fore, since the very beginning of the century, when Count Orsi edited a collective volume of replies to the French strictures on Italian literature, calling forth many attempts at the solution of the critical problem of literature, some urging good taste as a criterion and others striking out on less hackneyed lines. Aesthetics were frequently dealt with by the many essayists of the period. Among them was the fashionable man of letters, Francesco Algarotti (1712-64), as welcome in France, in England, Germany and Russia as he was in Italy, and as ready to write about philosophy, history and economics as he was to write on art, literature and politics. The Jesuit Bettinelli (1718-1808), an admirer of Voltaire, a satirical poet, was the author of *Lettere virgiliane* (1757), in which he denounced the evils of imitation and even criticised Dante ;

thus giving rise to a welcome reaction. Dante's defenders were led by Gasparo Gozzi (1713-86), a profuse essayist and journalist, the editor of the *Osservatore* (based on Addison's *Spectator*) and of the *Gazzetta Veneta* in which contemporary models and manners are severely censured. Gozzi has his counterpart in a Piedmontese Giuseppe Baretti (1719-89) who, during his first stay in London (1751-60), became a close friend of Dr. Johnson, and later edited in Italy a periodical (*La Frusta letteraria*) in which a less rigid classicism and the study of modern literatures were advocated in very spirited and occasionally unjust articles. Having re-turned to England in 1765, he wrote a lively pamphlet against Voltaire's strictures on Shakespeare. Baretti urged the use of a simpler prose style, and in this respect he agreed with Gozzi, Verri and Beccaria, though each differed in his conception of what this simple style should be ; the close adherence to the Italian classics preached by the Crusca Academy had never been so spiritedly attacked, for it was argued that it was impossible to find in old Tuscan authors appropriate words to express the new ideas of the epoch. This discussion suggested to Melchiorre Cesarotti (1730-1808), the translator of Homer's *Odyssey* and of Ossian's poems, a theory (*Saggio sulla filosofia delle lingue*) which struck a reasonable compromise between freedom and tradition, and succeeded in enlivening the discussion on the nature of language. These few remarks must suffice to show both the energy and the inconclusiveness of the reforming attempts in all departments of literature. Vico towered too high above the general reach to be properly understood, Metastasio was too closely tied to musical expression, and perhaps too easy-going, to echo the real problems of his period ; both he and Goldoni appeared to concentrate their efforts upon the technical improvement of a literary form, rather than upon making that form a vehicle for the expression of deeply felt human sentiments. Later reformers aimed higher. Both Parini and Alfieri were conscious of fighting for loftier than purely literary objects, and they have been justly considered to open out a new age in Italian literature.

Giuseppe Parini (1729-99), peasant born and forced by poverty to take Holy Orders, loved classical poetry and was especially fond of Horace ; thanks to a little volume of odes, he was elected to the Arcadian Accademia dei Trasformati in 1752. The fashionable poets of the age were cunning craftsmen who knew how to temper classical tradition with contemporary sentiment and voluptuousness ; there were legions of them, but among them Bertola, Vittorelli, Mazza and Fantoni (1755-1807) are the most deservingly praised. Here and there, in Fantoni's lyrics for instance, there is heard an echo of the problems of the day, but in general the tone is serenely artificial ; on the contrary Parini made his lyrics the means for the expression of a lofty idealism.   His odes after 1756 dealt with social problems, fearlessly attacking privilege and prejudice with the same courage with which the effete profligacy of the Lombard aristocracy was chastised by him in his satirical poem, *Il giorno*.   There had been other satirical poems in these years ; in Milan itself a friend of Parini, the Abbate G. C. Passeroni (1713-1803), had mildly criticised the vices of his day in his long poem *Cicerone ;* Gozzi had composed satires on the model of Horace, but Parini's work stands out as unique in its high-minded forcefulness and artistic polish.   Only minor weaknesses in Parini's character, and his tendency to pedantry, seem to have prevented this sterling moralist from producing a masterpiece.   In externals the *Giorno* was naturally much imitated, particularly by those who tried to ally satire with the fable in the manner of the French La Fontaine, such as T. Crudeli, Passeroni and G. Casti (1724-1803), a profuse and unclean writer who also composed a long semi-satirical poem (*Animali parlanti*), and a satirical presentation of the court of Catherine II of Russia (*Poema tartaro*).   In the circle of Parini there was also Lorenzo Mascheroni (1750-1800), a mathematician who described his scientific laboratories at the University of Pavia in a poem (*Invito a Lesbia Cidonia*), in which the poet is so evidently moved by the mystery of science as to touch greatness.

   Alfieri, as well as Parini, depended on his moral convictions for his literary success.   Parini had shown his moral integrity amid corruption and temptation ; Alfieri sacrificed his own position rather than forego the freedom of his movements.   But otherwise it would be difficult to imagine two men more dissimilar from one another.   Parini was learned, calm and saw perfection in moderation ; Alfieri was impulsive, impetuous and morbid.   He was the scion of a noble family, an orphan in early age, and had been trained as an officer, being free to do his own will from the age of fourteen.   He was fond of fleet-footed horses, of women and travel ; between 1766 and 1772 (he was born in 1749), he rushed through the best part of western Europe, always caring for his horses, often falling in love, sometimes fighting duels ; but, despite this turbulent mode of life, he came into touch with notable foreigners and favourably impressed them.   When he returned to Turin, he became the leading spirit in a semi-literary society.   He was then more familiar with French than with Italian, but he soon learned to consider himself an Italian

and to deprecate his French education, and he even tried his
hand at an Italian tragedy. He said himself that he decided
to dedicate his life to the writing of tragedies because this literary
form had been less successfully cultivated in Italy. Neither
this plan nor its cause was original, for P. J. Martelli had previously tried to import into Italian the tragic manner of France ;
Gravina had endeavoured to illustrate his dramatic theory by
most infelicitous plays ; the archæologist Maffei had successfully constructed a tragedy (*Merope*, 1712) as the outcome of a
discussion on dramatic theory ; and a learned friend of philosophy
and philosophers, Antonio Conti (1677-1749), had imitated
Corneille, though he was among the first Italians who read and
admired Shakespeare. And there were many others who aspired
to the laurels of tragic writers : Gozzi, Bettinelli, Varano and
the Jesuit writers. At any rate Alfieri himself later called this
first work of his, *Cleopatraccia*, though he admits that this partly
autobiographical play was successfully performed at Turin in
1775. This success altered the whole course of his life. He felt
he could do better, and that he must fit himself to do better by
assiduous study ; he cut himself adrift from society, from love and
even horses, gave up most of his property to his sister in order to
be free to live elsewhere than in Piedmont, and subjected himself
to the hard discipline of continuous study. His creed was simple
enough : liberty is the source of all good ; tyranny the source
of all evil ; poetry and the arts can only thrive in a free country,
for tyrants must persecute virtue ; and the majority of his
tragedies represent this contrast.

The French Revolution was greeted by Alfieri with unmeasured
enthusiasm ; but the excesses to which it led, and the personal
inconvenience and losses which he suffered through it, caused
a return of his original loathing of all things French, and he was
inspired to write a series of violent invectives against France
(*Il Misogallo*). He hated the French, but he accepted their
dramatic theory. His tragedies combined an uncompromising love
of political freedom (a subject with which he also dealt in two
long essays, *Del principe e delle lettere* and *Della tirannide*) with
the most rigid adherence to the dramatic theory of Voltaire,
observing the unities, excluding love from his plays and everything except the crudest presentation of the essential outlines
of his characters ; and all this he clothed in as bare and concise a
language, and as rugged a versification as could possibly be devised.
He trained himself to this art by rigid self-discipline and thus
no doubt impaired his dramatic possibilities, for, judging from
his admirable autobiography (*Vita di se stesso*), which may be

considered a dramatic, if intentionally sincere, presentation of
his own life, he would by nature appear to have been better
suited to a freer dramatic form.   But he did succeed in arousing
political passions among Italians, and he evinced a vigour in
the ruggedness of his verse that was new to his age.   *Saul*, the
chief tragedy in which the contrast between tyranny and liberty
is not exploited, is by far his best work ; the gloom of the aged
king, and his struggle against jealousy and against forebodings
of evil, are poetically depicted.   Among his other works—comedies,
satires and lyrics—the lyrics, many of which contain interesting
self revelations, are the most significant.   But he wished to be
considered as a playwright, and he certainly exercised a great
influence as a dramatist, although classical tragedy had then to
face the competition of middle class drama and of the early
Romanticist tragedies of A. Verri and G. Pindemonte and others
who dared to violate the unities.

The wars consequent upon the French Revolution broke down
all boundaries and facilitated the literary intercourse between
nations.   From the later eighteenth century a considerable attention had been paid in Italy to English poetry of the tomb,
to Ossian, Shakespeare, Milton and Pope, to French encyclopædists, to Molière, Corneille, Boileau and Voltaire, to German
idyllic and ballad poets, and to English novelists.   The results
of this interest are apparent in Ippolito Pindemonte's (1753-
1828) elegies and in Alessandro Verri's *Notti romane ;* while
Cesarotti, by his able translation, familiarised his contemporaries
with Ossianic poetry.   Vincenzo Monti, the most celebrated poet
of the Napoleonic period, echoed every one of these influences.
Born in 1754, he began his career as a follower of Arcadia, Dante
and Tasso, echoed Goethe and Young, and then responded to
the political and classical stimulus of the Directoire and imperial
periods.   His first tragedies were based on Alfieri (*Aristodemo*,
Galeotto Manfredi) ; he shows the influence of Shakespeare in his
later *Caio Gracco*.   He imitated Dante in the *Bassvilliana* (1793),
the poem of the Roman reaction against the Revolution.   Converted to the Revolution and passing to Milan under the French
rule, he rebuked its excesses (*Mascheroniana*), wrote excellent republican lyrics (*Per il congresso d'Udine, Il Congresso Cisalpino*),
and sang the praises of Napoleon in *Il bardo della Selva Nera*,
just as in later poems he welcomed the Austrian return.   He
changed political opinions as readily as literary models, and in
consequence he has been taxed with political fickleness and uncertainty of taste ; these charges are not really justified, for
Monti was, when writing, completely sincere, however contra-

dictory his successive opinions and discordant his different styles. It is significant, as showing his extraordinary pliability, that he translated with almost equal success two poems so different as Homer's *Iliad* and Voltaire's *Pucelle d'Orleans.* In later life he gave much attention to language and produced a witty and learned criticism of the dictionary of the Crusca Academy, as well as assailing the new romantic movement in his *Sermone su la Mitologia* (1825).

There stepped suddenly forward among these poets a young man of mixed Venetian and Greek parentage, Ugo (Niccolò) Foscolo (1778-1827). He was poor and proud of his poverty, ambitious, sensitive, pleasure-loving, as ardent as he was fickle in his loves, but, throughout a life in which there are events that had better be forgotten, he never was disloyal to poetry and literature, and never compromised with his duties as a citizen. He was born in 1778 at Zante, and he went to Venice in 1792 where he read feverishly and soon began to write and to love with little restraint. A lover of liberty, he came to the fore as a passionate partisan of democracy ; when Napoleon sold Venice to Austria, Foscolo's indignation knew no bounds ; he fought in the Italian army raised by the French, met Parini, Alfieri and Monti, as he had already met Cesarotti, loved and was loved ; and the story of these years, of his unhappy attachments and of the loss of his country, is portrayed in a repeatedly revised novel, *Le ultime lettere di Jacopo Ortis* (1799-1802), in which the hero ends by committing suicide. Foscolo did not commit suicide and conquered his sorrow ; he wrote lyrics of a Grecian perfection of form, a learned translation and commentary to Catullus (*Chioma di Berenice*), and excellent essays on the works of an Italian strategist. While in camp at Boulogne with the expeditionary army against England (1804-06), he translated Sterne's *Sentimental Journey*, possibly with the guidance of an English lady, and when he returned to Italy he composed a brief poem, *I sepolcri*, that is considered his masterpiece. The greatness of Italy's past inspired him to hopefulness, and he expressed this hopefulness with a magnificent rhetorical sweep and with consummate crafts-manship. His later fragmentary *Grazie* failed to rise to such heights of inspiration. His brief tenure of a professorship at Pavia provided the occasion for his early literary essays (*Origine e ufficio della letteratura*), and he also wrote three tragedies (*Tieste*, 1797, *Aiace*, 1811, and *Ricciarda*, 1813). When the Austrians returned to Italy, his position became difficult ; he sought a refuge in Switzerland in 1815 and thence passed, a year later, to England, where he died in 1827, after having enjoyed lavish hospitality and endured much hardship, written works on history and literature besides excellent articles for English reviews, and squandered the small patrimony of his illegitimate daughter.

Foscolo had scarcely left Italy, when the voices of two poets greater than he began to be heard. The period had been fertile in occasional poets—notably the satirical Carlo Porta (d. 1821), who wrote in the Milanese dialect—and in historical works, beginning with the *Saggio storico sulla rivoluzione di Napoli* (1801) of Vincenzo Cuoco. The eloquent and honest C. Botta (1766-1837) continued the history of Guicciardini until 1789, wrote a *Storia d'Italia*, 1789-1814, and a *Storia della guerra d'indipendenza degli Stati Uniti d'America* in a sonorous and effective prose ; more laboured and uneven was the manner of the high-minded general, Pietro Colletta (1775-1831), in his *Storia del Reame di Napoli* (1734-1825). A profound investigator of documents and a man endowed with the true historical instinct was Carlo Troya (1784-1858), the author of the *Storia d'Italia nel medio evo* and *Del veltro allegorico di Dante ;* Cesare Balbo (1789-1853) was straightforward, and M. Amari (1806-89) was more materially accurate (*Storia del Vespro Siciliano ; Storia dei Musulmani in Sicilia*). All endeavoured to react against the looseness of style of eighteenth-century writers, and some of them seemed to sympathise with P. Giordani (1774-1848) and his friends, who once again were leading a crusade against recent innovations in language and style. The question of the language had been revived by Monti and had brought into prominence Monti's son-in-law, G. Perticari, the narrow-minded A. Cesari, and Giordani himself, an ardent politician who had been divested of his ecclesiastical orders and had become a brilliant essayist. It was granted to him to be the first man of letters who befriended Leopardi.

Giacomo Leopardi (1798-1837), a precocious scion of a noble and impoverished family, in the course of his unceasing studies impaired his health, his good looks and his chances of happiness. He became a recluse because he pined for intellectual companionship, a morbid dreamer because he lacked normal intercourse with people of his own age, and a despairing pessimist because he saw happiness only in beautiful dreams and only sorrow in the bleak realities of nature. And from his shy seclusion he sent forth letters and poems like anguished cries for help. One of these letters Giordani answered, and a little later he visited Leopardi in his dreary house at Recanati. When Leopardi at last succeeded in going to Rome, he was disappointed in his excessive hope of intellectual companionship. And the same disappointment he

experienced in Milan, Bologna, Florence and Pisa ; everywhere
he suffered in the body and the spirit ; at one time his mind
was so oppressed that for over four years even the relief of writing
in verse was denied him. His later years were passed partly
in Florence and partly in Naples. He only wrote some forty
lyrics, forming a comparatively slim volume of *Canti ;* only two
of these, among the earliest and the least perfect, deal with those
patriotic sentiments which seemed mainly to inspire the literature
of the age, but the quality of his poetry is such that his contemporaries did not hesitate in placing him among the greatest poets
of the Italian language, a judgment that has been amply confirmed by posterity. Leopardi had gradually come to consider
nature as hostile to mankind, and happiness as unattainable.
His opinions cannot be briefly discussed ; it must suffice to say
that Leopardi's outlook, if always gloomy, varied considerably.
During his saddest years, between 1824 and 1828, when the gift
of song was withheld from him, he composed the *Operetti morali*,
a series of ironical and bitter dialogues, written in a crystal clear
prose and stripping bare the pet illusions in which men are wont
to enshroud the harsh realities of life.

During Leopardi's stay at Florence, G. Vieusseux, the founder
and editor of a famous review (*Antologia*), arranged for a meeting
between him and Manzoni. The two poets did not take kindly
to one another, owing partly to their shyness and partly to their
contrasting beliefs. By then Manzoni was already famous. He
was born of a noble family in 1785, his maternal grandfather
being Cesare Beccaria. As a youth he had imitated Monti,
and later Parini and Gozzi (*Sermoni*) ; it was only in a poem
written on the death of Carlo Imbonati (1806), that Manzoni
first attained literary individuality. The unadorned sincerity
of his inspiration struck Foscolo with admiration. Meanwhile
Manzoni had followed his mother to Paris and for a time lived in
close familiarity with French illuminists. But, following upon
his marriage in 1808 and upon his wife's conversion to Roman
Catholicism, he returned himself to the creed in which he had
been educated, and then decided to write twelve (of which he
only completed five) hymns on sacred subjects, among which
the *Pentecoste* is the finest. A shy, reticent man, if unswerving
in his moral courage, Manzoni took no open part in political
agitation, and showed a restraint as great as his logical power
in literary and religious discussions. Just at this time a letter
of Madame de Staël had started in Milan a discussion about
Romanticism ; its champions blaming the use of mythological
imagery, and urging the necessity of bringing literature within

the comprehension of the people. The polemic became very heated, for Romanticism had become in Italy an aspect of political liberalism. Its principal upholders were G. Berchet (1783-1851), L. Di Breme (1781-1820), Silvio Pellico (1789-1854), and others, who contributed to a periodical called *Il Conciliatore*. The connexion between liberalism and romanticism was revealed when, in 1820, the Austrian police arrested several of the contributors of this journal, Pellico among them, who, after his release in 1830, wrote a touching account of his life in prison (*Le mie prigioni*) ; others, as Berchet, went into exile. Manzoni, who had never identified himself with this group, remained unmolested. Meanwhile he had composed an inspired lyric on the death of Napoleon (1821) and two historical tragedies, carefully studying and reproducing the historical background, but almost wantonly violating all the unities. Neither *Carmagnola* (1820) nor *Adelchi* (1822) possesses real dramatic qualities ; they contain, however, some poetical scenes and three fine choruses, two of which unmistakably reveal Manzoni's patriotic feeling. At the same time (1821-23) he was at work on an historical novel which he so unweariedly revised that it appeared under the title *I promessi sposi* only in June, 1827. He had excellently reproduced the social conditions of the seventeenth century, but felt that his style lacked the vivacity of the spoken idiom owing to his habit of using the Milanese dialect in conversation, and he subjected his work to the most painstaking revision, so that the definitive edition was only published serially between 1840 and 1842 Its success was immediate. A whole array of perfectly drawn characters, well balanced, a simple story, leisurely but telling descriptions, and withal a perfect unity of conception and a profoundly Christian inspiration could not but impress the readers of this, one of the finest historical novels in any language. Strange to say, Manzoni soon became convinced that the admixture of history and imagination is not conducive to good results ; he wrote no other novels, and indeed wrote very little after 1840 apart from philosophical and critical essays and several articles on the Italian language, in which he successfully advocated the literary use of the Tuscan dialect. He died in 1873.

Though Manzoni abstained from writing more novels, his success, and the earlier success of Sir Walter Scott's novels, stimulated many Italians to enter this field. T. Grossi's *Marco Visconti* 1834, Massimo D'Azeglio's *Ettore Fieramosca*, 1833, and *Niccolò de' Lapi*, 1841, and Guerrazzi's *Assedio di Firenze*, 1836, may be recorded as the most notable works of this kind. Grossi closely imitated Manzoni, but though he succeeded in composing a readable novel, he was probably well advised in giving up literature for the practice of the law. D'Azeglio (1798-1866) showed as a writer the same grasp and facility that he evinced in painting and politics. The blunt directness of his style prepared the reader for the moving realism of his political pamphlet, *Gli ultimi casi di Romagna*, and for the discursive high-mindedness of his autobiography (*I miei ricordi*). Guerrazzi (1804-73), in this as well as in his other works, was eloquently patriotic, but he lacked power of characterisation ; he failed as a novelist just as he failed as a political leader in 1848-49.

Between 1821 and 1860, and particularly between 1830 and 1849, the new Italy was in the labour of birth. A universal genius such as Leopardi or a Christian gentleman such as Manzoni could keep aloof from the immediate suggestions of politics ; but most authors of this period must be principally considered as direct or indirect exponents of political aspirations and agitations. Of course there were exceptions, such as Pellico after his release, or C. Cantú (1804-95), a historian who dared single-handed to compile a universal history of the world, and wrote many useful monographs. Other writers, despite sentimental vagaries, were generally inspired by political feeling, as the poets A. Fusinato and L. Carrer. More notable was the Dalmatian, Niccolò Tommaseo (1802-74), well read in the classics and in Slav literature, who showed himself a penetrating critic of Dante, an inspired if occasionally turbid poet, a brilliant essayist, and an excellent lexicographer. He eked out a scant living by his literary exertions, but, though he had suffered in Austrian dungeons and had played an important part in Venice in 1849, he steadily refused every offer of assistance from the government. With him may be mentioned Giuseppe Mazzini, who gave promise in his youth to attain literary prominence, but later devoted himself solely to political agitation. The tragic stage was held by the Tuscan G. B. Niccolini (1782-1861). He passed from the imitation of Alfieri to that of Shakespeare, but never altered his political views or abated his patriotic feeling. Of all his plays the best is *Arnaldo da Brescia*, the least suitable for the stage, though much praised for its poetical merits.

Several of the most famous writers of the age were mainly inspired by politics, as Giuseppe Giusti (1809-50), who was gifted with a ready wit and a happy turn of verse ; after some experiments, he took to satirising in a popular way the vices of the political world and particular events and individuals ; his poems, which he composed almost impromptu, circulated in manuscript, for, of course, they could not be printed, and were greedily read ;

but few among his poems rise above the immediate contingencies and show the real possibilities with which Giusti was endowed ; ill-health, verbal facility, a certain carelessness prevented him from reaching as high a goal as his gifts would have allowed him to attain. But, even so, his works challenged comparison with other patriotic poets, such as the inspired Berchet, Gabriele Rossetti, P. Giannone, the lively A. Poerio, and the young Mameli, who died during the siege of Rome in 1849. Also the work of the philosopher V. Gioberti (1801-52) was mainly political. Owing to his liberal sympathies, he left Turin in 1833 and earned a modest living by teaching in Brussels. In 1843 he brought out a long treatise, *Primato morale e civile degli Italiani*, claiming Italy's right to independence on the ground of her past greatness, and planning a confederation of Italian states under the presidency of the pope and the protection of the Piedmontese army. His eloquence and his positive assertion of the birthright of Italians rendered his work most popular, thanks also to the almost contemporary appearance of D'Azeglio's *Ultimi casi di Romagna* and Balbo's *Speranze d'Italia*. In fact, Gioberti's treatise was considered a sort of sacred book during the Risorgimento. The events of 1848-49, in which Gioberti took part as premier in the Piedmontese government, showed that his plan was not practical, and, having returned to Belgium, he rapidly composed another treatise, the *Rinnovamento civile d'Italia* (1851), in which he prophetically advocated the unification of Italy under the rule of Vittorio Emanuele II and the leadership of Cavour.

The painful disillusionment of 1849 was not without its effect upon literature ; the revolutionary period was over ; it was generally realised that only careful preparation and planning could bring about success ; and many felt utterly discouraged and despondent. Despondency found expression in lachrymose sentimentality, such as was shown by Giovanni Prati (1814-84) in his numerous poems ; he lacked power of thought and grip, but the melodious facility and sincerity of his lines won him great praise. As sentimental, but less gifted, was Aleardo Aleardi (1812-78), and more romantic than either of them was Emilio Praga (1839-75), with whom must be mentioned, for both belonged to a small and noisy Milanese group, Giuseppe Rovani (1818-74), a journalist and the author of some historical novels which met with a temporary success. There was no counterpart in Venetia to this group, but in Vicenza and in Padua a learned and pious priest, Giacomo Zanella (1820-88), tried, according to his lights, to reconcile science with Christianity and to sing in honest verse the joys of scientific knowledge as he conceived them ; and Ippolito Nievo (1831-61), a young man of Padua who had been brought up in Friuli, enriched Italian literature with the finest historical novel since Manzoni's (*Confessioni di un Italiano*) ; it is a pseudo-autobiography of an old man written by a man of twenty-six, but it has unity, grip, power of characterisation and real poetic feeling, despite lack of polish due to the author's untimely death. Nievo fought with Garibaldi in Sicily, and was drowned in 1861, his death being a grievous loss to Italian literature.

After 1849 the course of political events was mainly controlled by Cavour, whose orderly and audacious leadership seemed to have a sobering effect on the Italian minds in general. Drama with Paolo Ferrari (1822-89) reached a notable perfection by the blend of able characterisation and careful reconstruction of the historical background ; and a little later, after 1860, Ferrari followed the French fashion and wrote several dramas which were intended to prove particular social or moral theories. Romanticism was slowly developing into positivism and realism ; and it had its critics. Francesco De Sanctis (1817-83), a Neapolitan who had lived as an exile in Switzerland and taught Italian literature at the University of Zürich, returning to Naples, wrote a series of critical works of outstanding merit. He possessed a vast store of information and sufficient penetration to bridge over gaps, while his philosophical training enabled him to build up for himself a theory as to the object and origin of good literature. Connecting literature with its political environment and creative genius with moral character, he regarded the study of Italian literature as the means of preaching the duty of acquiring and developing civic virtues which alone could save the country and originate great works of art. These views he expounded in his essays and in his history of Italian literature, a unique piece of work lit up by real flashes of genius. Only few among his pupils were at the time able to appreciate the import of his criticism, but his influence became paramount at the end of the century. For the time being the leadership was in other hands. During the early fifties, a group of young men tried in Tuscany to create a stir by their wholesale attack on the prevailing tendencies, and their outspoken and well-reasoned strictures on current literature. They called themselves " pedants," and claimed to be the champions of traditional classicism. Their leader was Giosuè Carducci, who quickly became known as a poet, and whose works will be more properly dealt with in a subsequent chapter. What Muratori, Maffei, Tiraboschi and other scholars of the eighteenth century had each endeavoured to accomplish single-handed, became the object during the following century, under German inspiration, of a co-operative effort. Its result was extreme specialisation ; the painstaking investigation of obscure points, with a certain indifference as to their bearing upon literature ; information for information's sake, without any accompanying attempt at co-ordinating the partial results. The leaders of this school (D'Ancona, Bartoli, Monaci, etc.) were scholars of real gifts, and all their followers, whatever their merit, had in common with them an amazing industry and a truly heroic spirit of self-sacrifice. Their monographs were published in books and, more often, in the learned and academical reviews that were then started or revived in great numbers. It was as if the country, having achieved political unity, wished to consolidate her position. No more dreams, but facts ; no more hopes for the future, if the present was disappointing, but records of the past. Just when the novel and drama were moving towards realism, and science was beginning to come to the fore, criticism strove to be factual and scientific. This effort entailed losses, but also permitted and encouraged a rapid and effective work of research which was to bear fruit a little later.

BIBLIOGRAPHY TO CHAPTER VII

GENERAL WORKS

In the " Storia letteraria d'Italia " (Milan) : A. Belloni, *Il Seicento* (2nd ed., 1929) ; G. Natali, *Il Settecento* (1929) ; G. Mazzoni, *L'Ottocento* (1913).

(a) LITERATURE OF THE SEICENTO :

B. Croce, *Saggi sulla letteratura italiana del Seicento* (Bari, 1911) ; *Storia della età barocca in Italia* (Bari, 1929) ; *Nuovi saggi sulla letteratura italiana del Seicento* (Bari, 1931).

V. di Tocco, *Ideali d'indipendenza in Italia durante la preponderanza spagnuola*. Messina, 1926.

V. Spampanato, *Vita di Giordano Bruno*. Messina, 1921.

G. Gentile, *Giordano Bruno e il pensiero del Rinascimento*. Florence, 1925.

C. Dentice di Accadia, *Tommaso Campanella* (Florence, 1921) ; Tommaso Campanella, *Poesie*, ed. Gentile (Bari, 1915) ; *Lettere*, ed. Spampanato (Bari, 1927) ; *Città del Sole*, ed. G. Paladino (Naples, 1920) ; R. De Mattei, *La politica di Campanella* (Rome, 1928).

Traiano Boccalini, *I ragguagli di Parnaso*, ed. G. Rua (Bari, 1912).

G. B. Marino, *Poesie varie*, ed. Croce (Bari, 1913) ; *Lirici Marinisti*, ed. Croce (Bari, 1911).

N. Vaccalluzzo, *Galileo Galilei, vita ed opere*. Milan, 1912.

R. Caverni, *Storia del metodo sperimentale in Italia*. Florence, 1891-95.

G. Basile, *The Pentamerone*, trans. N. M. Penzer. London, 1932.

(b) From Beginning of Eighteenth Century to 1870:

Vernon Lee, *Studies in the Eighteenth Century*. London, 1880.

P. Monnier, *Venice in the Eighteenth Century*. English trans. London, 1910.

G. Maugain, *L'évolution intellectuelle de l'Italie de 1657 à 1750*. Paris, 1909.

J. G. Robertson, *Studies in the Genesis of Romantic Theory in the Eighteenth Century*. Cambridge, 1923.

G. Toffanin, *L'eredità del Rinascimento in Arcadia*. Bologna, 1923.

H. C. Chatfield Taylor, *Goldoni : a Biography*. New York, 1913.

J. Spencer Kennard, *Goldoni and the Venice of his Time*. New York, 1920.

L. Collinson Morley, *G. Baretti and His Friends*. London, 1909.

G. Carducci, *Studi su Giuseppe Parini* (Opere, Vols. XIII, XIV). Bologna, 1907.

L. Valmaggi, *I cicisbei*. Turin, 1927.

E. Bertana, *Saggi pariniani*. Aquila, 1926.

E. Bellorini, *La vita e le opere di G. Parini*. Leghorn, 1918.

D. Petrini, *La poesia e l'arte di G. Parini*. Bari, 1929.

G. Megaro, *V. Alfieri, Forerunner of Italian Nationalism*. New York, 1930.

E. Bertana, *V. Alfieri studiato nella vita, nel pensiero e nell'arte*. Turin, 1904.

M. Porena, *V. Alfieri e la tragedia*. Milan, 1904.

P. Hazard, *La révolution française et les lettres italiennes, 1789-1815*. Paris, 1910.

J. Luchaire, *Essai sur l'évolution intellectuelle de l'Italie de 1815 à 1830*. Paris, 1906.

G. Natali, *Idee, costumi, uomini del settecento* (Turin, 1916) ; *Cultura e poesia in Italia nell' età napoleonica* (Turin, 1930).

E. Bevilacqua, *Vincenzo Monti : la vita, l'opera, i tempi*. Florence, 1928.

C. Antona Traversi e A. Ottolini, *Ugo Foscolo*. Milan, 1918.

G. Chiarini, *Vita di U. Foscolo*. Florence, 1910.

E. Donadoni, *U. Foscolo, pensatore, critico e poeta*. Palermo, 1910.

G. L. Bickersteth, *The Poems of Leopardi*. Cambridge, 1923.

F. De Sanctis, *Studio su G. Leopardi*. Naples, 1885 ; and later ed.

A. Zottoli, *Leopardi : storia di un' anima*. Bari, 1927.

B. Croce, *A. Manzoni : saggi*. Bari, 1930.

A. Momigliano, *A. Manzoni : la vita ; le opere*. Messina, 1915 and 1919.

L. Russo, *De Sanctis e la cultura napoletana*. Venice, 1929.

G. A. Borgese, *Storia della critica romantica in Italia*, 2nd ed. Milan, 1923.

B. Croce, *La letteratura della nuova Italia*, 2nd ed. Bari, 1921.

CHAPTER VIII

ITALIAN ARCHITECTURE AND SCULPTURE

ITALIAN art has as its immediate background early Christian art in Italy, centred in Rome and directly descended from Roman art. To this day, the type of the early Christian basilica, which set the main lines of the scheme of the church architecture of Europe, can, in spite of ravages and excrescences, due to the intervening centuries, best be studied in Rome— say at San Paolo fuori le mura or Santa Maria Maggiore ; while it is in Rome, too, that we find the most numerous surviving examples both of early Christian sculpture in the round and of the sarcophagi with bas-reliefs, which form the most important province of early Christian sculpture. Ravenna too, becoming in 402 the capital of the western empire, is an important centre for the student of early Christian art in Italy ; and the influence of Byzantine art soon made itself strongly felt in this city, which indeed, in 539, became the seat of the Exarch or Governor of Italy, appointed by the Byzantine emperor. San Vitale in Ravenna, commenced about 530, is a most remarkable centralised domed building, designed in close conformity with the schemes of archi- tecture prevalent in Byzantium.

Of the Germanic nations which invaded Italy, one which has left extensive traces in the art of that country is that of the Lombards. Coming from Hungary, they in 568 invaded Italy and founded a kingdom which comprised considerable parts of the peninsula : and this Lombard kingdom continued to exist for about two centuries, until, in 774, it was conquered by Charlemagne. The art which developed through the contact between the Lombards and those whom they found inhabiting Italy, is chiefly represented by a number of churches for the adornment of which—as regards both the actual structure and the furniture—it became customary to employ bas-reliefs in stone. Specimens of this art are still to be found in great numbers in Italy, and the manner in which they are executed— favouring designs of strapwork character—continued to be practised even after the fall of the Lombard kingdom : just as it penetrated into parts of Italy which never politically belonged to that monarchy, as for instance, Rome. The little town of Cividale in north-eastern Italy may be singled out as a place where you can obtain a particularly clear idea of this form of art.

The Carlovingian era in Italy was not marked by any very intensive architectural activity : as to plastic art, we do possess information, derived from written sources, of a considerable number of statues and bas-reliefs in metal, executed for the churches of Rome in the ninth century ; but, of all this, practically nothing has come down to us.

Once the year 1000 is past, we can, however, speak of a very great increase in building enterprise in Italy, and the history of Italian Romanesque architecture comprises a number of churches of great and varied interest, notably when the twelfth century is reached. There is, for one thing, the group of great vaulted churches in various cities of the Lombard plain—say San Zeno at Verona, the cathedrals at Modena, Parma, Piacenza, etc. Another important centre is Venice, where the edifice overshadowing everything else is St. Mark's, begun in the ninth century on a longitudinal plan, rebuilt in the eleventh century according to a centralised scheme after the Byzantine fashion. Further south we get to Tuscany, where memories of classical and early Christian art prove more powerful than in the north of the peninsula, and where flat wooden ceilings instead of vaulted ceilings are the rule : while on the exterior a very characteristic effect is obtained through the revetment with striped pattern of white and dark green marble. Pisa, Lucca and Pistoia may be mentioned among the cities where this Tuscan variety of Romanesque architecture may be seen to perfection : but no example surpasses the noble basilica of San Miniato al Monte, overlooking Florence, concerning which Jacob Burckhardt once said that it sums up the whole of Italy's pre-Gothic artistic capacities so brilliantly, that one is almost led to deplore the subsequent importation of the Gothic style from the north. Romanesque architecture in Rome is of little importance ; but the very opposite is true of southern Italy and Sicily, where the blending of many influences—Byzantine, Saracen, Norman—goes to produce results of peculiar interest and artistic fascination.

Of Italian sculpture of the period between the year 1000 and 1100 there is next to nothing to be said : it seems in the main to have been confined to the production of stone bas-reliefs containing patterns of the Lombard type. About the year 1100 the picture, however, changes ; and it is above all in the large

and powerful cities of northern Italy that sculpture begins to
be extensively practised, primarily for the purpose of decorating
the fronts and doorways of the great churches. And it is a
curious fact that, at the very beginning, the history of this north
Italian Romanesque sculpture should be associated with definite
artist's names. The first of these sculptors in order of time are
Master Wiligelmus and Master Nicholas, who are known to have
been engaged, either singly or conjointly, upon a considerable
number of works, between 1097 and 1150. Theirs is an art of
much vigorous narrative power, if still somewhat rude and uncouth : while a development towards greater accomplishment is
seen in the production of Benedetto Antelami of Parma (the second
half of the twelfth century).

The importance of northern Italy in Italian art of this period
is shown not only by the works which the artists of those parts
executed in their native land, but also by the fact that numerous
north Italian sculptors and architects wandered to other parts
of the peninsula and found plenty of employment there. The
district of Como was one which yielded a particularly large
number of these wandering stone-cutters and masons, so much so
that in the thirteenth century the word *Comacino* right down to
the south of Italy had become the regular appellation for a sculptor
or architect whether he hailed from Como or not. One of these
itinerant Lombard sculptors is probably responsible for the very
fine Romanesque bas-reliefs decorating the great porch of St.
Mark's in Venice.

Sculpture, as practised by native Tuscan artists, remained
for a very long time extraordinarily rude and formless. To
the more accomplished north Italian sculptors, Tuscany was
very hospitable ; and the most notable of these early Lombard
sculptors working in Tuscany is undoubtedly one Guido da Como
(*c.* 1200–*c.* 1250), whose excessively stiff bas-reliefs on the pulpit
of the church of San Bartolomeo at Pistoia (1250) by only ten
years antedate the first work of the great Tuscan sculptor
Niccolò Pisano. In southern Italy, work in metal under Byzantine influence, was extensively done, and we still possess
a whole series of large bronze doors, executed for south Italian
churches in the eleventh and twelfth centuries. In stone sculpture
an interesting attempt to revive the traditions of classical art
can be traced in southern Italy during the first half of the thirteenth century, chiefly as a result of the richly gifted Suabian
emperor, Frederick II, who lived a great deal in southern Italy,
where he died in 1250.

Gothic architecture may be said to have been fully developed in northern France, the country of its origin, by the middle of the twelfth century. It took some time in reaching Italy, where its pioneers were French Cistercian monks who, about the year 1200, built a number of fine edifices in central Italy (notably in the province of Sabina). The architecture here exemplified was, however, not so much a transplantation as an actual importation of the French Gothic style; for the most part, however, the system of French Gothic architecture was only adopted in Italy with very considerable modifications. To put it briefly, verticalism, the keynote of French Gothic architecture, has none of the same importance in Italy, where the churches are designed so as to convey a much greater sense of spaciousness; moreover, the windows of the churches were kept much smaller than to the north of the Alps, the church walls thereby offering incomparably greater opportunities for the fresco painter. The propagation of Gothic architecture in Italy was mainly the work of the two great new mendicant Orders, the Franciscans and the Dominicans; and the great central sanctuary of the Franciscan Order, the church of San Francesco at Assisi, is among the earliest examples of Italian Gothic architecture—begun in 1228 and completed in its main portions in 1253. Other early examples of importance take us further north in the peninsula: San Francesco at Bologna, Sant' Antonio in Padua, and Santa Maria Gloriosa dei Frari in Venice, all of them very large churches, built by Franciscans. Surpassing even these in size is Santa Croce, the noble church of the Franciscan Order in Florence, designed by Arnolfo di Cambio and begun in 1294, the nave and transept having an *open* roof; while the more normal, international Gothic usage of vaulted roofs all through is seen in the great Dominican church in the same city, Santa Maria Novella, commenced in 1278 from designs by Fra Sisto and Fra Ristoro. It was also Arnolfo di Cambio who was the first architect of the Duomo of Florence, with which he, however, remained in association only for four years (1296-1300) when death intervened. Building operations proceeded very slowly, and, as to the dome, it was not taken in hand until the dawn of the Renaissance.

Of great Tuscan Gothic churches, mention must not be omitted of the Duomo of Siena, a reconstruction of an older Romanesque edifice; its glorious façade, carried out in red, white and black marble, was designed by Giovanni Pisano, architect-in-chief since 1284. Derived from this is the façade of another great cathedral further south, Orvieto.

The epilogue of Gothic ecclesiastic architecture in Italy is supplied by the magnificent Cathedral of Milan, which was begun in 1386 and in the construction of which foreign, notably German architects took a prominent part. It shows in consequence an affinity to German Gothic architecture which is unusual in an Italian building ; the exterior, with its masses of pinnacles and 2000 statues, produces a superb, almost bewildering effect.

So far, reference has only been made to examples of ecclesiastical Gothic architecture ; but sight must not be lost of the fact that, all over the peninsula, there still exist numerous buildings of a non-ecclesiastical character, dating from this period. The *Palazzo Pubblico*, or Government House, supplied in the different municipalities one of the most important architectural tasks of a lay nature, and in addition there were the private houses, the castles, towers, etc. : the little town of San Gimignano, between Siena and Empoli, is justly famous on account of the faithful picture which it preserves of an Italian city of the time about 1300. In Florence, the Bargello, the Palazzo Vecchio and the Loggia dei Lanzi—begun respectively in 1250, 1298 and 1376— are the principal buildings to be mentioned in this connexion ; whilst Siena is graced—apart from various private palaces—by her incomparable Palazzo Pubblico, built in 1289-1305 of brick and travertine and having one of the finest towers ever designed, the lofty and slender *Torre del Mangia*. In the north, Venice possesses even now a considerable number of fine Gothic palaces, mirroring themselves in her canals : while the Ducal Palace, commenced early in the fourteenth century, is surely one of the most boldly original as well as splendidly successful buildings in the world. Of Gothic castles, Frederick the Suabian's noble and imposing Castel del Monte, overlooking the Apulian country for miles, must be mentioned in a class to itself.

It is customary to begin a new chapter in the history of Italian sculpture with the sculptor Niccolò Pisano ; and it is doubtless true that the art of Niccolò Pisano marks a new departure in the history of sculpture in the province of Tuscany, which, so far as our knowledge goes, was the principal sphere of Niccolò's activity—he is known to have worked also in various adjoining districts of central Italy. But, as a matter of fact, the striking return to the style of Classical art which is the essential characteristic of the early style of Niccolò Pisano had been very largely anticipated in the school of sculptors in the south of Italy which had been called into being by the Emperor Frederick II. It has indeed been supposed, and there is much to be said for the view, that Niccolò Pisano himself originally was a member of this South Italian Classical School. The first

authenticated work by Niccolò Pisano known to us is his famous
pulpit in the Baptistery of Pisa, dating from 1260. In the
sculptures with which this pulpit is adorned, we find the plainest
possible evidence of the study of Classical art ; but the result
is by no means of a purely derivative character, this art has a
severe grandeur all its own.   Niccolò's further evolution took him
well beyond this ; as may be seen from the sculptures executed
by him but a few years later—between 1265 and 1268—with
the assistance of various pupils, for the pulpit of the Cathedral
of Siena.   In these there is much greater flexibility of line and
gentleness of expression : the evidence of an approach to the
general trend of Gothic art.

The greatest Italian sculptor of the time about 1300 was
Niccolò's son, Giovanni Pisano (c. 1245–c. 1315), who collaborated
with his father in the pulpit at Siena.   The works of Giovanni
Pisano are distinguished by a force of dramatic expression, to
which there is no parallel in his father's works ; and the Classical
reminiscences in Giovanni Pisano's work claim but little attention in comparison with the features of style which show his
connexion with the main Gothic movement.   Among his works
his great pulpit in the church of Sant' Andrea at Pistoia, completed in 1301, may perhaps be singled out as the œuvre type ;
it evinces qualities of which the next great exponent in sculpture
was to be Donatello, while in some ways it anticipates the art
of Michelangelo.

All through the fourteenth century, sculpture continued to
be assiduously practised in Tuscany : among the most notable
of these later Gothic sculptors we may single out for mention
Andrea Pisano (a pupil, but no relation, of Giovanni Pisano),
Nino Pisano, and Andrea Orcagna whose masterpiece is the taber-
nacle in Or San Michele in Florence (1359).   In northern Italy,
the school of Venice comes to the fore towards the end of the
fourteenth century, and has left splendid examples of its work
in the reliefs in the corners of the Ducal palace.

The expression " Renaissance," which is one of the most
hard-worked items in the terminology of art history, might form
the basis of an interesting enquiry into the development of
conventional historic labels.   It is first used by Vasari in the
sense of the " rebirth " (rinascita) of the arts in Italy in the
thirteenth century ; but it has by now come to denote, in the
first instance, that movement in art which originated in Italy
at the beginning of the fifteenth century and in the country
of its origin lasted until the latter part of the sixteenth century.   In architecture, this means that the language of artistic

expression, developed by the Gothic style, is in the main discarded, and that the artistic vocabulary of Classical Rome is largely reverted to ; but it is modified so as to serve the needs of changed conditions, and the result bears but the vaguest resemblance to Classical architecture. The Italian Renaissance was essentially a period of creative power, not of pedantic retrospection ; and of any strictly " archæological " reconstructions such as were attempted say in the buildings of nineteenth-century Munich, there is scarcely any trace in the Italy of the period with which we are concerned.

It was Florence which led the way in this new artistic movement ; and at the head of the latter stands the great and imposing figure of Filippo Brunelleschi (1377-1446), a man of very many-sided gifts. Architecture became, however, the principal channel of expression for his genius ; and it is works such as the dome of Florence Cathedral (completed in 1436), the chapel of the Pazzi family in the cloisters of the church of Santa Croce (c. 1430-43), and the reconstruction of the church of San Lorenzo (which he did not live to see completed) that give us the clearest indication of Brunelleschi's aspirations as an architect—revealing as they do a close familiarity with Classical architecture and yet an entirely original, inventive spirit.

Florence of the fifteenth century—the Quattrocento—was primarily a field of operation for the designers of family palaces rather than churches ; and what is undoubtedly the most imposing of the series, the Palazzo Pitti, used to be ascribed to Brunelleschi and may indeed be his work, though for this there is no very early authority. It is of the utmost simplicity in the articulation of the exterior, in which exclusive use is made of stone blocks with rough (rustica) surface and hewn edges—a favourite device in Quattrocento Florence. As other important palaces in Florence of this period may be quoted the Palazzo Medici (now Riccardi), commenced in 1444 by Michelozzo di Bartolomeo (1396-1472), the Palazzo Strozzi designed by the sculptor Benedetto da Maiano (1442-97) and begun in 1489, and the Palazzo Rucellai (1446-51), in which the façade combines a modified rustica treatment with articulation by means of pilasters and other details in strict conformity with the rules governing the " Orders." The idea of this palace was evolved by Leone Battista Alberti (c. 1404-72), one of the greatest figures of the Italian Renaissance, again a universal genius, capable also of a very remarkable literary expression of his views on art. In Florence, the façade of Santa Maria Novella (completed in 1470) is yet another proof of Alberti's highly individual reaction to an architectural task ; but his activity took him to other parts of Italy as well, and that singularly effective architectural fantasy in the classical manner, the " Tempio Malatestiano " (strictly speaking, church of San Francesco) at Rimini is perhaps the most eloquent witness that exists to the extraordinary artistic gifts that were in Leone Battista Alberti.

In Rome, various buildings of great importance were erected after the middle of the century ; we will here only mention Giacomo di Pietrasanta's Palazzo di Venezia (commenced in 1455) and the Cancelleria, which used to be regarded as a work by Bramante, a view which the evidence of contemporary records contradicts. Again, in the mountain fastness of Urbino, the Dalmatian Luciano da Laurana (d. 1479) worked from 1465 onwards as architect to the Ducal Palace, and succeeded in creating the noblest princely residence of the early Renaissance. Nor must a review, howsoever rapid, of fifteenth-century architecture in central Italy, omit to make reference to the noble buildings which Aeneas Sylvius Piccolomini, eventually pope under the name Pius II (1458-64), in an amazingly short time caused to be erected in his native town Pienza, the chief architect in charge being the Florentine master, Bernardo Rossellino.

Turning to northern Italy, we find that in the fifteenth century a Florentine influence certainly penetrated into those parts, which became indeed a field of activity for several architects from central Italy : but a certain conservatism is not to be wondered at in districts which, as we have seen, had architectural traditions of very long standing. In Lombardy, the Ospedale Maggiore at Milan, designed by the Florentine architect Antonio Averlino, called Filarete, and begun in 1456, contains many concessions to Gothic ideas which must have been particularly galling to an architect who held the views on Gothic art which Filarete has expressed in his writings. Later in the century, the façade of the Certosa di Pavia presents an unsurpassed example of richness in decoration on Renaissance lines, carried out by a number of artists, foremost among whom was Giovan Antonio Amadeo, whose association with the work covered the years 1491-99. In Venice, the church of S. Maria dei Miracoli, built by three brothers of the name of Lombardi and completed in 1489, typifies admirably the tendencies current in the architecture of the City of the Lagoons during the Quattrocento ; particularly characteristic is the use of slabs of variegated marble for the purpose of making effective patterns on the walls— a device for which the previous architecture of Venice offered plenty of precedent. Of the Venetian palaces of the early

12

Renaissance, the finest is unquestionably the supremely elegant
Palazzo Vendramin Calerghi on the Grand Canal ; here the
many-windowed, richly colonnaded front denotes a definite departure from the earlier methods just indicated.

The architect who by preference to any other may be regarded as the link between the early and the mature Renaissance
is Donato d'Angelo known as Bramante (1444-1514). He was a
native of Urbino, but, so far as we can trace it, began his career
as an architect in Lombardy, being in 1476 appointed in that
capacity to the court of Ludovico il Moro, Duke of Milan. He
left Milan in 1499 for Rome, and worked there until his death,
busy with various great commissions, most of which he, however,
was unable to carry to completion. Much the most important
task given him was that of designing the new church of St.
Peter's, which had been decided upon by Pope Julius II in 1505.
The plans of Bramante for St. Peter's may be regarded as em-
bodying the ideal solution, in the spirit of his age, of the problem
of the centralised domed building, which haunted the imagination
of so many of the greatest architects of the Renaissance ; and,
through being able to erect the four immense piers supporting
the dome, as well as build the walls of the south transept, he
has left the stamp of his genius indelibly on the edifice, greatly
though his plans were subsequently departed from. Among
Bramante's completed works in Rome we may here single out
for mention the circular *Tempietto* built in 1499-1502 next to the
church of San Pietro in Montorio, since it is a work which, though
small in scale, shows to perfection that sense of harmonious
proportions and power of simple, monumental design, without
insistence on irrelevant detail, which substantiate Bramante's
claim to be regarded as the architect who ushered in the mature
Renaissance.

Of the many other distinguished architects, who were working in Rome at the beginning of the Cinquecento, we must
not omit to mention Baldassare Peruzzi (1481-1536), to whom
Vasari attributes the delightful little palace known as the Villa
Farnesina ; Antonio da Sangallo the younger (1483-1546), the
initial designer (before 1514) of the Palazzo Farnese, the most
impressive of the Roman palaces of the mature Renaissance, of
which we shall have more to say anon ; Raphael too, Bramante's
kinsman, found time in his short life to work as an architect,
and maintained a very close adherence to Bramante's manner.
As to Raphael's great rival, Michelangelo, he only began his
activity as an architect comparatively late in life. In the centre
of this activity stands his work as architect-in-chief of St. Peter's,

from 1547 until his death in 1564.   In contrast to his immediate
predecessors in that office, Michelangelo reverted to the centralised plan of Bramante which he, however, in conformity
with the spirit of the times, considerably simplified ; and he
was able to push the building operations so far forward, that
before his death the wonderful dome—one of the architectural
masterpieces of all time—had been begun according to his designs.
Later, unfortunately, the idea of a centralised building was again
departed from ;   Carlo Maderna designed and completed the
present nave and aisles and also built the fine atrium ;   and not
until 1616 was this new St. Peter's finally consecrated.   Among
Michelangelo's other works as an architect, we may mention
the completion, after Antonio da San Gallo's death (1546), of the
Palazzo Farnese, for which he designed the suberb cornice which
will ever be a *locus classicus* among architects; and the Porta
Pia (1561), a late work in which the tendencies of the Baroque
are already clearly anticipated.

   Two pupils of Bramante practised with much success in
northern Italy : namely Michele Sanmicheli (1484-1559), who
worked chiefly in his native town Verona ; and Jacopo Tatti
called Sansovino (1486-1570), a Florentine who settled at Venice
in 1527.   It was Sansovino who, in 1536, began the construction
of one of the most immediately attractive edifices of the mature
Renaissance, the glorious Libreria which occupies one side of
the Piazzetta in Venice, facing the Ducal Palace : the charming
Loggetta, nestling at the foot of the Campanile of St. Mark's
and rebuilt after its destruction in 1901, is also by Sansovino.
Florence, the city in which the style of the Renaissance had first
been developed, shrinks to comparative insignificance in the world
of Italian architecture during the first half of the sixteenth
century.

   As the first master of the " late " Renaissance it is usual
to regard Jacopo Barozzi (1507-73), usually called Vignola from
his native city near Modena.   The tendency of the late Renaissance architecture is towards an over-increased simplicity and
indeed severity : characteristics which are very patent in Vignola's
works, among which the most important are the castle of the
Farnese family at Caprarola in the Roman Campagna, not far
from Viterbo (1547-59), the Villa di Papa Giulio at Rome (1550-55),
and finally the church of Il Gesù in the same city, commenced
in 1568 and, as the principal church of the new and powerful
Order of the Jesuits, a creation destined to be of the widest
significance in the architectural history of Europe.   A single
lofty nave, with a barrel-vaulted ceiling and rows of chapels,

and a large dome are among the most notable features of this building, the façade of which was designed by Giacomo della Porta (1541-1604). Vignola was an architect of much learning, which, however, did not interfere with his creative power : his book on the " Orders " is still a classic. Giacomo della Porta also designed one of the famous villas in the neighbourhood of Rome, the Villa Aldobrandini at Frascati : the chief example of this category of architecture is, however, the Villa d'Este at Tivoli, built by Pirro Ligorio (c. 1550).

In the history of later Renaissance architecture an important position belongs to Genoa, where a style of magnificent palatial design was practised after the middle of the century : the principal architect's name to be mentioned in this connection is Galeazzo Alessi (1512-72). In the sister maritime republic, the great exponent of the tendencies of the late Renaissance is Andrea Palladio of Vicenza (1508-80), the designer of numerous palaces in his native town and villas in its neighbourhood ; while in Venice he is represented by various churches, among which the Redentore (begun in 1577) is specially notable. The noble, unaffected dignity of Palladio will never cease to elicit admiration ; and he is one of the individual forces in the history of architecture that have had the greatest and most lasting influence—not least in England.

The artist who in the history of Italian sculpture occupies a position corresponding to that held by Brunelleschi in the history of Italian architecture is Donato di Betto Bardi, called Donatello (1386-1466), a personal friend and to some extent a pupil of Brunelleschi's. The latter himself, indeed, came into prominence as a sculptor in the year 1400, when all the sculptors of Italy were invited to compete for the task of executing the pair of bronze doors for the northern gate of the Baptistery of Florence. Each of the competitors was to supply a bas-relief of the Sacrifice of Isaac, and the selecting jury hesitated long between two of the competitors, one being Brunelleschi, the other Lorenzo Ghiberti (1378-1455). It was the latter artist who eventually carried off the prize : and he is certainly a figure of considerable importance in the history of Florentine sculpture of the first half of the Quattrocento. Ghiberti is nothing like as great and original an artist as Donatello : he is a typical transitional artist, standing, so-to-speak, with one foot in each camp. The Gothic methods of design are echoed in his art to the last, but at the same time he assimilates a good deal of the new ideas of realism and study of the antique, and, as for his skill of execution, it is simply amazing. His most remarkable

Bartolomeo Colleoni, set up in a little square in Venice and modelled in 1481. In comparison with Donatello's *Gattamelata*, Verrocchio's statue inevitably strikes one as decidedly lacking in equipoise and harmony : but as a rendering of a Condottiere, loving the hand-to-hand fight for its own sake, the *Colleoni* is certainly unsurpassed in effectiveness.

As to Tuscan Quattrocento sculpture outside Florence, a word must be said of the school of Siena, whence issued Jacopo della Quercia (1367-1438), an important transitional master linking the Gothic period with the Renaissance, and Francesco di Giorgio (1439-1502), a remarkably many-sided artist, whose importance as a factor in the evolution of Italian art we are only beginning to realise. Lucca can claim a sculptor of considerable distinction in Matteo Civitali (1436-1501). Again, Agostino di Duccio (1418-81) was a Florentine with a keen sense of decoration, who is chiefly remembered on account of his work in the Tempio Malatestiano at Rimini and on the front of San Bernardino at Perugia ; while Francesco Laurana of Zara (*c.* 1425–*c.* 1502) found the principal centre for the practice of his charming art in southern Italy, before settling in France (after 1476).

In northern Italy a great deal of sculpture was produced during the Quattrocento. We may here mention among the principal centres immediately to the north of the Apennines Bologna (where the chief master was Niccolò dell' Arca, *c.* 1430-94) and Modena (where Guido Mazzoni, *c.* 1450-1518, practised a style of very vivid realism in his groups of figures in painted terra-cotta). In Lombardy, the Certosa di Pavia provided, as we have seen, ample opportunities for the local sculptors (Giovanni Antonio Amadeo, 1447-1522, the brothers Mantegazza, etc). In Padua, Donatello left behind him a tradition of plastic work in bronze, of which Andrea Riccio (1470-1532) is the chief exponent ; while in Venice, where the transition from the Gothic to the Renaissance style was a very gradual one, the principal names are those of Antonio Rizzo and the various members of the Lombardi family (Pietro, the father, and his sons, Antonio and Tullio). The greatest medallist of the Renaissance, Antonio Pisano, called Pisanello (*c.* 1395–*c.* 1455), was a native of Verona, whose career, however, took him all over the peninsula.

The central figure of Cinquecento sculpture is Michelangelo Buonarroti (1475-1564), with whom Florence splendidly reasserts her leading position in this branch of art. Michelangelo realises the Cinquecento ideal of monumental grandeur more completely in sculpture than anyone else : and through his art there runs a deeply subjective, heroic note, which will ever secure for it

the power profoundly to stir our emotions. The artistic medium
of expression most congenial to him was sculpture, and it was
certainly not a result of his own choice that the work which
both in aim and result is the most important he has left us—
the painted ceiling of the Sistine Chapel—should belong to a
different category of artistic production.

Early in Michelangelo's career come sculptures such as the
the *Pietà* in St. Peter's (1499) and the colossal figure of *David*
now in the Florence Academy (begun in 1501). In 1505 he
was called upon to undertake the task which offered him scope
for the realisation of his innermost aspirations and boldest
dreams—the tomb of Pope Julius II, a magnificent, most elaborately planned structure, which was to be set up in St. Peter's.
Preliminary work on this tomb was undertaken up to 1508,
when Michelangelo was prevailed upon to accept the task of
painting the ceiling of the Sistine Chapel ; and he was unable
to resume the work on the tomb until 1512. By 1516 Michelangelo
had completed three of the statues for the tomb—two figures of
prisoners, allegories of the provinces subjugated by Julius II,
and a statue of *Moses*. Then there came again an interruption
in the work and, after endless delays and difficulties, it was only
brought to a conclusion some thirty years later, on a scale,
comparatively speaking quite insignificant, in the church of
San Pietro in Vincoli. The *Moses* was used for this radically
modified scheme, while the two *Prisoners* are now in the Louvre.
Meanwhile (1524-27 and 1527-30) he had been busy with a pair
of tombs for two members of the Medici family in a mausoleum,
built in accordance with Michelangelo's designs, in communication with the church of San Lorenzo at Florence : these tombs
were also eventually set up on lines very much differing from
the original scheme, but remain nevertheless the completest
existing expression of Michelangelo's genius as a sculptor.

No other sculptor of the Cinquecento even approaches the
artistic rank of Michelangelo. Florence produced, however,
a large number of other masters illustrating this phase of art,
prominent among whom are Giovanni Francesco Rustici (1465-
1554), Andrea Sansovino (1460-1529), and Benvenuto Cellini
(1500-71), whose autobiography is one of the most notable literary
expressions of the spirit of the mature Renaissance ; artistically
he is, however, essentially the super-goldsmith. Among later
Florentine sculptors, all of them feeling the overwhelming influence of Michelangelo, we may note Bartolomeo Ammanati
(1511-92) and Jean de Boulogne, known as Giovanni da Bologna
(c. 1525-1608), a native of Douay. Elsewhere in Italy, Bologna

had a prominent master in Alfonso Lombardi (1497-1537), while
at Modena Antonio Begarelli (1498-1565) carried on the tradition
of Guido Mazzoni ; giving up, however, polychromy in his
groups of white-glazed terra-cotta figures.   We have already encountered Jacopo Sansovino when treating of Cinquecento architecture in Venice ; he was also a prolific sculptor, of whose gifts
his *Bacchus* in the Bargello, done before he settled in Venice,
gives perhaps the most favourable idea.   Among Sansovino's
pupils and followers in Venice, Alessandro Vittoria (*c.* 1525-
1608), an excellent portrait sculptor, and Girolamo Campagna
(*c.* 1550-1623 ?) are the most important.
   The period of the Baroque, which succeeds that of the Renaissance, may be said in Italy, the country where this next
movement originated, to begin towards the close of the sixteenth
century, and to last well into the eighteenth century.   The
tendency of the Baroque style may be said, in all provinces
of art, to be towards an increased effectiveness of impression
at first sight : there is indeed a definitely scenic quality in
Baroque art, and a note of extravagance is often struck in it.
As regards architecture, we note more especially a tendency
to operate with pictorial devices, as apart from such as are
dictated by strictly structural considerations.   For a considerable
time in the nineteenth century Baroque architecture and art
generally suffered a veritable eclipse as regards æsthetic appreciation : but this attitude is now entirely a thing of the past,
and there exists a practical unanimity in acknowledging the
Baroque as one of the great creative periods in the history of
Italian art.
   Upon the aspect of one city, Baroque architecture has left
an indelible impression—namely, Rome : and Rome was indeed
the cradle and all through the seventeenth century the main
focus of Baroque art.   The Baroque has many ancestors, but
nobody perhaps more important than Michelangelo, who spent
the last thirty years of his life in Rome.   Passing over the
earliest stages in the history of Baroque architecture, we come
upon its first full-blown representative in Lorenzo Bernini (1598-
1680), a native of Naples of Tuscan parentage, who accompanied
his father when the latter settled in Rome in 1605 and who
spent practically the whole of his life in the Eternal City, except
for a brief visit to the Paris of Louis-Quatorze in 1665.   Bernini
was an artist of very precocious development and with talents
in different directions ; his work as a sculptor will call for notice
a little later on.   One of Bernini's first patrons was the Cardinal
Maffeo Barberini, and when, in 1623, the latter was elected pope

under the name of Urban VIII he determined to avail himself fully of the talent of Bernini for the glorification of his reign : and the names of Urban VIII and Bernini are indeed linked together somewhat after the manner of those of Julius II and Michelangelo, though as regards their personal relations there is this important difference, that Urban and Bernini never quarrelled as Michelangelo and Julius II did. Urban VIII's reign was a long one, not terminating until 1644 ; his successor, Innocent XI, was at first not very favourably disposed towards Bernini, but before long he changed his attitude, and it has been truly said that, though Bernini could do very well without the popes, the popes were unable to do without Bernini.

The first great task undertaken by Bernini in the reign of Urban VIII, and standing as it were half-way between architecture and sculpture, was to execute a huge bronze canopy over the high altar of St. Peter's, the interior decoration of which was only then taken in hand and bears indeed all through the stamp of Bernini's genius. This canopy, which was begun in 1625 and took nine years to construct, is one of the works of Bernini concerning which there has been the greatest diversity of opinion : but an æsthetic defence of it is certainly possible. Great praise has, on the other hand, at all times been given to the great portico which between 1656 and 1667 he built in front of St. Peter's. The aim of Bernini was a twofold one : for one thing to counterbalance the excessive width of the front, which had been intended to show a tower at each end, and further to restore due prominence to Michelangelo's dome which —ever since the nave of the church was made longer than Michelangelo planned it—is concealed from view even at a considerable distance. Bernini has achieved this double end through a most brilliant use of artifices of perspective ; and, for nobility and grandeur of effect, the approach to St. Peter's undoubtedly takes rank among the greatest architectural achievements of all time. Other important architectural tasks carried out by Bernini include the magnificent Scala Regia of the Vatican— again a masterpiece of optical deception—and the church of Sant' Andrea al Quirinale designed on an elliptical plan.

A very remarkable group among the works of Bernini is also formed by his fountains ; and these once again go to prove how Bernini, whatever task he attacked, always succeeded in striking out fresh lines of expression : both by replacing the customary architectural framework with forms derived from nature and by his appreciation of the æsthetic possibilities of water, he became an absolute innovator in fountain design, and the squares of Rome depend to this day for their charm in a large measure directly or indirectly on Bernini's activities within this sphere.

As an architect, Bernini does not carry the style of the Baroque to its most advanced point—the principal milestones in that progress are marked by Bernini's pupil Francesco Borromini (1599-1667), a most extravagant designer whose chief field of activity was Rome, and the monk Guarino Guarini (1624-1683), who went even further than Borromini and who can be particularly well studied in Turin. Of the architects of the Venetian Baroque, Baldassare Longhena (1598-1682) possessed the greatest gifts : his masterpiece is the church of Santa Maria della Salute, boldly designed with a most admirable sense of architectural fitness for its position at the entrance to the Grand Canal.

Bernini the sculptor is intimately connected with Bernini the architect ; and in both capacities his influence was enormous. Immediate and striking effect is what Bernini's sculptures aim at : aided by an amazing technical virtuosity, he has the gift of the most vivid naturalism ; and, though the power of vigorous monumental effect is by no means denied him, he is above all the interpreter of palpitating vitality and restless agitation. Quite early in his career come a series of celebrated mythological groups in marble in the Casino Borghese ; later works of outstanding importance are two great papal tombs in St. Peter's—one, the tomb of Bernini's friend and patron Urban VIII, the other commemorating a later pope, Alexander VII : in these it is interesting to note how the dramatic note is increasingly stressed in the conception of the whole, whilst the use of variegated material indicates a characteristic tendency of Baroque sculpture. Finally, as one of the greatest and most typical works of Bernini, we must not omit his *Ecstasy of St. Theresa*, executed in 1645 for the church of Santa Maria della Vittoria in Rome. The sentiment in it has a most hectic, not to say hysterical, quality, and there can be no doubt of the absolutely convincing manner in which the artist has here succeeded in conveying a particular mood. Also, sculpture has here only become a means of " painting in marble "—and how marvellously Bernini does it.

Next to Bernini, the two most prominent sculptors working principally in Rome in the seventeenth century were François Duquesnoy, known from the country of his origin as Il Fiammingo (1594-1643), and Alessandro Algardi (1602-54). Both approximate on the whole very much to the manner of Bernini, though comparatively speaking they represent perhaps to some extent

a conservative tendency; Duquesnoy being specially noted
for his charming figures of children, while the excellence of
Algardi's portrait busts calls for particular mention. Florence plays
next to no part in the history of Baroque sculpture, though
it had one master of distinction in Giovanni Battista Foggini
(1652 – c. 1740); in Sicily the activities of a brilliant artist,
favouring the medium of stucco, Giacomo Serpotta (1656-1732),
take us already across the boundary of the Seicento. In and
around Venice sculpture continued to be practised extensively
until the downfall of the republic : as an illustration of the
grandiloquent manner of the Venetian Baroque, nothing could
be more graphic than the tomb of the Doge Giovanni Pesaro
(1669) in the Frari, designed by the architect Baldassare Longhena,
the statuary being executed by the German sculptor Melchior
Barthel.

The eighteenth century saw the transference of the hegemony
in the art world of Europe from Italy to France. Not that
this signified any abating of artistic activity in Italy, which also
continued to be a goal for art students from other countries ;
while Italian artists and craftsmen of every description found
employment from one end of our continent to the other—Ireland
in the West, Russia in the East. The Rococo style never became
fully at home in Italy, though to some extent Venice provides
the spectacle of a very attractive variety of it : Italian art of
the eighteenth century is largely a matter of a survival of the
Baroque style, and, as the century advances, the neo-Classical
movement gradually comes to the fore. Italy's architects were
still among the most distinguished of the time : as for instance
Filippo Juvara (1685-1735), the designer of many a noble building
in Turin with the classicist note strongly stressed ; Alessandro
Galilei (1691-1737) and Ferdinando Fuga (1699-1770), both of
whom worked in Rome ; and finally Luigi Vanvitelli (1700-73),
the son of a Flemish painter Gaspar Van Wittel, who designed
that magnificent pile for ever commemorating the Bourbon
Dynasty in the kingdom of Naples, the Palace of Caserta.

Southern Italy and Sicily play also an important part in
the history of Italian eighteenth-century sculpture. Generations
of tourists have wondered at the amazing technical skill dis-
played in the three celebrated marble statues in the Cappella
Sansevero at Naples : Giuseppe Sammartino's *Dead Christ*,
Antonio Corradini's *Pudicità*, and Francesco Queirolo's *Disinganno;*
while, in the neighbourhood of Palermo, the garden sculptures
of the Villa Palagonia at Bagheria take us to a world of extravagant fancy to which it would be difficult to quote a parallel.

Rome too continued an active centre of sculpture, the principal late Baroque master there being Pietro Bracci (1700-73). The excavations now being carried out with increased zest in and around Rome, and more particularly the sensational finds made (ever since 1719) at Herculaneum, resulted in a most enthusiastic appreciation of Classical sculpture ; and the man who first formulated the progress of the neo-Classical movement in art and became its most influential spokesman was the German archæologist Winckelmann, who settled in Rome in 1755, in which year he also published a book setting forth his views on art. These views may briefly be summarised thus, that the aim of art is not to imitate nature, but to achieve ideal beauty ; and that such is the perfection of the art of the ancient Greeks, that for the artists of subsequent ages there is nothing left but to imitate it straightway, since any change would inevitably be for the worse.

The first Italian sculptor to attempt the realisation of this programme was Antonio Canova (1757-1822), a native of the Venetian mainland, who settled at Rome in 1779 ; and he quickly achieved an international reputation, being acclaimed the greatest sculptor of his time and the equal of the ancients. Posterity has, however, failed to ratify this judgment, finding such positive qualities as Canova's art may exhibit marred by a tendency to cheap attractiveness and by the essential deadness of his form. Rome, however, from now onwards, became a great international centre of sculptural activity on neo-Classical lines, the long residence in the Eternal City of the once much-lauded Dane, Bertel Thorvaldsen (1770-1844), being one of the most characteristic episodes of this phase of art ; and, all through the nineteenth century, the neo-classic dogma still found exponents among the sculptors of Italy. Sculpture has, indeed, up to the present day remained a branch of art most extensively practised in Italy ; and the history of the political unification of the peninsula has provided the excuse for a statuomania, with results showing quality deplorably out of proportion to quantity. Among the most famous names in their day were Lorenzo Bartolini (1777-1850) and Giovanni Duprè (1817-82), who represent a gradual revolt against the tenets of neo-Classicism ; while *verismo*, as the Italian catchword is, came to the fore in the work of Vincenzo Vela (1820 - 91), an artist whose influence has been enormous though unfortunately not for the good. Much of modern Italian sculpture is marred by a cheap naturalism, pushed to tasteless extremes ; for the rest, the sculptors of Italy have been content to follow the international movements of the day, without starting any important development. From amongst the multitude of names of modern Italian sculptors, those of Giulio Monteverde (1837-1917) and Antonio dal Zotto (1841-1917) may here be singled out for mention: the latter was a Venetian, and his statue of Goldoni set up in a little *Campo* at Venice is undoubtedly one of the most successful public monuments of nineteenth-century Italy. Unfortunately, the same cannot be said of the huge and pretentious monument to Vittorio Emanuele II in Rome, designed in 1885 by Vittore Sacconi (1853-1905), agglomerating the work of a large number of sculptors, and not completed until 1911, some years after Sacconi's death. Architecture in Italy since the end of the eighteenth century has, beginning with neo-Classicism, followed a line of development somewhat analogous to that of sculpture. Great scope was naturally offered to the architects of Italy when Rome in 1870 was made the capital of the new kingdom; but few of the many ambitious new buildings erected since then may be regarded as having appreciably enriched the architectural physiognomy of the Eternal City. Two North Italians, working, however, in different parts of the peninsula—Camillo Boito (1830-1914) and Luca Beltrami (1854-1933)—can claim to rank among the principal Italian architects of their time; while, to mention a living Italian sculptor, Antonio Maraini (born 1881) has given evidence of a scholarly outlook and sense of historic tradition.

BIBLIOGRAPHY TO CHAPTER VIII

W. J. Anderson, *Architecture of the Renaissance in Italy*, 5th ed. London, 1927.

E. W. Anthony, *Early Florentine Architecture and Decoration*. Cambridge, Mass., 1927.

Emile Bertaux, *L'art dans l'Italie méridionale*. Paris, 1904.

Martin S. Briggs, *Baroque Architecture*. London, 1913.

Wilhelm Bode, *Denkmäler der Renaissance-Sculptur Toscanas*. Munich, 1892-1905.

Wilhelm Bode, *Florentiner Bildhauer der Renaissance*. Berlin, 1910.

Wilhelm Bode, *Die Italienischen Bronzestatuetten der Renaissance*, 3 vols. Berlin, 1907-12. (English edition, London, 1912.)

Camille Enlart, *Origines françaises de l'architecture gothique en Italie*. Paris, 1894.

R. W. Hammett, *Romanesque Architecture of Western Europe*. New York, 1927.

Arthur Haseloff, *Pre-Romanesque Sculpture in Italy*. Pegasus Press, 1931.

E. Hempel, *Francesco Borromini*. Vienna, 1924.

T. G. Jackson, *Byzantine and Romanesque Architecture*, 2 vols., 2nd ed. Chicago, Univ. of Chicago Press, 1920.

T. G. Jackson, *Gothic Architecture in France, England and Italy*, 2 vols. Cambridge, 1915.

T. G. Jackson, *The Renaissance of Roman Architecture*, vol. i. Cambridge, 1921.

Allan Marquand, *Luca della Robbia*. Princeton, 1914.

Allan Marquand, *Giovanni della Robbia*. Princeton, 1920.

André Michel, *Histoire de l'art*, 8 vols., each in two or three sections. Paris, 1905-29.

Leo Planiscig, *Venezianische Bildhauer der Renaissance*, 2 vols. Vienna, 1921.

Leo Planiscig, *Andrea Riccio*. Vienna, 1927.

A. Kingsley Porter, *Lombard Architecture*. New Haven, 1917.

C. R. Post, *A History of European and American Sculpture*, 2 vols. Cambridge, Mass., 1921.

Corrado Ricci, *Romanesque Architecture in Italy*. London, 1925.

Corrado Ricci, *Baroque Architecture and Sculpture in Italy*. London, 1912.

G. T. Rivoira, *Lombardic Architecture*. London, 1910.

Paul Schubring, *Donatello* (" Klassiker der Kunst," Vol. XI). Stuttgart, 1907.

Sacheverell Sitwell, *Southern Baroque Art*. London, 1924.

Pietro Toësca, *Storia dell' arte italiana*. In progress. Turin, 1913 *sqq.*

Adolfo Venturi, *Storia dell' arte italiana*, 9 vols. so far issued (some in several sections). Milan, 1901 *sqq.*

A. R. Willard, *History of Modern Italian Art*. London, 1900.

Heinrich Wölfflin, *Renaissance und Barock*, 3rd ed. Munich, 1908.

Heinrich Wölfflin, *Die Klassische Kunst*, 7th ed. Munich, 1924. (English translation, *The Art of the Italian Renaissance*, London, 1903.)

CHAPTER IX

ITALIAN PAINTING

IN popular conception, the history of Italian painting may be said to begin in the thirteenth century, the Duecento; but as students have long been aware, and as new discoveries continuously demonstrate with fresh emphasis, pictorial art was extensively practised in Italy for many centuries previously and the historian has no difficulty in tracing the descent of Italian painting, step by step, from painting of the early Christian period. Rome and Ravenna are the two cities which figure most prominently in a survey of the origins of Italian painting, thanks to the Catacomb paintings and to the mosaics which occur in the ancient churches of both places; and we are probably justified in assigning to the beginning of the seventh century the earliest items in the series of frescoes, which makes the church of Santa Maria Antiqua in the Forum a monument of such unique importance to the student of early medieval painting on a considerable scale. In these earliest frescoes, the features of style evincing a descent from Classical art are still very patent; in the frescoes of the eighth century, the influence of Byzantine art, which was to be of such enormous importance to Italian medieval painting in general, has already become very pronounced. Passing on to the Carlovingian period, and still remaining at Rome, we note the presence, in the lower church of San Clemente, of a series of wall paintings, which may be dated in the reign of Pope Leo IV (847-855) and among which an *Ascension* is particularly remarkable on account of its intensity of dramatic expression—a feature this which is common to a great deal of Carlovingian art. From the same century date the earliest surviving works (at San Vincenzo on the Volturno) of the great Benedictine School of Painting which was centred in the monastery of Montecassino, and gained particular importance in the eleventh century, from the second half of which dates the great cycle of frescoes in the church of Sant' Angelo in Formis near Capua. In Rome and the surrounding districts, meanwhile, pictorial activity had continued unabated; and in a sense the culminating point in the history of this great Roman medieval School of Painting is reached in the thirteenth century, when we come upon the painter Pietro Cavallini, who, probably about 1293, decorated the church of Santa Cecilia in Rome with a series of frescoes, of which those in the private choir of the nuns survive. What we see here is an art of singular force and monumental power, not uninfluenced to be sure by Byzantine art, nor out of touch with the great current of Gothic art, but, above everything else, giving clear evidence of an inspiration by Classical art.

If we turn to a survey of Romanesque painting in Italy outside the districts we have named, we shall find evidence of an activity extending practically over the whole peninsula during the twelfth century : as an especially important centre of painting late in this century we may mention Spoleto, where we come across a painter named Alberto Sotio signing a crucifix in the cathedral and dating it 1187 (or slightly later in the same decade). Crossing into the thirteenth century, we encounter a number of cities in Tuscany, where painting was actively practised, as shown by a string of surviving examples : Pisa, Lucca, Siena, in which latter place a painter named Guido signed a large Madonna enthroned (now in the Palazzo Pubblico) in the year 1221. As to Florence, she was rather slow in coming into prominence as a centre of painting ; but, in the second half of the thirteenth century, the Florentine school had evidently gained considerable vigour, and the first figure of outstanding importance to emerge in it is Cimabue, with whom Vasari begins his series of Lives of the Italian Artists, hailing him as the father of Italian painting. That Cimabue came into contact with the great School of Painting in Rome may be regarded as a certainty—in fact, it is in Rome that he is first heard of, in 1272. As to surviving works by him, there is now a virtual consensus of opinion, that he is the author of a series of very remarkable frescoes, painted in the choir and transepts of the Upper Church of San Francesco at Assisi, the great sanctuary of the Franciscan Order, to which reference has already been made as one of the most important early Gothic churches of Italy. These frescoes are compositions, evincing an extraordinary dramatic power, entitling the artist who painted them to a high rank among the masters of the Italian school.

Tradition has it that Cimabue was the teacher of the artist, who, about the turn of the century, brought about a most wonderful revolution in Italian painting—Giotto (1266/76-1337). There is, indeed, no impossibility in Giotto having studied under that leading master of Florence ; but his art shows at the same time the most evident affiliation to the great Roman School of Painting of the thirteenth century, and more especially to the work of Pietro Cavallini.

It is customary—though not without some considerable dissent—to regard as early works by Giotto (dating, say, from about 1295-1300) the series of frescoes in the nave of the Upper Church of San Francesco at Assisi, depicting a succession of scenes from the legend of St. Francis. At this time of day, the life of St. Francis was certainly not new to art ; but, in comparison with the scriptural subjects, it had iconographical traditions of not very long standing, and this, together with the fact that the incidents and the setting of the legend possessed at the time a colour of " modernity," provided exceptional opportunities for Giotto's creative genius. He has indeed risen to the occasion marvellously, producing a picture chronicle in which every scene is instinct with singular moving power ; his gift of keen observation, his simple, but convincing grasp of form, and his genuinely Italian dramatic sense being triumphantly vindicated all through the series.

As to whether the St. Francis series at Assisi is really by Giotto, or to what extent, will perhaps always remain a matter of dispute among critics. There is, however, no possibility of doubting the cycle of frescoes in the Scrovegni chapel in Santa Maria dell' Arena at Padua as Giotto's work ; and their probable date is about 1303-05. The subjects of this series are mainly derived from the life of Joachim and Anne and the Virgin and Christ : hence iconographically well-trodden ground. It is all the more remarkable how Giotto, while all the time remaining in touch with pictorial tradition, manages to infuse a new life into the old schemes ; and, in comparison with the St. Francis series, there is evidence in every direction of powers much more mature, of a far greater certainty of the means to be used.

The latest surviving wall paintings by Giotto are those in the Bardi and Peruzzi chapels in Santa Croce at Florence, which may with some probability be dated about 1320-30. These frescoes have, unfortunately, been very drastically repainted : but they are of enormous importance from the indications which they even so give of the direction in which Giotto's later development took him. His power of simple and effective monumental design is here seen grown still further intensfied : and it is with the tradition here created that Masaccio, at the beginning of the Quattrocento, most immediately links up.

The impulses received from Giotto meant a great deal to Italian painting in general, but most of all to the Florentine

School of Painting. At Florence, indeed, a tremendous pictorial activity now set in, it being a matter both of easel pictures and of frescoes, large cycles of which became a distinguishing feature of the school for a long time to come. Among Giotto's immediate followers, we may mention Taddeo Gaddi (*c.* 1300-63/66), Giotto's direct pupil and the orthodox " Giottesque," Bernardo Daddi (*c.* 1290-1348), an older and also more independent artist, remarkable through his great sensitiveness and dramatic power, and one Maso (perhaps also called Giottino), the author, according to Lorenzo Ghiberti's *Commentaries*, of the frescoes illustrating the life of St. Sylvester in a chapel in Santa Croce. An important figure in the Florentine School of about 1350 is Andrea Orcagna whom we have already encountered as a sculptor, and who painted in association with his two brothers, Nardo di Cione and Jacopo di Cione.   The famous, elaborately allegorical frescoes in the " Spanish Chapel " in Santa Maria Novella are the work of the painter Andrea Bonaiuti, painted about 1365 ; while Taddeo Gaddi's son, Agnolo Gaddi, dying in 1396, takes us practically to the end of the Trecento : in his frescoes, illustrating the Legend of the Cross, in the choir of Santa Croce, he gives evidence of a narrative tendency which, combined with a reckless application of what is known as " the method of continuous representation," at times causes him to produce compositions which precisely from the narrative point of view are almost unintelligible.

Retracing our steps from the chronological point reached, and envisaging Italian painting apart from the Florentine School, we may first note that the great Roman School of Painting came to an abrupt end at the beginning of the fourteenth century, when the pope was dragged into captivity at Avignon. A city which, on the other hand, towards the end of the thirteenth century rose to a position of prime importance in the realm of Italian painting was Siena : and here the name to be mentioned by preference to any other is that of a somewhat older contemporary of Giotto's, Duccio di Buoninsegna (*c.* 1260-1319). Unlike Giotto, Duccio is not primarily a painter of extensive series of large frescoes : there survives, as a matter of fact, not a single fresco by him. His production is restricted to panel pictures, and his principal work is the great altarpiece, or *Maestà*, which in 1308 he undertook to paint for the Siena Duomo ; the majority of its component parts is now in the Opera del Duomo at Siena. Duccio represents all that is best in the ancient Byzantine tradition, which in him is reflected through an artistic personality of singular refinement and distinction. Not that he

is not capable of modifying and enlivening the time-honoured
iconographical schemes in a thousand different ways : the keynote of his art yet remains conservative, aristocratic.   Endowed
with a wonderful sense of colour, his feeling for the rhythmic
harmony of line is also most keen ; and by effective silhouetting
he obtains dramatic effects of the utmost intensity.   For plastic
relief—a matter of the utmost concern to Giotto—Duccio cared
but little.   Upon the Sienese School, Duccio left his impress for
very long.   He had numerous immediate followers and imitators ;
while a profoundly original representative of the Ducciesque tradition is Simone Martini (1284 ?-1344), who practised his gentle
and sensitive art not only in his native Siena, but carried its
message very much further afield—to Assisi, to Naples, and at
last to Avignon, where Simone ended his days.   Contemporary
with Simone Martini were the two brothers Lorenzetti, Pietro
(c. 1280 – c. 1348) and Ambrogio : in these, an influence from
Giotto may be distinctly traced, which, however, does not by
any means obliterate their traditional Sienese feeling for harmony
of pattern.   The culminating point in Ambrogio Lorenzetti's work
is marked by the series of large frescoes, symbolising Good
and Bad Government, with which he between 1331 and 1340
decorated a hall in the Palazzo Pubblico of Siena.   Sienese elements of style, denoting an affinity to Ambrogio Lorenzetti,
mingled with features of different characteristics, occur in the
great fresco of the Triumph of Death, painted soon after the middle
of the century in the Camposanto at Pisa.   It has been suggested that this fresco—which interprets in such moving accents
the spiritual condition of Italy at the time of the Black Death—
may be the work of a Pisan master, Francesco Traini.

Practically the whole of the peninsula was studded by a
profusion of local schools of painting during the fourteenth century, even if Florence and Siena easily were the most important
centres.   Mention must, however, not be omitted of the activities of two Veronese masters of the last quarter of the century,
Altichiero and Avanzo, by whom we possess two important
series of frescoes in two Paduan churches, very notable on account of their fine sense of monumental design, their rich and
harmonious colouring and their keen observation of the facts
of life.

The close of the fourteenth century witnessed the diffusion,
all over Europe, of a movement in late Gothic painting, which
produced results remarkably similar in the different countries.
When analysed, this current of art will be found to present a
curious conflict of tendencies : for what is characteristic of it is,

on the one hand, a very minute and sensitive, literal realism, and on the other hand a complete disregard of verisimilitude, shown in the liberties taken with perspective, with anatomical structure and in the purely " rhythmic " use made of the curves of the draperies. In Europe, north of the Alps, the illuminations of the great Book of Hours of the Duc de Berry, painted by Pol de Limbourg and his brothers, about 1410, is the outstanding example of this phase in the history of European painting ; in Italy the three principal exponents of the same tendency are Don Lorenzo Monaco, Gentile da Fabriano and Pisanello. Don Lorenzo Monaco (c. 1370–c. 1425), a native of Siena, settled early in life at Florence, where, as a monk of the Order of the Camaldolese, he spent the rest of his life. His activity was principally that of the painter of panel pictures. The other two artists mentioned were itinerant painters and much sought after by various prominent patrons in different parts of the peninsula ; unfortunately a very extensive destruction has overtaken their work. The principal surviving example of the art of Gentile da Fabriano (c. 1390-1427) is his great *Adoration of the Magi* (1423) in the Florence Academy ; of the work of Antonio Pisano, called Pisanello, whom we have previously mentioned as a medallist, there remain, apart from a few small easel pictures, a couple of frescoes in churches of his native city Verona.

The great and fateful revolt against the tendencies now sketched is headed in Florentine painting by Masaccio (1401-1428/9), the founder of the Quattrocento style of painting and as such a figure of the most decisive importance in the history of western painting as a whole. His life was short, and, while a considerable proportion of what he did has been lost, we can be sure that his production did not reach a great extent as regards mere numbers. His works are, however, so definite and so masterly an expression of a new artistic creed, that they could not fail to exercise a most profound and lasting influence. Where the late Gothic painters went in for literal realism, interest in accidentals, charming melody of line, Masaccio takes as his aim general principles, solid structure, monumental grandeur. What Masaccio brought about was thus a revolution : but it was a revolution that linked up with tradition— the tradition of Giotto's monumental power, dramatic sense and keen observation of reality. Even Masaccio's use of light and shade with a view to articulating his compositions may be a device to some extent anticipated in the last works by Giotto— the condition of the latter is such that we cannot speak with certainty on this point. With all this, the temperamental

difference between the two artists is very great : Giotto has a
most extraordinary width of range and sympathy, Masaccio is
youthfully eager and *farouche*.

The chief place for the study of Masaccio is the Brancacci
Chapel in the church of Santa Maria del Carmine at Florence,
where he painted a number of frescoes, the authorship of which
is not in dispute : others in the same chapel have given rise
to some difference of opinion as to whether they are by him
or by the painter Masolino (1383-1447), who, according to Vasari,
was Masaccio's master and who undoubtedly is responsible for
some of the frescoes in the Brancacci Chapel.

An older Florentine contemporary of Masaccio's is a very
remarkable artist—Fra Angelico (1387-1455). His works breathe,
as regards the interpretation of the subjects, a spirit of medi-
evalism, which, together with certain features of his artistic
formula, have tended to obscure the fact that he is one of the
artists who did most to establish the new style of the Quattrocento in Florence. The principal scene of his activities was the
monastery of San Marco in Florence, where Fra Angelico spent
some eleven years (1436-47) as an inmate (he being a Dominican
friar) and where the walls contain a most impressive series of
frescoes by him ; he worked, however, in several other places,
dying in Rome, where his noble frescoes in the Oratory of Pope
Nicholas V in the Vatican show his style at the end of his career.
Alongside his frescoes, Fra Angelico also found time to execute
a large number of panel pictures, the pure and intense colours
of which show the perfection of his tempera technique, and which,
ever since taste in the nineteenth century veered in favour of the
" Primitives," have been great favourites in the galleries. Other
contemporaries of Masaccio in Florence are Paolo Uccello, Andrea
del Castagno and Domenico Veneziano—painters who, however
different they may be in their temperamental outlook, yet are
bound together by their sympathy with the aims of the movement ushered in by Masaccio, the exploration of the possibilities
of linear perspective being more particularly carried out by them.
Paolo Uccello (1397 ?-1475) is the name to be more especially
remembered in this connexion, but he was also an artist of
charming imaginative and delightful romantic feeling. Andrea
del Castagno (1410-57) is a forceful realist, favouring coarse
types expressive of very vehement feeling ; while of the life work
of Domenico Veneziano (*ob.* 1461) a mere fraction has reached
us, showing him, however, to have been an extremely interesting
and gifted artist. Contemporary with these artists but representing a very different artistic tendency was Fra Filippo Lippi

(1406 ?-69), endowed with a delightful wayward and Puckish imagination, and as a colourist of quite exceptional gifts : the scholarly aspects of art made on the other hand no appeal to him.

Passing from this first generation of Florentine Quattrocento masters to those who achieved distinction about the middle of the century, we may first notice Alesso Baldovinetti (1425-99), a pupil of Domenico Veneziano, and a figure of considerable importance in the history of the gradual artistic discovery of landscape. He was also keenly interested in technical experiments, and from now onwards one notices a widespread tendency in Florence to get away from the ancient tempera medium in the easel pictures : but the proper oil technique was very long in getting established. A younger contemporary of Baldovinetti's was Antonio del Pollaiuolo, known to us already as a sculptor, and also in his capacity as a painter intensely concerned about the theory of the nude and the rendering of vigorous, elastic movement. Francesco Pesellino (1422-57) was a gifted but shortlived pupil of Fra Filippo Lippi ; while a pupil of Fra Angelico, Benozzo Gozzoli (1420-97), inherited little of his master's scholarliness, but displays charming gifts as a story-teller in numerous series of wall paintings scattered across Tuscany and Umbria.

Among Florentine masters whose life's work mainly belongs to the second half of the Quattrocento, Sandro Botticelli (1444-1510) is doubtless the outstanding figure. The pupil of Fra Filippo Lippi, he may be said to represent the poetical and imaginative bent of the latter, though on a higher plane ; while a unique fascination attaches to his art through its typifying—in works like the *Primavera* or *The Birth of Venus*—the romantically-coloured, humanist conceptions of the Medicean court. Much of Botticelli's artistic formula can be explained as a result of a keen study of the work of Antonio del Pollaiuolo : and, as a master of sensitive line and of facial expression, Botticelli has few equals in the whole of European painting. Towards the end of his life, Botticelli's mind was profoundly stirred by the revivalist propaganda and tragic fate of Savonarola : and this experience is reflected in his art in a manner which fully discloses his highly strung temperament.

A great contrast to Botticelli is afforded by his most prominent rival for the favour of the contemporary Florentine public, Domenico Ghirlandaio (1449-94). Ghirlandaio's outlook is a very prosaic one : his realism is very literal and he is completely bereft of dramatic power : but, if inarticulate, there is a certain sense of monumental grandeur in him. Ghirlandaio is the

fresco painter *par préférence*—according to Vasari, it was his wish
to be allowed to decorate the town walls of Florence : and his
series of large wall paintings in the choir of Santa Maria Novella,
completed in 1490, is undoubtedly one of the spectacular triumphs
of Florentine painting, mirroring the life and manners of the times
in an admirable fashion.   Fra Filippo Lippi's son, Filippino
Lippi (1457-1504), a pupil of Botticelli, is yet another figure of
mark in the Florentine school of the second half of the fifteenth
century.   Gifted with great facility of invention and execution,
he lacked, however, deeper feeling and artistic backbone generally ;
and his evolution as an artist eventually resulted in exaggeration
and pointless freakishness.

In Quattrocento art generally, it was Florence which led
the way, exercising a great deal of influence through Florentine
artists working elsewhere in Italy ; and we also know of a large
number of artists from other centres who came to study and
work in Florence.   A case in point is offered by one of the greatest
masters of all time, with whom we may begin our consideration
of the Quattrocento School of Painting in Umbria—Piero della
Francesca (1416 ?-92).   A native of Borgo San Sepolcro, Piero
worked for a while as assistant to Domenico Veneziano at Florence.
The influence both of this master and of the other artists of
cognate tendencies then working in Florence meant certainly a
great deal for the formation of Piero's style : but he is essentially
one of the most intensely personal artists that ever existed,
gifted with a sense of severe, statuesque dignity coupled with
the most subtle feeling for harmonious composition ; while, in
his observation of values of tone and colour, he is absolutely
impressionistic.   At Borgo San Sepolcro he was looked upon as
a kind of local deity, and he always returned there from the
extensive wanderings which took him, in the words of one of his
pupils, as " the monarch of painting of his time " all over Italy :
unfortunately, a great deal of what he has painted has been
destroyed.   At Arezzo in the church of San Francesco may be
seen the only complete series of frescoes by him that survives ;
as to single frescoes, Borgo San Sepolcro, the neighbouring village
of Monterchio and Rimini still contain noble examples.   His
easel pictures are also very rare : the National Gallery possesses
two of the finest of them (*The Baptism of Christ* and the *Nativity*).

The three chief pupils of Piero della Francesca were Melozzo
da Forlì, Luca Signorelli and Pietro Perugino.   Of the productions of Melozzo da Forlì (1438-94) unfortunately very little
survives : his derivation from Piero is clearly seen in his interest
in problems of perspective, in his monumental style of design

and numerous points of detail ; but he differs very much from Piero's stability of movement and unrelenting austerity of line through the extraordinary intensity of vital power which marks his figures. Indeed Melozzo's art reflects to perfection the type of the free and strong individual which we associate with the Renaissance. Luca Signorelli (*c.* 1450 - 1523) was a native of Cortona in northern Umbria, and, though his work took him to most places of importance in central Italy, Cortona always remained his home and he occupied there much the same position as Piero della Francesca at Borgo San Sepolcro. Except in a very general way, Signorelli's art does not remind one of that of Piero : his affinities to Antonio del Pollaiuolo are much closer and he may indeed have studied for a while in Florence. His enquiry into the laws of anatomy is even more searching than that of Pollaiuolo, and he delights in dramatic situations of the utmost violence. His art thus forms in some ways the opposite pole to that of Piero, with its absolute restraint and balance of forces, and it is equally unlike that of Melozzo by reason of the rugged grandeur that marks his conceptions. His modelling is extraordinarily vigorous and sculpturesque, and he shows not the slightest concern about the atmospheric effects so dear to the heart of the great impressionist of Borgo San Sepolcro : but the powerful, sombre tones of iron and bronze which dominate his colour schemes are in admirable harmony with the masculine or rather Titanic character of his art. His greatest work is the series of frescoes painted in the Cappella di San Brizio in Orvieto Cathedral (1499-1503).

Pietro Vannucci (*c.* 1446-1523) is known as Pietro Perugino, from his long residence at Perugia, which was, however, frequently broken by sojourns at Florence. As to his predecessors at Perugia—amongst whom there are artists of such distinction as Benedetto Bonfigli and Fiorenzo di Lorenzo—this brief reference to them must suffice. The style which Perugino evolved for himself is intensely personal and marked by a lovely sense of spaciousness, by a very melodious, gentle flow of line and by a dreamy pensiveness in the facial expression of his figures. He is, too, the first interpreter of the Umbrian landscape, and achieves a fine effect of atmosphere both in his frescoes and his easel pictures ; the latter show him also as having eventually fully mastered an oil technique of no little complication. Unfortunately, there is a tendency in Perugino to become repetitious and monotonous, but at his best he may claim very high rank artistically ; and his achievement also possesses the great historical significance of having provided the preliminary to one

of the most splendid consummations of Renaissance art—the
art of Raphael.

Of Perugino's Umbrian contemporaries, Bernardino Pinto-
ricchio (c. 1454-1513) deserves special mention as the author
of some of the decoratively most effective series of frescoes
dating from this period—e.g. those in the Appartamento Borgia
in the Vatican and in the Libreria of the Siena Duomo.

Siena continued all through the fifteenth century a most
active centre of painting ; common to all her painters is a very
fine sense of decorative effect.   The late Gothic note is still very
marked in artists such as the delicately poetical Sassetta (1392-
1450) and the whimiscal, oddly graceful Giovanni di Paolo (1403-
1482).   The Renaissance note comes to the fore in the paintings
of Francesco di Giorgio, to whose activity as a sculptor reference
has previously been made, and in the works of Matteo di Giovanni
(c. 1435-95), a prolific master, capable of a great intensity of
expression.   The influence of this Sienese School on the destinies
of Italian painting in general became, however, very limited in
the fifteenth century : the pictorial output of Siena is henceforth marked by provincialism—though hers must be admitted
to be a most enchanting provincialism.

In northern Italy, the great centre of influence in Quattrocento painting became for a while Padua ; and that this came
about was ultimately due to the work of one man, Francesco
Squarcione (1397–c. 1470).   Not that Squarcione himself was an
artist of any remarkable talent : only he happened to hit upon
a formula of pictorial expression which appealed to his contemporaries, and owing to his enthusiasm, perseverance and faculty
for organisation he succeeded in giving a very wide diffusion to
that formula—he is said to have had 143 pupils from all parts
of northern Italy.   " Classicism " was the motto of Squarcione,
who himself only in a very limited sense lived up to it : but
that formula was raised to a degree of high artistic significance
by Squarcione's chief pupil, Andrea Mantegna (c. 1431-1506).
Mantegna had an absolute passion for anything that savoured
of Classicism, as he knew it, and he works in a strictly sculpturesque style, marked by a stern grandeur, which does not,
however, exclude the expression of intense passion—the example
of Donatello, who worked so long in Padua, was incidentally
by no means lost on Mantegna.   The principal work of his
early period is the series of frescoes which in 1448 he, in con-
junction with various other artists, undertook to carry out in
the Ovetari Chapel in the church of the Eremitani at Padua.
The greater part of his life, from 1460 onwards, was however

spent in Mantua. A North Italian School which rose to great importance in the fifteenth century, and owed a great deal to impulses received from Padua, was the School of Ferrara : it includes artists of such very marked individuality as Cosimo Tura (1420 ?-95), Francesco del Cossa (1435 ?-77), and Ercole de' Roberti (1450 ?-96). Verona, too, was the centre of a flourishing school in the Quattrocento, touched by Paduan influence, yet possessing a character of its own ; and that same influence also reached Vincenzo Foppa of Brescia and Pavia (1427/30-1515/6), the principal master of the Lombard School during the period which concerns us.

In the Venetian fifteenth-century school, the first master of outstanding importance to arise was Jacopo Bellini (c. 1395-1470), essentially still a late Gothic artist of whose paintings but few have come down to us : but there exist two sketch-books by him (in the British Museum and the Louvre) which enable us to measure the extraordinary width of this range : indeed it is not too much to say, that in a sense the whole of the subsequent development of the Venetian School, down to Tintoretto and Paul Veronese, is foreshadowed in these books. Jacopo's two sons, Gentile (1429 ?-1507) and Giovanni (c. 1430-1516), were the leading masters of Venice in their time : both were at the beginning of their career much influenced by their brother-in-law Mantegna, though their individuality was never obliterated by him : and both eventually grew to a supreme mastery of colour and atmosphere, thereby establishing what henceforth was to become the prime characteristic of the painters of the Venetian School. Of much importance in this connexion was the visit paid by a Sicilian artist, Antonello da Messina (c. 1430-79), to Venice in 1475-76. Antonello had acquired (perhaps through contact with Petrus Christus at Milan) a complete familiarity with the Flemish oil technique of the Van Eycks : and, largely thanks to his example, the oil medium soon became very popular in Venice. Of the two brothers Bellini, Gentile had the calmer temperament and excels in stately ceremonial subjects, which disclose his admirable gift of simple, monumental design and his exceptional powers as a portrait painter ; Giovanni, on the other hand, had a very emotional and poetical disposition, which finds ever varied and striking expression in the sacred subjects (notably groups of the Madonna and Child and scenes from the Passion of Christ) which make up the majority of his production. It was Giovanni who was the real *caposcuola* of his time : under him studied the artists who established the Cinquecento style of painting in the Venetian School, and many

others besides : also his influence affected powerfully numerous
artists who never stood to him in the active relation of pupil
to master. Among the minor Quattrocento masters of Venice,
Cima da Conegliano (*c.* 1460-1517/18) deserves mention as a
singularly lovable artist, gifted with a notable sense of calm,
harmonious design ; while Vittore Carpaccio (*c.* 1460–*c.* 1525)
is the very entertaining, though quite unscholarly story-teller,
reflecting in his canvases the glorious pageant of Venetian life
with peculiar vividness. The Vivarini family, represented by
three artists (two brothers, Antonio and Bartolomeo and Antonio's
son Alvise), formed a dynasty of painters decidedly inferior in
achievement and renown to the Bellini's ; while a contemporary
of Gentile's and Giovanni's, Carlo Crivelli (*c.* 1430–*c.* 1495), one
of the most gifted scions of the Squarcionesque movement, left
Venice early in life and found in the Marches the sphere of activity
for his weirdly eccentric genius.

Returning to Florence, the rise of the style of the mature
Renaissance in painting calls for a brief discussion. In Florence,
this style was very largely in the character of a reaction against
the tendencies which had become current in later Quattrocento
painting : the new style aims at grandeur, simplification, clarity,
where the late Quattrocento went in for quaintness, irrelevant
detail and a split-up general effect. And, whilst this denotes a
reaction against what went immediately before, it is at the same
time in many ways a return to Masaccio's standpoint : just as
Masaccio went back to the tradition of Giotto a century before him.

The painter who in Florence first established the new style
was Leonardo da Vinci (1452-1519), and the turning point may
be said to be marked by his unfinished *Adoration of the Magi*
in the Uffizi, begun in 1481. Through Leonardo, the birth of
what is often referred to as the Cinquecento style in painting
was thus brought about years before the Cinquecento had actually
begun. Consumed as he was by an endless curiosity about things,
Leonardo was much more inclined to experimenting and scheming
than to completing a given task : hence the paramount importance
of the study of his drawings for the proper understanding of
Leonardo. His one existing fresco—even that a wreck—is the
Last Supper in S. Maria delle Grazie at Milan, painted towards
the end (*c.* 1495-98) of his long stay at the court of Ludovico il
Moro. His easel pictures are not many, and in certain cases
the extent to which the actual execution is his remains a matter
of dispute. They all, however, serve to illuminate a variety
of aspects of a mind which is one of the most remarkable in the
whole history of European art and civilisation generally.

Of another great Florentine who has left profound traces in the history of painting—Michelangelo—I have already had occasion to speak, when treating of his activities as sculptor and architect. As a painter, he is pre-eminently to be studied in the Sistine Chapel, where the paintings on the ceiling (1508-12) disclose to us one of the most splendid embodiments of the Renaissance spirit, so intensely characteristic of Michelangelo in its limitation to the human figure as the one subject for the artist's brush—how different he is in this from the artistic universality of Leonardo ! The *Last Judgment* on the altar wall is a much later work (1534-41), overwhelming as a piece of pictorial rhetoric and fraught with destiny for the later development of Italian painting.

The trio of giants in the history of Cinquecento painting in central Italy is completed by Raphael (1483-1520). What Raphael above all stands for is a harmonious development and blending of different artistic features. His early training under Perugino at Perugia imbued him with the sense of melodious line and spacious composition ; and to this was added, as a result of a stay in Florence, a better grasp of form and structural drawing. Thus equipped, he proceeded to the great tasks which awaited him in Rome, where to this day the *Stanze* in the Vatican triumphantly vindicate Raphael's claim to rank among the world's truly great artists.

On the many more or less slavish followers of these three masters no word need be wasted ; but Cinquecento Florence contained a number of painters, who, if at times undoubtedly influenced by one or the other of them, yet possessed a sufficiency of individual character, and form a very interesting group. Fra Bartolomeo (1475-1517) gives the most theoretical expression to the Cinquecento idea of monumental design in Florence : his forms tend to be of shocking emptiness, but he had a sense of quiet, imposing grandeur which it is impossible to deny. Andrea del Sarto (1486-1531) is an artist almost irritatingly flawless—producing with an ease which leaves one speechless—but the genuine and essential nobility of his art should not be overlooked. Pontormo (1494-1556) had a very wayward, restless, and eccentric spirit, and banality is the last thing that one could impute to his art. He is singularly happy, as well as original, in the arrangement of highly stylised forms which characterise his subject compositions, of which the *Vertumnus and Pomona* in the Medicean Villa at Poggio a Caiano is an unforgettable poem on the theme of exhilaration ; and he is also a portrait painter of very great distinction, compelling and subtle in his interpretation of character and never failing in his sense of style. Finally, there is Agnolo Bronzino (1503-72), a painter of marvellously hard, enamel-like surface in his easel pictures, indulging in clusters of nude forms of cool marble beauty or else practising a superbly statuesque and monumental style of portrait painting.

One of the very greatest names in the history of Cinquecento painting is that of Correggio (c. 1489-1534), who worked principally at Parma, busy both on large schemes of fresco decoration and as a painter of easel pictures. Correggio's artistic ancestry can in a sense be traced back to Mantegna, the Ferrarese School and Leonardo, and there is some evidence that late in life he got to know the Sistine ceiling ; but, on the whole, Correggio is one of the most intensely personal, self-contained artists that ever existed. His art is all gracefulness and charm ; in his compositions he operates with the freest rhythms ; and what he is above all enamoured of is light. The transparence of his shadows is proverbial, and he renders with equal success effects of broad daylight and the magic interplay of light and shade caused when the radiance from a centre of illumination is contending with surrounding darkness. His feeling for harmony of colour is most exquisite : wonderful arrangements—unlike those of any other painter—in which the blondness of youthful flesh is set off against delicate greys and greens, rise to one's mind as one thinks of his pictures. In matters of design, chiaroscuro and technique of painting, his influence on subsequent painting was immense ; while in Parmigiano (1503-40) he had a follower who gives a personally coloured version of Correggio's formula, transformed by him into a vehicle of the most ultra-refined elegance.

Elsewhere in northern Italy, Ferrara also has a Cinquecento School of importance, including among its members the fiery romantic Dosso Dossi (1479-1541). In Milan and the surrounding districts this was equally a period of great pictorial activity. Among the most notable masters we may single out for mention Bernardino Luini (1475–c. 1532), an artist upon whose style Leonardo left an indelible impress, and the coarse and provincial, but at times very effective Gaudenzio Ferrari of Vercelli (1481-1546) ; while a native of the latter city, Sodoma (1477-1549) carried to Tuscany and notably to Siena a very individual adaptation of the manner of Leonardo.

It was, however, Venice which all through the Cinquecento was the principal centre of pictorial activity in northern Italy : and it was not only a matter of Venice herself, but also of her Hinterland on the *terra ferma*—notably cities such as Brescia, Bergamo and Verona, and also the Friulan district. In a fashion very characteristic of the conservative and traditional bent of Venice, the Cinquecento style came into being there not as a result of reaction against previous tendencies, but as a fulfilment of aspirations which had been present in the principal figure in the Venetian School of the late fifteenth century, Giovanni Bellini : and it was one of the pupils of Giovanni Bellini— Giorgione (c. 1477-1510)—who brought about this fulfilment. Giorgione is, and will probably always remain, one of the most mysterious figures in the history of art : the number of extant works, acknowledged as his by common consent, is very small, and there exist very conflicting opinions as to other attributions to him. The small nucleus of undoubted works by him—among which the Castelfranco Madonna, the Hermitage *Judith*, the *Tempest*, now in the Academy at Venice, the *Three Philosophers* at Vienna, and the Dresden *Venus* are the most important— is however absolutely sufficient to give us an idea of the character and significance of Giorgione's art. It is expressive of a lyrical mood, intensely romantic and with a definitely tragic note more or less perceptibly stressed ; and it uses as its vehicle forms of great simplicity, purity and indeed severity, evincing all the time a masterly sense of structure ; while his colours have a marvellous depth, intensity and atmospheric quality and his treatment of chiaroscuro is most effective. The interdependence of figures and landscape is another feature of prime importance in Giorgione's art : and herein, too, he was working fully within the tradition of Giovanni Bellini.

Few artists have had so powerful and lasting an influence as Giorgione : it was felt with particular strength at the beginning of his career by the artist who, after Giorgione's early death, succeeded to the headship of the Venetian School—Titian (1480 ?-1576). Titian forms, however, temperamentally a great contrast to Giorgione : for his is essentially not a lyrical, but a dramatic temperament. In the course of his long career, which brought him distinguished patronage from near and far, the dramatic note gets ever more emphatically stressed in his art : and when about 1555 he, in an artistic sense, entered upon his old age, this was by no means a period of decay, but on the contrary the one which marks the culmination of his greatness as an artist, being distinguished technically by a previously unparalleled freedom and breadth of handling and richness of atmosphere. The range of Titian's art is enormous : but it is perhaps in certain romantic mythological subjects—or *poesie* as he called them himself—of his last period that the innermost individuality of Titian is most clearly revealed.

Among the Venetian masters of Titian's own generation, Palma Vecchio (1480-1528) was an artist of somewhat phlegmatic temperament, but a colourist of very high order ; while Lorenzo Lotto (1480-1556), highly strung and erratic, is always psychologically interesting, and at times achieves results of real artistic distinction, notably in his portraits. Sebastiano del Piombo (c. 1485-1547) began as one of Giorgione's closest and most brilliant followers in Venice, and then, settling in Rome about 1510, came under the overwhelming influence of Michelangelo : his great gifts are, however, very apparent also in his later works. Of the provincials, Pordenone (1483-1539) found scope for his somewhat grandiloquent manner in numerous Friulan churches, but also further afield ; while Brescia had two remarkable colourists in Romanino (c. 1485-1566 ?) and Moretto (1498-1555), the one rich and fiery in tone, the other cool and silvery. From Brescia, too, came Savoldo (c. 1480–c. 1550), who, however, made his home in Venice. During a period of study at Florence he acquired a somewhat academic, vaguely Andrea del Sarto-like quality of drawing, but he has a fine sense of design and colour ; he cultivated the Giorgionesque sentiment, not without a touch of melodrama. A Bergamasque, like Palma Vecchio, was Cariani (c. 1490–c. 1550) and settled like him in Venice : the more obviously and exaggeratedly Giorgionesque vein was actively exploited by him. In Giambattista Moroni (1520/5-1578), Bergamo had an excellent portrait painter who, having studied under Moretto at Brescia, remained settled at Bergamo for the rest of his life.

In Venice the artist who, after Titian, carried the evolution of the school one important stage further was Tintoretto (1518-1594). " The colour of Titian and the drawing of Michelangelo " is said to have been Tintoretto's motto. It does, however, little justice to the essential character of Tintoretto's art, although it is doubtless true that he gave keen study to the art of Michelangelo ; but his colour is by no means Titian's, and altogether Tintoretto's artistic personality is one far too original and creative to be defined by an eclectic juxtaposition of exemplars. He aims above all at as complete and striking *scenic* effects as possible, the alertness and resource of his imagination within these limits being simply amazing : and the essential feature of his artistic method is his use of light and dark masses, one standing out against the other, in alternating succession. The magnificent sweep of line or tornado-like rush of movement ; the superb rhythmic beauty of his designs ; his consummate mastery of colour, atmosphere and brushwork—to all this

Tintoretto's method of contrasting lights and darks is ultimately the life-giving touch. He subordinates everything else to this obsession of his. There are anticipations of this device in earlier masters of the Venetian School, to be sure : but it was only in Tintoretto's hands that this method became an instrument of such amazing complexity and expressiveness ; and just as we may recognise in it the very quintessence of his style, so it also constitutes Tintoretto's great gift to subsequent art. The influence which Tintoretto's conception of the functions of lights and darks in a picture has exercised is almost boundless.

In Tintoretto's art, with its sombre and agitated drama, we feel the onrush of the autumn gales of the Renaissance. In the work of a younger contemporary of his, Paul Veronese (1528-88), the note of opulence and the majestic rhythm afford clear evidence that the style of the Cinquecento is ripening : but nothing occurs to trouble the delight in an existence which proceeds smoothly and free from care. In the period to which he belongs, Paul Veronese is the chief interpreter of the magnificent pageant of Venetian life for which he indeed—in the Doge's Palace and elsewhere—helped to provide such an effective background : the Carpaccio, as it were, of the Cinquecento. His sense of colour—luminous and silvery—is perfect, and equally to be enjoyed in his oil paintings and his frescoes, the latter decorating a number of villas on the Venetian mainland.

A slightly older contemporary of Tintoretto's who fills a niche of his own with real distinction is Jacopo da Ponte (1510 ?-92), known from the little mainland town where he lived as Bassano. As regards the interpretation of his subjects, he is notable for transposing them into a completely rural key, derived from the districts in which he lived : he is thus one of the pioneers of *genre* painting. His art achieved an enormous popularity and his descendants continued to paint in the same style : for purely pictorial qualities, none of them, however, rivals Jacopo, who really was a great master of the brush and one of the influences which most powerfully affected the youthful Greco.

Cinquecento Venice has detained us long, as she should : but we must now turn to the development of painting in central Italy after 1550. The influence which for a long time there outweighed all others, was that of Michelangelo : from 1550 to 1580, roughly speaking, the artists of Florence, Rome and Bologna confined themselves practically to an imitation of Michelangelo's mannerism. As a reaction against this one-sided adoption of the formula of one of the most subjective and one-sided of artists, there then arose the tendency to obtain perfection in art by

14

elaborating a style combining the various excellences of all the great masters of the Cinquecento. At the head of this " eclectic " movement stand three artists of Bologna, Lodovico Carracci and his two cousins Agostino and Annibale, the latter (1560-1609) the most gifted of the three ; and the *Accademia degli Incamminati* was opened by them at Bologna in 1589. This serious and scholarly movement attracted a number of followers, prominent among whom are Domenichino (1581-1641) and Guido Reni (1575-1642) ; and if in the past a great deal of exaggerated praise has been showered upon these artists, the purely derogatory view of them and " late Italian " painting in general which obtained during the latter part of the nineteenth century was equally mistaken. The masterpiece of the Carracci School is the really magnificent scheme of fresco decoration carried out between 1600 and 1604 in a hall in the Palazzo Farnese in Rome by a group of artists, headed by Annibale. And, indeed, it was Rome that during the Seicento was the principal centre of painting, as of art generally, in Italy : Venice and Florence are by no means up to their previous standard, Naples and Genoa acquire an importance which they had never before possessed in the history of Italian painting : but they are second to Rome. It was in Rome, too, that, even before the advent of the seventeenth century, there rose to fame the North Italian artist whose emergence in one sense may be said to open an entirely new chapter in the history of art—Caravaggio (1573-1610). For Caravaggio is the first representative of the type of the progressive modern artist whose works, in defiance of the existing standards of taste, bring about a violent taking of sides in the art world. " Naturalism " is the accepted label for Caravaggio's art. It lays appropriately strong emphasis on the feature of his style which differentiates it most markedly from the work of his contemporaries in central Italy ; but it should never be forgotten to what a large extent Caravaggio's style continues the traditions of some Venetian sixteenth-century painters, and above all of Tintoretto. The tendency of Caravaggio is then to treat any subject which he approaches in a spirit of frank realism, delighting indeed in emphasising the squalid aspects of life and sometimes going to quite intransigent heights of arrogance in this respect. His searching study of the individual model was equalled by his close attention to the disposition of light and shade throughout his compositions. The effect of light favoured by him is that of a ray penetrating into a dark cellar : and it serves undoubtedly a definite imaginative purpose : the few glaring lights lay an almost brutal emphasis on the squalid-ness of the facts represented, and the large masses of unbroken shadow increase the sinister impression. The formula of Caravaggio was one which lent itself easily to exaggeration, and only too many of Caravaggio's imitators give us nothing but chalky whites and smoky blacks in violent opposition, degrading the spirit of his art to that of crude melodrama. Caravaggio himself was undoubtedly working under a strong imaginative compulsion and had the true dramatic instinct ; while the secret of simple and monumental design had not been lost by him either. His dramatic force and his power of investing the most unselect and plebeian form with a feeling of stern grandeur make Caravaggio indeed appear a next-of-kin to one of the greatest figures of the Renaissance—Donatello.

Of Caravaggio's enormous influence outside Italy this is not the proper place to speak : among his most gifted followers in Italy I can only briefly refer to the Spaniard Ribera (1589-1652), who worked in Naples, where he in his turn strongly influenced Salvator Rosa (1615-73), the greater part of whose life was spent in Rome and whose defiant romanticism makes him a figure of the greatest interest in the history of art. From Naples, too, hailed one of the most brilliant decorators among the legion that flourished in Italy during the period of the Baroque— Luca Giordano (1632-1705), known from his sleight-of-hand as *Fa Presto*.

The study of Italian Seicento painting has only lately been taken seriously in hand : and, although enormous progress has been made in this field, we are still very far from being able to say that full justice has been done to an epoch which offers enormous interest both to the student of æsthetic values and of the history of civilisation. In the eighteenth century— the Settecento—there is undoubtedly a general lowering of the standard of Italian painting—with one great exception, the Venetian School which now enters upon a final phase of greatness. Representatives of it are, among the *veduta* painters, that incomparable classic Antonio Canale called Canaletto (1697-1770) and the delicious romanticist Francesco Guardi (1712-93), and among the figure painters Giovanni Battista Tiepolo (1696-1769), beyond question the most brilliant decorator of the whole Rococo period. During the nineteenth century and up to our own time, there has indeed been no lack of pictorial activity in Italy, though the results unfortunately are mostly on rather a low level æsthetically : and the history of Italian painting as a whole has ceased to be of more than local interest. Of sporadic individual talent there has, on the other hand, been no lack : as cases in point we may, perhaps more justly than that of Giovanni Segantini (1858-99), over-emotional rhapsodizer on Alpine themes, quote those offered by—to choose one representative of yesterday and to-day respectively—the names of Amedeo Modigliani (1884-1920) and Giorgio de Chirico (born 1888).

BIBLIOGRAPHY TO CHAPTER IX

For various standard works on the history of Italian art generally, see the Bibliography appended to the Chapter on Architecture and Sculpture.

Bernhard Berenson, *The Italian Painters of the Renaissance*. Oxford, 1930.
Bernhard Berenson, *Italian Pictures of the Renaissance*. Oxford, 1932.
Bernhard Berenson, *Drawings of the Florentine Painters*. London, 1903.
Bernhard Berenson, *The Study and Criticism of Italian Art*, 3 vols. London, 1901-16.
Tancred Borenius, *Florentine Frescoes*. London, 1930.
J. A. Crowe and G. B. Cavalcaselle, *A History of Painting in Italy*. New edition, 6 vols. Vols. I-IV edited by Langton Douglas, etc.; Vols. V-VI by Tancred Borenius. London, 1903-14.
J. A. Crowe and G. B. Cavalcaselle, *A History of Painting in North Italy*. New edition, 3 vols. Edited by Tancred Borenius. London, 1912.
J. A. Crowe and G. B. Cavalcaselle, *Titian*, 2 vols., 2nd ed. London, 1881.
J. A. Crowe and G. B. Cavalcaselle, *Raphael*, 2 vols. London, 1882-85.
Oskar Fischel, *Raphaels Zeichnungen*. In progress, 4 vols. so far published. Berlin, 1913 *sqq*.
Roger Fry, *Giovanni Bellini*. London, 1899.
Herbert P. Horne, *Alessandro Filipepi commonly called Botticelli*. London, 1908.
" Klassiker der Kunst " series: volumes on Raphael, Titian, Michelangelo, Correggio, Mantegna, Fra Angelico, Signorelli and Giovanni Bellini.
R. van Marle, *The Development of the Italian Schools of Painting*. In progress, 14 vols. so far published. The Hague, 1923 *sqq*.
Pompeo Molmenti, *G. B. Tiepolo*. Milan, 1909.
Giovanni Morelli, *Kunstkritische Studien über italienische Malerei*, 3 vols. Leipzig, 1890-93 (Vols. I and II translated into English under the title " Italian Painters." London, 1892-93).
Richard Offner, *A Critical and Historical Corpus of Florentine Painting*. In progress, New York, 1930 *sqq*.
Ugo Ojetti, *La pittura italiana dell' Ottocento*. Milan, Rome, 1929.
Eduard Sack, *Giambattista und Domenico Tiepolo*. Hamburg, 1910.
Paul Schubring, *Cassoni*, 2nd ed. Leipzig, 1923.
Osvald Sirén, *Giotto and Some of His Followers*, 2 vols. Cambridge, Mass., 1917.
Osvald Sirén, *Leonardo da Vinci*. London, 1916.
Osvald Sirén, *Toskanische Maler des XIII Jahrhunderts*. Berlin, 1922.
E. Somaré, *Storia dei pittori italiani dell' Ottocento*, 2 vols. Milan, 1928.
Ernst Steinmann, *Die Sixtinische Kapelle*, 2 vols. Munich, 1901-05.
Hermann Voss, *Die Malerei des Barock in Rom*. Berlin, 1924.
Yukio Yashiro, *Sandro Botticelli*, 2nd ed. London, 1929.

CHAPTER X

ITALIAN MUSIC

The Age of Dante

THE anticipation of the Renaissance which produced Dante, Petrarch and Boccaccio had its counterpart in music as well as in literature. During the previous centuries the most important centre of musical activity had been Paris. It was the northern countries, England and the Netherlands, which had first attempted the composition of music in parts; the troubadours had brought a new spirit into vernacular poetry and created a new type of secular music. As in the case of literature, so in music these influences began to be felt in Italy also. Dante tells us little about music, although he must have been keenly susceptible to it; his descriptions of music in the *Paradiso* are those of an ecstatic listener rather than of a professional musician. Boccaccio tells us more of the social aspect of music, and the most vivid picture of musical life in the Florence of those days is to be found in the *Paradiso degli Alberti*. We meet there a company of distinguished people who listen with rapture to the madrigals of Francesco Landino (d. 1397), the blind composer, who sings love-songs to the accompaniment of a little portable organ such as is often to be seen in the hands of angel musicians in the paintings of the period. Landino was the chief exponent of the *Ars Nova* in Italy. Many of his compositions are described by the name of *madrigals;* but the reader must be careful not to confuse the madrigals of the fourteenth century with those of the sixteenth, which are of an entirely different type. The madrigal of Landino's days is generally a song in two-part counterpoint. It often had an introduction and interludes for instruments, and its musical style was often characterised by long florid passages for the voices. Landino was no doubt influenced by the songs of Machaut, the troubadour composer, but the Italian music of this period has a quality of its own. Another favourite form of composition was the *caccia*, which had lively descriptive words, generally dealing with the pleasures of country life. The two voice-parts of the *caccia* are written in canon, which is carried out with great skill and at considerable length ; the style of the music is often extremely vivid and picturesque. The name *caccia* may originally have signified a hunting song, but it obviously applied equally well to the device by which one voice pursues the other.

This first period of madrigal-writing was short-lived, and during the fifteenth century there seems to have been very little native Italian music of any importance. The music of the churches was almost exclusively supplied by Flemish composers, many of whom were attached to the small Italian courts such as that of Ferrara. Teofilo Folengo (Merlinus Coccaius) tells us a good deal about music in his *Macaronica ;* he gives an amusing description of a musical priest collecting all his friends for the performance of some elaborate Mass on a festival day, and he launches out into a long and enthusiastic apostrophe to the Flemish composer Josquin des Prés, enumerating many of his works by name. In the room of Isabella d'Este in the palace of Mantua there are fragments of music inlaid in the panelling, and it may be noted that these are taken not from Italian composers, but from Heinrich Isaac, known as *Arrigo il tedesco*.

THE RENAISSANCE

It has often been said that the Renaissance did not make itself felt in music until about the year 1600, at which time an almost revolutionary change came over all music ; but it would be more true to say that signs of the Renaissance are to be traced in music even earlier than in literature. The secular style of Landino was transferred to the realm of church music by the English composer Dunstable, whose works were probably known and appreciated in Italy, since many of them are preserved in MSS. at Bologna and (until recently) at Trent. It is well known, and openly acknowledged by contemporary writers, that Dunstable had a great influence on the Flemish school of Dufay and Josquin, with whom the real Renaissance of music may be said to begin.

During the latter half of the fifteenth century Italy was overrun with Netherlandish musicians, many of whom are more commonly known under Italianised names. They were accomplished composers of church music, but in secular music they did not go beyond the *chanson*, a short type of song harmonised generally for four voices in counterpoint. The *chanson*, however, is of great importance in the history of music, because it was the standard form from which various later forms were derived. It was utilised in church music as early as the days of Dunstable ; right up to the end of the sixteenth century the practice continued of basing the composition of the Mass on secular *chansons*. This system has often been decried as blasphemous, but there can be no doubt that composers adopted it in all seriousness simply in order to provide musical themes for the setting of the conventional Latin words, and to give these compositions musical form. Occasional cases of scandal may have occurred, but in the vast majority of masses of this type (called *missa parodiata*) the music has not the least trace of frivolity.

The first music printed in Italy by Ottaviano Petrucci of Fossombrone in 1501 was a collection of French *chansons*. Within a generation the *chanson* began its development into the typical Italian madrigal, when the Flemish composers such as Adrian Willaert and Jacques Arcadelt came into close association with the Italian poets of Cardinal Bembo's circle. The early settings are very simple and hardly to be distinguished in style from some of the *Laudi spirituali* popular in devout congregations. Gradually the Flemish composers learned to treat these delicate Italian poems with more grace and subtlety. The madrigal was a form of music practised among highly cultivated people, and we can watch it becoming more and more literary in its methods until in the next century it disappears in the Opera. Along with the madrigal we meet a rival type—the *villanella*, ostensibly a rustic song, but actually written and composed by skilled poets and musicians as a satirical counterblast to the exaggerated " good taste " of the madrigalists.

For a long time the chief composers in Italy were Netherlanders —Adrian Willaert, Verdelot, Arcadelt, Cipriano de Rore, Orlando Lasso, Giaches de Wert and Filippo de Monte. The first Italian madrigalist of importance is Constanzo Festa (d. 1545). To the later half of the century belong the great Italian names—Luca Marenzio, Claudio Monteverdi and Gesualdo Principe di Venosa. The poems which they set were often by contemporary poets— Bembo, Guidiccioni, Sannazaro, Striggio ; naturally Petrarch was set to music by many, and also stanzas from Ariosto and Tasso. Marenzio's madrigals (now in course of publication) are of extraordinary beauty. The Italian madrigal was composed not so much for family entertainment as in England, as for court ceremonial, so that Italian madrigals of the later period exhibit a great dignity and magnificence of style. With Monteverdi the literary element comes into strong prominence ; the counterpoint of the Netherlanders is subordinated to intensely dramatic expression of the words. Gesualdo, an accomplished amateur, carries dramatic expression still farther, and is daringly experimental in his harmony.

Palestrina

During the nineteenth century it was commonly stated that the Council of Trent, after considering the state of church music at the time, had almost decided to abolish all contrapuntal settings of the Mass in view of the scandal caused by the employment of secular themes, and to order a return to simple plainsong ; but that, after three Masses composed by Palestrina (1525-94) in a purer style had been submitted to a commission of cardinals, it was agreed to permit music of this type, and the style of Palestrina was officially recognised as the correct style for the church. Palestrina has therefore been frequently described as the saviour of church music, and further as the last and greatest exponent of the " Gothic " style, as opposed to the " pagan " tendencies of the Renaissance.

Modern research has shown that there is no evidence for this story, and it is obviously absurd to suppose that a composer whose music was first heard under Michael Angelo's frescoes in the Sistine Chapel could have been representative of the Gothic period. Palestrina belongs clearly to the Counter-Reformation. Like his Flemish predecessors, he composed a certain number of Masses on secular themes, but those for which he is most famous are built on purely ecclesiastical material. What distinguishes Palestrina from his predecessors and contemporaries is, first, the fact that he devoted himself almost exclusively to church music (his few madrigals are of little importance) and, secondly, that he adopted a somewhat archaic style combined with exceptionally polished workmanship. His music has far less originality or force of expression than that of his contemporaries Lasso and Byrd, but no composer can equal him in sweetness and smoothness of harmony, or in the ingeniously contrived effects of pure vocal sound.

Church music has at all times followed the lead of secular music, even if reluctantly and under protest from ecclesiastical authority. As long as the enormous quantity of Italian madrigals remained comparatively unknown, musicians failed to see that the church composers of the sixteenth century achieved their often very expressive settings of sacred words through the technique of the madrigal, the perpetual aim of which was to set poetry with the subtlest attention to all its literary and emotional values. The motet differed little from the madrigal in style, and such gulf as there might be between them was bridged by the so-called *madrigale spirituale*. Both madrigals and motets were often used as themes for settings of the Mass. The style of Palestrina, polished and restrained as it is, could never have come into being but for the technical developments of the secular composers. Their methods are plainly visible in his exquisitely beautiful settings of the *Song of Solomon*.

It is certainly true that Palestrina represents the end of a period. His style may have obtained the seal of authority, but the church music, which continued to be written *alla Palestrina* for another two hundred years, is for the most part very conventional and is interesting only when it breaks away from a tradition which the composers accepted but hardly understood. What purported to be the style of Palestrina was taught continually as the basis of every composer's education, but, as the few existing copies of his works were jealously guarded until well on into the nineteenth century, it is easy to understand that the tradition gradually became corrupted.

The Beginnings of Opera

The word *madrigal* is often loosely used to cover all varieties of secular music composed for several voices, and during the latter half of the sixteenth century secular vocal music took various experimental forms, based partly on the technique of the madrigal and partly on dance forms and forms of more popular music. The whole life of the period is mirrored in it. The earlier madrigals were expressions of some lyrical emotion ; later on we find descriptive passages from Ariosto or Tasso, pictures of landscape in music and even of architecture. Croce of Chioggia sets the *gioco dell'oca* (the game of the goose, still played by Italian children) to music ; Striggio describes the chattering of women at the washing-place (*Il cicalamento delle donne al bucato*) with a group singing folksongs while the rest talk scandal about their mistresses or their lovers. In 1594 Orazio Vecchi (d. 1605), a canon of Modena, set the Comedy of Masks to music in the form of fourteen madrigals for five voices ; this work (*L'Amfiparnasso*, printed 1597) was never intended to be acted on the stage, but was simply a musical reproduction of the familiar improvised comedy with all its different characters and dialects. There is every probability that the words of it were written by the Bolognese popular poet Giulio Cesare Croce. Simultaneously Monteverdi and Gesualdo were intensifying to the utmost the musical expression of passion, and tending more and more to treat the various voices not as individuals, but as a homophonic group in which the uppermost voice took the principal part.

The moment was ripe for the emergence of musical drama. For

a long time it had been a frequent practice to perform madrigals with one solo voice, instruments playing the subordinate parts ; solo singing was nothing new. A group of poets and musicians in Florence, headed by Vincenzo Galilei, father of the astronomer, began experimenting with what they intended to be a reproduction of classical Greek drama with its musical declamation. Their first attempt was *La Dafne*, of which the poem was by Ottavio Rinuccini and the music by Jacopo Peri (1594). In 1597 they produced *Euridice*, by Rinuccini and Jacopo Peri, which was printed complete. It consists mostly of recitative, accompanied by harpsichord or theorbo, with a few attractive episodes in song or madrigal form ; the music in itself is of little interest, but serves to bring out the beauty of Rinuccini's poem. Another setting of the same poem was made in 1600 by Giulio Caccini. He was closely associated with the poet Chiabrera, and his collection of songs called *Le Nuove Musiche* (1602) show interesting examples of the new style that was called *monodia*. These monodies, some of which are purely lyrical and others more narrative and dramatic, were carried on by various composers, notably by Claudio Saracini of Siena, and eventually developed into the chamber cantata, of which many hundreds were composed in the later part of the century.

Stimulated by the example of Peri and Caccini, Emilio de' Cavalieri in 1600 composed what is often described as the first oratorio, because it was performed at the Oratory of St. Philip Neri in Rome. It is, however, a solitary experiment which was not followed up. The *Rappresentazione dell'Anima e del Corpo*, as it was called, is a musical setting of a morality play based on some of the older *Laudi* which were still printed and read, although ecclesiastical authority had for some time forbidden them to be publicly acted. Cavalieri's drama was intended to be acted to music and not given merely in concert form, as the copious stage directions plainly show. The music is extremely simple, and the unvarying rhythm of the 8-syllable verses rather monotonous, but Cavalieri presents the characters of the morality and the angels and devils in very picturesque style.

The first composer to see the possibilities of musical drama on a grander and more vividly dramatic scale was Monteverdi (1567-1643), whose *Orfeo* was produced at Mantua in 1608. Monteverdi was technically far more accomplished than Peri and Caccini, and he makes full use of the resources of madrigal technique. Peri and Caccini had assembled a small orchestra to accompany their dramas, but seem to have had little idea of what could be done with it. Monteverdi's orchestra was larger, although to modern ideas very heterogeneous ; he used instruments of different quality to accompany scenes of definite character, and occasionally wrote very daringly for instruments. His harmony is equally daring, and his recitative intensely expressive. *Orfeo* includes not only recitative, but half-lyrical, half-declamatory passages such as we find in Purcell's *Dido and Æneas*, of a type that we should now describe as *arioso*, as well as songs in clear-cut musical form, choruses and dances for instruments.

For some years to come opera depended on the munificence of princes, and performances were only occasional. The Barberini family in Rome were keen supporters of opera. In 1637 Francesco Cavalli (1602-1676) opened an opera house at Venice in which he produced opera on a commercial basis with great success, and during the course of the century there were no less than eleven theatres in Venice devoted to opera. When opera was carried on commercially its methods naturally became standardised. The string quartet was made the regular basis of the orchestra, and on that foundation the beginnings of classical orchestration were built up. Cavalli was a composer of considerable ability, especially in the picturesque use of the orchestra. The Venetian operas of the seventeenth century are typically baroque in the extravagance of their plots, which were taken generally from later Roman history rather than from Greek mythology ; they were baroque too in the magnificence of their scenery, which exhibited the skill and invention of the most accomplished architects and engineers. Monteverdi in 1642 wrote his opera *L'Incoronazione di Poppea* for Venice ; its methods are conventional as compared with the experiments of *Orfeo*, but its dramatic expression is even now astonishingly vivid and intense.

From Venice the opera spread to Paris, Munich and Vienna, always composed and executed by Italians. Naples did not become acquainted with opera until 1671, when a Venetian company visited the city. From that date onwards Naples gradually became the chief centre of operatic activity, mainly owing to the musical genius of Alessandro Scarlatti (1659-1725) and the dramatic reforms of the poet Apostolo Zeno.

Chamber Music in the Seventeenth Century

The favourite domestic instrument of the Renaissance was the lute, and an enormous mass of music was composed or arranged for it. As the lute was to that period what the pianoforte is to our own, the greater part of this music consists of arrangements, mostly of madrigals. There is also a large amount of more or less trivial dance music, but a certain number of collections of serious artistic music also were made. Early in the century much music was written for mixed instrumental combinations, some of which seem very odd to us nowadays ; these were largely used in churches. This instrumental style grew partly out of the vocal forms, such as the madrigal and the *balletto* or dance madrigal, and partly out of the contrapuntal style practised in the early Netherlandish *chansons*. Hence comes the word *canzona*, signifying a primitive type of fugue, employed largely in organ music and in serious instrumental music.

The most intellectual form of chamber music in the seventeenth century is represented not by instrumental works but by the chamber cantata, of which the chief exponents were Luigi Rossi (1598-1653), Stradella (1645-1682), and Alessandro Scarlatti. It consisted of two or more songs in set forms separated by recitatives, and accompanied generally by violoncello and harpsichord, sometimes with the addition of a few other instruments. Another favourite form was the cantata for two voices, often called *madrigale*, and derived from the accompanied madrigals of Luzzasco Luzzaschi (d. 1607). It was not until the middle of the century that composers began to realise the possibilities of the newly invented violin. The violin in its early years was regarded as harsh and violent in quality ; French musicians complained of the exaggerated passion of all Italian music, and English amateurs for a long time still preferred the gentler tones of the old viols. The violin, a typical product of baroque art in its outward shape, was eminently suitable to the expression of the baroque in music. During the whole of the seventeenth century it was seldom used to accompany the voice ; the songs in the operas were mostly accompanied by the harpsichord, the strings entering only in contrasting passages, so as not to overpower the singer.

In purely instrumental music the favourite form was the sonata for two violins and bass, consisting partly of dances and partly of more serious movements cast more or less in the form of fugue ; the best known sonatas of this type are those of Arcangelo Corelli (1653-1713), who learned much from the singers of his day in the development of expressive *cantabile* playing. Within Corelli's own output we may observe the change of attitude which took place at the turn of the century ; sonatas for two violins on equal terms give place to sonatas for one only, in a more operatic style. Tartini (1692-1770) further developed the technique of violin-playing, and about the same time we find the violins more habitually used to accompany voices, while the noisy and inexpressive harpsichord is reserved for loud instrumental passages.

Metastasio and the Opera

Italian opera in the eighteenth century owed perhaps less to its innumerable composers than to one single dramatic poet, Pietro Metastasio, who presents the unique example of a poet of high distinction devoting his life to the composition of operatic *libretti*. His first *libretto* was *Didone abbandonata*, first set to music by Leonardo Vinci of Naples in 1724. Metastasio, whose dramas for music (strongly influenced by Racine) show great nobility of literary style combined with much psychological insight into character, was set to music by so many composers that every operagoer in Italy must soon have come to know his works by heart, as the same *libretti* were set over and over again. The form of these operas was conventional in the extreme, and their artificiality was heightened by the practice of giving the heroes' parts to the artificial *soprani* or *castrati*, who dominated the operatic stage in Italy and abroad, except in France. The blame for the barbarous method of mutilation by which these voices were obtained has often been laid to the stage ; but modern research has shown clearly that the practice was begun in the church, owing to the difficulty of obtaining boy singers, and the papal restrictions on the appearance of women on the stage in Rome gave further encouragement to it.

Early in the eighteenth century a school of comic opera arose at Naples ; the first attempts were comedies in Neapolitan dialect, often satirising the absurdities of the serious opera. The success of Leo (1694-1744), Pergolesi (1710-36), and Logroscino (b. 1698) in this direction led to imitations in other cities, the most important examples being the comedies of Piccinni of Naples (1728-1800), and Galuppi of Venice (1706-85), who enjoyed a long collaboration with the playwright Goldoni.

Most of these eighteenth-century operas (with the exception of Pergolesi's *La Serva Padrona*, which is not a real comic opera but a series of *intermezzi* designed for performance in a serious opera) are completely forgotten ; but it must be remembered that in their day they represented the type of music that was popular all over Europe. Their melodies were imitated in instrumental music, especially in Germany, and the classical style of Haydn and Mozart is unmistakably derived from the trivial Italian musical

comedy tunes which the princes and archbishops of those days
wanted to have played to them during their meals. Operatic
melody of this type is equally to be found in the clavier sonatas
of Emmanuel Bach and in the innumerable violin sonatas of the
followers of Corelli and Tartini.

Italy remained entirely unaffected by the dramatic reforms of
Gluck, which bore fruit only in Paris and Vienna. Italian opera
was in demand everywhere, and after the famous *Guerre des
Bouffons*, caused by the visit of Italian comic singers to Paris in
1752, even France submitted to the charms of the Italian style.
The Florentine Lulli had been the creator of serious French opera
in the preceding century ; a hundred years later another Italian,
Egidio Romoaldo Duni (1709-1775), created French *opera-comique*.
At almost every court in Europe there was an Italian opera with
an Italian composer in charge of it—Ariosti at Berlin, Jommelli
at Stuttgart, Hasse, an Italianised German, at Dresden, Sarti
at St. Petersburg and Copenhagen. The Italian musicians soon
discovered that foreign countries had more success to offer them
than their own. The musical life of Italy, as described by Dr.
Burney and other travellers, was very provincial as compared with
that of the northern cities. The pianoforte had been invented in
1709 by Cristofori of Florence, but it seems to have been little
appreciated in its own country, and its later developments were
the work of German and English craftsmen. Domenico Scarlatti
(1685-1757), the most original composer of clavier music, spent
most of his life in Spain and belongs more to the history of Spanish
than of Italian music ; his later fame arose neither in Spain nor
Italy, but in London and Vienna.

ROSSINI AND THE ROMANTIC PERIOD

With the rise of symphonic music the leadership of the musical
world had passed from Naples to Vienna, and Vienna remained
the most important musical centre in Europe until the deaths of
Beethoven and Schubert. A new Italian genius made his appearance in Gioacchino Rossini (1792-1868), whom Italian writers
have often compared with Napoleon—a comparison not altogether
ridiculous, for Rossini, during a very short active career as a composer, rapidly conquered the whole of Europe. In his early days
he was regarded by his compatriots as too German in style. Vienna
had made the fame of his predecessors Anfossi and Cimarosa, whose
Matrimonio Segreto (1792) had so delighted the Emperor Leopold
II that he commanded an immediate repetition of the whole

opera the same evening. The fame of Rossini dates from the performance of his *Tancredi* (Venice, 1813) at Vienna in 1822. In Italy musical conditions had gone from bad to worse, as we may see from the letters of Liszt and the memoirs of Berlioz. The one and only Italian representative of serious Italian music, the austere Florentine Luigi Cherubini (1760-1842), had made his home in Paris. Paganini (1782-1840), the mysterious genius of the violin, whom half his hearers believed to be in league with the devil, travelled from place to place giving concerts until disease wore him out.

The Romantic movement which swept over England, France and Germany was hardly felt in Italy at all, at any rate as far as its influence on music was concerned. Yet the musical aspect of the Romantic movement in other countries derived perhaps more from Italy than has generally been admitted. E. T. A. Hoffmann, novelist, composer and musical critic, who forged the chief link for Germany between romantic music and romantic literature, was an ardent devotee of Italian music, as may be seen in his writings, although the music which he adored was the music which we should now call classical rather than romantic. If we consider the music of the period in its purely technical aspect, apart from all literary considerations, we shall see that Beethoven was influenced by Cherubini, for whom he openly professed his admiration, while the influence of Rossini is unmistakable on Schubert and Weber. In France Rossini reached his greatest height with *Guillaume Tell*, produced in 1829. Founded on Schiller's play, *Guillaume Tell* was the prototype of the French romantic grand operas of the school of Meyerbeer. Rossini had made a contract to compose five more operas for Paris, but the revolution of 1830 repudiated it, and Rossini retired to Bologna. He returned, however, to Paris a few years later, and lived there until his death in 1868 ; but he wrote no more operas, and his only compositions during those forty years were the few pianoforte pieces which were recently worked up into a ballet called *La Boutique Fantasque*. Those who have heard the ballet will have observed how Rossini seems to foreshadow much that sounds more characteristic of Chopin or Offenbach.

French music up to about 1870 or later is permeated with the influence of Rossini, especially as shown in his vivacious overtures and the overwhelming *entrain* of his concerted movements. A little junior to Rossini were Bellini (1801-35) and Donizetti (1797-1848), whose operas enjoyed equal popularity, especially in Paris. The touching melodies of Bellini's *Norma* and other operas were perpetuated by Chopin in his nocturnes.

The most interesting link between Italy and the Romantic movement is to be seen in the music of Liszt. Fascinated by the
diabolic figure of Paganini, Liszt, as a young man in Paris, living
in the thick of romanticism, set out, one may say, to be the
Paganini of the pianoforte. He transcribed Paganini's *Caprices*
for violin as *Etudes* for the pianoforte ; he improvised publicly
on themes from the operas of Rossini, Bellini and Donizetti,
and later on published his transcriptions. While Italy remained
indifferent to the movements which were convulsing German
music, Liszt created the most daring and original expressions
of romanticism out of his memories of the Italian opera, and
it was through Liszt that the spirit of Italy passed on into the
music of such composers as Wagner and Tchaikovsky.

VERDI AND THE RISORGIMENTO

For the romantics in other countries Italy had the romance
of a picturesque ruin ; the nearest approach to a romantic movement that the Italians themselves ever experienced was the
political movement that was to bring about Italy's restoration
as a unified kingdom. Giuseppe Verdi (1813-1901), sprung from
humble peasant stock, devoted most of his life to the production
of what was frankly commercial opera. Unlike his contemporary
Wagner in Germany, he had no problem to solve except that which
we find mentioned over and over again in his letters—*l'effetto*.
His earliest operas continue the style of Bellini and Donizetti,
but with a new spirit of energy which was at times almost brutal.
Looking back from the standards of the present to such operas
as *Il Trovatore* and *La Traviata*, we are easily tempted to imagine
that Verdi enjoyed a career of uninterrupted popular success ;
but this was far from being the case. Such early popularity as
he encountered was largely due to the political associations of
certain scenes in his operas which were interpreted as expressions
of contemporary patriotism, and, although Verdi himself stood
quite aloof from political intrigue, his name was used as a political
symbol, and audiences shouted *Evviva Verdi !* with the implied
meaning of *Evviva Vittorio Emanuele Re D'Italia*. What caught
the ear of the multitude were his full-blooded melodies which
have become popular all over the world ; but he had also a keen
sense of drama, and the dramatic element becomes more and
more prominent in his operas as he gradually achieved the musical
technique necessary for its full expression. *Rigoletto* (1851) shows

the first attempts at real dramatic intensity, and its conventional arias appear the more conventional by contrast with the originality of the recitatives. The next few years brought *La Traviata* (1853), an experiment in chamber tragedy, foreshadowed by *Luisa Miller* in 1849, *Il Trovatore* (1853), undoubtedly the best, as it is still the most popular, of his earlier operas, and *Un Ballo in Maschera* (1859). *Aïda*, commissioned for the opening of the Suez Canal in 1871, shows a broader accomplishment in every way ; Verdi had travelled widely after his name began to be well known, and had not only heard operas in other countries, but had made a careful study of his contemporaries. It was in 1871 that he heard Wagner's *Lohengrin* at Bologna ; but, although some of his critics complained that he was becoming more and more subject to Wagnerian influences, he preserved his own personality throughout with singular certainty and assurance.

Arrigo Boito (1842-1918), by natural gifts more of a poet than a musician, had in 1868 produced his *Mefistofele*, which skilfully adapts scenes from both parts of Goethe's *Faust*. The opera caused a scandal, and Boito for many years retired from the musical arena. But he revised *Mefistofele*, which still holds the stage in Italy, and he wrote libretti for other composers. Ponchielli's *La Gioconda* (1876) owes much of its success to the literary skill of Boito's drama ; he re-arranged Verdi's *Simone Boccanegra* (1857) for Verdi's revision of the music in 1880, and he provided the libretto of Verdi's *Otello* (1887). *Otello* marked a new departure in Italian opera ; here was a libretto of high literary quality, following Shakespeare's tragedy as closely as its form permitted, and set to music which welded the lyrical and dramatic elements into an organic whole. Another long interval passed ; Verdi had reached a stage when it was impossible for him to produce a new opera every year in the old-fashioned method of his young days. In 1892, in his eightieth year, he gave the world *Falstaff*, the libretto for which was again provided by Boito. Comic opera seemed to have died out in Italy since the days of Cimarosa and Rossini ; the operas of the nineteenth century had almost all been tragedies, generally in an ultra-romantic style. With *Falstaff* Verdi, in his old age, re-turned to comedy. *Falstaff* is not only a masterpiece of musical comedy, but a work which unexpectedly exhibited Verdi as a prophet of the future. The rest of Verdi's operas belong to an age that is dead and gone ; *Falstaff* pointed the way to a new type of music.

15

The Veristi

The influence of the realistic school in literature towards the end of the nineteenth century produced a reaction from old-fashioned romantic grand opera ; the new movement was initiated by the startling success of Mascagni's *Cavalleria Rusticana* (1890), and its inseparable partner, *Pagliacci*, by Ruggiero Leoncavallo. Neither Mascagni (b. 1863) nor Leoncavallo (b. 1858) ever achieved an equal success with their later works. Ermanno Wolf-Ferrari (b. 1876) followed in the same track with *I Giojelli della Madonna* (1908), but his comedy operas on plays of Goldoni, *Le Donne Curiose* and *I Quattro Rusteghi*, are more musically attractive, although they show little originality of style. The most successful composer of the early twentieth century was Giacomo Puccini (1858-1924), whose operas still enjoy unexampled popularity. His international reputation was made by *La Bohème* (1896), which belongs to the school of the *veristi* in its choice of a subject. *Tosca* and *Madame Butterfly* came out in 1900 ; *La Fanciulla del West* (1910) has failed to hold the stage. Puccini's best work is the little comic opera, *Gianni Schicchi* (1918). His style derives much from Massenet, and he was quick to assimilate various new types of technique ; his popularity is due chiefly to his sentimental melodies, and to an unfailing sense of the theatre. Since Puccini Italy has produced no successful composer of commercial opera.

Chamber and Symphonic Music

During the long period in which Italy exported opera to all other countries, other branches of music were almost totally neglected. Church music fared no better than concert music ; William Gardiner, travelling in Italy in 1846, gives a very depressing account of musical life. Liszt took holy orders at Rome in 1865, and from 1875 onwards he spent every winter there. Giovanni Sgambati (1841-1914) under his influence did much to raise the standard of musical life in Rome as conductor, pianist and composer of chamber music and symphonies, though his works are rather of an academic type. Other musicians who worked on similar lines were Giuseppe Martucci (1856 - 1909), Enrico Bossi (1861-1925), and Antonio Scontrino (1850-1922). They were all men of the highest artistic ideals, but their music was appreciated only in a limited circle. None the less they were pioneers and educators who did much to awaken interest in Italy for serious music, both native and foreign, and it is due to their

teaching that Italian music at the present day has reached a
far higher standard in the concert-room than in the theatre.
Scontrino's string quartets, which are admirably written, deserve
more than a passing mention.

Another nineteenth-century composer who achieved originality
in a limited sphere was Luigi Gordigiani (1806-1860) of Florence,
whose settings of Tuscan folk poetry have a singular charm ; one
of these songs, *Ogni sabato avrete il lume acceso*, is still often sung.

The school of Martucci is to-day represented by Ottorino
Respighi (b. 1879), an accomplished and prolific composer in all
forms. He has absorbed the various techniques of Rimsky-
Korsakoff, Richard Strauss and the modern French school, in
addition to his native Italian tradition ; his best-known work is
the symphonic poem, *Le Fontane di Roma*. Ildebrando Pizzetti
(b. 1880) has been closely associated with Gabriele d'Annunzio,
for some of whose plays he wrote music. His songs to words of
D'Annunzio are full of beauty, and his instrumental music,
notably the *Concerto dell' Estate*, combines the picturesque with
a serene thoughtfulness which makes him a notable figure in
European music of the present day. The influence of D'Annunzio
is further apparent on G. Francesco Malipiero (b. 1882), a composer
of more daring originality, whose somewhat experimental style
has often made his music difficult of acceptance. Alfredo Casella
(b. 1883) received his musical education in Paris under Fauré,
and was for some time known chiefly as a brilliant pianist.
Casella's technical accomplishment in composition is unrivalled,
and his outlook is more international than Italian, but despite
his extraordinary facility in the imitation of all possible styles,
he has more real originality than is often credited to him. His
deliberate intellectualism and his predilection for a light-hearted
(though by no means trivial) type of music have made him perhaps the most stimulating personality in the world of music
to-day.

Ferruccio Busoni (b. Empoli, 1866, d. Berlin, 1924) spent little
of his life in Italy and made his home for the most part at Berlin,
though for a year (1913-14) he was director of the Liceo Rossini
at Bologna. He was little appreciated in his native country, and
was known chiefly as a pianist of exceptional powers. But all
his life he was keenly conscious of his Italian nationality, and
it was always his hope to provide Italy with an opera that should
be a national possession such as *Die Meistersinger* is for Germany.
Although standing completely apart from Italian musical life,
he was linked up with it through his friendship with Sgambati
and his ardent discipleship of Liszt. His compositions carry

on the Italian tradition of Liszt, and his operas (to German words) are strongly influenced by *Falstaff*.

BIBLIOGRAPHY TO CHAPTER X

G. Adler, *Handbuch der Musikgeschichte*, 2nd ed.   Berlin, 1930.

A. Solerti, *Gli albori del Melodramma*.   Milan, 1904.

A. Solerti, *Musica, Ballo e Drammatica alla Corte Medicea dal 1600 al 1637*.   Milan, 1905.

A. Solerti, *Le origini del Melodramma*.   Turin, 1903.

R. Rolland, *Les origines du théâtre lyrique moderne*.   Paris, 1895.

M. Brenet, *Palestrina*.   Paris, 1905.

A. Cametti, *Palestrina*.   Milan, 1925.

M. Scherillo, *L'Opera buffa napoletana*.   Naples, 1916.

E. J. Dent, *Alessandro Scarlatti*.   London, 1905.

Vernon Lee, *Studies of the 18th Century in Italy*, 2nd ed.   London, 1907.

Corrado Ricci, *Vita Barocca*.   Milan, 1904.

G. Radiciotti, *Rossini*.   Tivoli, 1927-8.

Francis Toye, *Verdi*.   London, 1931.

H. Prunières, *Monteverdi* (English trans., London, 1926).

H. Prunières, *Cavalli*.   Paris, 1931.

L. Ronga, *Girolamo Frescobaldi*.   Turin, 1930.

C. Gray and P. Heseltine, *Carlo Gesualdo Prince of Venosa*.   London, 1926.

E. Bellasis, *Cherubini*, 2nd ed.   Birmingham, 1905.

E. J. Dent, *Ferruccio Busoni*.   London, 1933.

R. A. Streatfield, *The Opera*, 5th ed.   London, 1925.

CHAPTER XI

ITALY FROM 1870 TO THE FASCIST REVOLUTION

(a) POLITICAL AND SOCIAL HISTORY

ON 20th September, 1870, the Italian troops entered Rome and put an end to the political domination of the popes over the Eternal City and the central provinces of the peninsula. King Victor Emmanuel II and his ministers, on their arrival in Rome soon after, were very careful not to add insult to injury, but to secure that every due respect should be paid both by public officials and private citizens to the Vatican authorities and to the official religion of the state. Pope Pius IX took up an attitude which was to remain the official attitude of the Papacy for nearly sixty years to come ; he shut himself in the Vatican and claimed that he was a prisoner there, the head of the Church having been violently deprived of the age-old territorial possessions of St. Peter. He, therefore, would have no official intercourse with the " usurpers," nor would he take any heed of the " Legge delle Guarentigie " (Law of Guarantees) by which the Italian state fixed in 1871 the privileges of the popes and the ecclesiastical hierarchy within the borders of the young nation. The capital, which had been in Florence since 1865, was removed to Rome, also in 1871 ; and of all the foreign forces that, in ages far and near, had come to Italy to act as defenders of the Church, very often against the wishes and the interests of the Italians, only a French warship remained for some years yet in the port of Civitavecchia, ready to embark the pope and his household, had they wished to escape from their " prison " and take refuge in France.

That the pope should abandon Rome was within the sphere of possibility for some time after 1870. Most Italians would have deprecated such an event, either because they were good Catholics (though also, in many cases, enthusiastic supporters of the new state), or because they thought that the presence in Rome of the head of the Church would still give a world-wide importance to the city, with results not altogether indifferent to united

Italy. There was only a minority of people who would see the departure of the popes with satisfaction : these were either extreme revolutionaries or over-zealous patriots who feared lest clerical influence should become a serious drawback to the working of the new state. But after a few years it was evident, even to the eyes of many Catholic observers, that there were advantages in the new conditions in which the Papacy had to exist and to work. The rule over the city and the territories of the old papal state had proved, more and more, to be a most uncongenial burden on the prelates of the Vatican, often distracting or diverting their energies from their spiritual vocation ; also, a world power institution like the Catholic Church, being divested of every temporal and political interest as it appeared to be now, and living almost as an alien on the soil of a nation with which it had no official connexion, made a better appeal to the imaginations and feelings of many who had always looked suspiciously at the " worldly politics " of Rome.

Thus the new order of things did not prove to be too harmful either to the Italian state or the Vatican ; those powers, like France and Austria, who might have objected to the new arrangement in the name of the Church, found it expedient not to mix with such an entangled problem, and finally even the French warship was withdrawn from Civitavecchia. Pope Pius IX and his successor, Leo XIII, insisted upon the *non expedit* principle, namely, that Italian Catholics should take no active part in the politics of the new state, and should neither vote at the polls nor be political candidates ; but, in the process of time, Catholics were allowed to participate in municipal elections, and finally, under Pius X, they sent actual representatives to the Lower House, though the Vatican would insist on the fine distinction, that these were " *cattolici deputati, e non deputati cattolici.*" The Christian-Social movement, that had begun under the auspices of Leo XIII, found some following in Italy at the beginning of the present century, claiming to represent the Catholic solution of those social problems which had led to the development of Socialism and to the principle and practice of class war. " Christian Socialism " developed, in Italy, into a movement called " Democrazia Cristiana," which was not favoured by Pius X ; but later still, after the world war, a new Catholic party, unofficially supported by the Vatican, was formed, called " Partito Popolare Italiano," under the leadership of Don Sturzo, a very able and active Sicilian priest. This party, half-socialistic and half-conservative, lost most of its *raison d'être* with the advent of the Fascist regime in 1922, and ceased to exist two or three years later, with the tacit consent of the Vatican. |In fact, all problems concerning the religion of the Italians, and the position of the official religion in Italy, were better discussed outside the field of militant politics ; and the " Roman Question " was a national problem, such as no party officially labelled as " Catholic " could ever tackle and still less solve. It was left to Pope Pius XI on one side, and the Fascist Government on the other, to solve it finally and satisfactorily with the Treaty of the Lateran, signed on the 11th February, 1929, and the Concordat. The pope is now a full sovereign within the Vatican City, which includes St. Peter's, the Vatican palaces and gardens, and a few other spaces and buildings, and he has renounced all claims on his old territories. The position of the Church in Italy, on the other hand, is set on a basis resembling to some extent that of the Established Church of England.

Thus, after nearly sixty years, was solved one of the most delicate and serious problems confronting Italy in the hard, upward way of her new life. There were many other problems in 1870, and each of them seemed so grave and difficult that several Italians, at regular intervals of time, gave up hope that they could ever be satisfactorily overcome. And yet they have all been, to a great extent, conquered, so that the Italy of to-day, in her internal life, in many ways resembles other nations that have behind them centuries of unity and independence. | It was one of the commonplaces, and common illusions, of the period of the Risorgimento, that most of Italy's ills were a consequence of division and foreign domination. Now, " the garden of Europe " remained a beautiful garden after its liberation, despite many new and ugly commemorative monuments, but it proved to be a vastly unfertile garden ; and many evils that were ascribed to the previous rulers proved to be the results of the habits and tendencies of the population itself. The Bourbons in the South, the popes in the centre, the Grand Dukes in Tuscany, even the Austrians in the North, had generally followed the line of least resistance ; they had ruled very much according to the spirit and the character of their people ; they had, very often, become more Tuscan and more Neapolitan than the Tuscans and the Neapolitans themselves. In fact, the conquered had always prevailed over the conquerors, perhaps even too much. A foreign ruler, to be popular, must adapt himself even to the drawbacks and shortcomings of the ruled ; and only a native dictator may sometimes risk unpopularity in counteracting the most deeply rooted faults of his own nation. In this light, the Risorgimento appears to have been more an internal revolution of the Italians against themselves, of Italians trying to reform themselves, than the insurrection of an enslaved people against its foreign dominators.   Yet liberation and unification had been achieved, and only now were the Italians to discover that the gravest difficulties to be overcome were to be found in themselves and in their own country.

Much has been said about the local and regional egotism of the Italians. Perhaps too much. In fact, the real, genuine Italian never feels himself quite a stranger in any inhabited land, or among any kind of human creatures. Still less did a Tuscan, in 1870, feel a stranger to a Bolognese, or a Roman to a Neapolitan. There was a general knowledge, of course, of the profound differences between North and South ; but there was on both sides a great willingness to bridge those differences and make them vanish in the process of time. Local rivalries, between Pisa and Leghorn, between Modena and Reggio, were, and are, in the nature of things, and can be found as well in any other country. The problem was not so much one of repressing the evil side of so many local patriotisms, as one of bringing their good side to work within the range of a new and larger patriotism. Italy was a small country with so many capitals, and each capital had its own traditions of life, culture, politics and administration. The suppression of a capital very often meant the partial destruction of a tradition ; and all these traditions, taken together, meant a civilisation. Thus the unification of Italy resulted in a partial destruction of the older civilisation of the peninsula. No wonder that so many patriotic Italians began to ask themselves, after 1870, if it had been worth the while !

But many of the real and undisputable evils of the country could only be overcome, in course of time, by the united efforts of all the Italians. Roads and transports, for instance ; deforested mountains ; torrential rivers in the highlands, and pools and marshes in the plains ; insanitary conditions of life ; malaria, pellagra and other endemic diseases; large farms scarcely cultivated ; and drawbacks of many kinds to the development of a national industry. To these and other real problems, it was usual to add illiteracy (*analfabetismo*). It seemed almost unbearable to the patriots of 1870, that over one half of the Italian population should be illiterate, while there were already countries in Europe where the percentage of illiterates was practically nil. Much was attempted to modify this state of things, but the results were, for a long time, disheartening. Many Italians did not seem to want any form of scholar learning ; in fact, many

Italians did not need it at all. A shepherd may know many precious things, and he may be a model of a shepherd, and yet not know how to read and write. So for the able-bodied sailor, for the agricultural hand and the unskilled workman, for the miner and even for the artisan. Not a few of the greatest artists of the Renaissance could hardly do more than write their names ; yet we do not consider them uncivilised, or representing an inferior type of humanity. So many Italians were illiterate, because the general conditions of the peninsula did not make illiteracy a disadvantage for those concerned, nor even a drawback to national life. As those conditions were slowly altered and the life of the whole society adapted itself to new lines, illiteracy gradually disappeared, and in most parts of the country is nowadays nonexistent.

To such internal problems are to be added the external difficulties. Some of the dispossessed potentates had not lost hope of a restoration. Austria was definitely not a friend to the new kingdom, the formation of which had meant for her the loss of so many provinces and could mean, in the future, the loss of more. Furthermore, the new Italy could not avoid having a policy of her own in the Balkans, probably antagonistic to that of Vienna, and the occupation of Rome had been a blow to the legitimism of the Holy Emperors. And France was no less a suspicious neighbour : she had been, to the last day, the defender and protector of papal Rome, and she had an age-long tradition of interference with, or indirect control of, Italian affairs. Besides, she was, after England, the only great naval power in the Mediterranean. United Italy meant to her the rising of a new great nation largely dependent upon the sea for her life, possessing some of the best commercial and military strongholds in the Mediterranean, and keeping up a great tradition of seafaring. Between such two neighbours as France and Austria, Italy felt herself in a continuous danger, her feeling being, to some extent, merely a psychological result of her too recently acquired independence. It is certain that Austria always was to her a potential enemy, and France a rather unreliable, and sometimes uncomfortable, friend. Italy was thus obliged to develop an army and a military spirit, in which her people were lacking ; the very good and disciplined Piedmontese army became the seed out of which a national army could grow. And the scattered remains of the Piedmontese and Neapolitan fleets soon developed into one of the best navies in the world.

The foreign policy of the new kingdom was thus divided between a natural but never gratified inclination towards France, and an actual fear of Austria. But only the French occupation of Tunisia, which was gravely resented by the Italians, and the influence brought to bear by Bismarck both on Rome and Vienna, led to the signing of the first treaty of the Triple Alliance between Germany, Austria and Italy, in 1882 : a merely defensive treaty, which was renewed again and again until it fell in abeyance when Italy declared her neutrality in August, 1914, at the beginning of the World War, and was actually denounced by Italy in the early 1915. Parallel with this treaty, a naval agreement was signed with Great Britain, sanctioning the mutual interest of the two countries in the maintenance of the *status quo* in the Mediterranean.

Having thus gained a comparative security among the ever-stormy waves of European politics, Italy could now give more of her energies to her internal problems, and to the need for expansion and colonisation, which was more and more generally felt. The *Vecchia Destra Liberale*, a party inspired by a moderate and very critical liberalism, of the pattern left by Cavour, was defeated in Parliament by the Left-wing parties in 1876. The victorious *Sinistra* was a heterogeneous amalgam of Republicans, Radicals and Democrats, and their leader and new prime minister, Depretis, could do no better than try and attract to the service of the state all kinds of representative men, from whatever political quarter they came. Also, he had to persuade his direct followers to conciliate their internal differences, so that a majority could be relied upon. And the differences of opinion between the various parties were so vague and superficial, that a period of general transformation began : the period of *trasformismo*, as it was called with a sense of disgust by many who had too much at heart the old principles and political dogmas ; *Destra* and *Sinistra*, Liberalism, Conservatism, Democracy, Radicalism (and even, to some extent, Republicanism), became little more than empty words, useful to enflame the feelings and rouse the enthusiasms of provincial electorates, but hardly significant in the atmosphere of Montecitorio, the Lower House in Rome, where every deputy was mainly the representative of local interests, trying to secure for his constituency and for himself as many advantages as he could from the Government. *Trasformismo*, therefore, was not an evil in itself, because much that was being transformed was not worth keeping unaltered ; but it was, from another point of view, the unpleasant effect of an unwholesome cause : it implied a general vagueness and weakness of principles, and it showed how scanty was the critical power being brought to bear on political ideas, and how indifferent many Italians still

were to the life and the development of their new state. The
democratic parties, in their long tenure of office, did not show
themselves inspired by a strong sense of moral discipline and
social virtue ; on the contrary, they seemed to be only too op-
portunistic, and ever leaning towards that spirit of *combinazione*,
which has always been attributed to the Italians as one of their
less admirable qualities.

A sense of discouragement and even of disaffection was everywhere to be felt in the early eighties, partly due to the precarious
international position of Italy, and also to the increasing difficulty of internal and financial problems. The need for a
" strong hand " was voiced from many quarters, and many
Italians welcomed it in the person of Francesco Crispi, a
Sicilian who had taken a prominent part in Garibaldi's legendary
liberation of the South, and who had gradually modified his
original republican ideas until he became, to all practical purposes, the leader of the *Sinistra*. Crispi became Prime Minister
in 1887 and retained that office, with two short interruptions,
until 1896 ; and many Italians expected a good deal from him,
without being able to say even to themselves what they actually
expected. Crispi's main work consisted in giving more vigour
to Italy's external and colonial policy, using the Triple Alliance
as a means of securing some international recognition of Italy's
rights and needs ; Bismarck encouraged him on this line, with
the result of straining the relations between Italy and France
to the point that rumours of an imminent war between these
two countries were heard more than once ; it was partly due to
the good offices of a third and impartial power, Great Britain,
if the ill feeling on both sides did not lead to serious consequences.
From 1891 till 1896 Crispi persevered in extending the Italian
occupation of Abyssinia, trying to enforce the Treaty of Uccialla,
which, according to the Italian interpretation of it, gave Italy
a kind of protectorate over the Abyssinian Negus. The Negus,
having first secured the services of several rebellious tribes,
could face the Italian forces of occupation with a much superior
army, and, after a series of local successes had been scored by
the Italians, the latter suffered a severe reverse at Adua in 1896.
Italy had to content herself with a smaller colony along the
Red Sea (*Colonia Eritrea*), and Crispi, whose impatience and lack
of foresight had been partly responsible for the mishap, fell from
power and never recovered it again.

After the *Vecchia Destra*, Depretis and Crispi, several short-
lived ministries were held by men of more conservative ideas
or *moderati*, as they were called, whose internal policy was no

altogether successful, while in international affairs they allowed
the country to lose much of the prestige she had acquired under
Crispi, and only paved the way to a better understanding with
France. But their energetic repression of the more advanced
political tendencies in the country, and especially of Socialism,
finally led to the serious revolts which took place in Milan and
elsewhere in 1898, and had a tragic conclusion in the assassination
of King Humbert I in 1900. The new and young monarch, Victor
Emmanuel III, ascended the throne amid a general feeling of sorrow
and sympathy with the fate of his honest and popular father ;
the Left-wing parties, still more reconciled with the throne, came
to power again with the Zanardelli ministry, in which Giovanni
Giolitti, the Piedmontese statesman, was Home Secretary. In
1903 Giolitti became Prime Minister, and remained in that office,
but for two comparatively short interruptions, until the early
months of 1914. The last eminent feat of the Giolitti Government was the declaration of war against Turkey in 1911, and the
occupation of Lybia, a vast but mostly desert region which had
been earmarked to become an Italian colony since the establishment of the French rule in Tunisia. The war was ended
by the Treaty of Lausanne in October, 1912, in consequence
of which Lybia remained to Italy, who also maintained her
occupation of Rhodes and the Dodecanese islands. The guerrilla
war on the Lybian desert went on, the rebellious tribes being supported and sometimes led by Turkish emissaries ; and the complete occupation of the territory, implying also the submission
of the various tribes and local potentates, was not achieved until
the winter of 1931, when the oasis of Cufra, not far from the
Egyptian border, fell to the Italian troops. A third Italian
colony is Somaliland, the occupation of which began as a private
enterprise, and in recent years has been enlarged by agreement
with the British Government.

The last twenty years before the Great War were marked
in Italy by a growing prosperity. Peace at home and abroad,
better communications, improved methods of agriculture, the
large development of electricity and the growth of several specialised industries (like the motor-car industry) were the visible and
immediate causes of that prosperity ; but its deep-lying source
is to be found in the changed attitude of the Italian mind confronted with the circumstances and the problems of modern life.
Instead of paying a grudging and suspicious attention to the
novelties that were being developed in other countries, Italians
began to be more and more unprejudiced and energetic. In
certain fields they even succeeded in leading the way. Whenever

they found material or political circumstances barring them from
further progress, they developed a national consciousness of those
obstacles, and made them become national problems : so that the
nation was now kept together, more than by anything else, by the
consciousness of its own handicaps and drawbacks. One of these
was the total, or almost total, lack of those raw materials that are
essential to industry, such as coal, iron and petrol ; the second
one, in order of importance, was the overpopulation of the agricultural districts, and the fatality of emigration in unfavourable
conditions. The figures of emigration increased every year,
a maximum being reached in 1913, when over 600,000 Italians
left their country in search of work or of a better chance in life.
Although since the war emigration has diminished considerably,
it is estimated that in these days there are between 10 and 12
million Italians abroad ; adding these to the 42 million who
live in the country, the total figure surpasses that of the population of Great Britain. Yet the capital wealth of Italy is
roughly estimated at a total figure which is about twice as much
as the total income of all the British subjects for one year. This
might suggest the idea of a country living on the verge of starva-
tion ; but the contrary is true. Almost everybody is poor in
Italy, but practically nobody is a miser, and the recent economic
crisis has been felt there less tragically than in other countries.
All this is due to a fairly reasonable distribution of the means
of production, to agriculture being the fundamental resource of
the country, and to a very centralised system of administration,
of banking, of education and of all the social services and activities.
The first decades of united life brought to the country, if
nothing else, a numerical increase and a biological improvement
of the population, as is clearly shown by many statistics. Even
the Great War (which cost nearly 600,000 dead and about as
many crippled), and the ensuing plague of *grippe*, did not affect
considerably the growth of Italian population in number and
strength, as the losses were largely compensated by the stop-
page of emigration during the years of the war. It may be interesting to note that the total population of the peninsula at the
time of the wars of the Risorgimento is calculated to have been
about 20 millions, and in the first years after 1861 the number
of young people physically unfit for the compulsory military
service was appalling. In our days, the percentage of those
exempted from military service owing to physical unfitness is
almost irrelevant. Such a remarkable and sudden growth of the
Italian population in number and strength, and such widening
of the sphere of its activities, were not to take place without

an accompaniment of social and political troubles. New Italy
was like a vigorous and somewhat rough and riotous child growing
out of an old, noble and rather decayed family. Decadent habits
and feelings were still to be found in her, bound up with her sense
of being the descendant of a noble lineage and the heir to glorious
traditions. Yet all the fresh impulses of her new life pointed
to an ideal aim, which was to consist in the development of a
civilisation essentially Italian and completely modern at the
same time. This has been the obscure but persistent motive
underlying all the internal and international events of Italian
history in the present century. Socialism, which grew step by
step with industry, practically replaced all the older forms of
revolutionarism, such as anarchism and republicanism, though
absorbing some of the spirit that had been peculiar to them in
Italy ; and as industry, for many reasons, could not grow further
after the war, neither could Socialism grow, nor point to any
practical solution of the fundamental problems of the country
as a whole. The period of intensive *red* turbulence in the years
between 1919 and 1922 was but a *crisi di giovinezza,* though a
very serious crisis, and one that might have been fatal. Really
convinced Socialists were only a very small minority, and even
those were not so much interested in the political problems
concerning the constitution of the state, as in the economic and
social claims of the lower classes. Many of their ideas have been
adopted by Fascism and are now among the basic principles of
the Fascist state.

All historians agree in saying that Socialism in Italy contributed to bring large masses of the lower classes within the sphere
of political and social life, and to make them take an interest in
the working of the state. For having done this Socialism deserves
the gratitude of all good Italians ; indeed, the democratic system
of representation was so uncongenial to the Italian people as
a whole, that large masses of enfranchised workmen and peasants
never took the trouble of making use of their vote. Socialism,
by appealing to their sense of economic values, almost forced
them to take some active part in the life of the country. And,
here again, Fascism is the natural heir to Italian Socialism, as
the only bodies that are represented in the present Italian Parliament are syndicates and trade unions, and the " Corporative
System " is the most fundamental institution of the Fascist state.
But, when the European war broke out, Italian Socialism proved
unequal to the circumstances ; its purely economic mentality
made it impossible for it to see any reason why Italy should
ever enter the war ; it was, therefore, *neutralista.* And, during

the war, the support it gave to the cause of resistance was none, or rather negative. In fact, a more advanced and more energetic section of the party seceded at the end of 1914, following Benito Mussolini, who had been until then the young leader of the revolutionary section. These, with many other young elements from other advanced parties, even of the extreme Right (Nationalists), formed those " Fasci interventisti " which spread the campaign for the intervention of Italy on the side of the Allies, and were also, in some vague sense, the forerunners of Fascism.

The European war broke out during one of those intervals in the Giolittian rule which were meant to give the impression of a regular parliamentary life, with two parties, or groups of parties, being in power alternately. The Prime Minister was then Antonio Salandra, as the leader of the moderate Liberals and of most of the Right-wing groups. After the declaration of Italian neutrality, soon after the beginning of the war, Salandra denounced the treaty of the Triple Alliance, and drove towards intervention on the side of the Allies during the winter months of 1915. But Giolitti continued to keep in touch with the German ambassador, von Bülow, and expressed the opinion that *a fair amount (parecchio)* could be obtained from Austria without Italy entering the war. Soon after he proceeded to Rome, apparently with the intention of bringing all his authority to bear against intervention, and a considerable majority of the deputies called privately at his hotel. Nevertheless, war was declared on the 24th of May. But the impression remained that intervention had been wanted only by a comparatively small minority of the nation, which was probably true ; and that it had not been wanted merely for the sake of *redeeming* the Italian districts subject to Austria (Trento, Trieste and Dalmatia), but in order to test the powers of the young nation in a great enterprise, and to make her a first-rank power in the world. Mussolini and his group expressedly considered intervention as " the one condition for the beginning of a social revolution in Italy " ; and it was generally felt that most of the democratic and liberal parties of the Left, and Parliament in general, not to speak of the Socialists, had been against intervention.

The war, though carried on with great energy and a heavy sacrifice of human lives, remained scarcely popular in the country until the great Austro-German offensive of October, 1917, followed by the retreat which has taken the name of Caporetto, put the mass of the Italians face to face with complete disaster. The enemy was arrested on the Piave line by the younger recruits of the Italian army, boys of eighteen years of age who were taken directly from the barracks to the fire line; allied forces subsequently came to support them, and the main bulk of the Italian army was promptly reorganised and employed. The heavy offensive of the enemy on the Piave in May, 1918, was resisted, and this marked the end of a long period of unfavourable events for the Allies, which had begun with the Russian revolution in the summer of 1917. The battle of Vittorio Veneto, in October, 1918, put an end to the resistance of the Austrian army, and to the very existence of the Austrian empire. The armistice between Italy and Austria was signed at Villa Giusti (Padua) on the 4th of November, 1918. Once again, as so often before in history, one of the widest conflagrations in Europe had been decided on the battlefields of the Po valley. In one year Italy had recovered from the severest reverse in her history, and had become able to strike the mortal blow at the enemy. The important fact is that, after Caporetto, the largest majority of the Italians had chosen the hard path of resistance and recovery at any cost ; never before had the nation been so deeply united in a great effort for the salvation of the country, and there is truth in the now common saying that a new and very different period of Italian history began in those dramatic days.

Victory and peace did not bring to Italy all the advantages that Italians expected, nor even the territorial acquisitions that had been promised to her by the Allies before her intervention. This was one of the principal causes of the intense state of restlessness which prevailed in the country soon after the armistice. The years from 1919 to 1921 were particularly bad ; general strikes, communist propaganda, frequent ministerial crises due to the splitting up of Parliament into a number of groups, the state of utter inefficiency into which the traditional parties had fallen, and the energetic enterprise of the more youthful patriotic elements (like the occupation of Fiume by D'Annunzio and his legionaries), kept the country in a continuous turmoil. Nor did the return of Giolitti, who was in power again for over one year, alter the situation considerably.

The new and decisive factor, which drove Italy out of this state of affairs, was Fascism. The first "Fascio di Combattimento" was founded by Mussolini in Milan in March, 1919; their programme was to counteract Socialist and anti-national activities on their own ground, that is to say, opposing force to force whenever necessary ; they also expressed the need for a general reform of the constitution. Fascism spread rapidly. It was beaten in the general elections of 1919, but it scored a conspicuous success in many important centres in those of 1921.

Early in 1922 it had already become the prominent factor in
the life of the country. It was more than a party, it was a kind
of religion ; its ideals and aims were now better defined ; it
had ceased to be anti-monarchist. It was also like a huge private
army, perfectly organised, led by the best fighters who had returned from the war. But the regular army, though in sympathy
with the movement, never took an active part in it, thus maintaining a sound tradition. The *reds* proclaimed a general strike
in August, 1922, as a protest against Fascism. The Government
was powerless to take any measures whatever ; the strike was
counteracted and rapidly brought to an end by the Fascists
alone. Mussolini publicly declared that Fascism could not remain any longer a "state within the state" : it must take on
itself the main political responsibilities in the life of the country.
The March on Rome, at the end of October, 1922, was intended
to cut the Gordian knot of Italian politics. Mussolini was called
by the King to be Prime Minister, and since then the internal
history of Italy has been that of the development of the Fascist
regime.

It may hardly be within the scope of the present summary
to give an ample illustration of the Fascist state : on this subject
there is already a large and popular, though not always reliable,
literature in every European language. It will be enough here
to remember that Fascism means to be a new constitution, inspired by a philosophy of its own, and based on a peculiar organisation of society from economic and other points of view ;
that many outstanding features of its present-day life are meant
to be provisional, but that the regime aims at being durable in
its essentials ; and that the roots it has in the heart of the country
are so deep and wide that even the disappearance of the eminent
personality of its Founder could not shake it out of existence.

Our account of the political history of Italy in the last sixty
years has been comparatively ample, because that period has
been one of intense political and social experiences for all Italians.
The experiment of a united Italy was now being attempted for
the first time in history ; it was an entirely new thing, and it
developed an entirely new set of conditions and problems. These
problems were, *prima facie*, political, social and economical.
Unity and independence have so far resulted, as we said above,
in a remarkable growth of the population and of the economic
activities of the country. Italian economy, from being local
and regional, has become national and international. Millions
of Italians have emigrated beyond the Alps and the oceans,
and some have returned, bringing back, with their savings, new

16

ideas and experiences. The lever of a broader vision of life has stimulated many energies and possibilities that would have been killed by the mean provincialism of earlier days. At the same time, geographical conditions and the steady and conservative nature of the people, the majority of which still rely on agriculture for their life, all contribute to give tenacity to the old local traditions and habits. A Tuscan is still a Tuscan ; a Sicilian is a Sicilian. Although the official language is now spoken everywhere, dialects are far from dying : some of the best living poets and playwrights write in their dialects. Rome is not such an absorbing centre of national life as is London or Paris ; Milan is by far the greatest business centre of Italy ; Genoa and Naples are the capitals of the sea ; Turin and Bologna are very important centres, respectively, of industry and agriculture ; Venice, Trieste, Florence, Bari, Cagliari, Palermo, are so many other small capitals for their respective regions. Culture itself still moves round its traditional centres ; smaller towns, like Padua, Pavia, Pisa, and also Parma, Modena, Siena, Catania and several others, still remain the seats of more or less important universities. Unity, therefore, has not killed the traditional individuality of the different parts of the peninsula, and it is possible to foresee that a complete unification will never take place. Yet, as we have already stated, many local traditions of political, social and cultural life were submerged under the new conditions ensuing from unity. United Italy, in more than one way, had to start her own civilisation anew.

(b) LITERATURE

One of the most peculiar facts of the first period of unity was that the national tradition in literature (the one and only Italian tradition that might be called *national*) proved inadequate to express the soul of the nation, now that the latter had at last become united under an independent state. The tendency to derive inspiration from foreign models in literature became more marked after 1870 than it had ever been before. The various parts of the country acted differently in this respect, at least until about the end of the century : the North and the South, as a rule, though for different reasons, were more inclined to adopt or imitate foreign influences and fashions, whereas the diehards of indigenous and ancient tradition and taste were mostly to be found within an ideal triangle which might be traced from Bologna to Pisa, thus including most of Tuscany and Romagna, and then to Rome. This was the great entrenched camp of traditionalism and nationalism in literature and, more generally, in culture ; a zone that remained almost untouched by romanticism, in spite of the efforts of Tommaseo and others, and in spite of the vogue which made of *Manzonismo* the almost official literary tendency of the new kingdom in the first years of its existence. It was in Pisa and then in Florence that several young students of literature met in the late fifties, on a common ground of admiration for paganism and republicanism, and on a common deprecation of the romantic tendency of the age. They called themselves " gli amici pedanti," the adjective suggesting their vocation of school teachers and also, ironically, their fondness of the patient study of the classics, as opposed to the facile literary improvisation for which they reproached the romanticists. Some of them, like Chiarini and Targioni-Tozzetti, became well-known writers and professors of literature in later years ; another, Enrico Nencioni, was mainly a critic, and one of the first Italian students of the great English poets of the nineteenth century. But the greatest personality in the group was that of Giosuè Carducci (1835-1907), and it was mainly due to him that the tendencies of the " amici pedanti " became an important factor in the history of Italian culture. Carducci was a Tuscan in the deepest sense of the word. Born in Versilia, the son of a country doctor, he had spent some of his early years in the sad and marshy region of Maremma ; he had then been educated by the Scolopian friars and had followed the courses of literature at the University of Pisa. He was a high school teacher for some years, until he was appointed professor of Italian Literature at the University of Bologna, when still very young. Bologna became his adoptive city and the centre of his eminent activities as a lecturer, a scholar, a poet, and, one might say, the founder of a school of Humanities.

Carducci's importance can hardly be estimated from the mere perusal of his writings. It was due to some extent also to his personal qualities as a teacher and as the inspiring genius of an ever larger circle of pupils, friends and admirers. He left his personal stamp on a period of Italian culture, covering the last decades of the nineteenth century and extending into the next one. In politics he stood for a republicanism that was democratic in principle but aristocratic in fact ; but in his later years he came to admit more and more openly the great importance of the House of Savoy in the events of modern Italian history. Similarly, in the sphere of religion he stood for classic paganism as the greatest source of mythological inspiration for all men ; he believed in Reason over against Faith, and in the freedom of men from any bond of a transcendental nature. But, here again, in his old age he modified his attitude in some degree, and, in the beautiful poem *La Chiesa di Polenta*, wrote the epic of the civilising function of the Catholic Church in the Middle Ages. His philosophical attitude only can be said never to have been modified, but it consisted of a vague rationalism, and never achieved any deep and consistent form. His studies of literary history touched many of the most important points of Italian literature, and brought new light to them all : yet his method was not altogether new, nor of his own invention ; he followed the " metodo storico," concentrating on the analytical examination of texts and sources, and on the establishment of the philological links between the various works of literature. This method, which was to some extent opposed to the idealistic method of De Sanctis and others, who were more concerned with the æsthetical valuation of the single works, and tended to interpret literary history in the light of general history as an evidence of the moral and intellectual attitude of various countries in different times, was to some extent of Germanic origin, and was not, even in his early days, peculiar to Carducci alone. But what Carducci brought into his literary studies, and what made his teaching so efficient, was the magnetic power of his rich personality, the fascination of the style of his prose, one of the best in the whole of Italian literature, and his keen feeling of human and artistic values. Literature was, to him, a religion, involving a large and luminous outlook on life, a profound seriousness of purpose, an implicit vow to serve the cause of beauty and virtue at any cost. This kind of religion was only equalled in intensity by his deep and unflinching patriotism. The ruffled and sturdy figure of the great master and poet of Bologna, in the later years of his life, had almost become a national symbol of all that was most classically genuine in the tradition of Italian culture.

Such being, in a rough outline, the personality of the man, his poetry was its direct and natural expression. It began, with the *Juvenilia* and *Levia gravia*, as, for the most part, an avowed imitation of Greek, Latin and Italian classics, and of a few foreign romanticists. In *Rime nuove*, *Intermezzo*, and more especially in *Odi barbare*, it became more personal and direct. In *Odi barbare* Carducci follows the rhythms of Greek and Latin prosody, using Italian accented syllables in place of the *long* vowels of the classics ; and with them he may be said to have achieved his highest poetical results. It would not occur to one's mind that Carducci's poetry embodied a universally felt experience : as Petrarch's poetry suggests love, and Leopardi's sorrow and melancholy. To appreciate Carducci as a poet, one must keep in mind the historical, cultural or literary background to which practically all of his poems refer ; his *barbaric* rhythms seem to give us a sort of erudite pleasure by the mere fact of the successful transposition of ancient metres into a modern tongue. Whatever the occasion of the poems, Carducci's inspiration always seems to have come through a thick stratum of culture and literary learning ; his happiest and most direct intuitions express themselves indifferently in prose or verse, but in the majority of cases the inspiration of his poems is *learned*, and all of them are intensely *literary*. Every good poet must be also a student of poetry, who has learnt a lesson from his great predecessors and profited by it to produce original work ; yet, with Carducci, it seems that what he has to say would have never taken the form of verse in his mind if it had not been associated with some learned recollection. The subject of his inspiration is practically always a learned subject, and the form it takes in his poetry is one which always derives some intellectual majesty and beauty from illustrious literary precedents. He is not the sort of artist who ploughs his own furrow through uncharted lands ; he lives in the household of the classics, both ancient and modern, and works according to their rules and traditions ; even when he takes his start from recent and foreign poets, like Hugo or Uhland, which is often the case, he adapts them to his own familiar atmosphere of refined classicism. One would describe him as a poet belonging to a previous age, the last classicist of the early nineteenth century, coming after Monti, Foscolo and Leopardi. In his latest years he began to write a series of epic verses, the *Canzone di Legnano*, inspired by the struggle of the Lombard Communes against Barbarossa ; in these his aim seems to have been to achieve a perfect candour and objectivity of inspiration ; and yet, even here, the historian and the philologist that were in him could not entirely conceal themselves.

All this will help us to understand how Carducci, despite his impressive personality, and the enormous bulk of the work he left, did not appeal to the younger generation as he had appealed to his own. Those who were young at the beginning of the present century showed a widespread inclination to revolt against his teaching and his example, admiring rather Pascoli or D'Annunzio, or some French or German poets ; or else they showed a new interest in De Sanctis and his school of Romantic thought and criticism. Yet, even though they might not avow

it, Carducci had been the vital link between the greater and
older traditions of Italian art and culture, and the mentality of
Italians of the post-Risorgimento times ; he belonged, somehow,
to an older epoch than his own, but he taught his own age, and
the new nation that was now growing, to appreciate and to
maintain what was best in her ancient heritage of beauty.

In Carducci's time, Mario Rapisardi, from Catania, achieved
a certain popularity with lyrical and epic poems, the first of
which still preserve some significance. A Bolognese, Enrico
Panzacchi, was like a minor Carducci in the type of his inspiration,
and wrote a good deal to celebrate social and political occasions ;
some of his books of criticism would be of interest to the student
of the Italian culture of those days. Olindo Guerrini (" Lorenzo
Stecchetti ") achieved perhaps more popularity than he deserved
with his humorous and satirical poems, in which the paganism
of the school was often brought forward to exalt or justify a
sensual inspiration, while many motives were derived from such
romantic sources as Baudelaire. Among Carducci's own pupils,
only two achieved poetic distinction : Severino Ferrari, who
left a few delicate lyrics, some of them inspired by family life
and affections, and Giovanni Pascoli (1855-1912), who was to
obtain public recognition as a poet of great distinction only late
in his life. Both Ferrari and Pascoli brought an intimate touch
into their inspiration, which was sometimes lacking in Carducci ;
they found their poetic scenery, so to speak, more within themselves than in the external events of society or in the monuments
of the past. Pascoli in particular, although a keen student of the
classics, and himself a much-praised author of Latin poems, is
not a classicist, nor a *poeta letterato* in the same sense as Carducci.
He belongs to a later age of which he is one of the typical representatives.

How much of Pascoli's inspiration is due to the tragedy
that befell him and his family in the days of his childhood, is
still a matter of discussion. His father, a big farmer on the estates
of a noble family in Romagna, was shot dead one evening as he
was driving his grey mare back to the country house, bringing
with him two dolls which were meant as presents to his small
daughters. The mare found her way home unguided, and the
whole family saw her arrive with the cart carrying the dead body
and the presents. The murderer was not discovered, though
Pascoli, in many passages of his works, seems to hint at a strong
suspicion as to his identity, and even suggests that the impunity
of the culprit was due to some obscure collusion with local
authority. However, the widow and her many children were

left in a state of almost complete destitution ; she died not many years after, of privations and sorrow, and none of her children, except Giovanni, and even he rather late in his life, could obtain that position in society which they might have hoped for had their father survived. No wonder that Pascoli became a melancholy youth, a hard and solitary worker, and an advanced revolutionary. He felt a victim of society, and he sympathised with the surging aspirations of the lower classes ; Carducci's aristocratic and sturdy republicanism would not appeal to him : that was a creed for an energetic optimist, and Pascoli was not an optimist, nor could he display much energy except in his own work. Pascoli took his degree in classics at Bologna and became a high school teacher, in which capacity he had to spend long and dreary years in secluded provincial towns ; his only company was a younger sister, Maria, who lived with him ever afterwards. He never married ; his meagre salary was often needed to support brothers and sisters in distress. Besides, love does not seem to have played an important part in his life, and it has practically no part in his poetic inspiration. He has been described as a poet of nature, and has been often praised for being one of the few Italian poets who ever derived their inspiration from natural things, such as birds, trees, flowers, and sometimes the stars. This is true, yet it needs some qualification. The English " Lake poets " and some German romantics may have influenced Pascoli's mind, but he remains essentially a follower of Virgil and Hesiod. Nature to him is the nature of the *contadino* ; a nature which the incessant work of man has subdued, fertilised, somehow humanised ; it is the repository of perennial labour and ancestral tradition ; it is a nature endowed with a soul, and this is the soul of the multitudes who have toiled on it for millenniums. The Virgilian " Arbusta iuvant humilesque myricae " was Pascoli's favoured motto, *Myricae* being the title of his first collection of small Georgic poems : and the stress of the sentence should be on the verb, *iuvant.* " Let others "—the poet seems to say—" be inspired by great events, deep passions or majestic scenery ; we find pleasure in these humble things, and they are after all useful, and even necessary, to the life of our kind." Even in his intense, almost Franciscan, love of birds Pascoli seldom forgets to remind us that they are useful for agriculture. The *Primi poemetti* and the *Nuovi poemetti*, almost entirely dedicated to the labours and the events of rustic life, provide a continuous illustration of Pascoli's characteristic sense of nature. The *Canti di Castelvecchio*, on the other hand, show us more of Pascoli's

own personality : his melancholy longing for the past, his tragic
sense of the smallness and solitude of man in a universe which
is either soulless or inimical, his instinctive sympathy with the
humblest workers, his almost pessimistic and Leopardian feeling
of the necessity for human solidarity as a defence against sorrow
and death, his mild sentimental patriotism, these are all characteristics that enable us to see him as the best representative
of the national mind and feeling of Italy in the age of her discouragement, when the great dreams of the Risorgimento had
been dispelled by crude and squalid realities.   It was the age
of positivism and materialism in philosophy, of anti-clericalism
and " trasformismo " in home politics, of renouncements and
failures in international and colonial affairs ; the age when both
industrialism and socialism were beginning to spread.

One might say that Pascoli saw in Christianity what medieval
Christianity saw in Virgil : the intelligible expression of deep-
lying truths ; yet an expression which did not give exactly the
truth.   He was not even a pagan in the sense of Carducci ; he
was, for the greater part of his life, a sentimental materialist.
His classical scholarship provided him with one great poetical
opportunity : that of re-expressing some of the most solemn
myths of the past in terms of his own feeling of life.   Thus, for
instance, he represents the return of Ulysses to Ithaca as the
disconsolate experience of a man who has travelled and laboured
all his life to achieve greatness and knowledge, and who now
finds that he cannot even recognise his own dear native land.
Most of his poems of this kind are in *Poemi conviviali*.   His
later historical poems are of minor importance ; but he also left
some important studies on Dante, and for a few years was
Carducci's successor in the chair of Italian Literature at Bologna.
At his death, students of Bologna University clamoured that he
should be succeeded by the other popular poet of Italy, Gabriele
D'Annunzio.   But D'Annunzio hastened to decline the offer,
publicly stating that he preferred to live and work on open
sand-dunes than in stuffy classrooms.   Thus the tradition of
learned poets who were or became professors of literature was
broken ; poetry was being divorced from the academic traditions.
It seems probable that a long time will have to pass before the
two are reunited.

Born in Pescara (Abruzzo) in 1863, D'Annunzio was educated
in the old Collegio Cicognini of Prato, where he received a very
good classical training and learnt the best Tuscan of the Trecento
and Cinquecento.   He was precocious and restless, good in progress and unsatisfactory in conduct.   Once, to discountenance

a college priest whom he disliked, when serving him at mass, he made the responses in pure Greek instead of Latin.   On leaving college he did not join the university ; life was calling him with an irresistible attraction.   He was, for a time, the social editor of Roman papers, but soon adopted the policy, very risky in Italy, of expecting all his financial support from his literary activities ; the result was more than once disastrous, although one should not take without reserve all the popular legends about D'Annunzio's recklessness and irregularity.   A very sober and hard-working man, his " greed of life " mainly manifested itself in sensuous love adventures, and in his daring initiative during and after the Great War.   He began his poetical career at the age of sixteen with the publication of a booklet of lyrics, *Primo vere*, in 1879 ; but showed more of his personality in *Canto novo* ('82), *Intermezzo di Rime* ('83), *Isaotta Guttadauro* ('86), *La Chimera* ('90).   This first group of immature and yet remarkable poems already shows that marked sensuality which will remain typical of most of D'Annunzio's later work.   This is not simply because their subjects are mostly erotic, but because they always reveal a sensual way of appreciating the values of life. D'Annunzio seems to find a sort of sensual pleasure even in the actual work of composing his poetry.   Also, he is very much under the influence of certain models, partly Italian (Carducci and some classics), but very largely foreign and modern.   The influence on him of the late French and English romantics, or, as they have been called, Decadents, is obvious.   Hugo, Baudelaire, and, more especially in his later production, Swinburne, Verlaine, Rimbaud, Francis Jammes and a few others, appear to have exercised a deep influence on D'Annunzio's inspiration.   But in 1892 he published the *Elegie romane*, in "barbaric" distichs, which were only to be surpassed in poetic merit by some of the later works included in the volumes of *Laus Vitae*.   Rome, with the elegance of her modern society life developing itself on the background of medieval and pagan buildings and scenery, arouses the poet to an intensity of feeling and a terseness of expression that are sometimes unsurpassable.

More than ten years will elapse before D'Annunzio will display again his highest poetical gifts.   He is now attracted by prose and the theatre.   Already, in *Terra vergine* (1882), he had shown in a series of realistic sketches of peasant life in Abruzzo his powers of crude vision and direct expression.   His first important novel, *Il piacere* (1889), is a clear, though artistically imperfect, expression of D'Annunzio's philosophy : the hero of the novel is the author himself, a hedonist with an intense, lawless, almost

heroic sense of beauty.   One thinks of Oscar Wilde ; and, indeed,
not a little of Wilde's high-faluting complacency and æsthetic
snobbery has passed into the Italian's style.   Nietzsche is already
dawning on D'Annunzio's horizon ; his novels, *L'innocente* ('92),
Il trionfo della morte ('94), *Le vergini delle rocce* ('96), *Il fuoco*
(1900), *Forse che sì, forse che no* (1910), suggest more and more
distinctly a Nietzschean conception of life.   Very much the same
may be said of most of the plays : *La città morta* ('98), *La Gioconda*
('99), *Francesca da Rimini* (1902), *La Figlia di Jorio* (1904),
La fiaccola sotto il moggio (1905), *La Nave* (1908), *Fedra* (1909),
Più che l'amore (1907), *Parisina* (1913), *Il ferro* (1914), and the
two that were written in French : *Le martyre de St. Sébastien*
(1911) and *La Pisanella* (1913).   Space prevents us from entering
into a detailed description of these works ; they present a large
variety of subjects, and are also very different in manner.   *La
Figlia di Jorio*, like the *Novelle della Pescara* (1902), in its subject
and inspiration belongs to that school of " local realism " which
had been flourishing in the south of Italy since the days of Verga,
and of which we shall have to say more.   *Francesca da Rimini*
gives a new rendering of a popular subject and is, like *La Nave*
and *Fedra*, expressive of D'Annunzio's pleasure in reconstructing
milieux and characters of more primitive and less sophisticated
ages, and in showing the triumph of the same elementary instincts
and passions of which he feels the urge in himself.   At the same
time, it would be wrong to represent him as a *primitive* artist.
Side by side with the primitive, some even say "the barbarian,"
there is the decadent in him ; in many cases, his original inspiration is primitive, while its developments and the final form in
which it expresses itself may be called decadent.   One seldom
finds in his works that balanced proportion between conception
and expression, that harmony of thought and form, which is
in the best traditions of Italian poetry.   D'Annunzio indulges
in the pleasures of a luxuriant form, even though it may be
entirely out of harmony with the requirements of his subject,
just as he indulges lustily in the savage promptings of passion and
instinct.   He has been described as a primitive shepherd of the
Abruzzese mountains who has absorbed too much civilisation,
too quickly and undiscriminatingly.   And there is truth in this
description ; although one should not forget that here and there
in the works already mentioned, and especially in many pages
of the *Laudi* (*Laudi del cielo, del mare, della terra e degli eroi*,
several volumes, beginning 1903), he has achieved a perfection
of his own : he still appears there as a sensual poet, yet a great
poet.   The moralist may have a continuous reason for protest

against him ; but the critic must admit that he sometimes finds a perfect expression of human experiences that are too often badly expressed or not expressed at all.

Of D'Annunzio's later work, mainly inspired by his experiences in the war and in the adventure of Fiume, only *Notturno*, perhaps, will remain as a book of outstanding literary merit : it contains a series of notes which he set down during his temporary blindness after an aeroplane accident during the war, and might be described as this author's *De Profundis*, not because it contains any obvious trace of piety and repentance, but because here D'Annunzio has been compelled for once, by the mere force of circumstances, to look within himself instead of revelling in the enjoyment of the world without. Apart from this, and from the best pages of his earlier books, he remains now as a most remarkable artist who has outlived his own day ; a popular hero, but not a popular poet expressing the taste and the feeling of his nation at the present stage of her development. He had been the typical poet of the adolescence of the new Italian nation, from the early nineties until the first years of the present century. It was the age of Italy's sudden growth in population and economic outlook, one of peace and comparative prosperity both at home and abroad ; and there was a leisured class, a mixture of old decadents and new rich, to whom D'Annunzio appealed with his superhumanism and sensuality, with the crudeness of his passions and the exuberance of his style. Among the younger generation, a different and more sober vision of life was beginning to prevail ; but, to explain this, we must go back to see what developments the romantic tendency had found in Italy in the last decades of the nineteenth century.

The Lombard "scapigliati" (dishevelled), Emilio Praga, Giuseppe Rovani, Cletto Arrighi and others, gave an unexpected turn to the Manzonian school. The Manzonian ideal was truth with a moral aim ; these writers sought truth as a moral aim in itself. Manzoni was to them a literary and not a spiritual master ; they would not adopt his Catholic faith, nor his moderate liberalism ; they all shared to some extent a spirit of disaffection and discontentment, coupling the morbid and melancholy pessimism of other romantics with a kind of revolutionary spirit. The butt for their satires was no longer the foreign oppressor but the inborn *bourgeois*. " Épater le bourgeois " might have been their motto, as well as Baudelaire's. Indeed, French decadentism was their school ; they created a type which is still to be found in Italy : the type of the *advanced* artist, who leads a very unconventional existence, and keeps himself in line as

much as possible with the new literary fashions that come from
Paris, or through Paris. They discovered that there was a certain
kind of truth, and a certain way of expressing it, which is dis-
couraging and depressing to the moderate mind of the average
man ; and they found a sort of sadic pleasure in enlarging
upon that truth, and in that manner. Rovani (1818-74), in his
Giovinezza di Giulio Cesare, gives us a disappointing picture of
his hero's character, with an air of calm, unimpassioned objectivity. Thus the historical novel in the north of Italy was
already developing towards that crude and rebellious realism
which was to find its clearest expressions abroad, in Zola and
others. Rovani had a following : among the younger people
who took their lead from him, Carlo Dossi (1849-1910) deserves
a special mention. Born of an old and wealthy Lombard family,
he was for a time in the diplomatic service, but soon retired and
concentrated on his literary work : this resulted in a bizarre
mixture of fantasy and realism, of cynicism and sentimentality.
Dossi is an eccentric prose writer and an elusive poet. His
imagination, his wide curiosity, his delicate sensibility and taste
seem to be out of proportion with his rather limited creative
power, and he hints at many artistic possibilities which are
not always realised in his work. Another Lombard, Gianpietro
Lucini, followed in Dossi's footsteps, but his abundant and
varied production is mainly the document of an uncommon
personality. Eccentric romanticism still lingers among Lombard
artists of our days, as an element inherent in their genius. Apart
from this group, two northern writers of note were Edmondo
De Amicis (1846-1908), author of tales and sketches with an
educative purpose as well as of popular books of travel, and
Emilio De Marchi (1851-1901), a Milanese who continued the
Manzonian tradition in *Demetrio Pianelli* and other romances.

In the South, romantic realism took a peculiar direction
before the end of the nineteenth century : it devoted itself to
describing local and mostly primitive conditions of life. A
Sicilian, Giovanni Verga (1840-1922), after publishing several
novels of society life, rather artificial and melodramatic in tone,
gradually turned to take inspiration from his recollections of
peasant life in his native island. He thought that the art of fiction
should be turned to good purpose, to make people realise the
existence of obscure and little-known tragedies, the importance
of difficult social problems. In accordance with the general
tendency of the age, he considered science as the worthiest of
intellectual occupations, and art as subservient to science ; and
both science and fiction were to be directed towards a humani-

tarian purpose. This is the doctrine which he briefly expounded
in his introduction to the series of novels entitled " I Vinti ";
and for a time he did not seem to realise that these new works
were of so much artistic merit, that their importance as evidence
of the problems concerning the poor classes in the South became,
in comparison, almost irrelevant. Yet we ought not to forget
that Verga's profound humanity of inspiration is due to his deep
sympathy with the unfortunate heroes of his novels and short
stories ; and his objective and detached style is partly due to
his realisation of the profound differences in culture and temperament between the people of the South, of whom he was writing,
and those of the North, for whose enlightenment his works were
intended. Having spent a considerable part of his life in Milan,
among cultured and wealthy people, he felt that the appalling
ignorance of northerners about the conditions prevailing in the
South could only be met by a crude, immediate, poignant representation of tragic realities. The personality of the author
was to disappear entirely, so as to let reality speak for itself. *I
Malavoglia* (1881) and *Novelle rusticane* (1883) are the two masterpieces of Verga, but *Vita dei campi* (1880) and *Mastro don Gesualdo*
(1888) also deserve great praise. Verga's language, in its perfect
adherence to the subject, has almost ceased to be Italian ; these
works are thought in Sicilian and, as it were, translated into Italian ;
and the author's deep emotion and sympathy are concealed
by his calm, impersonal objectivity of exposition. The tragic
quality of Verga's realism naturally led him, at a later stage,
to make adaptations of some of his stories for the theatre.

Verga's example was to inspire many other writers, especially
from the South : Luigi Capuana, already well known for other
novels and for his literary criticisms, published *Il Marchese di
Roccaverdina* in 1901, a novel not unworthy of Verga's tradition ;
and, in 1893, another Sicilian, Federico De Roberto, had published
his long novel, *I Viceré*, a poignant presentation of the events
and characters of a noble family of Sicily. About the same time
Matilde Serao published her novels and short stories depicting
life in the poorest quarters of Naples, and Edoardo Scarfoglio,
also a Neapolitan, collected his impressions of travels in the Near
East and in Africa, giving literary perfection to a new kind of
realistic prose which was to develop and flourish in the following
century.

Local realism found adepts in most parts of the country,
very often giving new scope and a sense of higher dignity to the
efforts of dialectal poets, prose writers and dramatists. We
must here confine ourselves to mentioning Cesare Pascarella and

" Trilussa " (C. A. Salustri) in Rome ; Renato Fucini in Tuscany ;
Vittorio Bersezio in Piedmont ; Giacinto Gallina, Riccardo
Selvatico and Berto Barbarani in Venice and the Veneto ;
Alfredo Testoni in Bologna ; Cesare De Titta in Abruzzo. In
Naples, a poet who has written the best of his work in dialect
is Salvatore Di Giacomo (born in 1860), who is rightly praised
as being one of the truest poets of modern Italy (d. 1934).

In Trieste, " Italo Svevo " (Ettore Schmitz) has given notable
examples of a new type of realistic novel, based on psycho-
analysis ; some of his books have attracted more attention abroad
than in Italy, and represent a type of inspiration which seems rather
unnatural to the Italian mind. Realism of a kind may also be
said to have been the starting-point of the most popular novelist
of the late nineteenth century, Antonio Fogazzaro (b. at Vicenza in
1842—d. in 1911). His masterpiece is *Piccolo mondo antico* (1896),
the history of a Lombard family at the beginning of the Risorgimento. In his other novels Fogazzaro is also interested in contemporary social realities, but from a different standpoint than
that of the writers we have mentioned so far. His central
problem is that of the relation between the modern man and the
Catholic religion, meaning by " the modern man " the positivist
scientist ; but he brings to bear on the problem, to make it still
more insoluble, his own personal feeling of life, very vague and
sentimental, and a repressed eroticism that he can neither conceal
nor discountenance. *Il Santo*, published in 1906, gave vent to
his modernist tendencies, and brought on the author the dis-
approval of the Holy See. This contrast, between his religious
creed and his innermost feelings and beliefs, saddened Fogazzaro's last years, and in a sense it was typical of an age when the
conscience of cultured Italians was reawakening to problems of
thought and religion, never so deeply felt for a long time before.
It is this revival of a deeper feeling of the problems of life that
marks the beginning of the twentieth century in Italy.

A solitary Romagnole figure, Alfredo Oriani (1852-1909), a
realist in his novels, in his polemical and historical writings
(*La lotta politica in Italia, La rivolta ideale*) possessed a sense of
language as a weapon and an intuition of the meaning of history
which have profoundly influenced the mentality of Italians to-day.

Benedetto Croce, born in Abruzzo in 1866, published his first
treatise on *Estetica* in 1900, which was soon to be followed by
the *Logica* and the other two volumes of the *Filosofia dello Spirito*.
The whole of Croce's theory may be described as a criticism of
Positivism on Positivism's own ground. All that is *positive* to
the human mind, Croce would say, is its own working ; science

only gives approximate concepts, or pseudo-concepts, as he styles
them ; theology and metaphysics make into objects what are
merely desires or suppositions of the subject.   All that philosophy
has got to do is to make clear distinctions between the various
categories of spiritual activity.   He draws a first distinction
between practical and intellectual activities, and then distinguishes
the practical into moral and economic activities, and the intellectual into artistic and philosophical.   Language, and expression
in general, fall within the artistic, or poetic, category ; history,
within the philosophical.   Philosophy and history come to be
almost identified, both of them being, inextricably, our " logical
consciousness " of the spiritual world.   The importance thus given
to art as one of the four spiritual realities of life, and his clear
and very inclusive definition of art, has secured for Croce's theory
a wide popularity even abroad, while in Italy it has become the
foundation for further speculations, and almost the touchstone of
the new school of artistic and literary criticism.   Croce himself contributed to the rebirth of critical and historical activities in Italy
with many valuable works of literary criticism and historical
essays mainly concerning the south of Italy.   Parallel with that
of Croce grew another important school of thought, founded by
Giovanni Gentile (born in Sicily in 1875) ; it had its basis on the
traditions of Italian and German Idealism, and sought to interpret the whole of reality in terms of the dialectic of thought,
considered as a " pure act " of the mind.   Gentile's principal
books are *Teoria generale dello spirito come atto puro* (1916) and
the two volumes of the *Sistema di logica* (1917 and 1922).
    Both these eminent masters of thought have deeply in-
fluenced the process of rejuvenation of Italian culture in the
present century, suggesting or clarifying problems to which
the minds even of very cultured Italians had been unaccustomed
in the preceding period ; and, despite being both very unorthodox,
they have contributed to reawaken many spirits to the importance
of religion.   Critics, after Croce, have all felt the need for bringing
clear light into their theoretical conception of art, while creative
artists seem to have been all more or less intensely preoccupied
with speculative, religious or practical and political problems,
in a way quite unknown to their more refined, but also more
conventional, predecessors of the late nineteenth century.   Papini
and the Futurists were the most typical representatives of this
new direction.   Giovanni Papini, born in Florence in 1881 from
a family of the poorest middle class, would have become a skilled
artisan, a schoolmaster or an obscure clerk, had it not been for
his precocious curiosity for art, literature and philosophy ; he

had no teachers, and he followed no regular course of studies, but at the age of twenty-two could found a magazine, *Il Leonardo*, which attracted some of the best brains among the younger generation in Florence ; a few years later he was one of the founders of *La Voce* with Giuseppe Prezzolini, and from 1913 to 1915 he edited *Lacerba*, a futurist magazine, with Ardengo Soffici. His main work at this early stage was *Un uomo finito* (1912), an autobiographical novel which seemed to express, in some way, the dramatic failure of Papini's youth to achieve its great end : a supreme intellectual victory over the world round him. His witty but violent skits against personalities of great renown were collected in *Stroncature* ('16), and various critical appreciations of his friends in *24 cervelli* ('13). But Papini's eager and restless mind could not remain still in an attitude of discomfiture and uncertainty. After his futuristic excesses, and the experiences of the war period, his conversion to Catholicism began, and found expression in 1920 in the *Storia di Cristo*, to be followed by many other works of hagiography and debates on religious points. His poetic vein is expressed in *Cento pagine di poesia* ('15), *Opera prima* ('17), *Pane e vino* ('26).

Papini may be said to have brought back into Tuscan prose some of the strength and substantial elegance that it had found in Carducci ; while others of the group, like Soffici, also a painter and a poet, made it more versatile and familiar, and more varied in colour (*Lemmonio Boreo*, 1912 ; *Giornale di bordo*, '15 ; *Arlecchino*, '18 ; *Kobilek*, '18 ; *Elegia dell'Ambra*, '27, etc). In the same years before the war appeared a young Florentine poet, Aldo Palazzeschi, a Futurist in name, but essentially a Tuscan epigone of the French symbolists of the late nineteenth century.

Futurism was founded in 1905 by F. T. Marinetti, a Milanese born in Egypt and who had spent many years in Paris, where he had also published a few books in French. It has been described lately, with some reason, as one of the final derivations of romanticism ; certainly, it resembles the romantic *Sturm und Drang* in its reaction against all forms of static adoration of the past, and in its instinct for making the public participate immediately in the work and the inspiration of the artist. On the other hand, in its programmatic manifestations it sounds more like a theory of life than like an artistic school ; but, even as a theory of life, it suffers from being essentially inspired by æsthetic preoccupations, and lends itself to the charge that it is another manifestation of decadent æstheticism. Its gospel of energy at all costs, of broadmindedness, of liberation from rhetorical commonplaces and from " the slavery of the past,"

expresses a feeling of life which began to be felt by young Italians
before the war, had a part in determining Italy's intervention,
and in later years contributed to the growth of Fascism.   It
belongs, therefore, more to political history than to the history
of art.   In fact, not long after the end of the war, the futuristic
nd post-romantic craze for novelty and modernity found a
counterpoise in a more restful and vaguely ironical current of
taste which had its best expression in the Roman magazine,
La Ronda.   Writers like Vincenzo Cardarelli, Antonio Baldini,
Riccardo Bacchelli, Emilio Cecchi, Bruno Barilli, all became
known, or better known, through *La Ronda* (1919-23).   They had
several points in common among them, such as a great respect
for literary and other traditions, a delicate sense of form, a wish
that all the novelties of this modern age should not disturb
the old, essential characters of the nation.   Not many years
later, their attitude was taken up and developed, also politically,
by younger Fascist writers, and for polemical purposes it was
given the name of " Strapaese " (super-village), over against
" Stracittà " (super-city), by which word was meant the tendency
of extreme modernisers, futurists, post-romanticists in general.
Among the latter, a remarkable narrator may be mentioned,
Massimo Bontempelli, a vivid and rather paradoxical writer.

In our brief survey we have omitted the names of several
writers of merit.   Federigo Tozzi (1883-1920), in his *Tre Croci*
and *Il podere*, shows himself a Tuscan follower of Verga with his
centre in his native Siena.   Ercole Luigi Morselli (1882-1921)
dramatised ancient myths in an original and symbolical fashion
in his *Glauco* and *Orione*.   Among living writers, Alfredo Panzini
at his best is a fine novelist, who combines elegance, humour
and a clear sense of reality ; social and political problems were the
original motives of the Lombard poetess, Ada Negri, but she has
since been attracted by more intimate themes, and has achieved
notable results both in verse and prose ; Angelina Lanza is a
classically inspired Sicilian poetess ; Grazia Deledda has found
for her novels a copious source of inspiration in her native island,
Sardinia ; and G. A. Borgese, a scholar and critic as well as writer
of fiction, attracted considerable attention with his novels, *Rubè*
(1921) and *I vivi e i morti* (1923).   Among playwrights should
be mentioned Sem Benelli, whose able but somewhat melodramatic reconstructions of medieval scenes and characters
achieved great popularity, particularly *La cena delle beffe* (1909).
After the war, the prose theatre seemed infected by a general
inclination towards intellectual problems ; this tendency, in
spite of its drawbacks, was a refreshing novelty, and brought

17

new life to the Italian stage. Luigi Pirandello has been the best and most prolific representative of this new kind of drama, but the names of P. M. Rosso di San Secondo and Luigi Chiarelli should also be recorded. Pirandello from one point of view is the last of the southern realists, from another the reviver of the " dramma a tesi," reflecting the Italy of the after-war period, but only in a limited degree the new renovated Italy of Fascism.

BIBLIOGRAPHY TO CHAPTER XI

Collections of articles on modern Italian literature are numerous, but hardly relevant to the scope of this volume. Croce's *Letteratura e critica della letteratura contemporanea in Italia* (Bari, 1908), and *La letteratura della Nuova Italia* (4 vols., 2nd ed., Bari, 1921), are of the first importance. The following will also be found useful:—

R. Serra, *Le lettere* (2 vols., Rome, 1914) ; *Opere, scritti critici* (Rome, 1919 et seq.).
C. Vossler, *La letteratura italiana contemporanea*, 2nd ed. Naples, 1922.
G. Prezzolini, *La cultura italiana*, new ed. Florence, 1923.
B. Crémieux, *Panorama de la littérature italienne contemporaine*. Paris, 1928.
C. Pellizzi, *Le lettere italiane del nostro secolo*. Milan, 1929 ; with full bibliographies.

An important anthology of modern poetry was edited by G. Papini and P. Pancrazi, *Poeti d'oggi* (Milan, 1925). F. Guercio has edited an anthology of *Contemporary Italian Prose* in English (London, 1931).

On the period of Italian history dealt with in this chapter an important work is Croce's *Storia d'Italia dal 1870 al 1914* (Bari, 1928) ; but, also to correct Croce's own " personal equation " in treating many controversial points, we should read Gioacchino Volpe's *L'Italia in cammino* (Milan, 1927). For the period after 1914, we would recommend:—

G. Volpe, *Guerra, dopoguerra, Fascismo*. Venice, 1928.
L. Villari, *The Awakening of Italy*. London, 1924.
L. Villari, *Italy*. London, 1929.
A. Rocco, *La dottrina politica del Fascismo*. Rome, 1925.
G. Gentile, *Che cosa è il Fascismo?* Florence, 1925.
H. W. Schneider, *Making the Fascist State*. Oxford, 1928.
T. Sillani, *What is Fascism and Why*. London, 1931.
C. Delcroix, *Un uomo e un popolo*. Florence, 1928.
C. Petrie, *Mussolini*. London, 1931.
J. S. Barnes, *Fascism*. London, 1931.
U. Spirito, *I fondamenti dell' economia corporativa*. Milan, 1932.
H. E. Goad, *The Making of the Corporate State*. London, 1932.
P. Einzig, *The Economic Foundations of Fascism*. London, 1933.
A. Piccioli, *La Nuova Italia d'Oltre Mare*. Milan, 1933.

The definitive edition of the *Scritti e discorsi* of Benito Mussolini is now in course of publication at Milan (Hoepli).

INDEX

(Names in the Bibliographies are not included.)

A

Abruzzo, 21, 249, 250, 254

Abyssinia, 235

Academies : Arcadia, 152 ; del Cimento, 151 ; della Crusca, 15-17, 152, 157, 161 ; Fiorentina, 14 ; degli Incamminati, 210 ; dei Lincei, 151 ; dei Pugni, 156 ; dei Rozzi, 102 ; dei Trasformati, 157

Accent, Latin and Italian, 6

Accolti, Bernardo, 105

Acton, John, 128

Adrian IV, Pope (Nicholas Breakspear), 33

Adrian VI, Pope (Adrian Florent), 116

Adriani, Marcello, 97

Adua, battle of, 235

Agnadello, battle of, 115

Agostino di Duccio, 183

Aistulf, King of the Langobards, 28

Aix-la-Chapelle, Treaty of, 127, 129

Alamanni, Luigi, 103, 105, 108

Alaric, the Visigoth, 27

Alberico da Barbiano, 45, 52

Albericus of Montecassino, 65

Alberoni, Giulio, 126

Alberti, Leon Battista, 12, 93, 176, 177

Albertus Magnus, St., 76

Albizzi, family, 44, 52

Alboin, King of the Langobards, 28

Albornoz, Cardinal Giles de, 50, 51

Aldobrandini, Ippolito (Clement VIII), 122 ; villa, 180

Aleardi, Alearda, 166

Alessandria, 33

Alessi, Galeazzo, 180

Alexander III, Pope (Rolando Bandinelli), 33

Alexander V, Pope (Pietro Filargi), 54

Alexander VI, Pope (Rodrigo Borgia), 61, 62, 113-15

Alexander VII, Pope (Fabio Chigi), 124, 187

Alfieri, Vittorio, 157-60

Alfonso I (of Aragon), King of Naples and Sicily, 55, 56, 58, 59

Alfonso II, King of Naples, 62

Algardi, Alessandro, 187, 188

Algarotti, Francesco, 156

Alghero, 24

Alighieri, Dante, prophet of Italian unity, 1, 3 ; linguistic theory and influence upon Italian language, 11-14, 16 ; 24, 36, 37, 40, 67, 69, 70, 71, 72, 73 ; minor works, 74-8 ; *Divina Commedia*, 78-80 ; 81, 82, 83, 84, 87, 90, 97, 107, 151, 156, 157, 160, 162, 165, 213, 248

Allotropes, in Italian, 6

Altichiero da Zevio, 196

Alva, Duke of, 119

Amadeo, Giovanni Antonio, 185

Amalfi, 29

Amari, Michele, 162

Ambrosian Republic, 57

Amedeo VI, Duke of Savoy, 51

Amedeo VIII, Duke of Savoy, 55, 57

Ammanati, Bartolomeo, 184

Ampezzo, 20

Anacletus, antipope, 31

Anafesto, Paolo Lucio, 29

Anagni, 37

" Analfabetismo," 232

Ancona, 28, 32, 59, 67

Andrew of Hungary, 49

Andreini, Giambattista, 148

Anfossi, Pasquale, 222

Angelico, Fra (Giovanni da Fiesole), 198, 199

Angiolieri, Cecco, 80

Anguillaia, Ciacco dell', 70 *n.*

Anjou, House of, domination in Southern Italy, 4, 35, 38-40, 46, 49, 52, 54-6

Anselm, St., 65

Antelami, Benedetto, 172

Antologia, 163

Antonello da Messina, 203

Aosta, 20

Apulia, 21-3, 31, 35

Aquilano, Serafino, 92

Aquinas, St. Thomas, 73, 75, 76, 79, 87

Aquino, Rinaldo da, 69

259

Q

Quarto, 141
Queirolo, Francesco, 188
Quercia, Jacopo della, 183
" Questione della lingua," 13-17

R

Raffaelli, Bosono de', 82
Ragusa, 20
Raphael (Raffaello Sanzio), 25, 178, 205
Rapisardi, Mario, 246
Ravenna, 27-9, 192
Realism, 210, 226, 252-4 (see *Verismo*)
Rebellamentu de Sichilia, 74
Redi, Francesco, 151
Reggio, 23, 130
Renaissance, meaning of, 2, 24, 87, 90-92 ; in art, 175-6 ; in music, 214
René of Anjou, 56
Reni, Guido, 210
Respighi, Ottorino, 227
Revolution, French, 130, 131, 133, 159, 160
Rhodes, knights of, 117
Riario, Girolamo, 60
Ribera, Giuseppe, 211
Ricasoli, Bettino, 140
Riccio, Andrea, 183
Richelieu, Cardinal, 123, 124
Rienzi (Cola di Rienzo), 49, 50
Rimini, 59, 177, 200 ; Francesca da, 79
Rinaldo d'Aquino, 69
Rinuccini, Ottavio, 218
Risorgimento, 133-43, 224, 231, 232
Ristoro, Fra (O.P.), 173
Ristoro of Arezzo, Fra, 73
Ritmo, Bellunese, 68 ; *Cassinese*, 68
Rivoli, battle of, 130
Rizzo, Antonio, 183
Robert Guiscard (de Hauteville), 31, 66, 67
Robert of Anjou, King of Naples, 40, 46, 47, 49
Robert of Bavaria, emperor-elect, 53
Robert of Geneva (antipope, Clement VII), 51, 54
Roberti, Ercole dei, 203
Rococo, 188, 211
Roger I (de Hauteville), Count of Sicily, 31
Roger II, King of Sicily, 31-2, 33, 67
Rolandino, Paduan chronicler, 73
Rolli, Paolo, 153
Romagna, 18-19, 21, 130
Romanesque architecture and sculpture, 171, 172

Romanino, Girolamo, 208
Romanticism, 145, 149, 161, 163, 164, 167, 222-4, 243, 245, 251, 252
Rome, in Italian tradition, 2, 3, 4 ; medieval, 27-9, 32, 33, 38, 39, 49-53 ; in fifteenth century, 54-9, 62 ; in the Renaissance, 90, 92, 103 ; sack of, 117 ; French occupation, 131, 132 ; constitution, 130 ; republic, 137, 138 ; annexation to Italy, 142, 143 ; art, 177-80, 184-7, 189, 190, 192-5, 198, 202, 205, 209-11 ; music, 216, 218, 219, 221 ; capital of Italy, 229, 230, 239 ; Fascist march on, 241
Ronda, la, 257
Rosa, Salvator, 148, 211
Rossellino, Bernardo, 182
Rossetti, Dante Gabriel, 83
Rossetti, Gabriele, 166
Rossi, G. G. de, 155
Rossi, Luigi, 220
Rossini, Giovacchino, 222-5
Rosso di San Secondo, P. M., 258
Rosso, Niccolò del, 81
Rota, Berardino, 105
Rovani, Giuseppe, 166, 252
Rovere, della, Francesco Maria, 119 ; Giuliano, 60 (see Julius II)
" Rozzi," the, 102
Rucellai, Giovanni, 105
Ruffo, Cardinal, 131
Rustici, Giovanni Francesco, 184
Rustico di Filippo, 71
Rusticiano (Rustichello) of Pisa, 73

S

Sacchetti, Franco, 84, 106
Sacconi, Vittore, 190
Sagredo, Giovanni, 150
Salandra, Antonio, 239
Salerno, medical school, 65
Salimbene of Parma, friar, 73
Salustri, Carlo Alberto (" Trilussa "), 254
Salutati, Coluccio, 90
Salva lo vescovo senato, 68
Salviati, Lionardo, 14, 107
Saluzzo, 121
Sammartino, Giuseppe, 188
San Gallo, Antonio da, 178
San Gimignano, 174
Sanmicheli, Michele, 179
Sannazaro, Jacopo, 13, 93, 96, 101, 114
Sansovino, Andrea, 184
Sansovino, Jacopo, 179, 185, 215
Sanudo, Marin, 101
Sanzanome, Florentine chronicler, 74
Saracini, Claudio, 218

18

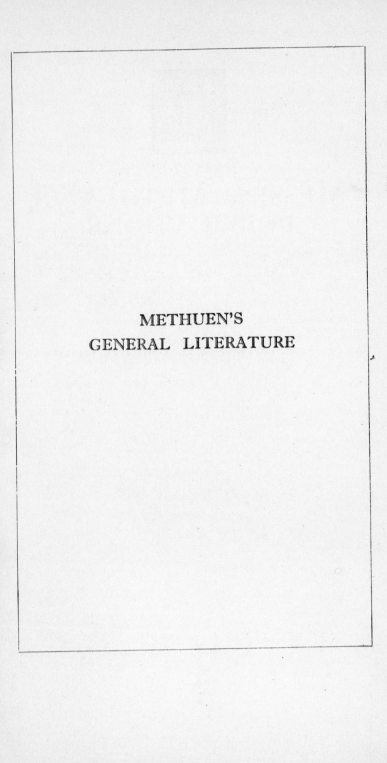

METHUEN'S
GENERAL LITERATURE

A SELECTION OF
MESSRS. METHUEN'S
PUBLICATIONS

This Catalogue contains only a selection of the more important books published by Messrs. Methuen. A complete catalogue of their publications may be obtained on application.

CHESTERTON (G. K.)—*continued*
GENERALLY SPEAKING
ALL THINGS CONSIDERED
TREMENDOUS TRIFLES
FANCIES VERSUS FADS
ALARMS AND DISCURSIONS
A MISCELLANY OF MEN
THE USES OF DIVERSITY
THE OUTLINE OF SANITY
THE FLYING INN
    Each 3s. 6d. net.
WINE, WATER AND SONG 1s. 6d. net.

CURLE (J. H.)
THE SHADOW-SHOW   6s. net.
    Also, 3s. 6d. net.
THIS WORLD OF OURS 7s. 6d. net.
TO-DAY AND TO-MORROW 6s. net.
THIS WORLD FIRST   6s. net.

DEXTER (Walter)
DAYS IN DICKENSLAND
    Illustrated. 7s. 6d. net.

DUGDALE (E. T. S.)
GERMAN DIPLOMATIC DOCUMENTS,
1871–1914
In 4 vols. Vol. I, 1871–90.
Vol. II, 1891–8. Vol. III, 1898–
1910. Vol. IV, 1911–14.
    Each £1 1s. net.

EDWARDES (Tickner)
THE LORE OF THE HONEY-BEE
Illustrated. 7s. 6d. and 3s. 6d. net.
BEE-KEEPING FOR ALL
    Illustrated. 3s. 6d. net.
THE BEE-MASTER OF WARRILOW
    Illustrated. 7s. 6d. net.
BEE-KEEPING DO'S AND DON'TS
    2s. 6d. net.
LIFT-LUCK ON SOUTHERN ROADS
    5s. net.

EINSTEIN (Albert)
RELATIVITY : THE SPECIAL AND
GENERAL THEORY   5s. net.
SIDELIGHTS ON RELATIVITY
    3s. 6d. net.
THE MEANING OF RELATIVITY
    5s. net.
THE BROWNIAN MOVEMENT
    5s. net.

EISLER (Robert)
THE MESSIAH JESUS AND JOHN THE
BAPTIST
    Illustrated. £2 2s. net.

EVANS (B. Ifor)
ENGLISH POETRY IN THE LATER
NINETEENTH CENTURY
    10s. 6d. net.

**EWING (Sir Alfred), President of
the British Association, 1932**
AN ENGINEER'S OUTLOOK
    8s. 6d. net.

FIELD (G. C.)
MORAL THEORY   6s. net.
PLATO AND HIS CONTEMPORARIES
    12s. 6d. net.
PREJUDICE AND IMPARTIALITY
    2s. 6d. net.

FINER (H.)
THE THEORY AND PRACTICE OF
MODERN GOVERNMENT 2 vols.
    £2 2s. net.
ENGLISH LOCAL GOVERNMENT
    £1 1s. net.

FITZGERALD (Edward)
A FITZGERALD MEDLEY. Edited
by CHARLES GANZ. 15s. net.

FYLEMAN (Rose)
FAIRIES AND CHIMNEYS
THE FAIRY GREEN
THE FAIRY FLUTE   *Each* 2s. net.
THE RAINBOW CAT
EIGHT LITTLE PLAYS FOR CHILDREN
FORTY GOOD-NIGHT TALES
FORTY GOOD-MORNING TALES
SEVEN LITTLE PLAYS FOR CHILDREN
TWENTY TEA-TIME TALES
    Each 3s. 6d. net.
THE EASTER HARE
    Illustrated. 3s. 6d. net.
FIFTY-ONE NEW NURSERY RHYMES
Illustrated by DOROTHY BUR-
ROUGHES.   6s. net.
THE STRANGE ADVENTURES OF
CAPTAIN MARWHOPPLE
    Illustrated. 3s. 6d. net.

GAVIN (C. I.)
LOUIS PHILIPPE, KING OF THE
FRENCH   7s. 6d. net.

GIBBON (Edward)
THE DECLINE AND FALL OF THE
ROMAN EMPIRE
With Notes, Appendixes and Maps,
by J. B. BURY. Illustrated. 7 vols.
15s. net each volume. Also, unillustrated, 7s. 6d. net each volume.

GLOVER (T. R.)
VIRGIL
THE CONFLICT OF RELIGIONS IN
THE EARLY ROMAN EMPIRE
POETS AND PURITANS
    Each 10s. 6d. net.
FROM PERICLES TO PHILIP
    12s. 6d. net.

GRAHAME (Kenneth)
THE WIND IN THE WILLOWS
7s. 6d. net.
Also illustrated by ERNEST H.
SHEPARD. Cloth, 7s. 6d. net.
Green Leather, 12s. 6d. net.
Pocket Edition, unillustrated.
Cloth, 3s. 6d. net.
Green Morocco, 7s. 6d. net.
THE KENNETH GRAHAME BOOK
(' The Wind in the Willows ',
' Dream Days ' and ' The Golden
Age ' in one volume).
7s. 6d. net.
See also Milne (A. A.)

HADFIELD (J. A.)
PSYCHOLOGY AND MORALS 6s. net.

HALL (H. R.)
THE ANCIENT HISTORY OF THE
NEAR EAST   £1 1s. net.
THE CIVILIZATION OF GREECE IN
THE BRONZE AGE   £1 10s. net.

HEATON (Rose Henniker)
THE PERFECT HOSTESS
Decorated by A. E. TAYLOR.
7s. 6d. net. Gift Edition, £1 1s. net.
THE PERFECT SCHOOLGIRL
3s. 6d. net.

HERBERT (A. P.)
HELEN   2s. 6d. net.
TANTIVY TOWERS and DERBY DAY
in one volume. Illustrated by
Lady VIOLET BARING.   5s. net.
Each, separately, unillustrated
2s. 6d. net.
HONEYBUBBLE & CO. 3s. 6d. net.
MISLEADING CASES IN THE COMMON
LAW.   5s. net.
MORE MISLEADING CASES 5s. net.
STILL MORE MISLEADING CASES.
5s. net.
THE WHEREFORE AND THE WHY
' TINKER, TAILOR . . . '
Each, Illustrated by GEORGE
MORROW.   2s. 6d. net.
THE SECRET BATTLE 3s. 6d. net.
THE HOUSE BY THE RIVER
3s. 6d. net.
' NO BOATS ON THE RIVER '
Illustrated. 5s. net.

HOLDSWORTH (Sir W. S.)
A HISTORY OF ENGLISH LAW
Nine Volumes.   £1 5s. net each.
Index Volume by EDWARD POTTON.
£1 1s. net.

HUDSON (W. H.)
A SHEPHERD'S LIFE
Illustrated. 10s. 6d. net.
Also unillustrated. 3s. 6d. net.

HUTTON (Edward)
CITIES OF SICILY
Illustrated. 10s. 6d. net.
MILAN AND LOMBARDY
THE CITIES OF ROMAGNA AND THE
MARCHES
SIENA AND SOUTHERN TUSCANY
NAPLES AND SOUTHERN ITALY
Illustrated. Each 8s. 6d. net.
A WAYFARER IN UNKNOWN TUSCANY
THE CITIES OF SPAIN
THE CITIES OF UMBRIA
COUNTRY WALKS ABOUT FLORENCE
ROME
FLORENCE AND NORTHERN TUSCANY
VENICE AND VENETIA
Illustrated. Each 7s. 6d. net.

HYAMSON (Albert M.)
PALESTINE OLD AND NEW
Illustrated.   7s. 6d. net.
A HISTORY OF THE JEWS IN
ENGLAND
Illustrated.   10s. 6d. net.

INGE (W. R.), D.D., Dean of St. Paul's
CHRISTIAN MYSTICISM. With a New
Preface.   7s. 6d. net.

JOHNS (Rowland)
DOGS YOU'D LIKE TO MEET
LET DOGS DELIGHT
ALL SORTS OF DOGS
LET'S TALK OF DOGS
PUPPIES
Each, Illustrated, 3s. 6d. net.
LUCKY DOGS Illustrated. 6s. net.
SO YOU LIKE DOGS !
THE ROWLAND JOHNS DOG BOOK
Each, Illustrated. 5s. net.

' OUR FRIEND THE DOG ' SERIES
Edited by ROWLAND JOHNS.
THE CAIRN
THE COCKER SPANIEL
THE FOX-TERRIER
THE PEKINGESE
THE AIREDALE
THE ALSATIAN
THE SCOTTISH TERRIER
THE CHOW-CHOW
THE IRISH SETTER
THE DALMATIAN
THE LABRADOR
THE SEALYHAM
THE DACHSHUND
Each 2s. 6d. net.

KIPLING (Rudyard)

BARRACK-ROOM BALLADS
THE SEVEN SEAS
THE FIVE NATIONS
DEPARTMENTAL DITTIES
THE YEARS BETWEEN
Four Editions of these famous
volumes of poems are now pub-
lished, viz. :—
Buckram, 7s. 6d. net.
Cloth, 6s. net.   Leather, 7s. 6d. net.
Service Edition. Two volumes
each book.   3s. net each vol.
A KIPLING ANTHOLOGY—VERSE
Leather, 7s. 6d. net.
Cloth, 6s. net and 3s. 6d. net.
TWENTY POEMS FROM RUDYARD
KIPLING   1s. net.
A CHOICE OF SONGS   2s. net.
SELECTED POEMS   1s. net

LAMB (Charles and Mary)

THE COMPLETE WORKS
Edited by E. V. LUCAS. Six
volumes.   6s. net each.
SELECTED LETTERS
Edited by G. T. CLAPTON.
3s. 6d. net.
THE CHARLES LAMB DAY-BOOK
Compiled by E. V. LUCAS. 6s. net.

LANKESTER (Sir Ray)

SCIENCE FROM AN EASY CHAIR
First Series
SCIENCE FROM AN EASY CHAIR
Second Series
DIVERSIONS OF A NATURALIST
GREAT AND SMALL THINGS
Each, Illustrated, 7s. 6d. net.
SECRETS OF EARTH AND SEA
Illustrated. 8s. 6d. net.

LINDRUM (Walter)

BILLIARDS. Illustrated. 2s. 6d. net.

LODGE (Sir Oliver)

MAN AND THE UNIVERSE
7s. 6d. net and 3s. 6d. net.
THE SURVIVAL OF MAN 7s. 6d. net.
RAYMOND   10s. 6d. net.
RAYMOND REVISED   6s. net.
MODERN PROBLEMS   3s. 6d. net.
REASON AND BELIEF   3s. 6d. net.
THE SUBSTANCE OF FAITH   2s. net.
RELATIVITY   1s. net.
CONVICTION OF SURVIVAL 2s. net.

LUCAS (E. V.), C.H.

READING, WRITING AND REMEM-
BERING   18s. net.
THE LIFE OF CHARLES LAMB
2 Vols.   £1 1s. net.
THE COLVINS AND THEIR FRIENDS
£1 1s. net.
VERMEER THE MAGICAL   5s. net.
A WANDERER IN ROME
A WANDERER IN HOLLAND
A WANDERER IN LONDON
LONDON REVISITED (Revised)
A WANDERER IN PARIS
A WANDERER IN FLORENCE
A WANDERER IN VENICE
Each 10s. 6d. net.
A WANDERER AMONG PICTURES
8s. 6d. net.
E. V. LUCAS'S LONDON   £1 net.
THE OPEN ROAD   6s. net.
Also, illustrated by CLAUDE A.
SHEPPERSON, A.R.W.S.
10s. 6d. net.
Also, India Paper.
Leather, 7s. 6d. net.
THE JOY OF LIFE   6s. net.
Leather Edition, 7s. 6d. net.
Also, India Paper.
Leather, 7s. 6d. net.
THE GENTLEST ART
THE SECOND POST
FIRESIDE AND SUNSHINE
CHARACTER AND COMEDY
GOOD COMPANY
ONE DAY AND ANOTHER
OLD LAMPS FOR NEW
LOITERER'S HARVEST
LUCK OF THE YEAR
EVENTS AND EMBROIDERIES
A FRONDED ISLE
A ROVER I WOULD BE
GIVING AND RECEIVING
HER INFINITE VARIETY
ENCOUNTERS AND DIVERSIONS
TURNING THINGS OVER
TRAVELLER'S LUCK
AT THE SIGN OF THE DOVE
VISIBILITY GOOD
Each 3s. 6d. net.
LEMON VERBENA
SAUNTERER'S REWARDS
Each 6s. net.
FRENCH LEAVES
ENGLISH LEAVES
THE BARBER'S CLOCK
Each 5s. net.

LUCAS (E. V.)—*continued*
'THE MORE I SEE OF MEN . . .'
OUT OF A CLEAR SKY
IF DOGS COULD WRITE
'. . . AND SUCH SMALL DEER'
Each 3s. 6d. net.
See also **Lamb (Charles).**

LYND (Robert)
THE COCKLESHELL
RAIN, RAIN, GO TO SPAIN
Each 5s. net.
IT'S A FINE WORLD
THE GREEN MAN
THE PLEASURES OF IGNORANCE
THE GOLDFISH
THE LITTLE ANGEL
THE BLUE LION
THE PEAL OF BELLS
THE ORANGE TREE
THE MONEY-BOX *Each* 3s. 6d. net.
'YY.' An Anthology of essays by
ROBERT LYND. Edited by EILEEN
SQUIRE. 7s. 6d. net.

McDOUGALL (William)
AN INTRODUCTION TO SOCIAL
PSYCHOLOGY 10s. 6d. net.
NATIONAL WELFARE AND NATIONAL
DECAY 6s. net.
AN OUTLINE OF PSYCHOLOGY
10s. 6d. net.
AN OUTLINE OF ABNORMAL PSYCHO-
LOGY 15s. net.
BODY AND MIND 12s. 6d. net.
CHARACTER AND THE CONDUCT OF
LIFE 10s. 6d. net.
MODERN MATERIALISM AND EMER-
GENT EVOLUTION 7s. 6d. net.
ETHICS AND SOME MODERN WORLD
PROBLEMS 7s. 6d. net.
THE ENERGIES OF MEN
8s. 6d. net.

MAETERLINCK (Maurice)
THE BLUE BIRD 6s. net.
Also, illustrated by F. CAYLEY
ROBINSON. 10s. 6d. net.
OUR ETERNITY 6s. net.
THE UNKNOWN GUEST 6s. net.
POEMS 5s. net.
THE WRACK OF THE STORM 6s. net.
THE BETROTHAL 6s. net.
MARY MAGDALENE 2s. net.

MARLOWE (Christopher)
THE WORKS. In 6 volumes.
General Editor, R. H. CASE.
THE LIFE OF MARLOWE and DIDO,
QUEEN OF CARTHAGE 8s. 6d. net.
TAMBURLAINE, I AND II 10s. 6d. net.

MARLOWE (Christopher)—*cont.*
THE JEW OF MALTA and THE
MASSACRE AT PARIS 10s. 6d. net.
POEMS 10s. 6d. net.
DOCTOR FAUSTUS 8s. 6d. net.
EDWARD II 8s. 6d. net.

MASEFIELD (John)
ON THE SPANISH MAIN 8s. 6d. net.
A SAILOR'S GARLAND 3s. 6d. net
SEA LIFE IN NELSON'S TIME
7s. 6d. net.

METHUEN (Sir A.)
AN ANTHOLOGY OF MODERN VERSE
SHAKESPEARE TO HARDY: An
Anthology of English Lyrics.
Each, Cloth, 6s. net.
Leather, 7s. 6d. net.

MILNE (A. A.)
TOAD OF TOAD HALL
A Play founded on Kenneth
Grahame's 'The Wind in the
Willows'. 5s. net.
THOSE WERE THE DAYS: Collected
Stories 7s. 6d. net.
BY WAY OF INTRODUCTION
NOT THAT IT MATTERS
IF I MAY
THE SUNNY SIDE
THE RED HOUSE MYSTERY
ONCE A WEEK
THE HOLIDAY ROUND
THE DAY'S PLAY
MR. PIM PASSES BY
Each 3s. 6d. net.
WHEN WE WERE VERY YOUNG
WINNIE-THE-POOH
NOW WE ARE SIX
THE HOUSE AT POOH CORNER
Each illustrated by E. H. SHEPARD.
7s. 6d. net. *Leather,* 10s. 6d. net.
THE CHRISTOPHER ROBIN VERSES
('When We were Very Young'
and 'Now We are Six' com-
plete in one volume). Illustrated
in colour and line by E. H.
SHEPARD. 8s. 6d. net.
THE CHRISTOPHER ROBIN STORY
BOOK
Illustrated by E. H. SHEPARD.
5s. net.
THE CHRISTOPHER ROBIN BIRTH-
DAY BOOK
Illustrated by E. H. SHEPARD.
3s. 6d. net.
FOURTEEN SONGS FROM 'WHEN WE
WERE VERY YOUNG' 7s. 6d. net.

MILNE (A. A.) and FRASER-SIM-SON (H.)—*continued*
> TEDDY BEAR AND OTHER SONGS FROM 'WHEN WE WERE VERY YOUNG' 7s. 6d. net.
> THE KING'S BREAKFAST 3s. 6d. net.
> SONGS FROM 'NOW WE ARE SIX' 7s. 6d. net.
> MORE 'VERY YOUNG' SONGS 7s. 6d. net.
> THE HUMS OF POOH 7s. 6d. net.
> In each case the words are by A. A. MILNE, the music by H. FRASER-SIMSON, and the decorations by E. H. SHEPARD.

MORTON (H. V.)
> A LONDON YEAR Illustrated, 6s. net.
> THE HEART OF LONDON 3s. 6d. net.
> Also, with Scissor Cuts by L. HUMMEL. 6s. net.
> THE SPELL OF LONDON
> THE NIGHTS OF LONDON
> BLUE DAYS AT SEA Each 3s. 6d. net.
> IN SEARCH OF ENGLAND
> THE CALL OF ENGLAND
> IN SEARCH OF SCOTLAND
> IN SCOTLAND AGAIN
> IN SEARCH OF IRELAND
> IN SEARCH OF WALES Each, illustrated, 7s. 6d. net.

OMAN (Sir Charles)
> THINGS I HAVE SEEN 8s. 6d. net.
> A HISTORY OF THE ART OF WAR IN THE MIDDLE AGES, A.D. 378–1485. 2 vols. Illustrated. £1 16s. net.
> STUDIES IN THE NAPOLEONIC WARS 8s. 6d. net.

PERRY (W. J.)
> THE ORIGIN OF MAGIC AND RELIGION
> THE GROWTH OF CIVILIZATION Each 6s. net.
> THE CHILDREN OF THE SUN £1 1s. net.

PETRIE (Sir Flinders)
> A HISTORY OF EGYPT
> In 6 Volumes.
> Vol. I. FROM THE 1ST TO THE XVITH DYNASTY 12s. net.
> Vol. II. THE XVIITH AND XVIIITH DYNASTIES 9s. net.
> Vol. III. XIXTH TO XXXTH DYNASTIES 12s. net.
> Vol. IV. EGYPT UNDER THE PTOLEMAIC DYNASTY By EDWYN BEVAN. 15s. net.

PETRIE (Sir Flinders)—*continued*
> Vol. V. EGYPT UNDER ROMAN RULE By J. G. MILNE. 12s. net.
> Vol. VI. EGYPT IN THE MIDDLE AGES By S. LANE POOLE. 10s. net.

PONSONBY OF SHULBREDE (Lord)
> ENGLISH DIARIES £1 1s. net.
> MORE ENGLISH DIARIES 12s. 6d. net.
> SCOTTISH AND IRISH DIARIES 10s. 6d. net.

RAGLAN (Lord)
> JOCASTA'S CRIME 6s. net.
> THE SCIENCE OF PEACE 3s. 6d. net.

SELLAR (W. C.) and YEATMAN (R. J.)
> 1066 AND ALL THAT Illustrated by JOHN REYNOLDS. 5s. net.
> AND NOW ALL THIS Illustrated by JOHN REYNOLDS. 5s. net.

STEVENSON (R. L.)
> THE LETTERS Edited by Sir SIDNEY COLVIN. 4 Vols. Each 6s. net.

SURTEES (R. S.)
> HANDLEY CROSS
> MR. SPONGE'S SPORTING TOUR
> ASK MAMMA
> MR. FACEY ROMFORD'S HOUNDS
> PLAIN OR RINGLETS?
> HILLINGDON HALL Each, illustrated, 7s. 6d. net.
> JORROCKS'S JAUNTS AND JOLLITIES
> HAWBUCK GRANGE Each, illustrated, 6s. net.

TAYLOR (A. E.)
> PLATO: THE MAN AND HIS WORK £1 1s. net.
> PLATO: TIMÆUS AND CRITIAS 6s. net.
> ELEMENTS OF METAPHYSICS 12s. 6d. net.

TILDEN (William T.)
> THE ART OF LAWN TENNIS Revised Edition.
> SINGLES AND DOUBLES Each, illustrated, 6s. net.
> THE COMMON SENSE OF LAWN TENNIS
> MATCH PLAY AND THE SPIN OF THE BALL Each, illustrated, 5s. net.

TILESTON (Mary W.)
DAILY STRENGTH FOR DAILY NEEDS
3s. 6d. net
India Paper.   Leather, 6s. net.

UNDERHILL (Evelyn)
MYSTICISM. Revised Edition.
15s. net.
THE LIFE OF THE SPIRIT AND THE
LIFE OF TO-DAY   7s. 6d. net.
MAN AND THE SUPERNATURAL
7s. 6d. net.
THE GOLDEN SEQUENCE
Paper boards, 3s. 6d. net ;
Cloth, 5s. net.
MIXED PASTURE : Essays and
Addresses   5s. net.
CONCERNING THE INNER LIFE
2s. net.
THE HOUSE OF THE SOUL. 2s. net.

VARDON (Harry)
HOW TO PLAY GOLF
Illustrated.   5s. net.

WILDE (Oscar)
LORD ARTHUR SAVILE'S CRIME AND
THE PORTRAIT OF MR. W. H.
6s. 6d. net.
THE DUCHESS OF PADUA
3s. 6d. net.

WILDE (Oscar)—continued
POEMS   6s. 6d. net.
LADY WINDERMERE'S FAN
6s. 6d. net.
A WOMAN OF NO IMPORTANCE
6s. 6d. net.
AN IDEAL HUSBAND 6s. 6d. net.
THE IMPORTANCE OF BEING EARNEST
6s. 6d. net.
A HOUSE OF POMEGRANATES
6s. 6d. net.
INTENTIONS   6s. 6d. net.
DE PROFUNDIS and PRISON LETTERS
6s. 6d. net.
ESSAYS AND LECTURES 6s. 6d. net.
SALOME, A FLORENTINE TRAGEDY,
and LA SAINTE COURTISANE
2s 6d. net.
SELECTED PROSE OF OSCAR WILDE
6s. 6d. net.
ART AND DECORATION
6s. 6d. net.
FOR LOVE OF THE KING
5s. net.
VERA, OR THE NIHILISTS
6s. 6d. net.

WILLIAMSON (G. C.)
THE BOOK OF FAMILLE ROSE
Richly illustrated.   £8 8s. net.

METHUEN'S COMPANIONS TO MODERN STUDIES
SPAIN. E. ALLISON PEERS. 12s. 6d. net.
GERMANY. J. BITHELL. 15s. net.
ITALY. E. G. GARDNER. 12s. 6d. net.

METHUEN'S HISTORY OF MEDIEVAL AND MODERN EUROPE
In 8 Vols. Each 16s. net.
I.   476 to 911.   By J. H. BAXTER.
II.   911 to 1198. By Z. N. BROOKE.
III. 1198 to 1378. By C. W. PREVITÉ-ORTON.
IV.   1378 to 1494. By W. T. WAUGH.
V.   1494 to 1610. By A. J. GRANT.
VI.   1610 to 1715. By E. R. ADAIR.
VII. 1715 to 1815. By W. F. REDDAWAY.
VIII. 1815 to 1923. By Sir J A. R. MARRIOTT